Who's Bashing Whom?

LAURA D'ANDREA TYSON

Who's Bashing Whom?
Trade Conflict
in High-Technology Industries

INSTITUTE FOR INTERNATIONAL ECONOMICS
Washington, DC
November 1992

Laura D'Andrea Tyson, a Visiting Fellow at the Institute for International Economics, is Professor of Economics and Business Administration, Director of the Institute of International Studies, and Research Director of the Berkeley Roundtable on the International Economy at the University of California, Berkeley. She received a B.A. summa cum laude from Smith College and a Ph.D. in economics from Massachusetts Institute of Technology.

Professor Tyson has written extensively on US competitiveness and on the economies of Eastern Europe. Her publications include *American Industry in International Competition* (1983); *Politics and Productivity: The Real Story of How Japan Works* (1989); and *Power, Purpose and Collective Choice; Economic Strategy in Socialist States* (1986).

INSTITUTE FOR INTERNATIONAL ECONOMICS
11 Dupont Circle, NW
Washington, DC 20036-1207
(202) 328-9000   FAX: (202) 328-5432

C. Fred Bergsten, Director

Printed in the United States of America
94 93 92   6 5

Library of Congress Cataloging-in-Publication Data

Tyson, Laura D'Andrea, 1947–
  Who's bashing whom? : trade conflict in high-technology industries / Laura D'Andrea Tyson.
  p.   cm.

  Includes bibliographical references and index.

  1. High technology industries—United States.
  2. United States—Commercial policy.
  3. Competition, International.
  I. Title.
  HC110.H53T94   1992
  382'.3'0973—dc20   92-15646
                                       CIP

ISBN 0-88132-151-6 (cloth)
ISBN 0-88132-106-0 (paper)

Marketed and Distributed outside the USA and Canada by Longman Group UK Limited, London

To Erik, my husband
and Elliot, my son
for their patience and support

VC gift

Contents

Preface   xiii

Acknowledgments   xvii

**1 America's High-Technology Trade Challenge: The Perspective of
a Cautious Activist**   **1**

Introduction   1

Setting the Stage: The Nature of Trade Conflict in High-
Technology Industries   3

High-Technology Trade Conflict with Japan and Europe   5

Should the United States Care? The Answer of a Cautious Activist   9

The Plan of the Book   14

2 Trade and System Conflict in Technology-Intensive Industries   **17**

Trends in High-Technology Competition Between the Developed
Countries   17

The Roots of High-Technology Trade Conflict: Trade Barriers,
Structural Impediments, and Structural Differences   29

Why High-Technology Industries Matter for US Economic Welfare   32

A Brief Concluding Comment   45

**3 From MOSS to Motorola and Cray: Managing Trade by Rules and
Outcomes**   **53**

The Real Japan Problem   53

The MOSS Talks in Technology-Intensive Products: Trade
Management Through Sectoral Rules   58

Motorola and Japan's Cellular Telephone Market: A Step Closer
to Managed Trade   66

The Third-Party Radio Conflict: A Successful Managed Trade
   Resolution   71
Lessons from Motorola's Experiences in Gaining Access to the
   Japanese Market   73
Cray and the Japanese Supercomputer Market: Procurement,
   Infant-Industry Tactics, and Reciprocity   76
Concluding Remarks   82

4 Managing Trade and Competition in the Semiconductor Industry   85
Industry Economics and the Evolution of Comparative Advantage   88
From Manipulated to Managed Trade: The US–Japan
   Semiconductor Trade Agreement   106
The Effects of the Agreement on Trade and Pricing   111
The New Semiconductor Trade Agreement: The Story Continues   130
An Overall Assessment of the SCTA   132
Lessons for US Trade Policy from the Semiconductor Experience   133

**5 Industrial Policy and Trade Management in the Commercial
Aircraft Industry   155**
Historical Decisions in a Strategic Industry   155
Economics of the Industry   161
History of the Industry   176
The Economic Analysis of Government Intervention in the
   Commercial Aircraft Industry: The Case of Airbus   192
Trade Friction in the Aircraft Industry   195
Challenges Facing the American Commercial Aircraft industry   210
Conclusions   214

**6 Managing Trade and Investment: Europe's Evolving Strategy in
the Electronics Industry   217**
Videocassette Recorders: From Managed Trade to Managing
   Investment   220
High-Definition Television: The Strategy to Create European
   Champions   237
Understanding Europe's Evolving Strategy Toward the
   Electronics Industry   244
Lessons for US Trade and Industrial Policy   249

**7 A Cautious Activist Agenda for U.S. Policy in High-Technology
Industries   253**
Expanding Market Access   255
The Pros and Cons of Antidumping Remedies   267
Strategic Threats in High-Technology Industries   274
Subsidies, Foreign Targeting, and Countervailing Duties   280

The Need for Complementary Technology and Industrial Policies   286
Some Concluding Thoughts   295

Index   **311**

Tables

1.1   Cases of trade conflict in technology-intensive industries treated in this book   15

2.1   Alternative classification schemes for high-technology industries   20

2.2   High-technology exports as a share of total manufactures exports, selected countries, 1970–86   22

2.3   Shares of world high-technology exports, selected countries, 1970–89   23

2.4   Revealed comparative advantage in selected high-technology products, selected countries, 1970–89   24

2.5   Shares of world trade in R&D–intensive electronics products, selected countries, 1970–89   25

2.6   United States, Japan, and Europe: export shares in selected electronics products, 1980–88   26

2.7   United States and Japan: trade in electronics products, by type of product, 1980–91   27

2.8   United States: trade in high-technology products, 1980–88   28

2.9   United States: high-technology exports and imports as a share of total value added, by industry, 1980–88   29

2.10 United States: high-technology expenditures for R&D, by industry, selected years, 1979–89   33

2.11 United States: production and value added in selected high-technology industries, 1989   34

2.12 United States: employment in selected high-technology industries, 1989   35

2.13 United States: scientists and engineers employed in selected high-technology industries, 1989   36

2.14 United States: value added per worker in selected high-technology industries, 1989   37

2.15 United States: compensation in selected high-technology industries, 1989   38

2A.1 Assessments of US and Japanese comparative standings in selected technologies, Japanese Ministry of International Trade and Industry, 1983 and 1988   46

2A.2 Relative US position in critical defense technologies   47

2A.3 Position of the US computer industry in selected critical computer technologies, 1990 and projected 1995   48

2A.4 Assessments of US standing in selected high technologies by the Council on Competitiveness   49

3.1 Relative performance of Japanese imports in industries addressed in the MOSS negotiations, 1985–88   62

4.1 United States: trade in semiconductors, by product type, 1966–91   94

4.2 Joint research and development projects in microelectronics sponsored by the Japanese Ministry of International Trade and Industry (MITI)   96

4.3 Japan: trade in semiconductors, 1967–90   104

4.4 Average selling prices for 256-kilobyte and 1-megabyte DRAMs, 1984–92   115

4.5 Average selling prices for 256-kilobyte and 1-megabyte EPROMs, 1984–89   122

4.6 United States: semiconductor imports as a share of total semiconductor consumption, 1982–89   129

4.7 Japan: semiconductor imports as a share of total semiconductor consumption, 1982–89   130

4.8 Japan: semiconductor imports from the United States and semiconductor sales by US companies in Japan, 1984–89   131

4.9 Shares of production of integrated circuits produced offshore, by home country of parent   144

5.1 Orders of narrow- and wide-body commercial aircraft, by company and model   158

5.2 Aircraft company revenues from military aircraft and related sales, 1989   160

5.3 Costs to develop selected commercial aircraft   163

5.4 Public launch aid for Airbus Industrie, by country and aircraft model   174

5.5 Production of narrow-body commercial jet aircraft, by model, 1952–90   178

5.6 Production of wide-body commercial jet aircraft, by model, 1969–90   180

5.7 Geographical composition of world imports of aircraft, 1976–87   196

5.8 Geographical composition of world exports of aircraft, 1976–87   197

5.9 Geographical composition of world imports of aircraft engines, 1976–87   198

5.10 Geographical composition of world exports of aircraft engines, 1976–87   199

6.1 Trade balances in information technology and telecommunications, by region, 1986–89   218

6.2 European Community: trade deficit in electronics, 1988 and 1989   219

6.3 Costs of protection in videocassette recorders   226

6.4 Europe: trade deficit in videocassette recorders, 1980–88   227

6.5 Japanese share of the European videocassette recorder market, 1986   229

6.6 Market shares in videocassette recorders, by country, 1988   235
6.7 Japan: exports of videocassette recorders, 1981–88   236
7.1 From multilateral rules to bilaterally managed outcomes: an
      anatomy of the cases   256

Figures

3.1 United States: trade surplus with Japan in selected commodities,
      1987 and 1990   54
3.2 United States: trade deficit with Japan in key machinery
      industries, 1987 and 1990   55
4.1 United States, Japan, and Europe: shares of the worldwide
      semiconductor market, 1981–90   105
4.2 United States, Japan, Europe, and Korea/Taiwan: shares of the
      worldwide DRAM market, 1978–91   106
4.3 United States, Japan, and Europe: shares of the worldwide
      EPROM market, 1978–89   108
4.4 Japan: shares of the semiconductor market held by non-Japanese
      companies, 1985–91   111
4.5 Prices for 256-kilobyte and 1-megabyte DRAMs, by country of
      manufacturer, 1987–89   116
4.6 Cost estimates and average selling prices for 1-megabyte DRAMs,
      1987–91   118
4.7 Cost estimates and average selling prices for 1-megabyte
      EPROMs, 1987–91   123
4.8 Prices for 256-kilobyte EPROMs, by country of manufacturer,
      1987–89   124
4.9 Shares of the worldwide 1-megabyte EPROM market, by
      company, 1990   125
4.10 Shares of the worldwide microprocessor market, by company, 1990   127
5.1 Commonality of components among Airbus models   164

Boxes

5.1 Excerpts from the GATT Agreement on Trade in Civil Aircraft   200
5.2 Provisions of the 1992 agreement between the United States and
      the European Community on trade in civil aircraft   208

Preface

For over a decade, the US scholarly and policy communities have debated the merits of freer trade versus managed trade. For the most part, this debate has been astonishingly sterile. The protagonists are rarely able to agree on what they mean by such terms as free, fair, managed or strategic trade policy. They differ on fundamental issues such as the degree of competition that prevails in specific industries, the magnitude and types of assistance that governments provide to national firms, and the capacity of politicians and government technocrats to outperform markets in picking industrial "winners."

Most of the studies published by this Institute have tended to endorse the freer trade and market-oriented point of view. We have certainly recognized cases where completely free markets do not produce socially desirable results in such analyses as *Trade Policy for Troubled Industries* (Hufbauer and Rosen 1986) and several that support a managed exchange rate system to avoid prolonged currency misalignments (which cause resource misallocations and protectionist pressures). In the main, however, Institute authors have argued that the primary roles of government are to maintain a stable macroeconomic environment and to eliminate, at home and abroad, governmental or privately imposed obstacles to international trade and investment.

We therefore decided that the Institute should launch an objective study of the case for "managed trade," to broaden the horizons of our own research and to test the conclusions of our earlier work. Originally titled "Managed or Mismanaged Trade," but in the writing extended quite appropriately to address the trade-off between trade and other policies to support high-technology industries, this book does not fit neatly into either the freer trade or the managed trade orbit. Our goal in publishing it is to encourage a deeper, more thoughtful and hopefully more constructive debate on these contentious issues.

The study was written by Dr. Laura Tyson of the Berkeley Roundtable on the International Economy. Dr. Tyson, a superbly trained neoclassical economist who understands both modern trade theory and the revisionist critique that free trade is irrelevant in a world of imperfect competition and government support for certain industries, is admirably qualified to move this debate forward. She excels at using case studies to understand how markets and government policy affect economic outcomes, a crucial tool for addressing problems in this area in the real world. We hope that her volume will help bridge the gap between the competing schools of thought and start developing a consensus on the proper course for policy in the future.

The Institute for International Economics is a private nonprofit institution for the study and discussion of international economic policy. Its purpose is to analyze important issues in that area, and to develop and communicate practical new approaches for dealing with them. The Institute is completely nonpartisan.

The Institute is funded largely by philanthropic foundations. Major institutional grants are now being received from the German Marshall Fund of the United States, which created the Institute with a generous commitment of funds in 1981, and from the Ford Foundation, the William and Flora Hewlett Foundation, the William M. Keck, Jr. Foundation, the C. V. Starr Foundation, and the United States–Japan Foundation. A number of other foundations and private corporations also contribute to the highly diversified financial resources of the Institute. About 14 percent of the Institute's resources in our latest fiscal year were provided by contributors outside the United States, including about 6 percent from Japan.

The Board of Directors bears overall responsibility for the Institute and gives general guidance and approval to its research program—including identification of topics that are likely to become important to international economic policymakers over the medium run (generally, one to three years), and which thus should be addressed by the Institute. The Director, working closely with the staff and outside Advisory Committee, is responsible for the development of particular projects and makes the final decision to publish an individual study.

The Institute hopes that its studies and other activities will contribute to building a stronger foundation for international economic policy around the world. We invite readers of these publications to let us know how they think we can best accomplish this objective.

C. FRED BERGSTEN
Director
November 1992

Acknowledgments

While researching and writing this book, I received encouragement and help from several institutions and individuals. I owe my deepest gratitude to my colleagues Michael Borrus, Steve Cohen, and John Zysman at the Berkeley Roundtable on the International Economy (BRIE). Their insights and knowledge have been critical to the evolution of my thinking. BRIE was established a decade ago, long before America's declining competitiveness in high-technology industries had attracted the attention of academics and policymakers. Since that time, concern about the nation's competitiveness has become commonplace, but many of the pioneering ideas are found in BRIE research.

I am also indebted to C. Fred Bergsten, the Director of the Institute for International Economics, who first approached me about the idea of writing a book on managed trade for the Institute during the summer of 1989. Since that time, as my research progressed and my thinking evolved, I moved away from the managed trade question to the broader questions examined here. At every step of the way, Dr. Bergsten encouraged my efforts and provided valuable guidance. Without his personal support and the financial support of the Institute, this book would not have been possible.

In addition to the Institute, I am also grateful to the Alfred P. Sloan Foundation, whose generous grant to BRIE financed the invaluable office backup for the project, and to the Harvard Business School for research assistance for chapters 4 and 6. Within the BRIE office, I am especially appreciative of the efforts of Ms. Marybeth Schubert, who provided outstanding editing, typing, and secretarial assistance, and of Ms. Konstantina Kiousis and Mr. Pei-Hsiung Chin, who provided outstanding research assistance.

Several individuals, including Thomas Bayard, William Cline, Richard Cooper, Kenneth Flamm, Jeffrey Hart, Richard Heimlich, Thomas Howell, Thomas Kalil, Peter Kenen, Robert Kuttner, Ted Moran, Richard Nelson, Clyde Prestowitz, David Richardson, Ray Vernon, Ray Waldman, Alan Wolff, David Yoffie, and members of the IIE study group for this project, supplied helpful comments on earlier drafts. Although not all of them agreed with my point of view, they contributed insights and information that strengthened the analysis. I am grateful for their help but absolve them of all responsibility for the final product.

Laura D'Andrea Tyson

The dogmas of the quiet past are inadequate to the stormy present. The occasion is piled high with difficulty, and we must rise to the occasion. As our case is new, so we must think anew and act anew. We must disenthrall ourselves and then we shall save our country.

Abraham Lincoln, Annual Message to Congress
December 1, 1862

America's High-Technology Trade Challenge: The Perspective of a Cautious Activist

Introduction

Setting the Stage: The Nature of Trade Conflict in High-Technology Industries

High-Technology Trade Conflict with Japan and Europe

Should the United States Care? The Answer of a Cautious Activist

The Plan of the Book

Introduction

During the last half century, America defined its priorities in geopolitical terms. Our preeminent goal was to contain the Soviet Union and win the Cold War. We have succeeded beyond our wildest dreams, emerging as the world's only military superpower. But we are no longer the world's only economic superpower. Indeed, in the full flush of geopolitical triumph, we are teetering over the abyss of economic decline.

The signs are everywhere: anemic productivity growth, falling real wages, a woefully inadequate educational system, and declining shares of world markets for many high-technology products. After more than a decade of faltering American economic performance, what was once considered an alarmist view has now become a mainstream opinion: our economic competitiveness—defined as our ability to produce goods and services that meet the test of international markets while our citizens enjoy a standard of living that is both rising and sustainable—is in slow but perceptible decline.[1] The debate in Washington has shifted from whether the nation has a competitiveness problem to what should be done to solve it.

Some of the most controversial questions emerging from the new debate concern the nation's trade policies. To what extent does responsibility for the

---

1. This definition of competitiveness was introduced in a report issued by a commission established by President Ronald Reagan in 1983 to study the nation's competitiveness problem. The definition was developed for the commission in a background report (Cohen et al. 1984) prepared by scholars associated with the Berkeley Roundtable on the International Economy (BRIE). This definition has since become the standard used in most studies of competitiveness. Since 1983 hundreds of books, articles, and reports have been written on competitiveness and related issues. For an insightful and up-to-date discussion, see Competitiveness Policy Council (1992).

nation's competitive decline lie with its trading partners, and to what extent does responsibility lie at home? How should the nation's existing trade laws be used to reverse this decline? Should trade policy remedies be used instead of, or in addition to, economy-wide or sector-specific measures to improve national competitiveness? Are new trade policies needed to reflect the fact that the United States is no longer the only economic superpower?

This book addresses these questions using case studies of trade conflict in several high-technology industries.[2] There are many reasons for focusing on these industries. First, they are of substantial and growing importance in trade between the advanced industrial nations (see chapter 2 for evidence). Second, as theory suggests and empirical evidence confirms (a somewhat rare occurrence), success in high-technology industries bestows national benefits on productivity, technology development, and high-wage job creation. As a consequence, such industries are major building blocks of national competitiveness. Third, trade in high-technology products is not generally "free" in the traditional sense. On the contrary, trade outcomes are influenced or "manipulated"—indeed, some would say rigged—by both promotional and protectionist government policies. In these industries, the answer to the question, "Who's bashing whom?" is, "To some degree, everybody's bashing everybody." Fourth and finally, many of the barriers to free trade in high-technology products are not covered by regulations under the General Agreement on Tariffs and Trade (GATT) or other multilateral agreements. Therefore, for the foreseeable future, the question facing the United States isn't whether to address these barriers unilaterally, but how to do so efficaciously.

This book's focus on trade policies and high-technology industries should not be misunderstood. America's competitiveness problem is broad-based, involving much more than its high-technology industries. Indeed, many of these industries are still doing extremely well. Flawed domestic choices, not unfair foreign trading practices, are the main cause of the nation's long-run economic slowdown. Nonetheless, as the case studies demonstrate, high-technology trade is plagued with market distortions, and well-designed, forward-looking trade policies can be an important adjunct to a constructive domestic environment. But even the most sensible and effective trade policies cannot compensate for domestic programs that remain impoverished both fiscally and intellectually. And misguided trade policies can be even worse than ineffective; they can be downright destructive.

Perhaps the book's most important lesson is that the traditional approaches to trade and domestic policy that served the nation so well when American companies had an unrivaled technological lead are no longer adequate. In particular, we can no longer afford to ignore the efforts of Japan and Europe to promote their own high-technology producers. Nor, as the current deadlock in the Uruguay Round of GATT negotiations reveals, can we realistically expect our trading partners to adopt international rules that reflect our own ideological preferences. Confronted with these realities, we must devise macroeconomic,

---

2. A formal definition of high-technology industries is presented, together with some alternative measures of their importance in the United States, Europe, and Japan, in chapter 2.

trade, and industrial policies that promote our own high-technology industries while continuing to lobby for a more liberal trading system. This is a tall order.

Moreover, even if we meet this challenge, the nation's economic ills will persist for some time—they are not restricted to the high-technology industries examined here, and they have been festering for decades. There is no panacea to reverse years of wrong-headed policymaking. Those who hope to find a quick fix or a silver bullet will come away from this book disapppointed. But those who seek an understanding of how trade and competition in high-technology industries really work (as opposed to how theory dictates they are meant to work in a free trade, free market world) should come away with some plausible policy options.

Setting the Stage: The Nature of Trade Conflict in High-Technology Industries

Technology-intensive industries violate the assumptions of free trade theory and the static economic concepts that are the traditional basis for US trade policy. In such industries, costs fall and product quality improves as the scale of production increases, the returns to technological advance create beneficial spillovers for other economic activities, and barriers to entry generate market structures rife with first-mover advantages and strategic behavior. A nation's competitive position in industries with these characteristics is less a function of its national factor endowments and more a function of strategic interactions between its firms and government, and between them and the firms and governments of other nations. In the words of Ernst and O'Connor (1992, 27), in a new study by the Organization for Economic Cooperation and Development (OECD), "Oligopolistic competition and strategic interaction among firms and governments rather than the invisible hand of market forces condition today's competitive advantage and international division of labor in high-technology industries." The case studies presented in this book are a resounding confirmation of this view.

During the last decade, new developments in trade theory have demonstrated that, under conditions of increasing returns, technological externalities, and imperfect competition, free trade is not necessarily and automatically the best policy.[3] Promotional and protectionist policies by foreign govenments can harm domestic economic welfare by shifting industries with high returns and beneficial externalities away from domestic producers and domestic production locations. Conversely, comparable policies at home can improve domestic economic welfare, sometimes at the expense of other nations.

---

3. The literature on the new trade theory is large and growing. Several excellent papers are included in Krugman (1986). For a recent summary of the major conclusions of the theory, see Krugman (1987). For a complete technical treatment of the theory, see Helpman and Krugman (1985). For one of the earlier pieces that focused on high technology, see Brander and Spencer (1985). Although the strategic trade theory literature is full of theoretical demonstrations that promotional or protectionist policies can improve economic welfare at home or reduce it abroad, whether such policies work in practice is another matter. The theoretical assumptions behind these demonstrations are very restrictive. The available evidence, albeit flawed by overly simple models and inadequate data, suggests that such policies often reduce national welfare (see Richardson 1989).

As an illustration, if the world aircraft industry is a high-wage, high-profit industry over the long run, then foreign government intervention to help foreign producers capture a larger share of the world market may be welfare-improving abroad and welfare-reducing at home. Such intervention, which is designed to shift excess returns or "rents" from one set of national producers to another, is inherently beggar-thy-neighbor in its intended effect. To take another example, domestic policies to promote research and development in the semiconductor industry or the computer display industry may improve national welfare by fostering beneficial spillovers for other industries. These policies may also improve global welfare if the spillovers are global in reach. In this case, domestic intervention may prove to be positive-sum or welfare-enhancing for all nations.

In short, the characteristic features of high-technology industries—imperfect competition, strategic behavior, dynamic economies of scale, and technological externalities—provide a fertile breeding ground for interventionist policies. Indeed, despite the recent trend toward economic "liberalization" around the world, many nations remain committed to the goal of supporting their high-technology producers. Certainly this is the case in the European Community, in Japan, and in many newly industrializing countries like Korea, Taiwan, and Brazil. Most of the high-technology industries targeted and nurtured by these nations are ones in which the United States has considerable competitive strength and which are important to the US industrial base in a variety of ways. Understandably, these targeting strategies have sparked trade friction between the United States and its trading partners.

Trade barriers and traditional forms of government support, however, are only one source of friction. National differences in competition policies, R&D policies, intellectual property protection, standards and testing procedures, and a host of other regulatory features of modern economies are another. Indeed, John Jackson (1989, 220–21) has argued that many national trade remedies, including antidumping and countervailing duty laws, act more as a buffer or interface mechanism between different economic systems than as a response to traditional trade barriers.

Most high-technology industries are global in scope, dominated by a relatively small number of relatively large multinational companies competing in one another's domestic markets through trade and transnational investment.[4] Scale requirements and strategic concerns motivate these companies to take a global perspective, establishing a presence in all major markets.[5] A low ratio of transportation costs to the value of the goods transported and a high degree of capital mobility allow high-technology firms to disperse production broadly and to separate research and manufacturing activities (Yoffie 1991).

---

4. According to a recent study by the secretariat of the OECD (1990, 17), global oligopoly structures now constitute "the dominant form of supply structure in most R&D intensive or high-tech industries."

5. According to John Dunning (1991), between 30 percent and 40 percent of the sales of leading multinational firms are now produced outside their home-country boundaries, and the value of these sales now exceeds that of international trade (i.e., exports by all countries). The dispersion of production is particularly dramatic in the electronics industries that are the focus of much of this study.

But although both the markets for high-technology products and the companies that serve them are global, most of the rules governing their competition in individual markets are not. National differences in these rules can be both a barrier to trade and transnational investment and a source of competitive advantage or disadvantage for companies in particular markets. As a result, such differences have come to be called "structural impediments to trade."

The global scope of powerful high-technology companies and the persistent intervention by governments to manipulate market outcomes necessitate deeper integration of the multilateral rules governing such markets. In the absence of such rules for "better trade management," bitter trade conflicts and managed trade arrangements[6] will recur, and the world may well continue down a neo-mercantilist path. The GATT may not be dead as some have proclaimed, but in its present form it is largely irrelevant to many of the government practices and structural impediments that give rise to high-technology trade friction. Nor does the ambitious agenda of the Uruguay Round address many of these issues.

The gaps in GATT coverage and the recurrent trade tensions in high-technology industries have encouraged proposals for new multilateral rules to regulate high-technology trade. Jagdish Bhagwati (1991) and Sylvia Ostry (1990a and b) have been particularly effective proponents of this position. Although such prescriptions are sound, they appear to be a long way from realization. It is highly unlikely that nations will agree to harmonize such sensitive domestic policies as competition policy and technology policy during the next several years. It seems even less likely that they will forswear the options of protecting or promoting their own high-technology producers and of using implicit local content measures to attract foreign direct investment. Indeed, as investment flows grow in importance compared with trade flows, competition for foreign capital is likely to intensify. Nations may finally be willing to retire costly programs to build their own national champions. But they are likely to cling to the idea that a substantial fraction of the high-technology goods they consume should be locally produced, even if by foreign-owned companies.

High-Technology Trade Conflict with Japan and Europe

This book examines cases of high-technology trade conflict between the United States, Europe, and Japan. Several of the newly industrializing countries (NICs) have made great strides in high-technology production, especially in parts of the electronics complex.[7] But the United States, Europe, and Japan still account for a disproportionate share of such production and related trade: as the data in chapter 2 indicate, together they provide approximately 75 percent of global

---

6. Bhagwati (1991, 46) draws a sharp contrast between what he calls trade management through agreements that establish fixed rules, and managed trade through agreements that set fixed quantitative trade outcomes.

7. Evidence of the dramatic increases in the shares of the NICs in world electronics trade is contained in Guerrieri (1991). Of course, the foreign operations of multinationals with headquarters in the developed countries account for a sizeable fraction of these increases.

exports of high-technology products. And each of the three is committed to maintaining a vibrant high-technology production base, both by strengthening domestic producers and by attracting "quality" foreign direct investment. Now that the United States, Japan, and Europe are economic superpowers, the dangers of escalating trade conflict among them should not be discounted.[8] Nowhere is this danger greater than in several high-technology industries such as semiconductors and aircraft, in which competition is intense and military as well as economic interests hang in the balance.

From the US perspective, Japan and Europe pose different trade challenges. In Japan, the primary problem is one of market access, whether by trade or by direct investment and local production. Barriers to market access in Japan resist any simple remedy because they are rooted in unique structural features of Japanese capitalism. A sheltered, rapidly growing domestic market and targeted industrial policies have catapulted Japan into head-to-head competition with the United States in several critical segments of the electronics sector. In this competition, differences in the behavior of Japanese and American firms and differences in the Japanese and American regulatory environments have become major bones of contention.

In the presence of such differences, the traditional principles underlying US trade policy—including nondiscrimination and national treatment—have been called into question. Should the United States treat Japan like its other trading partners when Japan is so obviously different in ways that disadvantage American producers? Should the United States recognize, as legitimate policy choices, Japanese regulatory practices that actively discriminate against foreign producers, or the official condoning of Japanese business practices that do so? Should Japanese firms be accorded national treatment in the American market when American firms are not accorded such treatment in the Japanese market?[9]

A growing number of American policymakers are inclined to answer these questions in the negative. In recent bilateral negotiations, the United States has lobbied—indeed, some would say arm-twisted—to bring Japanese practices into greater conformity with American practices. In these cases, which are discussed in chapter 3, the goal has been policy convergence to the American standard. The process has been tortuous, and progress has been halting and slow, usually requiring substantial US pressure up to and including the threat of retaliation. In the meantime, Japanese producers have made inexorable inroads in global high-technology markets.

The United States has also clashed with Europe over questions of market access. However, such questions have revolved around overt trade barriers, such as tariffs and preferential government procurement, not structural differences. Although such differences exist between the United States and Europe, they pale in comparison with those between American and Japanese capitalism.

---

8. C. Fred Bergsten (1992) also emphasizes the possibility of growing econmic conflicts between the United States, Europe, and Japan. A new book by Sandholtz et al. (1992) also examines the roots of such conflicts and analyzes their implications for national security.

9. These questions have been given considerable attention as a result of the writings of Clyde V. Prestowitz, Jr. See, for example, Prestowitz (1991, 22–29).

Recent European initiatives to create a more unified market have sparked several heated exchanges with the United States over potential access barriers. Procurement and standards have been of special concern to American high-technology producers.[10] On these issues as on others, the Europeans have often stressed the principle of bilateral reciprocity. Reciprocity clauses, extending specific benefits of the single European market to Europe's trading partners only if they provide reciprocal benefits to Europe, have been embodied in many EC 1992 directives. For example, a recent Community directive on public procurement in water, energy, transport, and telecommunications—sectors currently excluded from GATT procurement regulations—places foreign bids at a disadvantage when more than 50 percent of the products' content originates in countries with which the Community does not have an effective market access agreement. According to official EC statements, this disadvantage will not apply to nations that drop their own national procurement preferences in these sectors.[11]

Although the European principle of selective reciprocity needs to be defined precisely for particular industries as diverse as telecommunications and financial services, the general European idea seems clear enough: the competitive opportunities afforded to foreign companies in the European market should be matched by comparable foreign opportunities for European companies. (As the discussion in chapter 7 makes clear, a comparable reciprocity principle has been emerging in US trade policy as well, although so far it has been less explicit.) Although the Europeans stress the principle of reciprocity with all of their trading partners, it has taken on particular significance in their relations with Japan, with which they suffer a growing trade imbalance, especially in high-technology electronics goods. Most European companies and policymakers also believe that reciprocity is more easily achieved in trade with the United States than in trade with Japan. Indeed, some Europeans have even suggested that the United States and Europe join forces to agitate for more open markets in Japan.

Many American high-technology producers have chosen to hurdle overt trade barriers to the European market through direct investment in European production facilities. Until the late 1970s, explicit policies restricting foreign direct investment ruled out this option in Japan. Thereafter, a variety of structural impediments—most notably extensive cross-shareholding among Japanese companies, which prevents their acquisition by would-be foreign investors—has had the same effect. In contrast to the Japanese preference for containing direct

---

10. The US International Trade Commission estimates that public procurement purchases account for as much as 90 percent of telecommunications equipment sales and up to one-third of computer sales to the European Community by American companies (Flamm 1990). Talks between Europe and the United States in 1988, prompted by then–US Secretary of Commerce Robert A. Mosbacher, led to an agreement whereby the American National Standards Institute will exercise a voice in the two most important standards-setting bodies within the Community.

11. For the United States, the European directive poses a challenge: will the United States override its "buy American" provisions at the federal and state levels by subjecting a wide range of public purchases to the GATT procurement code? This challenge is especially important in the telecommunications industry, where the regulated Baby Bells are not currently covered by this code.

investment, Europe has frequently encouraged such investment as a substitute for imports.

The contrast between the Europeans and the Japanese shows up in the numbers. The local affiliates of foreign firms accounted for only 1 percent of aggregate Japanese sales and employment in 1986. The comparable figures for Germany were 18 percent and 13 percent. They were even larger for France and Great Britain (Julius and Thomson 1988). As the case studies indicate, differences in the extent of transnational investment in Japan and Europe are even more pronounced in such high-technology industries as semiconductors and computers.

Extensive direct investment by European and American companies to serve one another's markets has defused tensions between Europe and the United States on questions of market access. In contrast, the asymmetry between limited foreign direct investment in Japan and the recent explosion of direct investment by Japanese companies in both the United States and Europe has fed perceptions of Japan as an unfair trader.

So far, the European preference for local production over imports—a preference clearly exhibited in the semiconductor and videocassette recorder (VCR) cases analyzed in this book—has not caused much friction between the United States and Europe.[12] But the situation could change. In recent years, European antidumping and procurement regulations have been modified to embody explicit local content requirements.[13] These regulations have been interpreted in ways that discriminate against imports in favor of local European production and that raise the local content requirement for goods seeking to qualify as "European" production. As the case study of the European electronics industry in chapter 6 indicates, such requirements have deterred imports and served as a magnet for "quality" foreign investment. A European strategy of "creeping local content" threatens both the interests of American producers who prefer to serve the European market through trade and the interests of the United States as a production location. Consequently, this strategy may ignite US–Europe trade friction in the future.

For the present, however, European subsidies for high-technology industries are a more immediate source of conflict. Despite efforts by the European Commission to curb industrial subsidies, they remain much more significant in Europe than in either Japan or the United States. According to a recent study by the Office of Technology Assessment (1991), for example, industrial subsidies amount to about 3 percent of GDP in Europe, compared with only 1 percent in Japan and 0.5 percent in the United States.

A dispute over European subsidies to Airbus festered throughout the 1980s. Despite strong American pressure, the Europeans aggressively subsidized the Airbus consortium with the explicit goal of building a European producer that

---

12. European rules of origin combined with various local content tests to meet the rules can determine the eligibility of foreign firms for the following benefits of the unified European market: exemption from residual national quotas, eligibility for government procurement, avoidance of antidumping duties, and eligibility for EC–EFTA and other preferential trading arrangements.

13. The 50 percent local content rule proposed by the Community for the four excluded sectors is consistent with the GATT Code on Government Procurement, which permits a local content requirement provided it is nondiscriminatory in the sense that it can be met by goods or services furnished by any code signatory.

would be the competitive and technological equal of the American producers. By the end of the 1980s Europe had realized its goal, and the United States had lost its patience. In 1991 American trade officials lodged formal GATT complaints against European subsidies and openly threatened unilateral retaliation to stop them. Finally, in response to increasingly credible American threats and a GATT ruling against them, the Europeans negotiated a compromise bilateral agreement with the United States to limit—but not to end—future public support for Airbus.

In contrast to European subsidies in the commercial aircraft industry, European subsidies in the electronics sector have not antagonized the United States for two reasons: so far they have not created European companies that pose a real competitive challenge to American companies; and they have benefited the European affiliates of some American producers. Should either of these conditions change, the United States could easily end up locking horns with Europe over its subsidy programs for electronics. In the meantime, reciprocity definitions and overt protectionist measures are more likely to cause clashes between the two. As chapters 4 and 6 reveal, even though Japan is the primary target of such measures, they often have unintended adverse effects on American producers.

Should the United States Care? The Answer of a Cautious Activist

Many of the arguments made here are no longer as controversial as they once were. Nearly everyone now concedes that competitive advantage in high-technology industries is created, not endowed by nature, and that governments the world over have earmarked them for special support. Even the assumption that structural impediments influence competitive outcomes in global oligopolies has become commonplace in contemporary discussions of trade policy. Although some observers still deny the existence of structural barriers to the Japanese market, their opinion is called into question by a growing body of sophisticated empirical evidence, cited in chapter 3. Certainly, that chapter's story of Motorola's efforts to compete in Japan in pagers, cellular telephones, and third-party radios confirms the conviction of a growing number of mainstream economists that the problem of market access in Japan is real, not imagined.[14] And no serious observer, whether American or European, doubts the existence of substantial European subsidies for specific sectors. In short, the controversial questions are no longer whether foreign intervention in high-technology industries exists, whether such intervention influences competitive outcomes to the disadvantage of American producers, or whether structural differences among nations tilt the playing field, but rather how much the United States is harmed by such practices, and how it should respond.

Many economists, who might be called traditional free traders, believe that the harm is small and that unilateral responses that violate multilateral trading

---

14. Among the mainstream economists who have concluded that there are structural and policy barriers to Japan's markets are the late Bela Balassa, Rudiger Dornbusch, Paul R. Krugman, and Robert Z. Lawrence. For references to their work on this subject, see chapter 3.

rules should be avoided. They maintain that foreign promotional policies usually worsen the terms of trade for the country initiating them and benefit its trading partners. According to this logic, when the Japanese subsidize semiconductors or the Europeans subsidize aircraft, the United States enjoys the benefits of cheaper foreign products. A note of thanks is more appropriate than a threat of retaliation.

Similarly, traditional free traders contend that if the Japanese restrict access to their market, whether intentionally through overt trade barriers or unintentionally through regulatory policies, they will pay higher prices and reduce their own economic welfare. True, the United States and Japan's other trading partners will suffer some loss of efficiency, because the gains from trade will be reduced. But only the composition of trade between Japan and the rest of the world will be affected; overall trade balances will not change. And standard economic logic assumes that the composition of trade does not matter—a dollar's worth of exports or imports of shoes has the same effect on national economic welfare as a dollar's worth of exports or imports of computers.

Although they are skeptical about the actual damage done to the American economy by foreign trade barriers and structural impediments, many traditional free traders recognize that these barriers are likely to fan protectionist sentiments at home and retaliation abroad. Ultimately, the entire liberal trading order will come under fire without America's support and leadership. But traditional free traders believe that the appropriate response to such dangers is the development of new multilateral rules, not unilateral actions, particularly if those actions transgress existing rules.

A dwindling number of economists and very few policymakers espouse the traditional free trade arguments as an overall prescription for US trade policy. Instead, a growing number of academic and policy economists are best described as moderate free traders: although they support the free trade ideal, they grudgingly concede that it is a long way off and conclude that unilateral measures to serve the national interest may be justified under some circumstances.

Traditional economic theory provides moderate free traders with three such justifications: the risk of high adjustment costs, potential terms-of-trade losses, and the threat to national security that may result from significant injury to the nation's high-technology producers. Adjustment costs are the costs of writing off or reallocating resources from domestic industries forced to contract as a result of declining markets. When resources are not costlessly mobile—as assuredly they are not in technology-intensive industries with specialized human, capital, and technological assets—adjustment costs can be substantial. Such costs, however, are rarely estimated and even more rarely invoked as a rationale for trade policy.[15]

Potential terms-of-trade losses are another matter. American economic welfare is harmed by any foreign action that increases the prices of American imports or reduces the prices of American exports.[16] If foreigners subsidize their aircraft

---

15. The recent study of the NAFTA by Hufbauer and Schott (1992) is an important exception to this generalization.

16. So far, however, the available empirical evidence, although weak, suggests that the gradual decline in the US terms of trade over the past decade has had a small effect on US GNP. See, for example, Litan et al. (1990).

producers, US exporters of aircraft may have to lower their own prices to match their competition. Likewise if foreigners erect barriers to American computer exports (or if business practices allowable under foreign competition laws are themselves barriers), exports of other American products will have to be increased to maintain the overall level of US exports. To induce these higher sales, US export prices may have to be reduced, either directly or through a drop in the value of the dollar. Or again if foreign trade barriers or structural impediments reduce global competition, the prices of American imports may increase. In such cases, foreign actions jeopardize the nation's terms of trade and its economic welfare, and moderate free traders may find justification for a defensive American response.

Moderate free traders may also sanction such a response when national security interests are threatened by American dependence on concentrated foreign suppliers with substantial market power. According to this logic, when foreign suppliers of a particular product critical to the national defense are numerous and dispersed, national security is not imperiled. But when a small number of foreign suppliers account for the lion's share of global output, they have the power to place conditions or restrictions on its use, thereby undermining America's national autonomy. Under these circumstances, American policy intervention to secure a more competitive supply base may be warranted, even if such intervention violates free trade or free market principles.[17]

Although usually limited to national security, the dependency rationale for action can be logically extended to encompass the dangers of American reliance on concentrated foreign suppliers of any important product. Foreign market power in a particular high-technology industry can translate into higher prices— a terms-of-trade effect—and restrictions on access to frontier technologies by American consumers and producers—a strategic effect on market competition. These dangers are especially pronounced when foreign suppliers control inputs—for example, semiconductors—that are widely used throughout the economy.

All of the moderate free trade arguments described here can be used to justify the prescriptions for trade policy proposed in this book. In addition, both the trade policy *and* the domestic policy recommendations can be justified on the grounds that they are needed to quell protectionist pressures at home.[18] Without an adequate domestic capacity to respond to the difficulties of American industries and their workers, American policymakers are often driven to protectionist measures that are simultaneously counterproductive for American economic interests and threatening to the liberal trading order. American postwar economic history is replete with examples of trade policy actions that are best understood as inadequate substitutes for industrial policy.[19]

Although I could easily hide behind the moderate free trade disguises described here, it would be disingenuous for me to do so. Unlike most free traders, unilateral and moderate alike, I believe that what we as a nation make and what

---

17. Both Graham and Krugman (1991) and Moran (1992) have forcefully argued this point.

18. The first report of the Competitiveness Policy Council (1992) justifies several of its domestic economic policy recommendations along these lines.

19. For an earlier discussion of this phenomenon see Tyson and Zysman (1983).

we trade matter. The composition of our production and trade does influence our economic well-being. Technology-intensive industries, in particular, make special contributions to the long-term health of the American economy. A dollar's worth of shoes may have the same effect on the trade balance as a dollar's worth of computers. But, as the data in chapter 2 indicate, the two do not have the same effect on employment, wages, labor skills, productivity, and research—all major determinants of our long-term economic health. In addition, because technology-intensive industries finance a disproportionate share of the nation's R&D spending, there is a strong presumption—supported by the evidence and the arguments presented in chapter 2—that they generate positive externalities for the rest of the economy.

However, even economists who believe that the composition of the economy matters, and that high-technology industries create a virtuous cycle of economic growth, innovation, and learning by doing, harbor serious reservations about the policy implications of their views.[20] Even if one accepts the notion that competitive advantage in such industries can be created by government action, one need not conclude that such action is warranted—it all depends on the costs and the benefits. And these are devilishly difficult to measure with any precision. Any such calculation depends on a number of imponderables, including the exact form of the policy, its effects on other industries, and the reactions of both domestic firms and foreign firms and governments.

In imperfectly competitive industries, many kinds of strategic behavior are possible. For example, a promotional or protectionist policy to support American high-technology producers might increase their profits and discourage their foreign competitors. On the other hand, such a policy might result in excess capacity among domestic companies that hurts all of them. Prediction becomes even more perilous when foreign governments enter the picture as strategic players. Then the consequences of American policy depend on whether and how foreign governments respond.

Questions about geography also arise when one considers appropriate policies for high-technology industries. As already noted, most of the firms in such industries are global players, with extensive sales, production, and even research operations scattered around the world. Increasingly, they are also linked with their foreign competitors through a web of strategic alliances and joint ventures. Does a national trade and domestic policy agenda for such industries make sense? Should the United States use its trade policy to open foreign markets to American companies if those companies supply those markets from their off-shore production facilities? Should policies to promote a domestic high-technology production base be limited to American-owned companies, or should they include the American subsidiaries of foreign companies? Should the United States spend taxpayer dollars to finance R&D programs when the knowledge they create often ends up in the hands of foreign companies, sometimes through their joint ventures with American companies?

---

20. The so-called new growth theory literature elucidates the mechanisms that influence economic growth in knowledge-intensive industries. According to this developing body of literature, technological change and innovation are more important determinants of long-run growth than is saving. See Grossman and Helpman (1991) and Romer (1986).

The presence of externalities raises a related set of locational questions. Although high-technology industries may generate positive technological externalities, it does not follow that each nation must have its own domestically owned, or at least domestically based, companies to enjoy them. If externalities are international in scope and flow across national borders through trade in goods and technological information, each nation can benefit whether it has domestic producers or not. This reasoning reinforces the traditional free trade argument that foreign subsidies should be treated not as a threat but as a gift— one that brings not only lower prices but also new technological information free of charge.

Finally, even economists who might be persuaded that high-technology industries make special contributions to national economic welfare are likely to remain highly skeptical about the ability of the American government to intervene effectively on their behalf. A long history of misguided sectoral policies and pork-barrel politics indicates that a healthy degree of skepticism is certainly warranted.

Because I share many of the reservations about the wisdom of policy intervention described here, my recommendations for both trade and domestic policy are self-consciously cautious. Indeed, my perspective is one that Paul R. Krugman has described as "cautious activism" (see the introduction to Krugman 1986).

My trade policy agenda is a defensive one. I recommend that the nation's trade laws be used to deter or compensate for foreign practices that are not adequately regulated by existing multilateral rules. Unlike most traditional and even many moderate free traders, I am convinced that such practices can inflict substantial long-term injury on American producers. The case studies provide compelling evidence of such injury. In addition I believe that, in pursuit of defensive objectives, US policymakers should be guided by the principle of selective reciprocity and motivated by the goal of opening foreign markets. Wherever possible, they should favor approaches that encourage trade and competition over those that discourage them.

As the case studies demonstrate, cautious activism in trade policy is *not* synonymous with protectionism. Indeed, both the cases and the global logic of high-technology industries indicate that protectionist measures, such as voluntary restraint agreements and price floors on imports, are at least as ineffective or counterproductive in such industries as they have proven to be elsewhere in the economy. (See Hufbauer and Rosen 1986 for evidence on the negative consequences of protection in other industries.) But cautious activism does sometimes violate the principles of nondiscrimination and diffuse reciprocity that remain the mainstays of US trade policy. Moreover, cautious activism does sometimes involve forceful unilateralism. And, as Moran (1992) notes, "Arm-twisting is hardly an attractive remedy compared to multilateral agreements founded upon mutual concessions."

All too often, however, the choice between self-serving unilateralism and cooperative multilateralism does not exist. Sometimes the only real choice is between inaction on the one hand and bilateral deals or unilateral action on the other. Under some circumstances the costs of inaction for American economic welfare are unacceptably high. We must not be hoodwinked by the soothing notion that, in the absence of US intervention, the fate of America's high-technology industries will be determined by market forces. Instead, they will be manipulated by the trade, regulatory, and industrial policies of our trading partners. Cautious activism has implications for domestic economic policy as well as for trade policy. A cautious activist supports general policy measures such as a more generous R&D tax credit and increases in public funding for civilian R&D and education—initiatives that would promote all of the nation's high-technology producers without singling out any one of them for special favor. But a cautious activist is willing to go further, recognizing that measures to support particular technologies or industries are sometimes warranted.[21] To determine when such measures are required and what form they should take, the government needs an institutional capacity to monitor and respond to trends in global competition. Without such a capacity, America's policy has often been too little, too late. While we scramble to help our producers address crises that have been long in the making, both Japan and the European Community have forward-looking policies to nurture their high-technology industries. The American approach is no longer adequate, particularly at a time when cutbacks in defense R&D programs threaten to decimate public funding for science and technology unless new civilian programs are established to replace them.

Finally, I must emphasize that the policy agenda proposed in this book is not offered as a remedy for the US trade deficit. The experience of the 1980s confirms the orthodox view that the deficit is primarily a macroeconomic phenomenon (see, e.g, Bergsten 1991). As a recent study by Krugman (1991, 49) concludes, there are intellectually defensible arguments for activist trade and industrial policies. But the assertion that changes in exchange rates and macroeconomic policy cannot eliminate trade imbalances is not one of them. The trade and industry problems described here were not caused by macroeconomic factors, and they cannot be cured by them. Nor can the resolution of these problems substitute for macroeconomic measures both at home and abroad to restore sustainable balance of payments positions for the United States and its trading partners.

The Plan of the Book

My policy proposals are based on several case studies of trade conflict between the United States, Europe, and Japan. Table 1.1 contains a brief description of the industries, trade issues, and countries involved in each case. Each of the four case chapters (chapters 3 through 6) describes the sources of particular trade conflicts, the objectives of the trading partners, and the outcomes of the trade actions taken by them. Each chapter also contains a detailed discussion of policy lessons for the United States. Because the cases encompass different industries,

---

21. Paul Krugman is also a "cautious activist" on industrial policy in the sense used here (see Krugman 1990, 131). Several of the recommendations of the Competitiveness Policy Council (1992) are also consistent with a cautious activist agenda. As Richardson (1992) has recently noted, even cautious activists have the same preference ranking for policies as most mainstream economists: in descending order they are market-perfecting infrastructure; government promotion of saving, investment, R&D, and education; trade and industrial policies for whole industries; and firm-specific policies.

Table 1.1 Cases of trade conflict in technology-intensive industries treated in this book

Sector or industry	Drugs and medical equipment Telecommunications and cellular telephones Third-party radio systems Supercomputers	Semiconductors Liquid-crystal displays	Commercial aircraft	Consumer electronics (videocassette recorders and high-definition television)
Protagonists	United States and Japan	United States and Japan	United States and Europe	Europe and Japan
Issues in dispute	Nontariff barriers and structural impediments to Japanese market	Japanese dumping in US market; market access barriers in Japan, with emphasis on *keiretsu*	1979 GATT Civil Aircraft Code (tariff and nontariff barriers); European subsidies to Airbus; US defense subsidies	Temporary import relief in Europe via voluntary export restraint agreement with Japan; European antidumping and creeping local content vis-à-vis Japanese producers
Objectives of party initiating trade action	Improved market access in Japan for American and other foreign companies	Cessation of dumping; improved market access in Japan for American and other foreign companies	Creation of new multilateral rules for aircraft trade; reduction of European development subsidies to Airbus	Protection and promotion of European electronics producers
Treated in:	chapter 3	chapter 4	chapter 5	chapter 6

different trading partners, and different policy issues, each of them is written in a self-contained fashion so that it can be read independently of the others.

As a general introduction to the book, chapter 2 provides evidence of the changing competitive positions of the United States, Japan, and Europe in high-technology trade. The numbers confirm that the relative US position in a number of key industries and technologies has become steadily weaker. The advantage in high-technology industries we once took for granted has virtually disappeared.[22] Chapter 2 also describes the various sources of trade conflict in high-technology industries and suggests reasons why such conflict is likely to intensify in the future. Finally, chapter 2 examines the many reasons why the preservation of a strong high-technology production base should matter to the United States or any industrialized nation. Several measures are used to document the contributions of high-technology industries to national economic performance. Overall, the evidence supports the book's underlying premise that such industries are of special significance for long-term economic welfare.

Chapter 7 presents the trade policy conclusions that emerge from an overall assessment of the case studies. The chapter recapitulates some of the recommendations from the case chapters, but goes beyond them to provide some overarching conclusions. The recommendations encompass several issues that are hotly debated in discussions of American trade policy, including aggressive unilateralism under the rubric of the Section 301 and Super 301 legislation, selective reciprocity, managed trade, antidumping relief, responses to foreign targeting and subsidies, and the new kinds of multilateral rules that will be required to regulate high-technology trade in the future.

Chapter 7 also describes some new domestic initiatives to stem further erosion of the nation's competitiveness in high-technology industries. Even if used wisely, the nation's trade laws are by themselves inadequate to this task. They must be complemented by appropriate domestic measures. Ultimately, the fate of the nation's high-technology production base depends on the decisions that we make about our macroeconomic policy, our R&D policy, and our commitment of today's resources to tomorrow's economic well-being. We need an investment-led macroeconomic strategy and forward-looking technology and industrial policies to make these choices wisely.

---

22. For a detailed discussion of the rise and decline of American technological leadership during the postwar period, see Nelson (1990, 117–32).

2

Trade and System Conflict in Technology-Intensive Industries

Trends in High-Technology Competition Between the Developed Countries

The Roots of High-Technology Trade Conflict: Trade Barriers, Structural Impediments, and Structural Differences

Why High-Technology Industries Matter for US Economic Welfare

A Brief Concluding Comment

Appendix: Assessments of the US Position in Selected High-Technology Industries

Trends in High-Technology Competition Between the Developed Countries

Trade among nations is traditionally attributed to differences in their resource endowments. Australia exports wool because its climate and terrain are ideal for sheep grazing. Malaysia exports labor-intensive manufactures because it has a large supply of cheap labor. Japan is a net exporter of manufactured goods and a net importer of natural resources because of its abundance of capital and skilled industrial labor and its scarcity of raw materials.

Inherited national differences in resource endowments explain some world trade patterns but not others. Intraindustry trade between the advanced industrial countries in manufactured goods is a glaring exception. Such trade cannot be credibly attributed to national differences in availabilities of land, labor, and capital. Even a more finely grained analysis that distinguishes between different kinds of land, labor, and capital fails to do the trick. The advanced industrial countries are strikingly similar in their endowments of the resources essential for competitive strength in the production of most manufactured goods.

But if national differences in resource endowments do not explain intra-industry trade between the developed countries, what does? At first glance, the causes of such trade are not hard to find. They lie in the advantages of large-scale production—economies of scale, learning, and scope—that lead to a random division of labor in which those firms that first introduce a particular product gain cost advantages over new entrants. They lie in differences in national patterns of demand and subtle product differentiations designed to meet the desires of distinct national markets. And they lie in national differences in educational systems and technological capabilities.

But what, then, determines the kinds of technological capabilities a country fosters, the kinds of demand patterns it develops, or whether its firms are first-movers in scale-intensive industries? Such country-based sources of competitive advantage have something important in common—*they are created, not inherited.* They can be attributed, at least in part, to salient differences in how national economies are organized and in the economic objectives they pursue.[1]

As competition between the high-technology firms of the developed countries has intensified, the role of such differences in shaping competitive outcomes has commanded greater attention. Competition between American, European, and Japanese companies has spilled over into competition between the American, European, and Japanese models of capitalism.[2] Trade conflicts, once narrowly centered on national border policies, now often entail national differences in areas that have traditionally been the domain of domestic policy choice.

Nowhere are systemic competition and friction between the developed countries more heated than in technology-intensive industries. Conceptually, a high-technology industry is one in which knowledge is a prime source of competitive advantage for producers, who in turn make large investments in knowledge creation.[3] Reflecting this definition, high-technology industries are usually identified as those with above-average spending on research and development, above-average employment of scientists and engineers, or both. Several similar classification schemes have been developed for high-technology industries and are used throughout the following discussion. Table 2.1 contains a brief description of these schemes.

High-technology industries are disproportionately concentrated in the developed countries. In 1987, 82 percent of the world's R&D expenditure and 69 percent of the world's R&D personnel were located in just five industrial countries: the United States, Japan, France, the United Kingdom, and Germany. With the addition of five smaller European countries, the combined shares rise to 91 percent and 84 percent, respectively (Dunning 1990b). The share of technology-intensive production in total manufactured output has increased steadily in the developed countries during the past twenty years. According to preliminary estimates, high-technology goods accounted for about 30 percent of American, about 20 percent of European, and about 35 percent of Japanese manufactured output in 1990 (National Science Board, *Science and Engineering Indicators 1991,* appendix table 6-41, 404). Between 1980 and 1990, the shares of the United States and Europe in global high-technology production (as measured by the classification of the Organization for Economic Cooperation and Development, or OECD) declined by about 11 percent and 17 percent, respectively, while Japan's share increased by about 59 percent (National Science Board, *Science and Engineering Indicators 1991,* appendix table 6-3, 402).

In the 19 years between 1970 and 1989, exports of technology-intensive goods (as defined by Guerrieri and Milana 1991; see table 2.1) climbed from 12 percent to 21 percent of world manufactured exports. In 1986, 37 percent of America's,

---

1. For a recent popular discussion of how differences in the organization of national economies affect their competitive position in international trade, see Porter (1990).

2. The same conclusion is reached by Sylvia Ostry (1990a and b).

3. This definition is based on a similar definition by Paul Krugman (1991b).

one-third of Japan's, and 18 percent of Europe's manufactured exports were high-technology products (table 2.2). In that year the industrialized countries of the OECD accounted for almost 84 percent of world high-technology exports.

As a result of growing trade and investment, the import share of the domestic markets for high-technology products (as defined by the OECD) has increased in all three regions, but the increase has been larger in the United States and Europe than in Japan. Between 1980 and 1990, the share of imports in domestic high-technology markets jumped from about 8 percent to about 14 percent in the United States, from about 25 percent to about 41 percent in Germany, from about 33 percent to about 55 percent in France, and from about 7 percent to about 9 percent in Japan (National Science Board, *Science and Engineering Indicators 1991*, appendix table 6-5, 405). The figure for Japan not only remains the smallest but also increased the least during the 1980s.

Over the last two decades, significant changes have occurred in the competitive positions of the United States, Europe, and Japan in high-technology trade. According to the Guerrieri-Milana classification scheme, both the American and the European shares of global high-technology exports declined between 1970 and 1989, while the Japanese share steadily increased (table 2.3). A similar conclusion is suggested by the OECD classification scheme for the 1970–86 period (National Science Board, *Science and Technology Indicators,* appendix 7-10). According to Guerrieri and Milana (1991), Japan's share in global high-technology exports more than doubled from about 7 percent in 1970–73 to about 16 percent in 1988–89, while the US share declined from about 30 percent to about 21 percent. Significantly, the Japanese share continued to rise and the US share to fall after 1985, despite the sharp appreciation of the yen and depreciation of the dollar.[4] Meanwhile, the European share (here defined as that of the nine members of the European Community before 1981) declined steadily from about 46 percent in 1970–73 to about 37 percent in 1988–89. The overall European decline was reflected in similar declines for individual European countries.

Underlying these trends are changes in the revealed comparative advantage of the United States, Europe, and Japan. The revealed comparative advantage of the United States in high-technology products—measured by the ratio between the US share of global exports of these products and the US share of global exports of all manufactured products—declined between 1970 and 1989 (table 2.4). The ratio for the nine EC members also declined during this period, although by a smaller percentage. In contrast, Japan's revealed comparative advantage in high-technology products soared.

The revealed comparative advantage of the United States declined in four major high-technology product areas (mechanical equipment, electronics, scientific instruments, and aircraft and parts) while increasing in only one (chemicals and drugs; table 2.4). Europe also gained comparative advantage in chemicals

---

4. Although, as Krugman (1991a) has argued, the dollar's drop had the predicted effect of improving the overall US trade balance, it was unable to stem a further deterioration in the US share of many high-technology markets. Instead, the United States registered big gains in shares of global markets for nonmanufactured products and in resource-intensive manufactured products (such as steel and paper), traditional manufactured products (such as textiles, apparel, and furniture), and scale-intensive manufactured products (such as chemicals).

Table 2.1 Alternative classification schemes for high-technology industries

Classification scheme	Categories identified as high technology
Organization for Economic Cooperation and Development (OECD), International Standard Industrial Classification (ISIC)[a]	Drugs and medicines (ISIC 3522)
	Office machinery and computers (ISIC 3825)
	Electrical machinery (ISIC 383, but excluding 3832)
	Electronic components (ISIC 3832)
	Aerospace (ISIC 3845)
	Scientific instruments (ISIC 385)
US Department of Commerce, Standard Industrial Classification (SIC)	Guided missiles and spacecraft (SIC 376)
	Communications equipment and electronic components (SIC 365 and 366)
	Aircraft and parts (SIC 372)
	Office, computing, and accounting machines (SIC 367)
	Ordnance and accessories (SIC 348)
	Drugs and medicines (SIC 283)
	Industrial organic chemicals (SIC 351)
	Plastic materials, synthetic resins, rubber, and fibers (SIC 282)
Guerrieri and Milana[b]	Chemicals
	Synthetic organic coloring
	Products for agriculture
	Radioactive materials
	Polymers and plastics
	Pharmaceuticals
	Antibiotics and selected other products
	Power-generating machinery
	Turbines
	Piston engines
	Electrical
	Power machinery and selected apparatus
	Data processing
	Machines
	Processing and storage units
	Parts

Electronic office machines
Photocopying apparatus
Other
Telecommunications
Telephone, telegraphy, and transmission apparatus
Selected equipment, parts, and accessories
Electronic components
Integrated circuits and microassemblies
Semiconductors
Television picture tubes
Selected parts
Aircraft
Aircraft
Helicopters
Spacecraft
Reaction engines
Scientific instruments
Electronic measuring and controlling instruments
Particle accelerators
Optical instruments

a. OECD data in these ISIC categories was 96 percent coextensive with data in the US Department of Commerce categories in 1980, and 100 percent in 1986.

b. The Guerrieri-Milana classification scheme is a refinement of the OECD scheme. The authors use data on world trade flows at the five-digit SITC level to classify certain industrial products within the OECD high-technology industrial classification schemes as "high-technology" products. They base their classification decisions on experts' and analysts' judgments. This "subjective" approach to identifying high-technology trade is now used by the US Bureau of the Census to calculate high-technology trade balances for the United States. A recent paper by Abbot discusses the advantages and disadvantages of this approach and contrasts it with the more traditional OECD and Commerce approaches.

Sources: Paolo Guerrieri and Carlo Milana, "Technological and Trade Competition in High-Tech Products" BRIE Working Papers 54 (Berkeley: University of California, Berkeley), October 1991; T. A. Abbot, "Measuring High-Technology Trade: Contrasting International Trade Administration and Bureau of Census Methodologies and Results," Journal of Economic and Social Measurement 17: 17–44, 1991.

Table 2.2 High-technology exports as a share of total manufactures exports, selected countries, 1970–86 (percentages)[a]

Year	All countries[b]	France	Germany	Japan	United Kingdom	United States	Other	Europe[c]
1970	16	14	16	20	17	26	11	14
1975	16	14	15	18	19	25	11	14
1980	17	14	16	24	21	27	11	15
1982	19	18	18	26	24	31	12	16
1984	21	18	18	32	26	34	12	16
1985	22	19	18	32	27	36	13	17
1986	22	19	18	33	28	37	14	18

a. High-technology products are those defined by the OECD as "high-intensity technology products" (see table 2.1).
b. Includes, in addition to the countries listed, Australia, Austria, Belgium, Canada, Denmark, Greece, Iceland, Ireland, Italy, the Netherlands, New Zealand, Norway, Portugal, Spain, Switzerland, Turkey, and Yugoslavia.
c. Includes France, Germany, the United Kingdom, and the European countries listed in the preceding footnote.
Source: National Science Board, *Science and Engineering Indicators 1989*, appendix 7-11.

Table 2.3 Shares of world high-technology exports, selected countries, 1970–89 (percentages)[a]

Country	1970–73	1973–76	1976–79	1979–82	1982–85	1985–87	1988–89	Change 1970–89
OECD	95.57	93.93	91.52	88.79	86.80	85.40	83.64	−11.94
United States	29.54	27.36	24.37	25.07	25.24	22.29	20.64	−8.91
Canada	4.25	3.05	2.45	2.03	2.47	2.37	2.65	−1.61
Japan	7.07	7.54	9.21	10.06	12.93	15.03	16.01	8.94
EC-9[b]	46.38	47.50	47.48	44.14	39.26	38.60	37.38	−9.00
Germany	16.59	17.07	16.52	14.66	12.98	13.07	12.52	−4.08
France	7.22	8.06	8.78	8.10	7.26	7.07	6.80	−0.42
United Kingdom	10.12	9.47	9.70	9.87	8.45	7.54	7.64	−2.48
Italy	4.41	4.15	4.10	3.92	3.72	3.72	3.41	−1.00
Other EC-9	8.04	8.74	8.38	7.59	6.84	7.20	7.02	−1.02
Greece, Portugal, Spain	0.50	0.65	0.71	0.85	0.91	0.98	1.12	0.62
EFTA[c]	7.56	7.53	7.06	6.11	5.53	5.88	5.57	−1.99
Non-OECD	3.99	5.64	7.61	9.29	12.03	13.70	15.03	11.04
Asian NICS	1.3	2.28	3.18	4.06	6.05	7.56	8.76	7.46

NICS = newly industrializing countries (Hong Kong, Korea, Singapore, and Taiwan)

a. Each number is the average ratio of the country's or region's high-technology exports to total world high-technology exports (Guerrieri and Milana classification) for each subperiod.

b. The nine member countries of the European Community before the accession of Greece, Portugal, and Spain (includes, in addition to the four countries listed, Belgium, Denmark, Ireland, Luxembourg, and the Netherlands.

c. The countries of the European Free Trade Association: Austria, Iceland, Norway, Sweden, Switzerland, and (associate member) Finland.

Sources: SIE-World Trade Data Base; Paolo Guerrieri and Carlo Milana, "Technological and Trade Competition in High-Tech Products" BRIE Working Papers 54 (Berkeley: University of California, Berkeley), October 1991.

Table 2.4 Revealed comparative advantage in selected high-technology products, selected countries, 1970–89[a]

Product group	United States		Japan		Asian NICs[b]		EC-9[c]		Germany		France		United Kingdom		Italy	
	1970–73	1986–89	1970–73	1986–89	1970–73	1986–89	1970–73	1986–89	1970–73	1986–89	1970–73	1986–89	1970–73	1986–89	1970–73	1986–89
All high-technology products	219	192	80	133	54	110	99	91	111	91	97	105	132	133	79	62
Chemicals and drugs	111	124	86	47	45	46	123	130	159	132	99	156	103	122	114	84
Mechanical equipment	156	145	93	144	21	68	108	97	140	129	105	114	141	110	79	65
Electronics	212	168	110	200	132	190	95	71	99	57	97	72	113	122	88	53
Aircraft and parts	440	416	6	7	16	20	63	91	20	79	87	148	175	178	41	63
Scientific instruments	217	208	86	100	15	43	103	109	138	135	93	95	135	199	53	54

a. Ratio of a country's or region's world export share in the product group to that country's or region's share of total world exports of manufactures.

b. The newly industrializing countries of Hong Kong, Korea, Singapore, and Taiwan.

c. The member countries of the European Community before the accession of Greece, Portugal, and Spain.

High-technology products are those defined by the Guerrieri and Milana classification scheme (see table 2.1).

Source: SIE-World Trade Data Base; Paolo Guerrieri and Carlo Milana, "Technological and Trade Competition in High-Tech Products" *BRIE Working Papers* 54 (Berkeley: University of California, Berkeley), October 1991.

Table 2.5 Shares of world trade in R&D–intensive electronics products, selected countries, 1970–89ᵃ (percentages)

Country	1973–79	1979–82	1985–88	1988–89
United States	28.9	23.8	19.2	18.3
Japan	9.6	17.0	23.4	24.0
East Asian NICS	3.1	8.7	13.4	15.1
EC-9	44.7	37.4	30.8	28.6

ED-9 = the nine members of the European Community before the accession of Greece, Portugal, and Spain (data include intra-EC trade); NICS = newly industrializing countries (Hong Kong, Korea, Singapore, and Taiwan).
a. See the Guerrieri-Milana classification in table 2.1 for product coverage.
Source: Paolo Guerrieri and Carlo Milana, "Technological and Trade Competition in High-Tech Products" BRIE Working Papers 54 (Berkeley: University of California, Berkeley), October 1991.

and drugs but did so even more strongly in aircraft and parts. The analysis in chapter 5 implies that the gain in European strength in the aircraft complex came at the expense of the United States, a conclusion that is consistent with these results.

The erosion of the American and European positions was especially pronounced in electronics. Not surprisingly, both Japan and the East Asian newly industrializing countries scored dramatic gains in revealed comparative advantage in this sector. These findings are confirmed by data presented in the other chapters of this book and by the data on production and export shares in selected electronics products in tables 2.5 and 2.6.

Despite a strong competitive advantage in some electronics products, the United States has lost strength relative to Japan in the electronics complex as a whole. The deterioration of the US position began in consumer electronics and electronic office equipment and later extended to electronic components and most recently to data processing equipment. Because of the rapid growth in world electronics markets during the past twenty years, the offsetting shifts in the positions of the United States and Japan have ignited recurrent trade friction between the two nations. As table 2.7 indicates, despite the sharp drop in the dollar after 1985 the US trade deficit with Japan in electronics improved by only 3.4 percent between 1986 and 1991, and the 1991 deficit of $19.7 billion was dramatically higher than the 1980 deficit of $3.9 billion. In 1989, according to an industry source,[5] 1 percentage point of the global electronics market was worth approximately $7.3 billion. By this measure, the loss in the US share of this market between 1985 and 1989 meant forgone sales of approximately $105 billion. The lion's share of this loss was matched by an offsetting Japanese gain.

Before leaving this discussion of high-technology competition, it is useful to examine some trends in US high-technology trade. High-technology industries have contributed a significant share of both US exports and imports in recent years (table 2.8). In 1988, the last year for which a consistent time series is available, these industries contributed 41 percent of US manufactured exports and 26 percent of US manufactured imports. Three sectors—computers and

---

5. Estimate provided by a Motorola official in August 1991.

Table 2.6　United States, Japan, and Europe: export shares in selected electronics products, 1980–88 (percentages)

Product	1980			1988		
	United States	Japan	European Community	United States	Japan	European Community
Office and computing equipment	42	6	47	32	20	46
Semiconductors	44	29	21	31	40	17
DRAMS	60	39	1	16	74	2
Radio, television, and communications equipment	24	27	42	24	34	36

Sources: Office and computing equipment and radio, television, and communications equipment: Science and Engineering Indicators, 1991, appendix table 6–7, 408 (export shares); semiconductors and DRAMS: Dataquest (production shares). Dataquest data reproduced with permission.

office equipment, communications and electronics, and aircraft and parts—contributed a sizeable majority of America's high-technology exports. In 1988, according to US Department of Commerce data, they were responsible for 68 percent of the total. These sectors, along with a few other high-technology product lines such as engines and turbines, inorganic chemicals, and plastics, are considerably more export-intensive, as measured by the ratio of their exports to their value added, than US manufacturing as a whole (table 2.9). Aircraft and computers and office equipment have the highest export intensities of all manufacturing industries.[6]

As a result of both intensifying foreign competition and the globalization of production, however, many high-technology industries are also relatively import-intensive as well. In fact, with the notable exceptions of plastics and aircraft, the most export-intensive high-technology industries are also the most import-intensive (table 2.9). Since the United States is a major high-technology market, growing import penetration has contributed to the decline in the US share of global high-technology exports. This penetration has been particularly pronounced in high-technology electronics industries, in part because of the growing competitive strength of Japanese and East Asian producers, and in part because of the extensive globalization of production by American multinationals.

Several recent studies document the erosion of the US position in electronics and other high-technology industries. Studies by the Japanese Ministry of International Trade and Industry (MITI), the US National Research Council, defense and nondefense agencies of the US government, and private-sector business groups reach the same general conclusions (tables 2A.1 through 2A.4 in the appendix to this chapter). The number of technologies in which the United States has a clear lead over Japan and Europe has decreased over time, particularly during the last decade. In some critical technologies, the United States

---

6. According to the Council on Competitiveness, in 1988 the most export-intensive companies in terms of their exports-sales ratios included Boeing (46.3 percent), Intel (32.3 percent), Compaq Computer (29.6 percent), McDonnell Douglas (23.0 percent), Motorola (21.2 percent), Hewlett-Packard (21.0 percent), and Unisys (20.3 percent).

Table 2.7   United States: trade with Japan in electronics products, by type of product, 1980–91 (billions of dollars)

Product	SIC categories[a]	1980	1986	1989	1991
Computers and related products	3573, 3574, and 1579				
Exports	through 1987;	0.60	1.5	3.2	3.6
Imports	3571, 3572, 3575,	0.80	6.0	9.3	9.8
Balance	3577–9 thereafter	−0.20	−4.5	−6.0	−6.2
Consumer products	3651				
Exports		0.10	0.1	0.2	0.2
Imports		2.30	8.7	5.0	4.2
Balance		−2.30	−8.6	−4.7	−4.0
Telecommunications					
Exports	3661, 3662 through	0.10	0.3	0.5	0.6
Imports	1987; 3661, 3663,	0.60	2.9	4.2	4.3
Balance	3669, thereafter	0.50	−2.6	−3.8	−3.7
Other electronic equipment[b]	3699, 3812				
Exports		n.a.	n.a.	0.5	0.5
Imports		n.a.	n.a.	0.5	0.5
Balance		n.a.	n.a.	0.0	0.0
Semiconductors and other components	3674 (semicon-				
Exports	ductors); 367	0.30	0.7	1.7	2.2
Imports	through 1987, 367	0.90	4.1	6.5	6.6
Balance	less 3674, plus 3695 thereafter (other)	−0.60	−3.4	−4.8	−4.4
Medical					
Exports	3693 through 1987;	0.10	0.2	0.4	0.5
Imports	3844, 3845	0.05	0.3	0.5	0.7
Balance	thereafter	0.05	−0.1	−0.1	−0.2
Instruments					
Exports		0.40	0.7	1.3	Included
Imports		0.40	1.2	0.9	with
Balance		0.00	−0.5	−0.8	"Other"
Other[c]	3811, 3822–25, 3829,	0.01	0.1	0.1	0.7
Exports	3832 through 1987;	0.42	0.7	0.9	1.6
Imports	3822–26, 3829	0.41	−0.6	−0.8	−0.9
Balance	thereafter				
Total, all electronics products					
Exports		1.60	3.5	7.5	8.2
Imports		5.50	23.9	27.7	27.9
Balance		−3.90	−20.4	−20.2	−19.7

n.a. = not available; SIC = Standard International Classification.

a. Beginning in 1989, data use new SIC codes introduced that year. Therefore, segment data for 1989 and later are not directly comparable with earlier data. The change to a harmonized system beginning with 1989 data may have introduced a discontinuity between 1988 and 1989.

b. Included with telecommunications prior to 1989.

c. Data for 1991 also include SIC 3861 and EIA adjustment.

Source: American Electronics Association, as furnished by the US International Trade Administration (1980 data) and the US Bureau of the Census (other years). Data reprinted with permission.

Table 2.8　United States: trade in high-technology products, 1980–88 (billions of dollars except as noted)

	1980	1981	1982	1983	1984	1985	1986	1987	1988
Exports									
Total high-technology	55	60	58	60	66	68	73	84	104
Total manufactures	161	172	155	149	164	168	180	200	255
High-technology share of total (percentages)	34	35	37	40	40	41	41	42	41
Imports									
Total high-technology	27	33	34	40	58	63	73	81	96
Total manufactures	139	156	158	178	242	270	309	338	374
High-technology share of total (percentages)	19	21	22	22	24	23	24	24	26

a. High-technology products are defined according to the US Department of Commerce classification scheme (table 2.1).
Source: US Department of Commerce, International Trade Administration, Office of Trade and Investment Analysis.

now lags behind Japan, in some cases significantly (see *The Economist*, 11 January 1992, 17–19). Even in the computer industry, private-sector analysts see emerging signs of technological weakness. (table 2A.3). In the aircraft industry, the other major source of US high-technology exports, Europe has reached technological parity (see chapter 5 for evidence).

In short, "the advantage in high-technology industries [the United States] once took for granted has virtually disappeared" (Bloch 1991). To some extent, this development should not be cause for concern—indeed, as Richard Nelson (1990, 130–31) has argued, it was inevitable for several reasons. First, trade liberalization around the world neutralized the advantages of American firms deriving from the size of the US market. Second, technology became more generally accessible to those with the requisite skills and willing to make the requisite investments. The other developed countries and a handful of newly industrializing countries proved to be the main beneficiaries of the global diffusion of technological knowledge. Finally, as a result of a decline in spillovers from military R&D to the civilian economy, America's military preeminence no longer guarantees its technological preeminence (see Alic et al. 1992; Mowery and Rosenberg 1989a, 137–50; and Stowsky 1986).

The convergence of technological capabilities and productivity levels among the developed countries has been beneficial both economically, by providing growing foreign markets and technological knowledge for US producers, and geopolitically, by providing the foundation for a stable and prosperous Western alliance. Nonetheless, the fact that the United States no longer holds the lead in many critical process and product technologies, coupled with the fact that these technologies have been targeted for promotion abroad, worries many US policymakers and US companies. Some observers dismiss this anxiety as the petulant whimpering of a "diminished economic giant" (see, e.g., Bhagwati 1991). In contrast, this author considers the loss of America's technological leadership to be a justifiable policy concern.

Table 2.9   United States: high-technology exports and imports as a share of total value added, by industry, 1980–88
(percentages except as noted)[a]

Industry	Export shares			Import shares		
	1980	1984	1988	1980	1984	1988
Industrial organic chemicals	33.0	34.0	32.3	25.3	30.0	27.9
Plastic materials and synthetics	49.1	32.1	35.8	5.4	9.8	10.2
Drugs	14.7	13.0	13.0	7.1	8.2	11.8
Ordnance and accessories	23.9	19.6	13.9	5.2	4.6	8.3
Engines and turbines	54.9	41.2	49.5	25.5	28.7	61.1
Computers and office equipment	47.6	50.2	72.3	14.0	34.3	61.0
Communications and electronics	23.9	20.5	36.4	27.5	39.2	70.0
Aircraft and parts	52.7	40.3	61.9	9.6	10.9	15.4
Missiles and spacecraft	10.2	6.6	5.6	0.0	1.5	0.3
Scientific instruments	26.7	20.9	17.1	19.6	22.1	19.2
Average for high-technology industries	33.8	27.4	34.7	16.9	24.1	32.0
Average for all industries	20.8	16.6	20.2	17.9	24.6	29.7
Relative export intensity of high-technology industries[b]	1.63	1.74	n.a.			
Relative import intensity of high-technology industries[b]				0.94	0.98	1.08

n.a. = not available.
a. Both exports and value added are in current dollars.
b. Relative export (import) intensity is defined as the high-technology export (import) ratio divided by the all-industries export (import) ratio.
Source: US Department of Commerce, *Annual Survey of Manufactures, Census of Manufactures,* various years; US Department of Commerce, International Trade Administration, Office of Trade and Investment Analysis.

The Roots of High-Technology Trade Conflict: Trade Barriers, Structural Impediments, and Structural Differences

Trade friction between the developed countries in technology-intensive industries takes many forms, including conflicts over market access, dumping, rules of origin, import quotas, government procurement, industrial subsidies and targeting, standards and testing, and patent protection.

Some of these conflicts involve the standard fare of trade disputes—border and nonborder policies that *by intent or design* discriminate between domestic and foreign products, between domestic and foreign producers, or between foreign products imported from abroad and foreign products produced locally. For want of a better term, such policies will be called "trade barriers" throughout this discussion. Trade barriers include tariffs, import quotas, dumping laws, rules of origin, preferential procurement policies, subsidies, and other forms of industrial targeting.

Trade barriers, broadly defined in this way, encompass policy instruments that go far beyond traditional border measures. Both Japan and Europe, as well as the newly industrializing countries, have consciously employed various trade barriers to foster their high-technology industries. Their efforts have been motivated by a number of anticipated benefits, including more productive and better-paying jobs, enhanced national security, a more competitive supply base for critical inputs, and technological spillovers between technology-intensive industries and the rest of the economy. As the case studies in this book demonstrate, many of their policies have been beggar-thy-neighbor or mercantilist in character, sometimes encouraging a comparable US reaction.[7] Not surprisingly, trade barriers deployed to promote national high-technology producers are recurrent sources of friction between the United States and its trading partners.

Other trade conflicts emanate from national differences in a wide variety of policies and institutions that affect the terms of international competition. At issue in such conflicts are a potpourri of things including standards and testing, intellectual property protection, health and safety regulations, competition policy, the organization and support of R&D, corporate financial structures, and the nature of business-government relations. Even when not designed to advantage one set of national producers over another, structural differences may nevertheless have that effect. Perhaps because of this, such differences have come to be called "structural impediments" to trade—a term used by the OECD and by the United States in its recent bilateral negotiations with Japan.

To some extent, the broadening of trade conflict to encompass structural differences is the inevitable consequence of the dramatic growth of trade and transnational investment. In Bhagwati's (1991, 16) colorful words, expanding trade and investment are turning the "globalized world economy into a veritable spider's web, where everyone is now in everyone else's backyard, making import competition in one's own market and export competition in the other's market and in third markets ever more fierce." In technology-intensive industries, as in finance and other services, the ferocity of competition has sparked conflicts about national policies and institutions that appear to favor one or more of the players. Sometimes these effects are imagined or overdrawn, but sometimes they are real and significant.

Broad structural differences influence the terms of international competition in global high-technology industries in two ways. First, such differences affect the accessibility of different national markets to foreign competitors. Differences in language are the most obvious example. National differences in regulatory institutions, in antitrust laws and their enforcement, in patent procedures, and

---

7. Indeed, sometimes these policies are nothing short of a kind of technological mercantilism. The recent expulsion of the Fujitsu-owned company ICL from JESSI, Europe's publicly funded semiconductor research project, comes to mind.

even in land use policies may have large but unintended effects on the ability of foreign firms to break into a particular national market. Such differences can pose very real "structural impediments" to market access.

Second, structural differences create different incentive environments and behavioral tendencies for firms of different nationality. The long-term vision of Japanese companies is partly an outgrowth of the financial environment in which they operate (see chapter 3). The seeming inability of American firms to cooperate with one another is fostered—indeed, in some instances mandated—by the antitrust environment in which they function. The relatively open and rapid flow of technological information in the United States is encouraged by the high job turnover of scientific and engineering personnel and by the concentration of basic research in academic institutions. In Japan, lifetime employment and the concentration of basic research in proprietary laboratories produce the opposite result.

The home-country environments of global companies create a pattern of country-based advantages or disadvantages that shape outcomes in global markets. As Porter and others have observed, the black box of profit-maximizing capitalist firms obscures substantial diversity in national behavior, bred by diversity in national economic institutions and historical traditions.[8] Competition between firms gestated in different national systems is, to some extent, competition among the systems themselves (a point also made by Sylvia Ostry 1990b).

Because of the special production characteristics of high-technology industries—economies of scale, scope, and learning, and large and increasing entry barriers—policies designed to discriminate between domestic and foreign producers, as well as systemic differences that do so unintentionally, can have long-term consequences that are not easily reversed. Under such conditions, barriers to a lucrative foreign market can mean more for an American company than just a temporary loss in profits. Over time the company may face higher costs, a profit squeeze on R&D expenditures for future generations of products, restrictions on access to the latest technological information, and ultimately, extinction by their foreign competitors who have benefited from the sanctuary conditions of their home markets.

To summarize, technology-intensive industries are a source of growing trade friction between the United States and its trading partners for several reasons. First, these industries account for large and growing shares of their trade and investment with one another. Second, most of the nations with which the United States trades are committed to maintaining a national or a regional high-technology production base, even if it takes overtly neomercantilist trade barriers to do so. Third, even in the absence of such barriers, the global playing field is littered with structural impediments. Finally, because of increasing returns and market imperfections in high-technology industries, both trade barriers and structural differences can have long-term consequences for global competitive outcomes. Taken together, these four ingredients are a recipe for trade conflict.

---

8. As the evidence presented by Porter (1990) indicates, there are still striking similarities in the capabilities and strategies of individual firms of the same national origin. Many multinational high-technology firms are global in perspective, but they are still significantly national in terms of the behaviors they adopt.

Why High-Technology Industries Matter for US Economic Welfare

As already noted in chapter 1, an underlying premise of this book is that technology-intensive industries make special contributions to the performance of the American economy. In the following discussion, I present data and analytical arguments to justify this premise.

R&D and Spillover Benefits

By definition, high-technology industries sustain a disproportionate share of private R&D spending. Over the last decade, the 10 three-digit industries classified as high-technology industries by the US Department of Commerce funded nearly 60 percent of private industrial R&D in the United States. Together, the electronics complex (computers and office equipment, communications, electronic components, and audio and video equipment) and the aerospace complex (aircraft and missiles) accounted for about two-thirds of total high-technology R&D (table 2.10). Because of their military significance, aerospace, communications equipment, and electronic components also received nearly 80 percent of all federal funds for manufacturing R&D (table 2.10).

Private R&D provides benefits not just to the company funding it but to other producers and consumers, both at home and abroad. These spillover benefits occur in a variety of ways. Sometimes company research yields a scientific breakthrough with potential uses extending far beyond the applications of a specific producer. Often, even with effective patent protection, competitors are able to copy or reverse-engineer a private innovation. Competitors may also hire away key personnel, who bring technological information with them. Alternatively, scientists and engineers may leave one company to establish a competing one, as they have regularly done in the semiconductor and computer industries.

As a result of spillovers of all kinds, the social returns to R&D spending far exceed the private returns. According to a 1988 study, "a substantial gap exists between the private and social returns [to R&D] despite the availability of patents. The social rate of return is between 50 and 100 percent, so to be conservative we will say that the excess return to R&D is 35 to 60 percent above the return to ordinary capital."[9]

These findings contrast with Paul Krugman's (1991b) assertion that "on the whole the case that high-technology sectors generate strong returns over and above their direct returns is at best unsupported by the evidence." High-technology industries account for only about 20 percent of the nation's manufacturing output and 24 percent of its manufacturing value added (table 2.11) but nearly 60 percent of its industrial R&D (table 2.10). This fact, combined with evidence that such R&D produces substantial spillover benefits, is perhaps the most compelling reason for the long-run importance of these industries to the American economy.

---

9. Baily and Chakrabarti (1988, 39). A more recent survey of the empirical evidence (Griliches 1990) concludes that "There have been a significant number of reasonably well done studies all pointing in the same direction: R&D spillovers are present, their magnitude may be quite large, and the social rates of return remain significantly above private rates."

Table 2.10 United States: high-technology expenditures for R&D, by industry, selected years, 1979–89 (millions of dollars except where noted)

Industry	Industry funding[a]			Share of total R&D expenditures by all manufacturing firms, 1989	Federal funding		
	1979	1984	1989		1979	1984	1989
Industrial chemicals[b]	1,617	3,057	3,972	5.7	345	183	84
Drugs	n.a.	3,310	5,206	7.4	n.a.	n.a.	n.a.
Computers and office equipment	2,958	7,011	10,533	15.0	256	n.a.	n.a.
Audio and video equipment	192	362	85	0.1	53	n.a.	0
Communications equipment	2,049	5,147	5,842	8.3	1,586	3,538	4,666
Electronics components and accessories	n.a.	2,354	4,362	6.2	n.a.	477	522
Aircraft and missiles	2,201	4,764	6,020	8.6	5,840	14,094	19,634
Scientific instruments[c]	2,012	4,211	5,638	8.0	493	391	125
All high-technology industries	n.a.	30,216	41,658	59.3	n.a.	n.a.	n.a.
All industries	25,708	51,404	70,233		12,518	23,396	31,366
High-technology share of total R&D (percentages)[d]	n.a.	59	59		n.a.	n.a.	n.a.

n.a. = not available (for some industries, data are withheld by the National Science Foundation to avoid disclosing the operations of individual companies).

a. Funds from all sources except the federal government.

b. Includes SICs 281 (inorganic chemicals), 282 (plastics), and 286 (organic chemicals) rather than only the two high-technology categories (281 and 282).

c. Includes SIC 3825 (electrical test and measurement instruments).

d. These estimates understate the actual share because ordnance and engines are excluded from the high-technology total but included in the all-industries total.

Source: Data supplied by the National Science Foundation.

Table 2.11 United States: production and value added in selected high-technology industries, 1989

Industry	Value added		Production[a]	
	Millions of dollars	As a percentage of US manufacturing value added	Millions of dollars	As a percentage of US manufacturing production
Industrial organic chemicals	14,400	1.1	24,158	0.9
Plastic materials and synthetics	21,289	1.6	50,530	1.8
Drugs	34,358	2.6	49,114	1.8
Ordnance and accessories	5,118	0.4	7,342	0.3
Engines and turbines	7,637	0.6	16,931	0.6
Computers and office equipment	33,179	2.5	65,426	2.3
Audio and video equipment	3,402	0.3	9,421	0.3
Communications equipment	20,649	1.6	35,118	1.3
Electronic components and accessories	36,958	2.8	59,914	2.1
Aircraft and parts	44,889	3.4	83,980	3.0
Missiles and spacecraft	19,143	1.5	29,498	1.1
Scientific instruments	73,341	5.6	110,566	4.0
Total, all manufacturing	314,363	24.0	541,998	19.4

a. Production figures are less meaningful than value-added figures because of double counting of inputs in the former.
Source: US Department of Commerce, *Annual Survey of Manufactures 1989.*

34

Table 2.12 United States: employment in selected high-technology industries, 1989 (thousands of workers except as noted)

Industry	All workers	Production workers	Share of total US manufacturing employment (percentages)[a]
Industrial organic chemicals	97	54	0.5
Plastic materials and synthetics	131	89	0.7
Drugs	184	83	1.0
Ordnance and accessories	77	90	0.4
Engines and turbines	85	57	0.4
Computers and office equipment	305	114	1.6
Audio and video equipment	47	35	0.2
Communications equipment	254	122	1.3
Electronic components and accessories	551	339	2.9
Aircraft and parts	602	320	3.2
Missiles and spacecraft	221	80	1.2
Scientific instruments	890	453	4.7
Total	3,444	1,836	18.1

a. Share of industry employment (all workers) in total US manufacturing employment.
Source: US Department of Commerce, *Annual Survey of Manufactures 1989.*

Employment and Wages

A second reason, which is also intuitive given the way in which high-technology industries are defined, is their contribution to the nation's high-skill, high-wage employment opportunities. Together these industries account for only 18 percent (table 2.12) of total US manufacturing employment, but they account for at least one-third of US employment of scientists and engineers (table 2.13). On average, there are 82 R&D scientists and engineers per 1,000 employees in high-technology industries in the United States, compared with 45 per 1,000 employees in all of manufacturing.

Partly as a consequence of their greater skill intensity, most high-technology industries are also high-productivity industries that pay higher compensation than do other manufacturing industries, which in turn enjoy higher productivity and levels of compensation than do most service activities. In 1989, value added per worker in all high-technology industries was one-third higher than the average for all manufacturing, and two-thirds higher if only production workers are included in the calculations (table 2.14). In that year, average annual compensation in high-technology industries was 22 percent higher than the average for all manufacturing (table 2.15). Even for the category of production workers—a category that excludes most white-collar scientists and engineers—high-technology industries on average paid compensation 15 percent higher than that offered in manufacturing as a whole. And several high-technology industries paid their production workers 20 percent to 40 percent more than the average manufacturing wage, which in turn was more than twice the wage paid in retail services (which accounted for about 21 percent of all nonagricultural employment in the United States in 1989; *Economic Report of the President*, 1992, appendix tables B-41 and B-42). More disaggregated data, correcting for differences in the skill

Table 2.13   United States: scientists and engineers employed in selected high-technology industries, 1989

Industry	Scientists and engineers per thousand employees	Ratio to average for manufacturing	Imputed absolute number of scientists and engineers	Percentage of total for all US firms
Industrial organic chemicals[a]	53	1.18	18,115	2
Drugs	97	2.16	16,674	2
Ordnance and accessories	n.a.	n.a.	n.a.	n.a.
Engines and turbines	n.a.	n.a.	n.a.	n.a.
Computers and office equipment	113	2.51	37,030	4
Audio and video equipment	44	0.98	1,945	0
Communications equipment	72	1.60	18,734	2
Electronic components and accessories	90	2.00	49,176	6
Aircraft and missiles	89	1.98	72,063	8
Scientific instruments[b]	75	1.67	73,680	9
Average for all high-technology industries[c]	82	1.83	287,418	34
Average for all manufacturing	45	1.00	852,764	100

a. Includes SIC 281 (inorganic chemicals), SIC 282 (plastics), and SIC 286 (organic chemicals) rather than only the two high-technology SIC categories (281 and 282).
b. Includes SIC 3825 (electrical test and measurement instruments).
c. Calculated as the weighted average of all categories in table except ordnance and ammunition, and engines and turbines, using total industry employment as weights. The imputed number of scientists and engineers for all high-technology industry is the sum for the individual industries.
Source: National Science Foundation, *Research and Development in Industry, 1989.*

Table 2.14 United States: value added per worker in selected high-technology industries, 1989

Industry	All workers		Production workers	
	Value added per worker (dollars)	Ratio to US manufacturing average	Value added per worker (dollars)	Ratio to US manufacturing average
Industrial inorganic chemicals	148,301	2.16	269,159	2.54
Plastic materials and synthetics	162,264	2.36	397,925	3.75
Drugs	186,931	2.72	386,914	3.65
Ordnance and accessories	66,468	0.97	61,886	0.58
Engines and turbines	89,741	1.31	135,168	1.28
Computers and office equipment	108,712	1.58	290,026	2.74
Audio and video equipment	72,692	1.06	96,102	0.91
Communications equipment	81,391	1.18	169,671	1.60
Electronic components and accessories	67,074	0.98	109,149	1.03
Aircraft and parts	74,517	1.08	140,410	1.32
Missiles and spacecraft	86,659	1.26	239,887	2.26
Scientific instruments	82,489	1.20	161,828	1.53
Average for all high-technology industries	91,297	1.33	175,504	1.66
Average for all manufacturing industries	68,700	1.00	105,992	1.00

Source: US Department of Commerce, Annual Survey of Manufactures 1989.

Table 2.15 United States: compensation in selected high-technology industries, 1989

Industry	All workers		Production workers			
	Average annual compensation (dollars)	Ratio to US manufacturing average	Average annual compensation (dollars)	Ratio to US manufacturing average	Weekly wages (dollars)[a]	Ratio to US manufacturing average
Industrial inorganic chemicals	36,000	1.32	30,593	1.40	629	1.42
Plastic materials and synthetics	35,305	1.29	31,169	1.43	596	1.35
Drugs	35,185	1.29	26,145	1.20	538	1.22
Ordnance and accessories	29,727	1.09	12,911	0.59	492	1.11
Engines and turbines	35,259	1.29	32,228	1.48	620	1.40
Computers and office equipment	35,957	1.32	23,351	1.07	483	1.09
Audio and video equipment	21,064	0.77	17,286	0.79	397	0.90
Communications equipment	33,476	1.23	25,180	1.15	472	1.07
Electronic components and accessories	27,515	1.01	19,617	0.90	403	0.91
Aircraft and parts	36,184	1.33	30,856	1.41	626	1.42
Missiles and spacecraft	40,679	1.49	34,025	1.56	612	1.38
Scientific instruments	31,627	1.16	24,079	1.10	465	1.05
Average for all high-technology industries	33,223	1.22	25,102	1.15	510	1.15
Average for all manufacturing industries	27,272	1.00	21,822	1.00	442	2.00

a. Data are for 1990.
Source: US Department of Labor, Bureau of Labor Statistics, "Employment and Earnings," March 1991; US Department of Commerce, *Annual Survey of Manufactures 1989.*

composition and degree of unionization of the work force, tell a similar story (Dickens and Lang 1988, Katz and Summers 1989).

Labor economists have found that such persistent and large wage differentials cannot be wholly attributed to differences in skill or working conditions. High-technology industries are among the high-wage industries identified in recent studies of such "noncompetitive wage differentials" by Dickens and Lang (1988) and by Katz and Summers (1989). Both studies find that the interindustry wage structure is remarkably stable over both time and space. Most high-technology industries are high-wage industries in both the United States and the other developed countries, and they are likely to remain so for decades.

Higher Returns to Capital?

According to the new trade theory, industries can be of special or "strategic" significance to economic welfare in either of two ways: by providing a higher return to factors of production than they could earn elsewhere in the economy, or by providing spillover benefits for the rest of the economy (see the introduction to Krugman 1986, 14). The evidence presented here indicates that most high-technology industries are strategic in both ways. They fund a disproportionate amount of industrial R&D, and thus generate spillover effects, and they provide quasi-rents or higher returns to labor than those available in most other economic activities.

On the other hand, neither the evidence provided in the cases in this book nor the more systematic evidence reported by Katz and Summers confirms the hypothesis that high-technology industries generate higher returns to *capital* than those available elsewhere in the economy. According to Katz and Summers, "Whereas the recent literature on strategic trade policy has examined policy measures that can shift monopoly rents between nations, our estimates suggest that capital owners in the American economy receive few monopoly rents" (Katz and Summers 1989, 210). However, the cash flow generated in such industries, as distinct from their returns to capital, appears to be an important determinant of their R&D activity (see Hall 1990 and 1991, Fazzari et al. 1988, Hoshi et al. 1988, and Jorgenson 1971). This is understandable given the risks associated with R&D investment and the failures of private capital markets in the presence of such risks. As the case studies demonstrate, trade barriers and foreign market impediments that cut company sales and earnings can reduce R&D and its potential spillover benefits.

The Local Character of High-Technology Spillovers

There is an important difference between the possible strategic benefits of high-technology industries in the form of "rents" earned by their employees and their possible strategic benefits in the form of R&D spillovers. The former benefits are local or national in character, whereas often the latter are not. The competitive struggle between nations to secure a bigger share of the global rents from high-technology production is inherently beggar-thy-neighbor or zero-sum in nature. What one nation gains, others lose. Understandably, one nation's measures to promote its high-wage, high-technology producers can easily raise the ire of its trading partners. The case of Europe's aggressive promotion of Airbus Industrie comes quickly to mind. Even moderate free traders like Katz and Summers (1989, 270–271) conclude that labor rents in the commercial aircraft industry may be sufficiently large to tip the balance in favor of interventionist policies.

Unlike rents, R&D spillovers are not necessarily national in scope. Indeed, given the diffusion of production and information made possible by modern communications systems, they are increasingly global in reach. Whether through such dubious channels as industrial espionage and patent infringement, or through such acceptable channels as joint ventures, cooperative transnational R&D projects, and professional journals, much of the technological knowledge generated by a private company in a particular national setting can generate spillover benefits for the rest of the world.

Of course, there are delays in the international diffusion of knowledge— delays that are sometimes long enough to allow first-movers to appropriate a hefty take of private returns before losing monopoly control. And the extent and speed of knowledge diffusion are not insensitive to national institutions and regulations. Indeed, one of the objectives of US trade policy has been to impose tougher intellectual property conventions on its trading partners. When they are successful, such efforts reduce the global social returns to R&D funded by American companies. Finally, not all knowledge is footloose, even absent institutional and legal impediments to its diffusion.[10] A second kind of knowledge, such as that embodied in the design and operation of a company-specific production process, can be internalized by the firm, often for long periods of time.[11] The R&D that gives rise to such firm-specific knowledge may yield only narrowly private, fully appropriable returns.

Conceptually, a third kind of knowledge can be identified, although it is hard to measure. This is knowledge the benefits of which extend beyond the individual firm but tend to be "local" in character. The tendency of particular industries to cluster in particular locations within individual nations is an indication that such local externalities exist.[12] The concentration of much of

---

10. The following distinction between three types of technological knowledge was originally made by Krugman (1987).

11. Sometimes it is even difficult for a company to transfer process knowledge from one of its own plants to another. According to company sources, it took Texas Instruments much longer than expected to transfer the production process used in its DRAM production facilities in Japan to its dram production facilities in Texas. Another important early source on the developmental impact of local externalities is Young (1928). See also Kaldor (1970) and the more recent work of economic geographers Allen J. Scott, Richard Walker, and Michael Storper (Scott 1988, Scott and Storper 1987, and Storper and Walker 1989). See also Stowsky (1989).

12. Alfred Marshall first suggested the existence of economies external to the firm but internal to a network or cluster of firms located in a particular geographical area and the effects of such economies on competitive advantage. For an economist located on the West Coast of the United States, but contemplating a move to the East Coast, the existence of local external economies generated by the economics community in Boston and Washington, DC, seems obvious.

the American electronics industry in Silicon Valley, California, is only one celebrated example of this tendency. Several contemporary examples drawn from other nations are provided in a recent study by Michael Porter (1990).[13]

According to ongoing theoretical work on economic geography by Paul Krugman (1991), local external economies are the key to understanding such phenomena.[14] Firms in an industry tend to concentrate in particular locations because there are externalities provided by being near one another. These externalities can take several forms, including a labor supply with specialized skills, specialized suppliers of inputs and supporting services, and informational networks or a common knowledge pool through which firms can learn from each other. There is strong anecdotal evidence that these kinds of external economies continue to be strongly national and sometimes even local in character.[15]

Local externalities are often self-reinforcing[16]—regions or nations that have a strong presence in a particular industry germinate specialized inputs and informational networks that in turn make the industry even more competitive over time. Conversely, when an industry is forced to contract, its specialized inputs and knowledge are endangered. When a domestic industry declines as a result of foreign competition, as the US semiconductor industry did in the mid-1980s, the specialized labor force and suppliers supported by that industry are also threatened (Stowsky 1987).

Although local external economies are not unique to high-technology industries, they have special relevance for them. According to the blossoming literature on the generation and diffusion of technological knowledge, an important part of such knowledge resides in local accumulations of experience and know-how.[17] These local assets include specialized skills, specialized suppliers and ancillary services, and networks of social and professional contacts through which technological information is developed and exchanged.

Studies of technological change demonstrate that technological capabilities develop in conjunction with production. In other words, they cannot be acquired simply by purchasing a product; rather they are "hands-on" or "tacit" capabilities that depend on active involvement in the production process itself.[18] The kinds of learning that build such capabilities—learning by doing

---

13. See also Sabel (1989), Thurow (1992), and Storper and Walker (1989). Various regional studies also point to the existence of external economies. See, for example, Dunning and Morgan (1971), Scott and Angel (1987), and Malerba (1990).

14. Of course, the existence of external economies has long been recognized by regional theorists and geographers.

15. In addition to Porter's case studies see Storper and Walker (1989), Andersen (1991), von Hippel (1988), and Lundvall (1988).

16. See Arthur (1987 and 1990). This work has some roots in the older "cumulative causation" and "forward linkage" theories of development economists Gunnar Myrdal (1957) and Albert O. Hirschman (1958).

17. The literature on the process of technological learning and diffusion is growing rapidly. Some useful references include Dosi (1988), Dosi et al. (1990), Stowsky (1990, chapter 7), Storper and Walker (1989), Gore (1984), and Castells (1989).

18. Winter (1987); the seminal work in the economics of this issue is probably Arrow (1962). For a theoretical treatment of technological benefits see Krugman (1988).

in production, learning by using in consumption, and learning by partnering with engineers and scientists in different firms that specialize in different parts of the production process—are slow to diffuse outside the firm or the network of firms in which they were created, and thus slow to diffuse across national borders.

A nation that sacrifices a particular high-technology industry will gradually sacrifice many of the local technological capabilities nurtured by it. And the ultimate loss is likely to be even greater, since without these capabilities the nation will find it difficult to exploit the footloose technological knowledge created abroad. As Richard Nelson has observed, even access to generic technological knowledge—of the sort taught in graduate schools, written down in books and articles, and exchanged among high-level professionals—is limited to those with the requisite training and often to those actually doing related research. In Nelson's words:

> To take industrial advantage of generic knowledge or technology that is licensed . . . requires significant inputs of trained scientists and engineers, often involving research and development, aimed to tailor what has been learned to the specific relevant uses (Nelson 1990, 131).

Sometimes even footloose knowledge is a public good only for those who have made the local investments necessary to understand it.

What does this admittedly speculative discussion of local externalities imply for the questions motivating this study? A cautious activist answer is that high-technology industries are important to the nation's well-being not only because of their measurable contributions to exports, high-wage and high-skill jobs, productivity, and R&D, but also because of their unmeasurable contributions to the nation's technological capabilities. A long and rich body of evidence from the literatures on economic geography and technological change suggests that the latter contributions are substantial.

Foreign Direct Investment

The local externalities argument also has relevance for debates about the desirability of foreign direct investment in high-technology industries. Recently there has been growing anxiety in the United States about such investment, particularly when it takes the form of foreign acquisitions of American companies rather than new "greenfield" investment. This anxiety is largely unwarranted. Most studies indicate that foreign direct investment of either type usually provides substantial benefits to the United States in the form of jobs, capital, and technological and managerial know-how. The highly influential study by Graham and Krugman (1991) finds that American affiliates of foreign companies are, on average, virtually indistinguishable from the domestic operations of American-owned companies in terms of value added per worker, compensation per worker, and R&D per worker. Moreover, foreign direct investment must be evaluated against its alternative—it is certainly likely to be preferable to increasing dependence on imports or to failure to develop a new technology because of limited domestic capital and manufacturing capabilities. Even foreign direct investment in assembly operations provides employment that might otherwise have gone offshore. More extensive "quality" investment provides even greater national benefits in the form of high-wage, high-skill employment, R&D, and the local external economies and technological capabilities created by local production.

Whether foreign investment strengthens or undermines local economies and capabilities, however, depends on a number of factors. For example, Dunning (1989, 1990), who has studied foreign direct investment in a wide range of countries and industries, concludes that when a country has its own indigenous technological capacity in a particular industry based on its own firms and work force, foreign investment is more likely to enhance local economies. In contrast, if the host country has limited technological capabilities in an industry, foreign investment is more likely to drive out local competitors and further reduce such capabilities. Both Dunning's work and the evidence in chapters 4 and 6 of this book demonstrate that government policies exercise an important influence on the kinds of foreign direct investment a nation attracts and its effects on the domestic economy (see Tyson 1991 for more on this point). In this regard, the United States has much to learn from Europe's strategy of creeping local content. Although this strategy has raised prices for European consumers, it has succeeded in attracting extensive direct investment by both American and Japanese high-technology companies.

But are there exceptions to the general presumption that foreign direct investment is on balance good for the American economy? The answer is yes.[19] First, an open-door policy in favor of such investment may make sense when private investors are involved, but it must be more carefully considered when foreign governments are involved. In the former case, market objectives can be presumed to motivate the investment decision, and the usual presumption in favor of market forces applies. When a foreign government is the investor, however, foreign national interests are at play, and these may conflict with American national interests. Nor, in the case of an acquisition of an American company by a foreign government, can the interests of the American seller be assumed to be synonymous with the American national interest.

The proposed purchase of a 40 percent equity share in the commercial operations of McDonnell Douglas by Taiwan Aerospace Corporation, a company in which the Taiwanese government is a major investor, illustrates these points (this case is analyzed in chapter 5). Because McDonnell Douglas is the nation's largest military contractor, if the deal is finalized, it will be reviewed by the Committee on Foreign Investment in the United States (CFIUS), but only on narrow national security grounds. But much more than American national security writ small is involved. Also at stake are significant American economic interests, in particular the production, employment, exports, and local technological and production capabilities of the many domestic firms that do subcontracting work for McDonnell Douglas. Currently, however, the American government has neither the mandate nor the capacity to review this deal or any other foreign direct investment involving a foreign government for its effects on national economic welfare.

---

19. The following discussion draws on the author's written testimony before the Subcommittee on International Finance and Monetary Policy of the Senate Banking Committee, 4 June 1992.

Second, even foreign investments that do not jeopardize national security and do not involve foreign governments may sometimes have potentially harmful effects if they increase industry concentration and reduce competition. For example, if a foreign acquisition eliminates an American competitor, the result may be higher prices for American consumers and producers who use the product in question or limitations on their timely access to new technologies. These dangers are likely to be especially great in input industries, such as energy and electronic components, on which many other American industries depend. By controlling the terms of access to these inputs, foreign suppliers can restrict the market options and impair the market performance of their American rivals. Such anticompetitive dangers of foreign direct investment are discussed in chapter 4 in the context of the semiconductor and semiconductor equipment industries.

On balance, the evidence suggests that foreign direct investment is good for the American economy. However, when foreign governments are the investors, or when a foreign investment threatens to impair our economic or our defense security by concentrating market power in the hands of a few suppliers, that investment should be carefully reviewed and in some cases modified or blocked altogether in favor of a national solution.

National Security Concerns

So far the discussion has highlighted the special contributions of high-technology industries to economic welfare. Using Krugman's terminology, such industries are often "strategic" in the economic sense of providing spillover benefits and/or excess returns. Many of them are also strategic in the more traditional military sense.[20] America's defense strategy emphasizes high-technology weapons systems that depend heavily on the electronics and aerospace complexes. The 1991 Gulf War only served to confirm the wisdom of this strategy in the eyes of the nation's defense policymakers. National security concerns are often a legitimate consideration in devising sensible policies for trade and foreign investment. In addressing such concerns, however, it is necessary to accept two realities: first, many leading-edge technologies used by the military are now generated in the commercial marketplace; and second, in many so-called dual-use technologies (those with both military and civilian applications), US producers have lost their competitive edge. As table 2A.2 indicates, out of a recent list of 22 technological capabilities judged by the US Department of Defense to be "critical" to national defense, 14 are dual-use technologies, including microelectronics circuits, compound semiconductors, software, robotics, fiber optics, superconductivity, and biotechnology. In several of these technologies, the Defense Department believes that Japanese producers are significantly ahead of American producers, at least in some areas.

In an insightful study, Theodore H. Moran (1990) proposes that the United States adopt three principles for trade and investment policies in defense-related industries. First, US policy should use requirements for national ownership or

---

20. For a recent insightful discussion of the links between a nation's high-technology industries and its national security, see Sandholtz et al. (1992).

local production by foreign suppliers to enhance national control. Second, it should seek to stimulate a diversity of suppliers to maintain an honest and competitive supply base. And third, it should avoid condemning the nation to mediocre technologies and unnecessarily high costs in the process.

Edward M. Graham and Paul R. Krugman (1991) also argue that new policy approaches are necessary to safeguard national security. In particular, they recommend that the Exon-Florio amendment to the 1988 Omnibus Trade and Competitiveness Act be linked with US antitrust law to determine when a foreign takeover poses a national security threat by creating significant market power in a defense-related industry. In cases in which a positive determination is made, Graham and Krugman recommend several possible remedies, including blocking the takeover, promoting the entry or deterring the exit of alternative American suppliers, and imposing local content and performance requirements, including provisions that R&D facilities be maintained in the United States. Similar remedies are also proposed in chapters 4, 5, and 7 of this book, but they are not strictly limited to defense-related industries. As argued earlier, whenever foreign control of a high-technology industry poses strategic threats to commercial users, such remedies may also be advised.

A Brief Concluding Comment

For most trade policy questions, it is not necessary to determine whether a particular high-technology industry is "strategic" for either economic or national security reasons. Trade barriers and structural impediments often justify defensive responses for conventional "moderate" reasons—they threaten the international trading order; they encourage protectionist backlash; they impose unnecessary adjustment costs; they weaken the nation's terms of trade; and they expose American consumers to dependence on concentrated foreign suppliers. The possibility that the industry in question might also be "strategic" merely reinforces the weight of these conventional arguments. The general policy recommendations remain unaltered.

Many of America's trading partners, however, do not espouse the logic of moderate free traders. Instead, they are convinced that high-technology industries are strategic, and they are willing to protect and promote them. Consequently, the US preference for new multilateral rules to regulate and harmonize foreign interventions to American standards will not be easily or fully realized. Neither Japan nor Europe shares the dominant American view that policies to foster specific high-technology industries are at best unnecessary and at worst counterproductive. Nor do they share American views on competition policy, R&D policy, and intellectual property protection, all of which have important consequences for global competition.

Since it is utopian to imagine that the world will have enforceable multilateral rules for high-technology trade and investment any time soon, the relevant question for US policy is, What should be done in the meantime? The case studies presented in the remainder of this book provide some guidelines for a defensive trade and domestic policy response, as seen from the perspective of an avowedly cautious activist.

Appendix: Assessments of the US Position in Selected High-Technology Industries

Table 2A.1 Assessments of US and Japanese comparative standings in selected technologies, Japanese Ministry of International Trade and Industry, 1983 and 1988

Technology	1983 Level of technology	1983 Technical development capability	1988 Level of technology	1988 Technical development capability
Database systems	US	US	US	US
Semiconductor memory devices	Equal	Equal	Japan	Japan
Computers	US	Equal	Equal	Equal
Videocassette recorders	Japan	Japan	Japan	Japan
D-PBXS	US	US	Equal	Japan
Microprocessors	Equal	Equal	Equal	Japan
Laser printers	US	Equal	Equal	Japan
Copying machines	Equal	Equal	Equal	Japan
Assembly robots	Equal	Japan	Equal	Japan
CAD/CAM	US	Equal	Equal	Japan
Communications satellites	US	Equal	Equal	Equal
Photovoltaics	Japan	Equal	Japan	Japan
Aircraft engines	US	US	US	Equal
Skyscrapers	US	US	Equal	Equal
Advanced composite materials	US	US	Equal	Equal
Fine ceramics	Equal	Japan	Japan	Japan

CAD/CAM = computer-assisted design, computer-assisted manufacturing; D-PBX = digital private branch exchanges.
Source: Ministry of International Trade and Industry, *Trends and Future Tasks in Industrial Technology, 1988 White Paper.*

Table 2A.2   Relative US position in critical defense technologies

Technology	Dual-use[a]	US lagging in some important areas	US holding its own	US leading
Biotechnology	Yes	X		
Gallium arsenide (for use in advanced semiconductors)	Yes	X		
High-power microwaves for weaponry	No	X		
Integrated optics (for chip memories and signal processing)	Yes	X		
Machine intelligence and robotics	Yes	X		
Microchips	Yes	X		
Pulsed-power lasers and microwave devices	No	X		
Superconductors	Yes	X		
Advanced composite materials	Yes		X	
Air-breathing propulsion (jet engines)	Yes		X	
Fiber optics	Yes		X	
Hypervelocity projectiles	No		X	
Automatic target recognition	No			X
Computational fluid dynamics	Yes			X
Data fusion (for processing large amounts of raw data)	Yes			X
Highly sensitive radars	No			X
Parallel processing	Yes			X
Passive sensors	No			X
Phased-array radars	No			X
Signature controls	No			X
Simulation modeling	Yes			X
Software development	Yes			X

a. Dual-use technologies are those with potential civilian as well as military applications.
Source: US Department of Defense.

**Table 2A.3 Position of the US computer industry in selected
critical computer technologies, 1990 and
projected 1995**

Technology	1990	1995
Database systems	Ahead	Ahead
Processor architecture	Ahead	Diminished lead
Network and communications	Slightly ahead	Parity
Human interface	Ahead	Diminished lead
Visualization	Ahead	Diminished lead
Operating systems	Ahead	Diminished lead
Software engineering	Ahead	Diminished lead
Application technology	Ahead	Diminished lead
Displays	Behind	Further behind
Hard-copy technology	Parity	Behind
Storage	Slightly ahead	Slightly behind
Manufacturing technology	Slightly behind	Further behind
Integrated circuit fabrication equipment	Behind	Behind
Microelectronics	Parity	Behind
Optoelectronics	Slightly ahead	Parity
Electronics packaging	Parity	Behind

Source: Computer Systems Policy Project.

Table 2A.4 Assessments of US standing in selected high technologies by the Council on Competitiveness

Technology	Areas in which the United States is:			
	Strong	Competitive	Weak	Losing badly or has lost
Materials and associated processing technologies				
Advanced structural materials		Metal matrix composites Polymers Polymer matrix composites	Advanced metals	Structural ceramics
Electronic and photonic materials		Magnetic materials Optical materials Photoresists Superconductors		Display materials Electronic ceramics Electronic packaging materials Gallium arsenide Silicon
Biotechnologies	Bioactive and biocompatible materials Bioprocessing Drug discovery techniques Genetic engineering			
Materials processing		Catalysts Chemical synthesis Net shape forming Process controls	Membranes Precision coating	

Table 2A.4 Assessments of US standing in selected high technologies by the Council on Competitiveness Continued

Technology	Areas in which the United States is:			
	Strong	Competitive	Weak	Losing badly or has lost
Environmental technologies		Emissions reduction Recycling and waste processing		
Engineering and production technologies Design and engineering tools	Computer-aided engineering Systems engineering	Human factors engineering Measurement techniques Structural dynamics	Leading-edge scientific instruments	
Commercialization and production systems		Computer-integrated manufacturing	Design for manufacturing Design of manufacturing processes Flexible manufacturing Integration of research, design, and manufacturing Total quality management	
Process equipment				
Electronic components Microelectronics	Microprocessors	Logic chips Submicron technology		Memory chips
Electronic controls		Sensors	Actuators	

Optoelectronics components	Laser devices	
	Photonics	
Electronics packaging and interconnections	Multichip packaging systems	
	Printed circuit board technology	
Displays	Electroluminescent	
	Liquid crystal	
	Plasma	
	Vacuum fluorescent	
Hard-copy technology	Electrophotography	
	Electrostatic	
Information storage	Magnetic information storage	
	Optical information storage	
Information technologies		
Software	Applications software	
	Artificial intelligence	
	Computer modeling and simulation	
	Expert systems	
	High-level software languages	
	Software engineering	
Computers	Neural networks	
	Operating systems	
		Hardware integration
Human interface and visualization techniques	Animation and full-motion video	
	Graphics hardware and software	

table continued next page

Table 2A.4   Assessments of US standing in selected high technologies by the Council on Competitiveness
Continued

Technology	Areas in which the United States is:			
	Strong	Competitive	Weak	Losing badly or has lost
	Handwriting and speech recognition Natural language Optical character recognition			
Database systems	Data representation Retrieval and update Semantic modeling and interpretation			
Networks and communications		Broadband switching Digital infrastructure Fiber optic systems Multiplexing		
Portable telecommunications equipment and systems	Transmitters and receivers	Digital signal processing		
Powertrain and propulsion technologies Powertrain	Low-emission engines	Alternative-fuel engines	High-fuel-economy and power density engines	
Propulsion	Air-breathing propulsion Rocket propulsion			

Source: Council on Competitiveness. *Gaining New Ground: Technology Priorities for America's Future* (Washington: Council on Competitiveness, 1991). Adapted with permission.

3

From MOSS to Motorola and Cray: Managing Trade by Rules and Outcomes

The Real Japan Problem

The MOSS Talks in Technology-Intensive Products: Trade Management Through Sectoral Rules

Motorola and Japan's Cellular Telephone Market: A Step Closer to Managed Trade

The Third-Party Radio Conflict: A Successful Managed Trade Resolution

Lessons from Motorola's Experiences in Gaining Access to the Japanese Market

Cray and the Japanese Supercomputer Market: Procurement, Infant-Industry Tactics, and Reciprocity

Concluding Remarks

The Real Japan Problem

Between 1987 and 1991 Japan's merchandise trade surplus with the United States declined by about $10 billion. In 1991 Japan imported $30.0 billion in manufactured goods from the United States, up from only $16.3 billion in 1987. Do numbers like these mean that we have seen the last of the "Japan problem?" If so, why does trade friction with Japan endure? Is it simply a case of what Jagdish Bhagwati has called the "diminished giant syndrome,"[1] as the United States lashes out in frustration over the inexorable rise of Japan as a major competitive threat?

Certainly, some of Japan's ongoing troubles with the United States are the predictable and unfortunate result of its astonishing successes. Japan's growing ascendance in technology-intensive industries is a particular cause for concern. Although the US trade deficit with Japan has improved markedly since 1987,

---

1. According to Bhagwati (1991), the "diminished giant syndrome" of the United States today parallels that suffered by the United Kingdom at the end of the 19th century, when the United States and Germany arrived as major industrial powers on the world scene. In each case, concerns with the trading success of the newly triumphant countries became the order of the day.

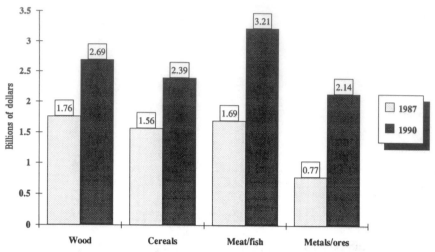

Figure 3.1 United States: trade surplus with Japan in selected commodities, 1987 and 1990. *Source:* Economic Strategy Institute. Data used with permission.

low-technology products account for most of the American gains. Indeed, the imbalance in many high-technology industries actually increased between 1987 and 1990 despite the appreciation of the yen after 1985 (figures 3.1 and 3.2). Japanese producers continue to gain market share in world telecommunications and computer markets at the expense of American producers. Reflecting Japan's remarkable success in these markets, between 1983 and 1989 the share of telecommunications equipment, integrated circuits, and data processing machines in total Japanese exports doubled (Corker 1990). If current trends continue, the Japanese share of the global computer market will surpass the American share sometime during this decade, mimicking a similar development in the world semiconductor market during the 1980s.

There is no denying Japan's growing competitive capabilities in high-technology industries, especially electronics. Despite the dramatic decline in the dollar's value after 1985, the US trade deficit with Japan in electronics declined by only 3.4 percent between 1986 and 1991. The bilateral electronics deficit in 1991 was more than five times as great as it was in 1980. In 1988, according to data provided by the American Electronics Association, electronic equipment accounted for 46 percent of the overall US–Japan trade imbalance; the economic consulting and forecasting firm DRI projects that the comparable figure for 1994 will be 59 percent.

According to a committee of the National Academy of Sciences, experts in both the United States and Japan "share the conclusion that Japan's high-technology capabilities are now on par with or ahead of the United States in many areas" (National Research Council, Committee on Japan, 1990, 7). But technological parity does not mean that trade outcomes between the two nations are simply the result of market forces. Nor should complaints by US producers about impediments to the Japanese market be glibly dismissed as protectionism in disguise. Although protectionist impulses are part of the story of trade friction with Japan, they are not the whole story. The openness or accessibility of the

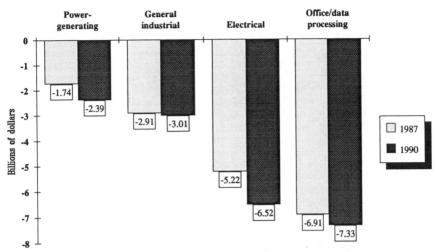

Figure 3.2 United States: trade deficit with Japan in key machinery industries, 1987 and 1990. *Source:* Economic Strategy Institute. Data used with permission.

Japanese market also plays a role. A number of serious scholarly studies have recently confirmed what the world business community has contended for years: the Japanese market remains significantly more closed to foreign trade and investment than the markets of most of the other advanced industrial nations (see, e.g., Balassa and Noland 1988, Encarnation 1992, Lincoln 1990, Lawrence 1987 and 1991, Salvatore 1990, and Tyson and Zysman 1990).

The real Japan problem, the one that lingers despite significant macroeconomic adjustments, is this problem of market closure. As a recent study by the General Agreement on Tariffs and Trade (GATT 1990) confirms, traditional trade barriers are not the source of this problem.[2] Japan has low tariffs and few import quotas. There is no smoking gun in the form of overt trade barriers—these were largely eliminated in nonagricultural trade by the end of the 1970s in response to US pressure. Rather, the most important impediments to the Japanese market are structural in nature. Bergsten and Cline (1987, 116) estimated that such impediments are roughly equivalent to tariff protection of the Japanese market on the order of 25 percent. According to their admittedly tentative estimates, US exports to Japan would be at least 30 percent higher in the absence of such impediments.

Structural barriers to the Japanese market are rooted in the unique character of Japanese business organizations and their distinctive relationships with one another and with the Japanese government. These distinctive features of Japanese capitalism have been well documented (see, for example, Johnson 1982, Dore 1986, Prestowitz 1988, Johnson et al. 1990, and Yamamura 1990). Within the business community, they include a high degree of vertical integration in many large firms and the existence of huge interlinked industrial groups or

---

2. The GATT Council established to carry out the Trade Policy Review Mechanism for Japan noted such nontariff impediments to trade as the "anti-competitive business practices" of certain Japanese firms, standards, health and sanitary regulations, certification and other import procedures, and a lack of transparency in policymaking.

keiretsu. All of the companies identified in this chapter and the next as major players in the Japanese electronics industry are both vertically integrated and members of such groups.

Vertical integration gives Japanese companies several advantages:[3] the ability to cross-subsidize product lines, using profits from strong divisions to support weak ones or to start new ones; the ability to rely on internal demand when external markets falter; the ability to tailor-make equipment for downstream uses; and the ability to maintain secure supplies of critical inputs.

Keiretsu membership strengthens many of these advantages.[4] As a result of stable shareholding arrangements between group members and with other institutions, approximately 60 percent to 80 percent of the shares of group member firms are never traded.[5] As a consequence, Japanese managers need not worry as much as their American counterparts about takeovers or short-term fluctuations in stock prices. Cross-shareholding also limits the ability of foreigners to acquire Japanese firms as a strategy for entering the Japanese market.

Group membership, like vertical integration, also provides member firms with a partially captive market. This is particularly important when a firm's products are not yet fully competitive. Sales to group members can provide breathing space to gain economies of scale and technological expertise at the expense of more competitive outsiders.

Finally, most of Japan's business groups are centered around a major bank. These "main banks" give member firms preferential access to low-cost capital and provide a financial buffer during hard times. Together, links to a main bank, stable shareholding arrangements, and vertical integration are largely responsible for the long time horizons and deep pockets of major Japanese companies.

Keiretsu links are a powerful barrier to both new domestic firms and foreign firms attempting to enter the Japanese market. Honda's difficulties in gaining a share of the Japanese automobile market in the 1970s and NMB Semiconductor's difficulties in gaining a share of the Japanese semiconductor market in the 1980s illustrate how hard it is even for new Japanese players to compete with well-connected, well-financed incumbents. In both of these cases, access to more open American markets has been important to the development of new Japanese competitors.

The evidence from the electronics industry presented in this chapter and the next confirms anecdotal evidence that *keiretsu* links pose powerful barriers to foreign competitors (see, e.g., Yamamura 1986). In a recent econometric study, Robert Z. Lawrence (1991) reaches a similar conclusion. According to his results, the larger the share of industry output produced by firms that are *keiretsu* members, the smaller the import penetration in that industry. Recent studies by Peter

---

3. The following discussion of the advantages of vertical integration and *keiretsu* membership is based on a discussion by Anchordoguy (1990).

4. For a more complete discussion of the implications of group behavior see Gerlach (1990).

5. A 1988 survey conducted by the Japanese Ministry of International Trade and Industry (MITI) of 300 large manufacturing firms in the United States and 300 in Japan found that 79 percent of the Japanese shares were held by relationship-oriented investors, usually other companies in related businesses. In the United States the corresponding share was only 34 percent. These results are reported in Blinder (1992).

A. Petri (1991) and K. C. Fung (1991) also document the import-restricting effects of *keiretsu*.

In principle, anticompetitive or restrictive business practices resulting from the distinctive structural features of Japanese industry can be controlled by Japanese antitrust laws, which are modeled on American laws. In practice, however, the Japanese have not actively enforced their antitrust regulations. Repeated violations have been overlooked, and penalties, when assessed, have been low (see, e.g., Ramseyer 1984–85, Sanekata 1986). In addition, a 1957 law explicitly exempted the electronics industry from prosecution for antitrust violations. Similar exemptions have been granted to other industries when they have encountered hard times.

Indeed, the Japanese government has actually exhibited a penchant for working with large, vertically integrated *keiretsu* firms to "control" competition, to "rationalize" industry structure, and to encourage business cooperation on price, production, investment, and R&D. This preference has been pronounced in industries, like the electronics industry, that the government has targeted because of their "strategic" economic significance. Preferential policies for targeted industries have usually benefited large, vertically integrated firms, especially those that are *keiretsu* members.[6] In the words of one MITI official, "MITI promotes the larger, more stable, more promising firms."[7]

However, to imagine that the Japanese government simply promotes powerful Japanese companies and turns a blind eye to their restrictive business practices overlooks the extent to which informal bureaucratic interference in business activity is acceptable in Japan. Japanese policymakers not only support Japanese companies in a variety of formal and informal ways, but they also "lean" on them to realize policy goals. Thus, it is not surprising to find Japanese semiconductor companies regularly reporting output and investment plans to MITI in the year following the first semiconductor trade agreement with the United States, or to find a Japanese company bowing out of a supercomputer bid or buying an American supercomputer in response to public pressure. Such behavior would be shocking in the United States, where, with the exception of the defense sector, the distinction between big government and big business is a meaningful one, and where business jealously guards its independence. In Japan, in contrast, this distinction is much more nuanced, leading many observers to conclude that discretionary bureaucratic power and big-business power are impossible to disentangle.[8] The invisible hand is at work in Japan, but it is not Adam Smith's invisible hand—it is the invisible hand of the government working with Japanese industry.

The Japanese government also has a different relationship with consumers than the American government does. In technology-intensive industries this

---

6. MITI's preferences for the large and powerful Japanese firms in targeted industries have been particularly pronounced in the electronics industry. For a full description see Anchordoguy (1989).

7. This remark was made in an interview with Marie Anchordoguy (reported in Anchordoguy 1991). See also Office of Technology Assessment (1991a).

8. For more detail on the nature of business-government relations in Japan, see Johnson (1982), van Wolferen (1989), Prestowitz (1989), and Fallows (1989).

difference shows up most clearly in procedures for product standards, testing, and certification. According to Daniel I. Okimoto (1989, 14–15), "In Tokyo, the regulatory philosophy is to push as close as possible to eliminating all risk." Whereas the US system of more lax standards and certification places heavy reliance on the common-law system of product liability, the Japanese system places heavy reliance on elaborate certification standards and administrative rulemaking.[9]

Such standards have hindered the sale of several American products in Japan, including air conditioners, baseball bats, skis, electrical appliances, telecommunications equipment, and drugs and medical equipment. Each has become the focus of a prolonged trade dispute. The cases of telecommunications and drugs and medical equipment are analyzed below. In these and other instances, foreign producers have been frustrated by Japan's reliance on design rather than performance characteristics for certification, because this approach allows foreign products to be denied certification even when they perform better than Japanese products. In addition, design standards are often drafted by committees of Japanese companies working with the relevant regulatory agency to guarantee that their products meet certification requirements. Foreign companies have traditionally been excluded from these committees.

The distinctive features of Japanese capitalism—vertical integration, *keiretsu* groups, cooperative business-government relations, and strict, often paternalistic regulatory arrangements—hamper the efforts of foreign producers to sell in Japan. Small wonder that American companies often complain that they are not competing with Japanese companies but with the entire Japanese system. They are right.

During the 1980s the United States repeatedly pressured the Japanese into bilateral negotiations to eliminate structural impediments to specific Japanese markets. This chapter examines three examples of such negotiations: the so-called market-oriented, sector-specific (MOSS) talks on telecommunications, drugs and medical equipment, and electronics; the negotiations over Motorola's access to the Japanese market for cellular telephones and third-party radios; and the negotiations over Cray Research's access to the Japanese market for supercomputers.

The MOSS Talks in Technology-Intensive Products: Trade Management Through Sectoral Rules

As the mid-1980s approached, the overall US trade imbalance with Japan was climbing rapidly, feeding frustration over a perceived lack of progress in recurrent bilateral trade talks.[10] The Reagan administration was under pressure to conclude successful negotiations or run the risk of a congressional protectionist backlash. The administration reacted by initiating a round of intensive, high-level negotiations with Japan to reduce or eliminate barriers to the Japanese

---

9. This point is made by Vogel (1992). This paper contains an excellent survey of Japan's regulatory practices in a variety of industries.

10. For other discussions of the MOSS talks, see Lincoln (1990) and Prestowitz (1988).

market in a few industries in which US companies were undeniably competitive. The sectors finally chosen also reflected domestic political considerations and included telecommunications; some other parts of the electronics industry, including computers and supercomputers (but largely excluding semiconductors, which were the focus of separate negotiations); forest products, including both wood and paper products; and medical equipment and pharmaceuticals.

The overarching goal of these negotiations was to improve access to the Japanese market, not to reduce access to the American market. Moreover, this goal was to be achieved not by specifying quantitative outcomes but by negotiating new rules for trade in specific industries. The new rules were to be multilateral in the sense that they would apply to all of Japan's trading partners. Thus, if the United States succeeded in reducing a structural impediment to the Japanese market in a particular industry, all of Japan's trading partners stood to benefit.

MOSS in Electronics

A major goal of the MOSS talks in electronics was adequate protection of US technology, in particular US semiconductor technology (especially original chip design), and copyright protection for intellectual property, especially computer software created and produced in the United States.[11] In the absence of such protection, many US semiconductor companies had seen their intellectual property rights in proprietary chip design dissipated by their Japanese competitors; many US software companies faced similar prospects. US negotiators also placed other requests on the MOSS electronics agenda, including opportunities for US companies to participate in government-sponsored R&D projects in Japan and to license patents from the Japanese government.[12]

Even before the talks started, the Japanese acquiesced to US demands for tougher intellectual property protection. In conformance with US practice, the Japanese adopted legislation that provided 50-year copyright protection for computer software and 10-year protection for original chip design. Japanese practice was harmonized to US standards, eliminating a serious structural impediment to competition between the two nations.

The Japanese government also invited US firms to participate in the Sigma project, a publicly funded cooperative R&D project for software development. In addition, US firms were granted access, under certain circumstances, to computer-related patents held by the Japanese government. Although these were largely token gestures, the MOSS talks set an important precedent by putting membership in government-sponsored R&D projects on the bilateral trade agenda.

Research in Japan is largely done by private industry, although it is often partially funded by the government. Consequently, even basic research results are often proprietary and not in the public domain. In contrast, because of the way in which the American research establishment is organized, a large portion

---

11. For more detail on the MOSS talks in electronics, see Prestowitz (1988), Lincoln (1990), and US General Accounting Office, National Security and International Affairs Division (1988a).

12. Two issues relating to access barriers to American supercomputer sales in Japan—procurement procedures and price discounting—were also included in the original MOSS framework but were ultimately negotiated in a separate agreement discussed below.

of basic research in the United States is funded by the government and is done in universities and public laboratories (Mowery and Rosenberg 1989b). Consequently, research results are widely and freely available. These national differences in the organization and funding of research sometimes give Japanese firms an advantage over American firms and limit reciprocal access of American companies to the Japanese market. In the MOSS electronics talks and in later negotiations with the Japanese (and the Europeans), American policymakers addressed these structural asymmetries by pressing foreign governments to allow American companies to participate in publicly funded R&D projects on an industry-by-industry and reciprocal basis. This approach is a necessary stopgap measure. Ultimately, multilateral guidelines regulating membership conditions and licensing rights in such projects are required.

MOSS in Medical Equipment and Pharmaceuticals

When the MOSS talks started, Japanese health care regulations posed several barriers to sales by American producers of pharmaceuticals and medical equipment. Moreover, these regulations, like product safety and testing regulations in other industries, tended to be stricter, more focused on product design than product performance, and more influenced by domestic-company interests than they are in the United States.[13]

The talks focused on testing and test data, approval and licensing procedures, linkages between approval and pricing mechanisms, the National Health Insurance reimbursement system, and greater transparency in the regulatory system.[14] Prior to the talks, Japan required all test data submitted in support of product approval applications to be generated by clinical trials in Japan involving resident Japanese citizens.[15] For American and other foreign producers this meant costly delays and the duplication of clinical procedures. As a result of the MOSS negotiations, Japan agreed to accept foreign clinical test data for most pharmaceuticals. Retesting of approved foreign products was required only to find the best dosage for Japanese bodies, which, according to Japanese regulations, may absorb substances differently from American bodies.

The US sought harmonization of Japanese regulatory practices to American standards in procedures for product approval and licensing. Prior to the talks, the Japanese Ministry of Health and Welfare (MHW) required two separate approvals for producers and their Japanese representatives wishing to participate in Japan's health care system. Any firm, whether domestic or foreign, first had to obtain a manufacturing or import approval for its drug or medical device and then had to obtain a second license to manufacture or import and market the

13. Despite these stringent Japanese regulations, American suppliers had about 14 percent of the Japanese medical equipment market and about 4 percent of total imports of medical equipment in Japan when the MOSS talks began. In pharmaceuticals, the comparable figures were about 10 percent and 40 percent (US General Accounting Office, National Security and International Affairs Division 1988b, 26).

14. See US General Accounting Office, National Security and International Affairs Division (1988a and b) for more detail.

15. For a broader discussion of Japanese regulatory principles, see Vogel (1992).

approved product. This two-stage system specified no standard processing times for new approvals and licenses, nor did it allow for their orderly transfer between companies. The MOSS talks produced significant changes in this system that benefited Japanese, American, and other foreign producers. In particular, regulations were rewritten to include so-called time clock standards or standard processing times for approvals similar to those used by the US Food and Drug Administration. In addition, in conformance with US practice, standard procedures were specified to let companies transfer their approvals to other producers or distributors.

Negotiations over the reimbursement system used by Japan's National Health Insurance concentrated on pricing and regulatory practices. Prior to the talks, after securing approval for a drug or medical device, a Japanese or foreign company had to apply for a price listing for its product. US companies were concerned about the irregular and infrequent listing of reimbursement rates and about the lack of transparency in the criteria used to set prices (the criteria frequently discriminated against imports). As a result of the MOSS talks, the Japanese regulatory authorities agreed to provide quarterly price listings for all new drugs and many medical devices, limiting delays between approval and price listing to no more than 90 days. On the issue of transparency, MHW agreed that its advisory body, the Central Pharmaceutical Affairs Council, would hold informational meetings explaining its procedures and would give both domestic and foreign firms opportunities to present their views on general reimbursement policy and on particular pricing decisions. MHW also agreed to make public the formulas used for calculating new drug prices and for revising drug tariff standards. Both Japanese and foreign producers stood to benefit from these regulatory changes.

In a follow-up survey evaluating the MOSS talks, a majority of American producers reported improved regulatory treatment for their products, but few reported actual increases in their sales in Japan (US General Accounting Office, National Security and International Affairs Division 1988a). Trade statistics confirm their evaluation. As the data in table 3.1 indicate, between 1985 and 1988, imports by Japan of medical equipment and pharmaceuticals from all countries grew more slowly than did total manufactured imports. Likewise, imports of medical equipment and pharmaceuticals from the United States grew more slowly than did manufactured imports from the United States as a whole. In fact, the share of American producers in Japanese imports of medical equipment and pharmaceuticals declined between 1985 and 1988, while the European share increased.

These results highlight the danger of assessing the efficacy of trade negotiations by quantitative trade outcomes alone. There seems to be widespread agreement that the MOSS talks improved the regulatory environment for doing business in drugs and medical equipment in Japan, thereby cutting costs for both foreign and domestic companies. These gains were real but difficult to measure. Nonetheless, some problems remained. Initially, there were delays in adopting new testing procedures, and as late as 1988 some American companies reported that MHW testing requirements were largely unchanged. According to a 1989 study, moreover, the reimbursement rates set by Japan's National Health Insurance continued to favor domestic manufacturers of medical devices (Foote and Mitchell 1989).

Table 3.1 Relative performance of Japanese imports in industries addressed in the MOSS negotiations, 1985–88

| | | Average annual rate of growth of Japanese imports (percentages) | | | | | |
| | | European Community | | United States | | World | |
SITC no.	Description	1985–88	1986–88	1985–88	1986–88	1985–88	1986–88
	Wood	76.4	59.3	36.8	41.7	34.3	41
245–48	Unprocessed	63.2	58.7	35.8	40.4	29.3	36
634–35	Processed	79.4	59.4	109.7	138.4	128.5	109.6
	Paper	119.1	122.3	36.8	36.1	39.6	37.9
251	Unprocessed	110.6	75.6	47.3	50	40.4	43.9
	Processed	120.4	132.1	23.5	19	38.1	28
541	Medical and pharmaceutical products	61.1	43	12.2	13.1	35.3	27.1
752	Automatic data processing equipment	43.9	34	37.6	47	33.5	39.8
764	Telecommunications equipment and parts	66.4	15.1	40.8	42.9	62.8	58
774	Electrical medical equipment	70.2	27.5	29.2	24.7	42.5	26.3
	MOSS sectors	62.6	42	33.3	37.3	36.8	38.7
	All manufactures sectors	56.7	36.9	21.8	16.7	42.9	37
	All sectors	52.6	35.2	11.2	21.9	7.8	23.4
Memoranda:							
	Ratio of growth in MOSS sectors to growth in all manufactures	1.1	1.14	1.53	2.23	0.86	1.05
		1.19	1.19	2.97	1.71	4.71	1.65

Source: Author's calculations based on data from International Monetary Fund, *Direction of Trade Statistics Yearbook 1989*, United Nations SITC data.

Many of the themes of the MOSS talks in pharmaceuticals and medical devices are likely to resurface in the 1990s as environmental and health and safety concerns become more salient, and as differing national standards threaten to become even greater structural impediments to trade. Ultimately, trading partners like the United States and Japan will have to agree either to harmonize their regulatory practices or to recognize and accept differences in their regulatory standards. Detailed bilateral or multilateral negotiations at the industry level will be the only way to achieve either outcome.

MOSS in Telecommunications Products

The MOSS talks in telecommunications were another in a series of bilateral negotiations between the United States and Japan on telecommunications trade. These negotiations reflected US frustration over the repeated attempts by American companies to gain access to the highly protected and regulated Japanese market, which was dominated by NTT (Nippon Telegraph and Telephone), a state-owned monopoly until 1985. Even after agreement on the GATT government procurement code in 1979, business-government ties in the Japanese telecommunications industry discriminated against foreign suppliers. In 1984 imports still accounted for only 3 percent to 4 percent of NTT's purchases (Bergsten and Cline 1987, 97). NTT's procurement practices and research support were also important ingredients in Japan's targeting strategy for electronics.

According to Clyde V. Prestowitz, Jr. (1988, 297), the goal of the MOSS talks in telecommunications was "to obtain an environment similar to that in the United States with regard to telecommunication enterprises, equipment standards, and certification." This goal was similar to that of the MOSS talks on drugs and medical equipment, namely, to bring Japanese regulatory practices closer to American practices. Even after the privatization of NTT in 1985, the Japanese telecommunications market remained much more highly regulated than the American market. The difference in regulatory stringency was perhaps most apparent in the area of standards. The basic American principle was that any equipment was acceptable provided it did "no harm to the network." In contrast, the basic Japanese principle required equipment to meet administratively determined "voice-quality" standards.

Japanese officials argued that they did not discriminate between domestic and foreign producers—that perceived access problems in Japan were simply the result of a different regulatory tradition. As the story (presented later in this chapter) of Motorola's efforts to enter the Japanese markets for beeper-pagers, cellular telephones, and third-party radios reveals, such arguments were misleading at best and disingenuous at worst.[16] Even accepting the Japanese at their word, however, Japanese regulations still posed major structural barriers to American companies. National treatment was simply not an adequate substitute for some policy harmonization. Standards and testing-certification procedures in the Japanese telecommunications market, as in the pharmaceutical and medical equipment markets, constituted technical barriers to trade that violated the spirit if not the letter of the GATT standards code.

---

16. Prestowitz (1988, 287–299) describes how proposed changes in Japan's telecommunications regulations were designed to restrict access to foreign companies.

The MOSS talks on telecommunications, like those on pharmaceuticals and medical equipment, focused on procedures for product testing and certification. But there was a significant difference between the two sets of talks as well. Both American and Japanese companies stood to gain from proposed regulatory changes in the medical field. In contrast, a handful of powerful Japanese companies accustomed to cozy, preferential arrangements with NTT and the Ministry of Posts and Telecommunications (MPT) stood to lose from the regulatory changes proposed by their American counterparts. In the short run, the telecommunications talks promised a zero-sum outcome—what American companies won, their Japanese competitors would lose.

Predictably, the telecommunications negotiations were bitter: the Japanese regulatory authorities dragged their feet, and the US Congress threatened retaliation if the talks were not successfully concluded. After a year of haggling, the Japanese agreed to several US proposals.[17] First, self-certification was allowed for value-added networks. Companies were permitted to use their own protocols (the rules determining how computers interconnect within a network), and prior registration and notification to install such networks were no longer required. Second, technical standards and requirements for terminal equipment were reduced in number and restricted to those necessary for protection of the network.

Japanese procedures for setting standards were also modified. The NTT privatization law gave the authority to establish product standards to the Telecommunications Deliberation Council, appointed by and attached to MPT. Neither foreign companies nor domestic companies with a foreign institutional connection were permitted to be council members. In addition, certification and testing of equipment according to the standards determined by the council were entrusted to an association of Japanese manufacturers of telecommunications equipment. American producers believed that these institutional arrangements discriminated against them. As part of the MOSS deal, MPT agreed to appoint experts from five American companies to the council's board of technical advisers. American companies also gained membership on an independent private-sector standards-setting body. Finally, an independent agency was established to carry out testing and certification without the direct participation of Japanese manufacturers.

On other telecommunications issues, channels for satellite communications were expanded, and two private firms using American satellites were allowed to enter satellite communications. An agreement was also reached to begin deregulation of cellular telephone service in Japan. By the end of the 1980s, this agreement was to become the source of a bitter trade dispute involving Motorola.

Overall, the MOSS talks on telecommmunications achieved most of their objectives. Except in the area of voice-quality standards, the Japanese adjusted their regulatory practices toward greater conformity with American practices. Acquiescing to American demands, the Japanese also committed themselves to the principles of transparency, national treatment, comparable market access, and nondiscrimination in their telecommunications market.

---

17. Prestowitz, who was a participant in the MOSS talks on telecommunications, gives a detailed discussion (Prestowitz 1988, chapter 10).

The trade figures presented in table 3.1 suggest that the MOSS agreement did indeed make the Japanese market somewhat more accessible to foreign producers. Between 1985 and 1988 Japan's imports of telecommunications products from all sources grew substantially faster than did its imports of all manufactured products, and imports of telecommunications products from the United States grew substantially faster than imports of all manufactured products from the United States. However, Japanese imports of telecommunications products from the United States grew more slowly than Japanese imports of such products from the rest of the world—in other words, the US share of the Japanese market actually declined. The talks may have succeeded in making the Japanese market more open, but the evidence suggests that American producers were not the main beneficiaries.

Nor did American telecommunications exports to Japan increase as much as anticipated. Whereas American officials had optimistically predicted that annual telecommunications exports to Japan would increase by $300 million in the three years following the agreement, they actually increased by only $160 million. And throughout this period the bilateral telecommunications trade balance continued to move against the United States (table 2.7).

Friction between the United States and Japan over telecommunications trade did not end with the MOSS agreement. Soon after, MPT changed its position, announcing that companies providing value-added services would have to replace their proprietary protocols with standard protocols recommended by an international standards-setting body.[18] MPT defended its about-face by emphasizing the fairness of using an international body and international rules for both domestic and foreign companies. But this reasoning appeared disingenuous, since it disadvantaged American firms such as IBM, which had already spent billions of dollars developing their own protocols, and advantaged Japanese companies, which were new to the field and had no protocols (Prestowitz 1988). The US government complained that MPT's decision was discriminatory and violated its MOSS commitments. MPT bowed to US pressure in mid-1988, agreeing to license any company that used a unique protocol, as long as the company was willing to provide the technology necessary to connect with other, incompatible networks.

This incident and the friction involving Motorola's efforts to compete in the Japanese market for cellular services demonstrate that trade agreements with Japan must be carefully monitored for compliance. Often such agreements specify principles for action but are vague on the details of implementation.[19] After the heat of negotiations dies down, there is a natural and understandable tendency for the relevant Japanese authorities to backslide, especially when to go forward necessitates changes in business-government practices that disadvantage powerful Japanese business interests.

---

18. For the story of MPT's growing regulatory conflict with MITI over control of the Japanese telecommunications industry, see Johnson (1990).

19. This observation applies to the so-called Global Partnership Plan of Action agreed to by the United States and Japan during President George Bush's trip to Tokyo in February 1992. The plan commits Japanese government and industry to take steps to boost US sales of computers to Japan by $5.5 billion and US sales of auto parts to Japan by $10 billion. But there are no detailed proposals indicating how these goals will be realized.

Overall Lessons from the MOSS Talks

Despite their shortcomings, the MOSS agreements between the United States and Japan on trade in electronics, drugs, medical equipment, and telecommunications had some common strengths. They addressed structural impediments that posed significant barriers to trade and were not adequately covered by existing bilateral or multilateral agreements. They targeted rules rather than outcomes. They had multilateral applicability—all of Japan's trading partners stood to benefit from the negotiated changes in Japanese regulatory practices, as did many Japanese producers themselves. They concentrated on industries in which American companies were strong enough to take advantage of greater market opportunities in Japan. And they established procedures for regular monitoring of Japanese commitments. For all of these reasons, the MOSS agreements provide good models for future sectoral agreements between the United States and Japan or between the United States and its other trading partners.

Motorola and Japan's Cellular Telephone Market: A Step Closer to Managed Trade

During the 1980s, Motorola became one of American industry's most outspoken critics of Japan's trading practices. Motorola's criticisms were based on its own experiences in Japan's semiconductor and telecommunications markets.

Motorola first attempted to break into Japan's telecommunications market in the early 1980s by selling beeper-pagers to NTT, which had agreed to open its procurement to foreign bidders during the Tokyo Round of GATT negotiations. At that time Motorola was the lowest-cost, highest-volume producer of beepers in the world. NTT was a publicly owned monopoly provider of telecommunications services in Japan and a monopsonistic buyer of telephone equipment to provide these services. It was NTT's practice to set an attractive price for its equipment purchases and divide them among NEC, Fujitsu, Oki, Hitachi, and Matsushita or smaller firms related to the same business groups. In the case of pagers, NTT's traditional Japanese suppliers included Matsushita, NEC, Totsu, Toshiba, and Kokusai. Relations between NTT and these companies were extremely close—indeed they often hired retiring NTT officials into management positions. In this industry, even more than in others, the distinction between the Japanese bureaucracy and Japanese industry was largely meaningless.

Motorola's initial efforts to sell beepers in Japan met with silence: Motorola was not even able to secure an appointment with NTT officials until the Office of the US Trade Representative (USTR) intervened. Then, in violation of GATT Article X, NTT refused to disclose its proposal procedures or specifications. Such violations led the United States to negotiate the NTT procurement procedure agreement with Japan in December 1980. This agreement simply stipulated national treatment: foreign firms responding to NTT's requests for proposals were to be treated in a manner no less favorable than responding domestic firms.

At first NTT denied that beeper-pagers were covered by the agreement, but after a personal intervention by US Secretary of State George P. Shultz, NTT reversed its position. After a lengthy delay—during which NTT claimed that its specifications were proprietary and had to be worked out by individual firms over several years—these specifications were released. In keeping with Japanese regulatory tradition, they included both product design and performance criteria. Motorola had an initial disadvantage in meeting these criteria because they had been developed by its Japanese competitors in collaboration with NTT. Nor was Motorola able to compete on price, because NTT set a price above what Motorola was prepared to bid and invited proposals at that price. Traditionally, NTT reserved 60 percent of its equipment purchases for NEC and Matsushita, its two main suppliers, dividing the remaining 40 percent among its other Japanese suppliers.[20] A gain in market share for Motorola in pagers would mean a loss in market share for its Japanese competitors. A *de facto* cartel arrangement existed—the question thus was whether Motorola would be allowed to participate in the arrangement.

Finally, after two years of pressure, in 1981 Motorola obtained an initial small contract of $9 million for 60,000 of its pagers, thus breaking into the family. When NTT was privatized in April 1985 and its links with its traditional Japanese suppliers further weakened, Motorola's sales of pagers increased significantly. By 1987 Motorola had sold 500,000 pagers to NTT and had achieved the largest share of NTT's pocket pager business.

Motorola next encountered barriers to the Japanese market when it tried to sell third-party radio service and cellular telephone service. This time around the barriers took different forms because NTT had been privatized in the meantime. Procurement procedures were no longer the major obstacle. Instead, standards, testing and certification, and licensing came to the fore. Although the means by which Japanese producers were favored had changed, the goal of favoring them had not.

Motorola had invented the cellular phone concept in the 1950s. By 1983 the company had spent $150 million to develop both the telephone and station equipment technology necessary for cellular service. Motorola first explored sales of cellular equipment in Japan's budding market in 1984, but it soon ran into the hurdle of technical standards. According to new laws introduced in conjunction with NTT's privatization and MPT's new regulatory functions, technical standards were to be established by the Telecommunications Deliberation Council, appointed by and attached to MPT, while certification and testing were assigned to an association of Japanese manufacturers of telecommunications equipment. Foreign firms had no representation in either group. As noted earlier, this became a key issue in the MOSS telecommunications talks. As part of its MOSS commitments, MPT appointed experts from five American companies, including Motorola and AT&T, to the council's board of technical advisers.

In March 1986 the council recommended that any of three existing protocols, including those of Motorola and NTT, could be adopted for cellular service in Japan. MPT, however, decided that Japan should be divided into geographic

---

20. Although Motorola could not compete with Matsushita on price in the Japanese telecommunications market, Matsushita could and did compete with Motorola on price in the US market. Indeed, premium prices in Japan allowed Matsushita to sell at very low prices in the United States. Motorola ultimately brought and won a dumping suit against Matsushita on its sales of beeper-pagers in the US market. To avoid higher duties after the finding of dumping, however, Matsushita stopped selling beepers in the United States, moving instead into alphanumeric display pagers, which it began to assemble in US locations.

regions. NTT would be allowed to operate in all of these regions, and one additional company would be allowed to compete with NTT in each of them. A non–NTT protocol could be used if a carrier had a franchise in a particular region and chose to do so. Only NTT's protocol could be used throughout the nation.

Motorola had been working for several years with a Japanese company, Daini Denden (DDI), to develop cellular phone service for the Japanese market using Motorola's standard. The DDI–Motorola partnership was to compete with NTT, with DDI operating the network and Motorola providing the equipment. In 1986 DDI approached MPT to apply for a license for cellular service and began the extensive technical discussions typical of the Japanese license application process. Shortly thereafter, and unexpectedly, a rival consortium, Nippon Idou Tsushin Corporation (IDO), which included Toyota, NEC, Japan Highway Authority, and Tokyo Electric Power, applied for a license to provide cellular service using the NTT system, the equipment for which was manufactured by NEC. The firms in the IDO consortium had much stronger industrial and government connections than DDI, which was a new Japanese entrant to the telecommunications field. The stakes in the competition between IDO and DDI were enormous: in 1986 the Japanese cellular market was valued at $400 million and was expected to grow by 40 percent to 50 percent a year during the next five years.

MPT officials argued that there were insufficient radio frequencies for both IDO and DDI, and they initially proposed that the two applicants form a joint venture to compete with NTT. Private negotiations among the companies to develop such a venture failed to reach agreement, however. In 1987 MPT announced its licensing decisions—IDO was allocated the eastern half of Japan, including Tokyo, with 60 percent to 70 percent of the potential market, while DDI was awarded the remaining 30 percent to 40 percent. It is important to note that these decisions represented the right to compete with NTT in a particular market, not the competitive outcome itself. Nonetheless, by licensing the right to compete in this way, MPT was in effect restricting Motorola's potential share in the Japanese market, a share that was already held in check by NTT's preferential access to the entire Japanese market.

DDI accepted MPT's decision, but Motorola, which had encountered discriminatory treatment by Japanese regulatory authorities in the pager market, was suspicious of MPT's motives and complained to US officials. Motorola's public dissatisfaction set off months of negotiations between American and Japanese officials, at the end of which DDI was given a license to operate throughout all of Japan, with the exception of the Tokyo-Nagoya corridor. This decision effectively divided the Japanese population between DDI and IDO and gave Motorola a more equitable chance to compete. Nonetheless, Motorola remained handicapped. MPT's decision meant that NTT's protocol was the only one licensed for the Tokyo-Nagoya corridor, while all other regions of the country were licensed for two protocols: NTT's and Motorola's. As a result, Motorola customers would not be able to use their cellular phones when entering the Tokyo-Nagoya area, whereas an NTT standard cellular phone could be used anywhere in Japan. In principle, a Motorola car phone could be used in Tokyo with an adapter. But adapters could not be used on portable cellular phones, which accounted for more than 80 percent of Japan's cellular market.

Initially, Motorola accepted MPT's new allocation. But in 1988, MPT allocated 40 megahertz bandwidth to a new service called Convenience Radio Phone (CRP), which was inferior to cellular service but was promoted by some well-connected Japanese business interests. This allocation called into question MPT's claim that insufficient frequency precluded DDI's competition in the Tokyo-Nagoya region. Motorola reasoned that if additional frequencies could be created for CRP, they could also be created for DDI's cellular service. Motorola complained once again to American trade officials.

This time Motorola's hand was strengthened by the 1988 Omnibus Trade and Competitiveness Act. Section 1377 of the act gave special priority to telecommunications and was designed to ensure that Japan honored its 1986 MOSS commitments. In addition, the so-called Super 301 provision of the act authorized the USTR to retaliate against particular trading partners for persistent unfair trading practices. In early 1989 Motorola filed a 301 complaint with the USTR, charging that MPT had violated the MOSS agreement by failing to grant Motorola equal access to Japan's markets for third-party radio systems and cellular telephone service.

Initially, MPT officials denied any violation of the MOSS agreement in the cellular area, arguing that CRP was a totally different medium, allocated a bandwidth unusable for cellular phones. In addition, MPT contended that the technical barrier to Motorola's competition in the Tokyo-Nagoya region would disappear in two to three years when digital cellular phones replaced analog models.

Motorola thought MPT's response was a delaying tactic, designed to give IDO and its Japanese suppliers a chance to bring their products up to Motorola's design and quality standards. Such a tactic was a hallmark of Japan's infant-industry strategy in other parts of the electronics complex (for example, in supercomputers and semiconductors as described later in this chapter and the next). Motorola maintained that it would be hurt by a two-to-three-year delay, since NTT and IDO would realize first-mover advantages in marketing their systems and give the Japanese producers of cellular equipment time to challenge Motorola's product leadership.

Confirming its technology advantage, in April 1989 Motorola announced its new pocket-sized cellular MicroTac phone, which was both sleeker and a third lighter than the next-closest cellular phone available from Matsushita. The Japanese were incredulous. Said one MPT official, "Who would have believed that an American firm could come up with a smaller, better mobile phone than those made in Japan?" (*Business Tokyo*, September 1990, 38).

Four days later, on 28 April 1989, the USTR issued the first annual report required by the 1988 trade act and announced that Japan had violated the MOSS telecommunications agreement; the USTR specifically cited MPT for limiting the access of American companies to the Japanese markets for third-party radio and cellular telephone systems. Telecommunications equipment was the first sector slated for Super 301 retaliation, with 100 percent duties to become effective on a variety of Japanese imports in 30 days if negotiations between the United States and Japan failed to resolve the conflict. Motorola's right to compete in the Tokyo-Nagoya cellular phone market was the major issue of contention.

After two months of bitter negotiations, marked by open conflict between MITI and MPT (with the latter adamantly opposed to Motorola's demands), meetings between high-level officials, a visit by Motorola's chief executive officer to MPT's vice-minister, and several all-night meetings, in June 1990 MPT finally agreed to reallocate frequencies to allow Motorola to compete in the Tokyo-Nagoya region. MPT's decision revealed what Motorola had argued all along—that there was no technical barrier to this outcome.

Consistent with its preference for limiting cellular service to two suppliers (one of which was NTT) in each region, MPT designated IDO rather than DDI to serve as Motorola's operating company in the Tokyo-Nagoya corridor. In this way, MPT continued to manage competition. Cellular service in the Tokyo-Nagoya area continued to be a market-sharing arrangement—but Motorola was dealt a place. As part of the deal, MPT made 20 percent of IDO's spectrum allocation immediately available for a "North-American type analog cellular telephone system." Both IDO and DDI were also allocated additional spectrum to enable users to shift between the IDO–based Motorola system and the DDI– based Motorola system as they travelled between the Tokyo-Nagoya area and the rest of Japan. This arrangement made the Motorola system fully portable and accessible nationwide.

As part of this deal, MPT required IDO to spend $60 million of its own funds to erect the station infrastructure equipment to accommodate the Motorola system. IDO's position in this arrangement was an ambiguous one. On the one hand, it was forced to spend a substantial sum up front. It was also forced to allocate 20 percent of its initial spectrum allocation to the Motorola system, although it received an additional allocation to make this system functional nationwide. Finally, it was forced to operate a system that directly competed with its already functioning NTT system and its Japanese equipment suppliers. These suppliers had an incentive to encourage IDO to delay the installation of the equipment necessary for Motorola's service.

Whatever the reason, IDO did delay. After first entertaining a competing bid from AT&T, IDO finally ordered the necessary equipment from Motorola in May 1990, almost one year after the United States and Japan had signed a formal agreement ending the Super 301 investigation. Another year went by before installation of the equipment actually began.[21] In the meantime the market for cellular telephone service in Tokyo exploded. In 1990, for example, IDO realized a 400 percent increase in its revenues, mainly as a result of growth in this market. Motorola in the meantime had to sit and watch its major Japanese competitors enjoy the fruits of this market boom.

It also watched its leadership in cellular technology temporarily disappear. Motorola officials estimate that the two-year delay in gaining access to the Tokyo-Nagoya market turned their 18-month lead in cellular technology in 1989 into a six-month lag behind Fujitsu, which introduced the world's lightest cellular telephone in November 1990. Motorola regained product leadership with the introduction of its new cellular telephone, the MicroTac Lite, in August 1991, just in time to be used by IDO in its introduction of the Motorola system in Tokyo.

Because of the delays involved in getting the Motorola system up and running in the Tokyo-Nagoya corridor, it is too early to evaluate the results of the 1989 agreement with Japan on cellular telephone service. According to Motorola officials, the payoff in terms of greater sales and profits for Motorola

---

21. Motorola's station equipment was finally installed in Tokyo by the end of 1991.

will not be fully apparent until at least mid-1994. In the meantime, Motorola has successfully sold cellular equipment in other parts of Japan, but its estimated 20 percent share of Japan's market is less than its estimated 33 percent or more share of the world market. And Motorola's Japanese competitors have done even better in the United States, where they hold an estimated 50 percent share of the cellular telephone market. Overall, the results of the agreement to date indicate that Motorola has been able to establish a viable although not fully equitable foothold in Japan's market for cellular telephones (Vietor and Yoffie 1991).

Ironically, Motorola's analog system is finally becoming operational in Japan just at the time that MPT has announced its intention to promote a digital system for mobile communication and has allocated bandwidth for that purpose. The anticipated move to digital has spawned the entry of a number of new Japanese telecommunication service companies in the metropolitan Tokyo area. It is too early to predict what Motorola's competitive position will be in Japan's digital market. On a positive note, in 1991 MPT chose Motorola's design for a digital cellular car phone system as the nationwide standard over the designs of six Japanese companies and one European company. Perhaps, after a series of frustrations that would have deterred many a smaller and less competitive company, Motorola has finally gained access to Japan commensurate with its underlying technical and productive capabilities.[22]

The Third-Party Radio Conflict: A Successful Managed Trade Resolution

Third-party radio systems, also called shared mobile radio systems (SMRSS), link several mobile radio users together through a single dispatch point or base station. User companies are able to share the expensive central facility and receive service on a more economical basis. SMRSS are particularly attractive for such businesses as delivery services, couriers, towing services, and trucking. Motorola is a major provider of third-party radio systems in the United States and lobbied to have them included in the MOSS talks. As part of the 1986 telecommunications agreement, Japan agreed to open its markets to foreign providers of such systems.

However, this required a change in Japan's Radio Law, which granted exclusive right to operate a similar service, called MCA, to a government-created monopoly called MRC (Mobile Radio Center). MRC was a nonprofit company staffed largely by retired Japanese government officials. After extensive lobbying by Motorola and the US government, MPT made an official request to the Japanese Diet to change the Radio Law to allow foreign competition. It took until the end of 1986 to effectuate the change and to issue the necessary official regulations.

Motorola's initial strategy was to introduce its service (under the name JSMR) in cities in which MCA service was not yet available. Motorola formed a 50-50

---

22. As Aho and Aronson (1985, 85) have observed, Japanese regulatory practices and standards are often designed to exhaust all but the largest and most determined foreign firms wishing to sell in Japan. Motorola may be willing and able to combat these practices at considerable costs. Smaller, less profitable companies are not.

joint partnership with one of its best Japanese equipment dealers, Shikoku Tsuhan, whose responsibility was to enlist subscribers and provide local service to equipment and customers. Motorola's strategy met with some initial success. By the end of 1988, it had established 14 systems throughout Japan, one of which was in Tokyo. By early 1989, however, Motorola was convinced that MPT had not fully liberalized its regulations and was acting in ways that both limited the overall growth of the Japanese market for mobile business services and benefited MCA in the provision of these services.

Motorola's complaints against MPT involved both spectrum allocation and licensing requirements. By controlling the amount of spectrum available for Motorola's JSMR system, MPT had effectively restricted Motorola's share of the lucrative Tokyo market to 4 percent, with the remaining share protected for MCA. In addition, to obtain a license for operation of a new JSMR system, Motorola was required to sign customers in advance to demonstrate full system loading. No such requirement was imposed on MCA. Motorola estimated that MPT took twice as long to process its license requests as it took to process similar requests from MCA. Finally, both Motorola and MCA were harmed by MPT's refusal to allow interconnection of the JSMR and MCA systems with public telephone lines, without which intra- and intersystem connection was impossible.

Motorola brought these complaints before the USTR as violations of the MOSS telecommunications agreement at the same time that it brought complaints about violations in Japan's cellular service market. The June 1989 agreement that ended the ensuing negotiations addressed all of Motorola's complaints in the third-party radio market. MPT guaranteed transparency in future decisions about frequency allocation by agreeing to hold public hearings that would be announced in advance and would be open to all interested parties, including foreign suppliers. MPT also committed itself to expedite licensing procedures so that they would be completed within four months. If more than one application were pending at the same time, MPT promised to process them simultaneously. MPT also gave way on the issue of interconnection. According to the agreement, each user of a third-party radio system could connect its system to the public telephone network. In addition, users of one third-party system who were also users of another system could interconnect these systems at the relay station, thereby permitting the development of broader regional communications networks.

These regulatory changes benefited all actual and potential suppliers of third-party radio systems and their users in Japan. They also mirrored similar regulatory practices in the United States. As a result of these changes, the Japanese market for such systems grew rapidly after the agreement was signed.

Motorola's share in this market was also directly influenced by temporary provisions of the 1989 agreement, which established quantitative guidelines for MPT's allocation of frequencies for additional third-party radio systems in Tokyo. According to these guidelines, MPT agreed to grant licenses to operate in Tokyo on a one-to-one basis to MRC and JSMR, provided the latter had enough subscribers to qualify. MPT proposed that the 50-50 split last until new bandwidth made possible an expansion in the number of available licenses for Tokyo. The scheme lasted from June 1989 through November 1990 when new bandwidth was finally opened. Revealingly, this arrangement was not requested by the American negotiators but was offered by Japanese bureaucrats who have often used quantitative allocations to apportion limited opportunities between competing claimants. The difference in this case was that one of the claimants was foreign.

Motorola's sales of third-party radio systems have clearly benefited from the 1981 agreement. In mid-1989, when it was announced, Motorola had 16 third-party systems operating in Japan. By August 1991 it had 75 systems in place. According to Motorola officials, after the agreement was signed, Motorola's systems in Japan expanded more quickly than did MCA's, and Motorola's share of the Japanese market expanded accordingly. Reflecting the managed aspects of the agreement, the increase in Motorola's systems in Tokyo temporarily matched the increase in MCA's systems in Tokyo.

In light of these results, Motorola judges the 1989 agreement on third-party radio systems to be an unqualified success. As already noted, its enthusiasm for the agreement on cellular telephone service is much more muted, in large part because of the long delays involved in its implementation. Although MPT was able to act expeditiously on its own to honor Japan's commitments in third-party radio, its commitments in the cellular telephone market depended on complementary actions by Japanese producers who stood to benefit from delaying Motorola's entry to the Tokyo market.

Lessons from Motorola's Experiences in Gaining Access to the Japanese Market

The story of Motorola's efforts to compete in pagers, cellular telephones, and third-party radios yields several lessons about access barriers to the Japanese market and appropriate US responses. First, the story flies in the face of those who question the existence of such barriers in Japan.[23] Even after the privatization of NTT, the telecommunications market in Japan remained heavily managed. MPT's cartelization of the right to compete replaced NTT's cartelization of sales, but NTT and its family firms remained the main beneficiaries of the new arrangements (Johnson 1990). In this industry more than most, there was a close alliance between Japanese bureaucratic authorities and Japanese business interests, an alliance that worked to the disadvantage of outsiders. Over time, often in response to US pressure, the Japanese authorities changed the methods by which they shaped the competition to the advantage of Japanese producers, but the overall objective remained the same. As each skin of the promotional onion was peeled off, another was revealed.

Second, it is hard to imagine an effective "fixed-rule" approach for dealing with the kinds of market barriers at play in this case. No set of rules, however detailed, could have anticipated the methods employed to thwart Motorola's repeated attempts to sell its products. Certainly, most of these methods fell outside the purview of GATT regulations, since they involved structural impediments rather than trade barriers. Moreover, the impediments in question were specific to the organization of the telecommunications industry in Japan. A general set of rules that abstracted from industry and national specificity would have been largely irrelevant.

---

23. One who questions the existence of such barriers in persuasive language is Jagdish Bhagwati (1991).

Even if more detailed, industry-specific, multilateral rules had existed, their enforcement would have been an issue. If Motorola had been able to threaten legal action for damages against NTT or MPT for violation of such rules through some global equivalent of the European Court of Justice, then their enforcement might have been a credible option. But in the absence of such a mechanism, unilateral pressure and bilateral negotiations were essential for the enforcement of negotiated agreements. It took direct personal pressure from the US Secretary of State to compel NTT to honor its multilateral procurement commitments in the case of pagers, and it took the threat of unilateral tariff retaliation to compel MPT to grant Motorola the right to compete in the Tokyo-Nagoya cellular market. In both instances, the stakes in the trade conflict were zero-sum from the point of view of allied bureaucratic and business interests in Japan—what Motorola stood to gain, they stood to lose. Japanese consumer interests that stood to benefit from greater competition were simply not accorded a place on the Japanese side of the negotiating table. In such situations, it is not surprising that the Japanese would give way to American interests only as much as they had to and only when they had something to lose.

Third, under such circumstances the Japanese often employ delaying tactics. For example, MPT argued that Motorola would be able to compete in Japan's digital cellular telephone market after a two-to-three-year delay. But as the sorry story of the semiconductor industry demonstrates, to delay access to Japan is often to deny access to Japan. Japanese producers and regulatory authorities can easily exhaust all but the largest and most determined foreign firms who want to sell in Japan. Even those firms that stick it out can be harmed financially by significant delays. Meanwhile things do not stand still, especially in technology-intensive industries where learning curve effects, scale economies, and investments that lock in standards create powerful first-mover advantages, and where infant enterprises can be nurtured into mature competitors. Time is often of the essence in establishing a presence in rapidly growing markets in such industries. The two-year delay in Motorola's access to the Tokyo cellular market cost Motorola sales and revenues it otherwise would have enjoyed from the initial 18-month product lead of its MicroTac technology.

Fourth, the Motorola story indicates that the distinction between trade management through establishing better rules and managed trade through establishing trade outcomes or results is overly simplistic and misleading.[24] The recurrent negotiations on pagers and cellular telephones were not designed to establish general multilateral rules for international competition. Nor, however, were they designed to give Motorola a targeted share of the Japanese market. But they were quite specific about the product in question, the geographical market in question, and even the firms in question. On a continuum between trade management through better rules and managed trade through quantitative targets, these negotiations were clearly closer to the latter. Nonetheless, their purpose was to increase competition, not to reduce competition and cartelize the market. The same can be said of the temporary quantitative sharing arrangement used by MPT for the allocation

24. This distinction between trade management through rules and managed trade through quantitative targets is made by Bhagwati (1991). A similar distinction—managed trade by rules and managing trade by outcomes—is made in Tyson (1990).

of scarce bandwidth for third-party radio service in Tokyo. This arrangement was designed to compensate Motorola for past disadvantages resulting from discriminatory allocations in favor of MRC. An increase in Motorola's allocation meant more rather than less competition. Paradoxically, in Japan's heavily "managed" markets for pagers, cellular phone service, and third-party radio systems, something akin to managed trade was needed to achieve something akin to market competition. As the next chapter will demonstrate, a similar conclusion applies to Japan's semiconductor market.

Fifth, US trade policy in the Motorola case won some significant victories. As a result of the 1989 negotiations, the Japanese market for third-party radio was deregulated in conformance with US practice, benefiting both producers and users. Motorola's sales of such systems grew rapidly, in part as a result of overall market growth and in part as a result of MPT's commitment to allocate a minimum share of the increase in the Tokyo market to Motorola systems. After a significant and costly delay, Motorola may finally see significant sales of its analog cellular phone system in Tokyo-Nagoya, and its digital technology has been adopted as the standard for Japan's budding digital cellular car phone market. On a broader level, NTT's and MPT's regulatory hold over the Japanese telecommunications industry was weakened during the course of the 1980s, largely in response to US pressure. Not only Motorola but other foreign producers, new Japanese entrants, and Japanese consumers are beneficiaries of this development.

Although the competitive situation has improved, however, vestiges of the old system remain. According to a recent study, many standards are still set and many procurement contracts are still distributed through informal company discussions with NTT and through participation in NTT's R&D projects. Foreign suppliers are rarely involved in such channels of decision making (Anchordoguy 1990, 16).

The successful use of trade policy in the Motorola case was not without its costs. Motorola's struggles contributed to worsening trade tensions between the United States and Japan. The conflict strengthened American perceptions of the Japanese as unfair and predatory traders, and Japanese perceptions of the Americans as unreliable and whining bullies. The Motorola case was also dangerous because it strengthened incentives for American companies to resort to trade policy to win their competitive battles. The Motorola case was clear-cut. Few would deny Motorola's real productive and technological capabilities. The company used trade policy to win the opportunity to compete on the basis of these capabilities, not as a substitute for them. But Motorola's case is an exceptional one as well. More often than not, weak producers, not strong ones, fall back on trade policy to protect themselves at home rather than to exploit market opportunities abroad. Unfortunately, given the politics of trade policy decisions in the United States and the understaffing and underfinancing of its trade policy institutions, it is hard to be optimistic that deserving cases will always be distinguished from undeserving ones. This is particularly true in an election year such as 1992, when recessionary conditions at home flame protectionist sentiments. In 1989, Motorola wanted to gain access to Japan's market; in contrast, in 1992, some American automobile manufacturers want to restrict access at home.

Finally, even when a company's underlying competitive position is strong and its complaint about structural impediments to the Japanese market is valid, trade policy may not be the most effective response. The efforts of Cray Research to sell its supercomputers in Japan illustrate this point.

Cray and the Japanese Supercomputer Market: Procurement, Infant-Industry Tactics, and Reciprocity

There are some striking similarities in the efforts of Cray and Motorola to improve their access to the Japanese market in the 1980s.[25] Both companies resorted to trade policy to sell more in Japan, not to reduce imports of Japanese products in the United States. Both companies were recognized global leaders in their product lines. Cray supercomputers were consistently ranked first in benchmark tests by independent experts. Although the best Japanese machines had achieved very high theoretical peak performance by the end of the 1980s, they were still regarded as inferior to Cray machines when run on real-world problems with realistic workloads. During most of the 1980s there was little doubt that Cray machines had the edge—an edge that was bolstered by the fact that most supercomputer software was developed for Cray machines because of their dominant world market share.

Cray introduced the world's first supercomputer in 1976. The first Japanese supercomputers were not produced until 1983, also the year of the first Japanese purchases of supercomputers. Not surprisingly, these purchases were from Japanese suppliers. Nor was it an accident that the first Japanese production coincided with the first Japanese purchases. Given the vertically integrated structure of the Japanese electronics industry, the firms with which Cray competed after 1983 were also among the same firms that competed with Motorola—NEC, Hitachi, and Fujitsu—all of which were closely knit members of NTT's family and all of which had benefited from infant-industry policies to promote the computer industry.[26] These firms were able to cover low prices and investment in new and risky products such as supercomputers with profits earned in their other business lines. Obviously, the premium prices paid by NTT for telecommunications products aided this cross-subsidization strategy.

The Japanese firms also benefited from their *keiretsu* membership. As noted earlier, group membership provides a source of demand for the products of affiliated firms. The evidence in the supercomputer industry suggests that group members were more likely to buy a supercomputer from an affiliated firm than from a member of another *keiretsu* (Anchordoguy 1991). On the other hand, Cray was able to sell some of its machines to *keiretsu* members despite substantial group pressure from competing affiliated firms.[27] Nonetheless, Cray's biggest

---

25. For a detailed and compelling study of the supercomputer trade negotiations with Japan, see Anchordoguy (1991). Most of the findings of this report are contained in OTA (1991). Many of the facts used in the following discussion are drawn from Anchordoguy's analysis.

26. For a full discussion of these infant-industry policies and their effects see Anchordoguy (1989).

27. As an illustration, Nissan's first purchase of a Cray in 1986 came only after Nissan engineers leaked to the US embassy in Tokyo that they wanted to buy a Cray, but that top company executives had decided to purchase a Hitachi because of their relationship with that firm. The leak had an effect. The USTR and Department of Commerce officials discussed the issue with MITI, which in turn pressured Nissan to purchase a Cray. This incident was reported in a series of interviews with US and Cray officials by Marie Anchordoguy (see Anchordoguy 1991 for more details).

Japanese customers were firms that did not belong to the groups with which NEC, Fujitsu, and Hitachi were affiliated: through 1989, of the 22 Crays purchased by private Japanese institutions, 14 were bought by companies unrelated to Cray's Japanese competitors (Anchordoguy 1991). Overall, *keiretsu* relations were a barrier to Cray's access to private-sector customers in Japan. But this barrier was not impenetrable. By the end of 1990, Cray had captured over 21 percent of the private Japanese market for supercomputers (Cray Research, Inc. 1991).

But Cray had considerably less success finding public-sector customers in Japan, and the company attributed its difficulties to public procurement practices. Cray argued that it was effectively excluded from bidding for public purchases of supercomputers because of several distinctive features of these practices. First, public agencies did not issue public notices of their intentions to procure supercomputers. Second, they did not require performance criteria on the bids they solicited. Third, Japanese companies regularly submitted bids on which prices were discounted 80 percent to 90 percent.

The first and second of Cray's complaints about Japanese procurement practices—namely, that procurements were not publicized and that performance criteria on bids were not required—were similar to complaints voiced by Motorola when it tried to sell beeper-pagers to NTT. Like Motorola, Cray argued that the GATT procurement code required public notification of procurement competitions to all potential suppliers. Like Motorola, Cray also argued that Japanese bidding practices should require performance criteria as American bidding practices do. Cray stood to benefit from such criteria because of the documented performance superiority of its machines.

Unlike Motorola, which had contended that it could not compete in the Japanese beeper-pager market because NTT set a price floor, Cray argued that it could not compete in the supercomputer market because of excessive discounting by Japanese companies willing and able to sell at a loss to public agencies. In essence, Cray argued that Japanese companies were dumping in their home market. Whereas Motorola had requested that it be allowed to compete on price, as it could in the American marketplace, Cray requested that Japanese companies be restricted from "unfair" price competition. In response to Cray's complaints, the United States initiated an inquiry into Japan's procurement practices under Section 305 of the 1974 trade act and included supercomputers in the MOSS talks on electronics. During these negotiations, MITI Vice Minister Makuto Kuroda repeatedly told US negotiators that "no matter how much the United States tried, it would not be able to sell supercomputers in Japan" (Office of Technology Assessment 1991a, 273). But under considerable US pressure, the Japanese authorities finally yielded, convincing NTT to buy a Cray supercomputer to ease trade tensions (Anchordoguy 1991). In addition, the Japanese government passed an emergency budget to enlarge public funding for supercomputer procurement by universities. Shortly thereafter, two public institutions bought American machines, one from Cray and one from Control Data. Extensive interviews with Japanese officials indicate that the invisible hand of bureaucratic intervention rather than the invisible hand of open bidding and market competition managed these outcomes (Anchordoguy 1991). The Japanese government made sure that American companies won these two public purchases.

A final agreement on supercomputers was negotiated by the United States and Japan in the summer of 1987. The agreement established an open bidding process, including advance notification of procurement, publication of specifications, and procedures for making complaints and protests. However, the agreement did not require that bids be based on benchmarks of real workload performance—theoretical peak performance was sufficient. Nor did the agreement address the discounting problem, in part because many US trade officials believed that if Japanese producers dumped their machines at below-cost prices they would only hurt themselves. The same officials might have added that an agreement to limit price discounting would probably not benefit American producers, since higher prices were likely to boost the profits of their Japanese competitors.

The 1987 agreement achieved its goal of making the procurement process in Japan more transparent. Thereafter, American producers were notified of public procurements, and they could submit bids if they wished. But given the circumstances prevailing in the Japanese public market, it was still highly unlikely that the bid of a foreign producer would be the winning one. As an illustration, in October 1987 Tohoku University announced its decision to procure a supercomputer, and Cray decided to tender a bid. In real benchmark tests of the competing equipment, Cray machines were judged superior. But Cray finally dropped out of the bidding under pressure to discount its price substantially. Meanwhile NEC, Tohoku's traditional supplier of computer hardware, went through seven bidding rounds, finally slashing its list price by 80 percent and winning the contract.

Hinting at the informal cartelization of the procurement process in Japan, the Director of the Computer Center at Tohoku predicted that he would buy an NEC machine well before Cray withdrew its bid (Cray Research, Inc. 1991). There is other evidence of such cartelization. For example, government procurements were often scheduled immediately after a new product had been announced by a Japanese company and were based on that product's specifications, even though it had yet to be manufactured, let alone tested. In such cases, there were telling matches between the companies that announced new products and the public agencies that announced identical procurement specifications (Cray Research, Inc. 1991).

The 1987 supercomputer agreement did little to dislodge these preferential links between Japanese companies and their public-sector customers. Through 1989, only 5 of 51 public purchases of supercomputers in Japan involved foreign machines. Even more striking, four out of five of these purchases occurred after the 1987 agreement, and at least three of them were "managed" by Japanese government pressure (Cray Research, Inc. 1991).

Largely as a result of Cray's difficulties in selling to public agencies in Japan, Cray's share of the Japanese supercomputer market remained considerably smaller than its share of other world markets. In 1989 Cray held an estimated 63 percent of the world market, 84 percent of the European market, and 81 percent of the North American market, but only 15 percent of the Japanese market (Cray Research, Inc. 1991). In that year, Japanese companies held 85 percent of the Japanese market, compared with only 10 percent of the European market (which accounted for a quarter of the world market).

In 1989, convinced that Japan's discriminatory procurement practices persisted, and concerned about CDC's withdrawal from the supercomputer industry in the wake of NEC's announcement of a superior machine, the US government targeted supercomputers in its Super 301 negotiations with Japan. During the 1990 negotiations, the Japanese government once again "managed" public procurement of a Cray machine, this time by convincing a Japanese firm to drop out of the bidding.

The 1990 agreement on supercomputers differed from the 1987 agreement in several ways. First, it required that bids contain real-world performance criteria rather than theoretical peak performance data. Second, it required that suppliers who won the bid deliver the machine by the announced delivery date or the entire procurement would be subject to rebidding. This restriction was designed to counter the tendency of Japanese companies to bid a product that did not yet exist (a "paper machine"). Finally, the agreement limited price discounting by voiding bids that violated Japan's Anti-Monopoly Law.

Between June 1990, when the supercomputer agreement was signed, and the middle of 1992, Cray sold only two additional supercomputers to Japanese public-sector agencies. During this period there were five additional public procurements of supercomputers in Japan, all from Japanese vendors.[28] History suggests that bureacractic maneuvering played an important role in Cray's winning bids and in the temporary boost to Cray's share of the Japanese market. As far as short-term results are concerned, it is difficult not to conclude that a major trade push by the United States has yielded only token sales arranged by the Japanese authorities to placate their American counterparts.

Nor is it likely that the 1990 agreement will significantly improve the prospects for public sales of Cray or other foreign supercomputers in Japan over the longer run. Policies of promotion and closure in the Japanese supercomputer market are now beginning to pay off. Many experts in both the United States and Japan now agree that Japanese companies will match or surpass American companies in advanced computing during the next five years. As has happened before in many other markets, the supercomputer market in Japan may finally become more open only when Japanese companies are strong enough to meet foreign competition head on and win.[29] Improved access for Cray at that point will mean fewer sales than it would have ten years earlier when Cray was the clear-cut technological leader. Moreover, greater access now or in the future cannot compensate for the damages suffered by Cray as a result of forgone sales in the past. According to a conservative estimate by Anchordoguy, forgone public sales alone cost Cray nearly $400 million in revenues and $59 million in extra R&D during the 1980s.[30]

Whatever its ultimate effect on foreign sales, however, the 1990 supercomputer agreement, like its 1987 predecessor, did address bona fide structural impediments to the Japanese market. In this sense, both agreements embody both the stated American goal of making the Japanese market more open and transparent and the traditional American emphasis on rules rather than results in trade negotiations. Revealingly, several times during the course of the supercomputer

---

28. Personal communication from the US Department of Commerce, July 1992.

29. This is an illustration of the so-called "moving band of protection" characteristic of Japanese industrial targeting (see Tyson and Zysman 1990).

30. Taking into account sales to private institutions, Cray's total forgone revenues jump to $684 million and $102.6 million in extra R&D revenues, enough to fund a whole new generation of supercomputers (Anchordoguy 1991, 51).

negotiations the Japanese authorities acted to "manage" trade results by leaning on Japanese companies and public agencies to make room for foreign suppliers. Orchestrated sales of this sort simply confirm Cray's contention that public procurement decisions in Japan were not the outcome of market competition.

Unfortunately, however, neither are most such decisions in the United States when it comes to supercomputers. A lack of reciprocity is a weakness of the supercomputer agreements. In both the MOSS talks and the Motorola negotiations, the United States urged Japan to harmonize its practices with US practices, which encouraged competition between domestic and foreign firms. In the supercomputer case, however, while insisting that Japan loosen its public procurement restrictions, the United States maintained tight national security restrictions over supercomputer purchases at home. Moreover, although formal restrictions were limited to the defense-related market, in practice the US government actively monitored potential procurements by private institutions for possible violations of antidumping laws. As a result of such monitoring, in 1987, under pressure from the Department of Commerce, the Massachusetts Institute of Technology withdrew its plan to buy an NEC supercomputer, which had won in a bidding competition against Cray, CDC, and Amdahl.[31]

Similarly, in late 1991 Fujitsu, by then the world's second-largest supercomputer manufacturer after Cray, dropped an offer to donate a supercomputer to an environmental research project based in Colorado after members of Congress protested the donation to the President's science and technology adviser. Ironically, this project received no US government funding, although it did get funding from electric utility organizations in France, Italy, and Japan.

Partly as a result of national security restrictions, partly as a result of such informal monitoring, but mainly as a result of the performance superiority of American machines, American suppliers held an estimated 98 percent of the North American supercomputer market in 1989, with Japanese suppliers taking the remaining 2 percent (Cray Research, Inc. 1991, 3-2). Reciprocity is likely to become a more important issue, however, as the Japanese companies continue to close to gap with their American competitors.[32] In the words of a report by the Institute of Electrical and Electronics Engineers (1988, 8), "Is it realistic to believe that the Japanese can long be required to give unbiased consideration to U.S. supercomputers while Japanese machines are foreclosed from U.S. institutions?" The answer is certainly no. If the United States adheres to its free-trade, open-market principles, sooner or later it will have to make the supercomputer agreement reciprocal.[33] And with reciprocity, as the Japanese com-

---

31. The available evidence about this case suggests that the NEC bid did violate US anti-dumping law, because the bid price was lower than NEC's average costs (Anchordoguy 1991). For more on the shortcomings of this cost-based approach to assessing dumping in high-technology industries, see chapter 7.

32. As an illustration, Fujitsu recently announced plans to reenter the American market with a new family of supercomputers, known as vector supercomputers, that achieve their speed with a handful of extremely fast processors. The vector approach, according to Fujitsu, will serve as a reliable interim vehicle to run many kinds of applications software until the software problems associated with massively parallel processing are solved (*New York Times*, 15 March 1992, section 3, 10).

33. According to the US Federal Acquisition Regulations, civilian agencies using federal

panies become more competitive, they will gradually increase their share of the American market (Cray Research, Inc. 1991, 14).

A second criticism of the US approach in the supercomputer negotiations relates to pricing. US producers, led by Cray, sharply criticized the discount pricing of Japanese companies. Even Cray conceded, however, that its Japanese competitors were not enthusiastic about large discounts, but were forced to offer them because of the tight procurement budgets of their Japanese customers. Nonetheless, Cray contended that such discounts were "unfair competition," and that they violated Japan's antitrust regulations. Ultimately, Japanese negotiators accepted Cray's arguments and outlawed bids that violated the prohibition against "unjust low-priced sales" in Japan's Anti-Monopoly Law (Office of the US Trade Representative 1990). At the same time, Japanese companies were encouraged to charge higher prices and to limit price discounting to 20 percent to 30 percent. Moreover, the Japanese government agreed to a US request to "budget sufficient funds to enable public procurement of supercomputers based on prices of similar supercomputers in the private sector."[34]

Since the 1990 agreement was powerless to break the informal preferential links between Japanese public agencies and their traditional Japanese suppliers, the likely consequences of such Japanese "concessions" were higher prices and greater profits for the Japanese companies, which had never wanted to discount their prices as much as they had been forced to in the first place. Such concessions, like Japanese concessions to raise prices in a variety of other trade conflicts with the United States (for example, those involving semiconductors and automobiles) only serve to strengthen Japanese companies at the expense of their American competitors over the long run.

At the root of the ability of Japanese firms to compete aggressively on price, even when it means selling products below cost and running losses, are the unique structural features of the Japanese economy. The companies competing with Cray and Motorola have deep pockets and long time horizons. They can afford to cross-subsidize losses in one market with profits from another. They continue to benefit from a variety of promotional policies and from lax enforcement of regulations on restrictive business practices. They also continue to benefit from the insulated nature of the Japanese market, fostered by these and other structural impediments. In short, the pricing behavior of Japanese companies is a natural outgrowth of Japan's business and government environment.

Any trade policy that encourages Japanese companies to charge higher prices does nothing to address the underlying causes of such behavior, nor does it offset the damages to American companies caused by lack of access to the Japanese market or by Japan's promotional policies. Instead, the winners of such a policy are usually the Japanese companies themselves, while the losers are their customers, many of whom are American companies.

In the supercomputer case, a US subsidy enabling Cray to meet the price competition in Japan's public procurement market would have been preferable

---

funds to buy supercomputers may not discriminate on the basis of nationality except for specific national security reasons. But the exception is vague and allows for interpretation by the purchasing unit.

34. US Trade Representative Carla A. Hills in a letter to the Ambassador of Japan to the United States, 15 June 1990. See also Anchordoguy (1991, 45).

to a trade agreement compelling its Japanese competitors to charge higher prices. Such a subsidy would have been justifiable on broader grounds as well, if it had been extended as part of a US initiative to support joint research between American and Japanese universities on common national concerns like global environmental change. In addition, such an initiative could have addressed some of the structural asymmetries in the organization of science and research in the United States and Japan.

For all its strengths, however, a subsidy approach would have been sharply criticized in the United States as a form of industrial policy. But this criticism would have overlooked a key historical fact: a defense-based industrial policy has played an essential nurturing role in the supercomputer industry—as in many other high-technology industries in which American firms have competitive strength. Now that American producers are confronted by strong foreign challengers, the real policy question is not whether to have an industrial policy for a high-technology industry like supercomputers, but whether to have an industrial policy with commercial as distinct from national security objectives.

Perhaps the most fundamental lesson to emerge from the supercomputer conflict with Japan is that trade policy is usually not an adequate substitute for a defensive industrial policy. By the end of the 1980s, the dismantling of preferential Japanese procurement practices, although a justifiable goal of American trade policy, provided no guarantee that American producers would survive intensifying Japanese competition. If a strong American supercomputer industry is itself a policy goal, some direct public support, preferably in the form of funding for cooperative, generic R&D programs, is warranted. The so-called federal high-performance computing and communications initiative is a step in the right direction. Initially submitted to Congress by the Bush administration in 1989, the initiative is a five-year, federally funded program to support research on advanced computing technologies. As designed, the program does not support any one firm or technology. Instead, the approach is a generic one: the goal is to encourage improvements in high-performance computing that will benefit a wide range of industries. The program is designed to foster joint research among government, business, and universities on basic scientific questions whose solutions require superior computing capabilities. If successful, the program will encourage cooperative research on such fundamental issues as global climate change and superconductivity, while simultaneously promoting technological change away from current supercomputer designs to the massively parallel processing designs that most experts believe are essential to enhanced computing capabilities in the future. In addition, the generic approach channels federal research monies toward basic scientific puzzles whose resolutions promise large social benefits.

Concluding Remarks

"Japan bashing" has become shorthand for American criticism of Japanese trading practices. Implicit in this phrase is the assumption that such criticism is a demagogic, unjustified assault on the blameless victor in a trade rivalry. On the other side, commonly voiced complaints about "Japan, Inc." imply that current trade discrepancies result solely from the unfair trading practices of a mercantilist monolith. A dispassionate interpretation of the facts indicates that both of these views are misleading.

A decade of research has confirmed that the Japanese market is significantly more closed to foreign competition than the markets of most of the other advanced industrial nations. There are those who argue that the closure problem ended with the reduction or elimination of overt Japanese trade and investment barriers by the late 1970s. But the evidence in this chapter and the next suggests otherwise. The means of blocking access may have changed, but the goal has not.

The major impediments to the Japanese market are rooted in the unique character of Japanese business organizations and their distinctive relationships with one another and with the Japanese government. Overt trade barriers are easy to identify and can be challenged under GATT rules. The structural impediments to Japan's market, in contrast, are less visible and fall outside the GATT's purview. Such impediments would be best remedied by enforceable multilateral regulations on the restrictive business practices characteristic of many Japanese companies and the promotional policies that give them a preferential advantage in the Japanese market. As an illustration, had Motorola and Cray been able to threaten for damages before a neutral multilateral institution, they might have been able to deter the preferential regulatory practices of public institutions in Japan and the aggressive pricing tactics of their Japanese competitors. In the absence of enforceable multilateral rules on competition policy and regulatory customs, however, both Motorola and Cray were forced to seek remedies through American trade law.

Even an optimist would have to admit that the prospects for the quick development of such rules are poor. GATT members have spent six years trying to agree on the more straightforward issue of agricultural subsidies. For policymakers interested in a meaningful time horizon—one measured in months or years, not decades—the question is what to do in the meantime. This question is of greatest importance to the United States, which remains Japan's largest trading partner and which accounts for 50 percent of the Japanese trade surplus (70 percent if the flow of Japanese goods through East Asian countries to US destinations is included). The stories of the MOSS negotiations, Motorola's efforts in cellular telephones and third-party radios, and Cray's efforts in supercomputers provide some answers. In all of these cases, US negotiators concentrated their energies on improving market access in Japan in specific industries. An industry focus allowed the participants in the negotiations to identify and address industry-specific impediments.

Such a focus contrasts with the economy-wide focus of the Structural Impediments Initiative (SII) between the United States and Japan that commenced in 1989. In principle, the SII approach was designed to reduce general structural impediments affecting trade between the two nations in all industries. In practice, the negotiations also included many macroeconomic issues, such as Japan's "excessive" saving rate and America's excessive budget deficit. However, some important economy-wide structural impediments to the Japanese market—including the organization of the distribution system, exclusionary business practices, and *keiretsu* relationships—did make it to the negotiating table. Revealingly, Japanese complaints about the US market concentrated on macroeconomic policy and overt trade barriers—there were few complaints about genuine structural impediments because the US market is remarkably free of them, especially in comparison with the Japanese market.

Getting the Japanese to add personnel to their Fair Trade Commission or to increase their antitrust penalties, as they agreed to do as part of their SII commitments, may have payoffs in the long run. Indeed, some actions to tighten regulations on anticompetitive business practices in Japan have already been taken, and more are under consideration.[35] In the short run, however, industry-specific talks and precise sectoral commitments are likely to prove more effective at enhancing access to Japan than the economy-wide SII approach.

On the other hand, the sectoral approach has several drawbacks. First, it is costly. The understaffed and underfinanced agencies of the US government responsible for negotiating sectoral deals can only manage a few at a time. There is an ever-present danger that political influence rather than economic significance will determine which industries are chosen for such negotiations. Second, although structural impediments to the Japanese market are real, they are not the primary cause of the overall US–Japan trade imbalance. Sectoral talks to eliminate these impediments cannot substitute for coordinated macroeconomic adjustments on both sides. Third, if sector-specific disputes are allowed to dominate trade negotiations between the United States and Japan, and if they are resolved by ad hoc deals in which power politics determines the outcome, economic relations between the two countries are likely to deteriorate still further, endangering their much-needed cooperation on a wide range of global issues. In addition, bilateral deals with Japan for specific sectors, when not explicitly designed with multilateral applicability, are likely to antagonize America's other trading partners as well.

For all of these reasons, the United States should judiciously restrict its sectoral talks with Japan to those industries in which there are well-documented structural impediments, in which American producers have demonstrated competitive strength in other global markets, and in which the gains to greater market access in Japan are likely to be large. In addition, such talks should explicitly target the removal of structural impediments that disadvantage all non-Japanese producers, not just American producers. Deals that favor American producers over their foreign competitors should be avoided. Finally, sectoral talks should be complemented by ongoing negotiations to address economy-wide structural impediments and to coordinate macroeconomic policies.

---

35. It is too early to judge whether these actions will have much effect. The main problem with Japanese antitrust has not been the regulations themselves but their enforcement. In an unpromising development, the first policy action taken in the name of stricter antitrust enforcement was aimed at foreign importers in Japan (including Apple Computer), not at domestic companies. For greater detail on the SII talks, see US Department of Commerce, International Trade Administration (1990). For an analysis of some of the preliminary results of the talks see Noland (1991). For an analysis of some their long-run consequences, see Frankel (1990).

4

Managing Trade and Competition in the Semiconductor Industry

Industry Economics and the Evolution of Comparative Advantage

From Manipulated to Managed Trade: The US–Japan Semiconductor Trade Agreement

The Effects of the Agreement on Trade and Pricing

The New Semiconductor Trade Agreement: The Story Continues

An Overall Assessment of the SCTA

Lessons for U.S. Trade Policy from the Semiconductor Experience

The semiconductor industry has never been free of the visible hand of government intervention. Competitive advantage in production and trade has been heavily influenced by policy choices, particularly in the United States and Japan. Some of these choices, such as the provision of public support for basic science, R&D, and education in the United States, have had general, not industry-specific, objectives. But other choices, such as the provision of secured demand for industry output through military procurement in the United States and through preferential procurement of computers and telecommunications equipment in Japan, have been industry specific in intent and implementation. In short, the semiconductor industry, *wherever it has developed*, has been an explicit target of industrial policy—whether in the guise of military policy in the United States or in the guise of commercial policy elsewhere in the world.

Conditions that create advantage in this industry are not inherited like features of the national landscape; they have been created and manipulated by policy. Nor has trade in this industry ever been "free" in the classical sense; it has been manipulated by a host of formal and informal policies that affect both trade and foreign investment. Over time, these policies—such as formal tariffs and quotas, restrictive or promotional policies for investment, and preferential procurement arrangements—have had powerful effects on trade among nations.

Why has the visible hand been so omnipresent and forceful in this industry? The answer lies in its strategic significance, in both the military and the economic

Portions of this chapter were coauthored with David B. Yoffie and will also appear in "Semiconductors: From Manipulated to Managed Trade," by Laura D'Andrea Tyson and David B. Yoffie, in David B. Yoffie, ed., *Global Trade and Competition* (Cambridge, MA: Harvard Business School, forthcoming). I also wish to express my special gratitude to my BRIE colleague Michael Borrus for his invaluable information and insights on the semiconductor industry.

sense. The semiconductor industry was born out of the US effort to develop ever more reliable and sophisticated military equipment, and indeed its military significance has never been doubted. Advances in semiconductor technology have supported all of the major advanced weapons systems, including the smart bombs and Patriot missiles that had their spectacular debut in the 1991 Gulf War.

In contrast, the Japanese, the Europeans, and the newly developing countries have focused on the commercial significance of semiconductors. Their governments have given the industry special promotional and protectionist treatment in the hope of realizing various economic benefits. The most notable of these are more-productive, higher-paying jobs for their workers; increased exports, as a result of an expanded national share of growing world markets; the development of an indigenous technological infrastructure, with spillover benefits for other industries; and the provision of linkage externalities—lower-cost, higher-quality inputs—for downstream user industries, such as computers and telecommunications equipment, that are also thought to have long-term economic significance.

Despite a general liberalization trend in many industries around the world, national governments have not forsworn measures to support their semiconductor industries. Moreover, although government regulation has been widely discredited in many sectors, there is no presumption that the visible hand of policy in semiconductors will lead to lower economic welfare than the invisible hand of the market. Increasing returns to scale, substantial learning curve economies, linkage externalities, and technological spillovers are not the stuff of perfect competition and market optimality.

This chapter attempts to demonstrate how the visible hand of government has influenced patterns of competition and trade in the semiconductor industry. The first part of the chapter examines how government policy encouraged the development of the industry in the United States and how policies at home and abroad affected the trade and foreign direct investment decisions of American companies. There is nothing particularly surprising in this part of the story. A combination of factor endowments, technological skills, and growing demand, all fostered by concerted government policies, gave American companies a competitive edge. Global trade patterns reflected these companies' strategies as they attempted to gain global market share in a context of changing production conditions and policy environments. Given the substantial first-mover advantages in the semiconductor industry and the characteristics of industry production, there was every reason to predict that the dominant position of US companies in the industry would endure.

This prediction, however, proved erroneous: instead a classic strategy of infant-industry protection and promotion in Japan "worked" to create a competitive Japanese industry capable of challenging American supremacy. What is surprising about this part of the story is not that the Japanese targeted the semiconductor industry for development or that they relied on protectionist policies to do so, but that their strategy was so effective at realizing its objective: the creation of a competitive domestic industry.[1] A European strategy, similar in some respects to the Japanese, was singularly unsuccessful.

1. It is important to emphasize that the objective of Japanese industrial policy in the

Barriers to both imports and foreign direct investment by American companies were a key ingredient of Japan's infant-industry policy in semiconductors. Initially, American companies tended to discount the significance of these barriers, treating them as mildly irritating rather than life-threatening. But as the protected Japanese market grew and ominous evidence of the successful Japanese challenge mounted, American companies began a 15-year struggle to open the Japanese market and to deter predatory Japanese business practices through various trade policy initiatives.

This struggle reaped little in the way of real gains, and by the early 1980s the American companies watched in disbelief as the Japanese companies surged into the open American market. Finally, in a crisis atmosphere brought on by a sustained cyclical downturn in industry demand, an aggressive price war by the Japanese producers, and the exit of all but two merchant American companies[2] from production of dynamic random access memory (DRAM) chips, the US industry mounted a trade policy initiative that resulted in a major five-year trade agreement with Japan, which is described in the second part of the chapter.

The third part of the chapter offers an assessment of the effects of this agreement. Was it a complete failure, as many observers have argued (e.g., Mowery and Rosenberg 1989b), or did it realize at least some of its objectives? The analysis indicates that the agreement had different effects on different segments of the industry. These effects in turn depended on the nature of competition within these different segments and on the nature of company strategies. Contrary to popular belief, the agreement was not ineffective at realizing many of its aims, including those of stabilizing the share of US producers in the global DRAM market, reversing the precipitous decline of the US share in the global market for EPROMS (erasable programmable read-only memories), and increasing the share of US producers in the Japanese market. Nor did the agreement reduce competition across the board, as is widely believed. Instead, the effects on competition also varied by industry segment and over time. On the other hand, the agreement did generate significant profits for the Japanese companies, and the investment of these profits in capital and R&D strengthened their position in future rounds of competition.

Drawing on the experience of the semiconductor trade agreement and its 1991 successor (described in the fourth part of the chapter), the concluding sections

---

semiconductor industry, as in other industries targeted for development, was not consumer welfare. The Japanese government never asked itself whether the costs of the policies it pursued in terms of forgone consumer welfare or the opportunity costs imposed on other industries exceeded the benefits of its policies for the semiconductor industry. A study by Baldwin and Krugman (1988a), which attempts to address these characteristically "un-Japanese" questions, concludes that infant-industry policies succeeded in gaining a share of the global 16K DRAM market for Japanese producers, but only at the expense of a net reduction in Japanese economic welfare. Their findings, although suggestive, are not conclusive because they fail to incorporate the possible dynamic effects of a Japanese position in the 16K DRAM market on profits and technological externalities in future generations of semiconductor products and in systems products incorporating semiconductor technology. As a consequence, their measure of economic welfare includes only the extra profits generated in the 16K DRAM market itself.

2. Merchant companies are those that produce semiconductors for resale rather than as inputs for their own products.

of the chapter provide some general lessons about managed trade arrangements, antidumping remedies, foreign direct investment, and industrial policies.

Industry Economics and the Evolution of Comparative Advantage

The Ascent of the U.S. Firms

The modern semiconductor industry originated in the United States with the invention of the transistor by Bell Laboratories in 1947.[3] That the industry was born in the United States is not surprising. Indeed, it is consistent with theories of trade that emphasize two kinds of country-based variables: the availability of factors of production and the level of domestic demand. In the early postwar era, the United States was the unchallenged leader in technological, scientific, and engineering capabilities—the single most important factors behind the development of the semiconductor industry and the driving force behind competition in the industry through the 1970s.

American leadership in these general capabilities was partly a reflection of America's commitment to scientific training and basic research. This commitment in turn was reflected in a number of indicators of technological superiority, including R&D spending as a percentage of GNP, engineering and scientific personnel as a percentage of the total labor force, and US dominance in world patents through the early 1960s.[4] In other words, US policy priorities nurtured the scientific capabilities that were the single most important factor advantage in the industry's birth and early evolution.

The industry's development in the United States was also supported by demand conditions in the form of a reliable defense market. In its early years, up to 100 percent of the industry's output was purchased by the military, and even as late as 1968 the military claimed nearly 40 percent (Borrus et al. 1983). In addition, there was a derived defense demand for semiconductor output from the military's large procurement of computer output throughout the 1960s.[5] Direct and indirect defense purchases reduced the risk of investment in both R&D and equipment for semiconductor producers, who were assured that a significant part of their output would be sold to the military. The willingness and ability of the US government to purchase chips in quantity at premium prices allowed a growing number of companies to refine their production skills and develop elaborate manufacturing facilities.

These improvements resulted in a continuous increase in the number of elements contained on a single integrated circuit, coupled with significant decreases in price. In 1964, for example, a chip containing about 64 components was priced

---

3. For more-comprehensive, in-depth studies of the evolution of the American and Japanese semiconductor industries, see Borrus et al. (1983), Borrus (1988), Prestowitz (1988), and Howell et al. (1992).

4. For comparative numbers on these and other indicators of US technological structure, see Nelson (1990).

5. For an in-depth study of the US Defense Department's involvement in the creation of the nation's semiconductor and computer industries, see Flamm (1988).

at around \$32. By 1971, the price of a chip containing over a thousand components was about \$1 (Yoffie 1991a, Borrus 1988). It came to be a rule of thumb in the semiconductor industry that costs would fall by 30 percent to 40 percent with every doubling in volume.

A steep learning curve lay behind these steep declines in costs. Semiconductor manufacturing routinely yielded more defective than sound chips early in the production run. For complex new products, yields as low as 25 percent were quite common, while mature products might yield 90 percent. The need to raise yields led firms to manufacture "technology drivers." A technology driver was generally a high-volume product that had a relatively simple design. When a firm mass-produced a technology driver, it would hone its manufacturing skills and then transfer its learning to more complicated, lower-volume, higher-value-added devices. DRAMS were particularly well suited for this task because they had a less complex structure than other types of circuits; DRAMS allowed firms to distinguish quickly between a flaw in the design and a flaw in the manufacturing process. For particular products, other high-volume integrated circuits such as EPROMS and static RAMS (SRAMS) could also serve as technology drivers.

Since American firms had invented DRAMS, EPROMS, and SRAMS, the US industry enjoyed obvious first-mover advantages. In addition to learning economies, product cycles were quite long, so the returns to a first-mover position in a given product could be substantial. These profits in turn were an important source of funds for R&D and capital spending for the next product generation.

From its inception, the semiconductor industry has been one of the most R&D–intensive industries, with R&D expenditures averaging over 10 percent of revenues. It has also been a highly capital-intensive industry, with as much as 30 percent of sales spent on capital equipment. Variable costs, on the other hand, have always been small and have declined over time. The basic inputs into semiconductor production are sand (silicon) and electricity. Distribution and transportation costs have been tiny (between 1 percent and 2 percent). The only significant variable costs have been labor costs for the final assembly of chips. And by the 1980s variable labor costs could be largely avoided through automation.

Investment patterns in semiconductors have been lumpy, producing chronic booms and busts, with excess capacity emerging approximately every five years. The cyclical nature of the industry, in conjunction with its steep learning curves, has promoted a practice of forward pricing. For example, Texas Instruments was well known in the 1960s and early 1970s for pricing well below costs in the early stages of a product in order to build volume, gain market share, and move down the learning curve. It was Texas Instruments and not the Japanese semiconductor producers that pioneered this strategy of "preemptive price cutting," made possible by the company's reliance on cheap, second-source producers (Ernst and O'Connor 1992). By the early 1980s, however, American producers were sharply critical of their Japanese competitors for similar pricing tactics.

In addition to their first-mover advantages, US firms continued to benefit from the nation's commitment to R&D and its pool of engineering and scientific talent. The government continued to pay for a large share of R&D through the early 1970s, providing roughly one-half of the total between 1958 and 1970. As late as 1958, federal funding covered an estimated 85 percent of overall American R&D in electronics (Flamm 1989).

The history of the American industry through the mid-1970s is a history of product innovation driven by the entry of new firms into the market. Between 1966 and 1972, for example, 30 new merchant firms were formed, mainly by managers and technical personnel who had left established companies. The US environment nurtured this pattern of competition in several ways. First, there were no policies or norms favoring permanent employment relationships between firms and their most valued employees. Indeed, the mobility of salaried employees has always been comparatively high in the United States in all industries. Second, the venture market supplied the financial capital necessary for entry on attractive terms. Third, the military, which remained the largest single consumer of leading-edge components throughout the 1960s, was willing to buy very expensive products from brand-new firms that offered the ultimate in performance in lieu of an established track record.[6] Fourth, some of the technological information required for successful operation was freely available from universities and other academic institutions where research continued to be funded by huge federal investments.[7] Indeed, the conditions of federal funding often required cooperation between industry and the government-supported university infrastructure. And fifth, the US antitrust environment favored the merchant firms and worked to the disadvantage of firms that might have been formidable vertically integrated competitors—IBM and AT&T, for example.

As a result of a 1956 consent decree, AT&T was precluded from entering into competition in the emerging US semiconductor market and was required to give access to its technologies to any other company that wished it—at a royalty to be set by the court, if the private parties could not agree. The entry of Texas Instruments, Fairchild, and other firms was greatly facilitated by the low-cost availability of AT&T's technological information. In the case of IBM, there was no court order precluding its competition in the semiconductor market. But the credible threat of antitrust action, combined with limitations on the profitability of semiconductors compared with computer systems and proprietary circuits, kept IBM out of the developing merchant market (Steinmueller 1986).

The US antitrust and patent environment also encouraged the flow of technological information through the process of cross-licensing. Cross-licensing, which became a popular mechanism for avoiding prolonged and risky patent disputes between individual producers, promoted technological exchange and reciprocal access among them.

As a result of all of these factors—the availability of venture capital and a mobile technical labor force, the diffusion of technological information through open university research and cross-licensing, continued defense procurement, and the antitrust environment—the US semiconductor industry developed a distinctive structure: merchant firms specializing in semiconductor products, not vertically integrated systems manufacturers, became the most important sup-

---

6. Indeed, Ernst and O'Connor (1992) argue that the Defense Department's support of small-scale merchant firms was critical to semiconductor development in the United States, since the predominant firms in the 1950s were committed to the previous discrete technology based on germanium and were extremely slow to adopt new circuit technologies based on silicon.

7. For a complete discussion of the role of American universities in the creation and diffusion of technological knowledge, see Mowery and Rosenberg (1990).

pliers. This distinctive structure gave rise to distinctive strategies and forms of competition, which were a source of vitality for the US industry through the mid-1970s.[8]

The potential sustainability of America's advantages in semiconductors was reinforced by the industry's underlying economics. Learning curve effects were so significant that the US merchant industry remained relatively concentrated despite the proliferation of new vendors. In 1965, for example, the four largest merchants accounted for 69 percent of total industry shipments, and the eight largest accounted for 91 percent. In 1972, even with significant new entry, the comparable figures remained high, at 53 percent and 67 percent, respectively (Steinmueller 1986). Nor did US industry leaders rest on their laurels; instead they sought to exploit their first-mover and country-based advantages by developing global strategies right from the beginning. Even the smallest semiconductor companies had international sales offices with exports that averaged about 20 percent of total sales (Borrus et al. 1983). Since transportation costs were insignificant and there were no credible foreign competitors, American companies aggressively exported their products to serve foreign markets.

Initially, global strategies focused on exporting, but foreign direct investment became more important over time, for two reasons. First, US firms in this increasingly cost-competitive industry moved aggressively to shift assembly operations to low-wage locations in Southeast Asia. The natural division of production into wafer fabrication, assembly, and testing meant that assembly plants could be located a continent away from fabrication and testing facilities without any significant impact on learning economics. And the assembly stage required relatively low-skilled labor that was available abroad at a substantial discount, yielding up to a 50 percent reduction in total manufacturing costs. It was not until a decade later that a high percentage of labor costs could be automated out of the assembly process.

Second, government policies in the United States and several newly industrializing countries also supported the offshore assembly strategy. Under items 807 and 806.3 of the US Tariff Schedules as amended in 1963, imported articles assembled in whole or in part from US–fabricated components became dutiable only to the extent of the value added abroad. This meant a substantial tariff break on the offshore assembly of chips. And beginning in 1967 the governments of Mexico, Taiwan, Singapore, Malaysia, and Korea established "export platforms" to encourage foreign direct investment. These platforms offered a wide variety of inducements, including tax-free exports, import tax reductions, and tax holidays. By 1978 the top nine US producers had among them 35 offshore

---

8. Porter (1990) emphasizes the effects of industry structure on distinctive national patterns of competitive behavior. Although it is impossible to rerun history, we may speculate about the consequences for industry behavior had the US industry developed in a different environment—one more conducive to an industry structure comparable to the Japanese. If the US industry had been dominated by large, vertically integrated producers, each of which produced chips for its own use and for sale to other users, it is likely that an even more concentrated industry structure would have developed. This might have had two kinds of incentive effects. First, there would have been an incentive for these producers to sell to one another on terms that would prevent the entry of merchant competitors. And second, the incentive to compete through product innovation might have been reduced.

assembly operations in 10 developing countries in Latin America and Southeast Asia. By that time more than 80 percent of the semiconductors shipped in the United States were assembled and tested overseas, mainly in these five countries (Borrus et al. 1983, 37).

The second type of foreign direct investment—point-of-sales affiliates—occurred mainly in Europe, encouraged by high tariff rates (17 percent of value), preferential procurement procedures, and subtle pressure by the European governments (especially the British and the French). The first major period of investment in Europe occurred between 1969 and 1974, by which time 46 affiliates, 18 of which were engaged in complete manufacturing operations including fabrication, had been established (Flamm 1990).

Tariffs, quotas, and other forms of border protection also encouraged US companies to consider foreign direct investment to serve the Japanese market. But the Japanese, in contrast to the Europeans, actively restricted such investment. The Japanese strategy was avowedly one of import substitution through the creation and promotion of indigenous suppliers, whereas the European strategy was one of import substitution, at least in part, through substituting the local production of American companies for imports from them. The difference in these strategies is apparent in the numbers: Japanese companies have always supplied the lion's share (90 percent) of the Japanese market, while American companies, through export or local production, have supplied 50 percent to 70 percent of the European market, with the remainder supplied primarily by European companies.[9]

Only Texas Instruments, by refusing to license its key integrated circuit patents to Japanese firms and by petitioning the US government for trade protection on grounds of patent infringement, was able to extract permission from the Japanese government to establish a wholly owned manufacturing subsidiary in Japan prior to 1968.[10] The Japanese government's requirements for investment by other US companies were so unattractive that few chose to invest until after direct controls were abolished in 1978. But by that time, for the reasons noted below, the growing strength of the Japanese firms had reduced the incentives for many American suppliers to invest in the Japanese market.

Implications for Trade

Both the level and the composition of US trade in semiconductors have been heavily influenced by the foreign direct investment decisions of American companies. Initially, the United States ran a trade surplus in integrated circuits; but even while US firms remained dominant in the world semiconductor market, direct investment abroad reduced net export earnings. The United States began

---

9. On the American share of the European market, see Flamm (1990). On the American share of the Japanese market, see Borrus et al. (1983) and Prestowitz (1988).

10. Initially, Texas Instruments was only allowed to establish a 50-50 joint venture with Sony in 1968; four years later, Sony sold out to the American firm. The Japanese Ministry of International Trade and Industry finally agreed to Texas Instruments' request for a wholly owned subsidiary only after the firm threatened any Japanese exports of consumer electronics using its technology with an immediate patent infringement lawsuit. For more on the history of joint ventures in the semiconductor industry, see Steinmueller (1987).

to run a trade deficit in integrated circuits as early as 1971, although overall semiconductor trade showed a surplus through 1977 (table 4.1). Initially, most US imports were products assembled by US affiliates in the newly industrializing countries; toward the end of the 1970s, however, the Japanese share of US imports began to rise sharply. On the export side, most US exports of finished integrated circuits served four markets: Great Britain, France, Germany, and Japan. US exports of unfinished circuits were primarily to five Southeast Asian locations for final assembly and packaging. These products were then reexported either to the United States or to the other four final markets.

In a manner consistent with these trade trends, by the late 1970s an estimated 80 percent of the fabrication by US firms was still done in the United States, and 20 percent was done abroad, mainly in Europe. The reverse numbers applied in assembly—about 80 percent was performed abroad and only 20 percent at home (Borrus et al. 1983).

The Creation and Rise of the Japanese Industry

The history of the Japanese semiconductor industry is a dramatic story of successful infant-industry promotion and protection. The overarching purpose of government support was to create a competitive indigenous computer industry; the creation of a semiconductor industry was a means toward that end. In the United States the government objective in these industries was a military one, but in Japan it was purely commercial. And whereas US support was designed to expand the technological frontier, Japanese support was designed to catch up.

From the birth of the industry through the mid-1970s, the Japanese market was formally protected by a variety of measures. The government consistently rejected all applications for wholly owned foreign subsidiaries and for joint ventures in which foreign firms would hold majority ownership (Encarnation 1992). It also restricted foreign purchases of equity in Japanese firms. High tariffs, restrictive quotas, and approval registration requirements were used to control imports. Approval was also required for all patent and technical assistance and licensing agreements. Through its controls on the acquisition of foreign technology, MITI acted as a monopsonist buyer of such technology and controlled its diffusion among Japanese firms.

These tight border controls held the US share of the Japanese semiconductor market substantially below what it was in the rest of the world. For example, by 1975 US firms had 98 percent of the US market and 78 percent of the European market, but only 20 percent of the Japanese market (Borrus et al. 1983, 38). Moreover, the effective prohibition of direct investment by American companies in Japan was to have long-term consequences for their market share. A 1985 study commissioned by the Office of the US Trade Representative concluded that the share of the Japanese semiconductor market in the 1980s was about half what it would have been had American firms been able to establish marketing and production facilities in Japan in the 1960s and 1970s (Quick Finan Associates 1985).

Initially, the Japanese industry grew out of the application of transistors to consumer electronics products, followed by the substitution of semiconductors for such applications. Consequently, during this first phase production was

Table 4.1 United States: trade in semiconductors, by product type, 1966–91 (millions of dollars)

	Exports				Imports			
Year	Total	Integrated circuits	Transistors, diodes, and rectifiers	Other devices	Total	Integrated circuits	Transistors, diodes, and rectifiers	Other devices
1966	130.4	8.9	91	30.5	44.6	n.a.	28.7	15.9
1967	152.4	26.5	81.4	44.1	46.5	n.a.	26.7	19.8
1968	204.5	36.2	89.5	78.8	76.6	n.a.	44.7	31.9
1969	345.7	72.4	138.6	134.7	111.2	n.a.	59.0	52.2
1970	416.9	99.8	146.2	170.9	167.7	69.4	59.8	38.5
1971	370.5	91.2	99.9	179.4	187	94.2	60.4	32.4
1972	469.6	103.5	126	240.1	328.8	180.5	100.1	48.2
1973	848.6	217.7	195.8	435.1	610.5	365.3	160.6	84.6
1974	1,247.5	313.5	215.6	718.4	953.5	606.3	235.9	111.3
1975	1,037.0	262.1	111.6	663.3	802.0	581.5	138.5	82.0
1976	1,385.9	320.4	120.3	945.2	1,098.0	813.7	153.1	131.2
1977	1,490.5	348.1	70.6	1,071.8	1,403.2	1,025.0	173.5	204.7
1978	1,521.4	471.9	85.4	964.1	1,827.4	1,405.2	179.1	243.1
1979	2,075.1	650.1	90.9	1,334.1	2,587.7	2,035.4	195.0	357.3
1980	2,782.3	833.5	95.2	1,853.6	3,395.6	2,780.4	212.2	403.0
1981	2,832.7	768.4	87.3	1,977.0	3,645.5	2,982.1	264.0	399.4
1982	3,058.9	836.3	81.8	2,140.8	4,397.0	3,501.0	263.9	632.1
1983	3,673.5	1,025.7	97.9	2,549.9	5,330.1	4,150.2	257.4	922.5
1984	4,651.5	1,391.3	118.8	3,141.4	8,284.2	6,135.8	345.9	1,802.5
1985	3,693.1	1,140.6	123.1	2,429.4	6,377.7	4,423.9	259.4	1,686.4
1986	4,185.4	1,148.1	138.8	2,898.5	6,685.7	4,539.0	303.7	1,843.0
1987	6,229.0	1,622.8	131.4	4,474.9	8,561.9	6,038.1	336.8	2,187.0
1988	8,035.4	2,588.5	168.4	5,278.5	12,089.8	8,767.6	425.2	2,896.9
1989	9,530.6	n.a.	n.a.	n.a.	12,301.6	n.a.	n.a.	n.a.
1990	10,709.6	n.a.	n.a.	n.a.	12,143.5	n.a.	n.a.	n.a.
1991	11,572	n.a.	n.a.	n.a.	12,335	n.a.	n.a.	n.a.

Sources: US Department of Commerce publications ES-2:15 (1966–72), ES-2:17 (1973–76), ES-2:19 (1977–82), ES-2:20 (1983–86), and FT-246 (1987–88). Data for 1989–90 were compiled from official US Department of Commerce statistics. Estimates for 1992 from US Department of Commerce, *U.S. Industrial Outlook*, 1992. Product breakdowns for 1989–90 were unavailable because of a change in classification from the sic system to a harmonized system.

94

dominated by a consumer electronics orientation. In 1968, for example, 60 percent of all Japanese semiconductor production went to consumer electronics products. The Japanese continually lagged in the introduction of new products and in the most advanced semiconductor technologies.

The Japanese firms also lagged in research during this phase. Through 1970, private-company funding of R&D was not competitive with US funding. Indeed, in the early 1970s combined spending by Fujitsu, Hitachi, and NEC on semiconductor and computer R&D was less than Texas Instruments' R&D budget alone. Moreover, direct Japanese government funding of advanced R&D on integrated circuits by Japanese firms was not significant, although a great deal of basic research was carried out in government and NTT laboratories (Borrus 1988).

The 1970s marked the second phase of the industry's development in Japan. In response to external pressure, the Japanese government gradually eliminated formal trade barriers by 1976 and formal foreign investment restrictions by 1978. At the same time, beginning in 1971, the government formally targeted a series of advanced technologies, including semiconductor technologies, and provided financing to stimulate their cooperative development with industry. Between 1971 and 1977, over 60 different projects received substantial public support in such areas as electron-beam exposure and large-scale integration (LSI) production equipment, discrete devices, basic materials research, and low-power, high-performance semiconductors (table 4.2; Borrus et al. 1983). All of these projects involved cooperation and cofinancing by competitors, because in the precommercial stages of developing a new technology it is difficult to exclude others from the use of results, and not easy to appropriate the returns to knowledge creation.[11]

These programs, along with others designed to support Japan's developing computer industry, succeeded in raising the value of more-sophisticated integrated circuits as a share of total Japanese semiconductor output from 27 percent in 1971 to about 42 percent by the end of 1975. By 1976 the Japanese companies had developed a significant LSI capability, and they dominated their domestic market in all but the most sophisticated integrated circuit devices. They had also succeeded in raising their share of the domestic installed base of general-purpose digital computers to over 60 percent (Borrus 1988).

According to all accounts, this performance was realized despite the fact that US semiconductor and computer products were available at lower prices and at higher quality, capability, and reliability levels than Japanese products. The counterliberalization measures taken by the Japanese government with the aim of preventing any "adverse effect on domestic firms which might produce confusion in the market" seemed to work.[12] Despite the abolition of formal barriers, foreign penetration of the Japanese market was held in check by a variety of offsetting policies. These included R&D support, government-sponsored formation of joint R&D and production ventures among the Japanese companies, preferential procurement policies (NTT would not buy any foreign systems prod-

---

11. Note that, although this research was precommercial, it was not generic—it was avowedly industry-specific, like that of the later US semiconductor consortium Sematech (discussed below).

12. The quote is attributed to Minister of International Trade and Industry Toshio Komoto by Prestowitz (1988, 37).

Table 4.2 Joint research and development projects in microelectronics sponsored by the Japanese Ministry of International Trade and Industry (MITI)

Project	Time frame	Technological focus	Government funding (millions of dollars)[a]	Participants
MITI VLSI	1975–79	VLSI manufacturing	112	NEC, Hitachi, Fujitsu, Toshiba, Mitsubishi
Optoelectronics	1979–86	Optical semiconductors	80	NEC, Hitachi, Fujitsu, Toshiba, Mitsubishi, Oki, Sumitomo
Supercomputer	1981–89	High-speed computing devices	135	NEC, Hitachi, Fujitsu, Toshiba, Mitsubishi, Oki, Sharp
New function elements	1981–90	VLSI device and processes	140	NEC, Hitachi, Fujitsu, Toshiba, Mitsubishi, Oki, Sharp, Sanyo, Sumitomo, Matsushita
SORTEC[b]	1986–96	Synchrotron lithography	62	NEC, Hitachi, Fujitsu, Toshiba, Mitsubishi, Oki, Sharp, Sanyo, Sumitomo, Nippon Sheet Glass, Matsushita, Nippon Kogaku
Optoelectronic devices	1986–96	Optical semiconductors	42	NEC, Hitachi, Fujitsu, Toshiba, Mitsubishi, Oki, Sharp, Sanyo, Sumitomo, Nippon Sheet Glass, Fujikura
Fifth-generation computer	1981–91	VLSI logic	n.a.	NEC, Hitachi, Fujitsu, Toshiba, Mitsubishi, Oki, Sharp

VLSI = very large scale integration.
a. Dollar figures are calculated using the period-average yen-dollar exchange rate.
b. Funded through the Japan Key Technology Center.

Sources: Thomas Howell, William A. Noellert, Janet J. MacLaughlin, and Alan W. Wolff, *The Microelectronics Race: The Impact of Government Policy on International Competition* (Boulder, CO: Westview Press, 1988). Reprinted with permission.

ucts or any domestic systems products containing foreign semiconductors), administrative guidance, and the purchasing decisions of the Japanese companies themselves.

Of all the Japanese support programs of the 1970s, the most successful was the VLSI (very large scale integration) cooperative R&D program designed to help Japanese firms reach state-of-the-art capabilities in the production of both memory devices and logic circuits. The Japanese strategy to move into the most sophisticated memory products reflected their aims and needs in telecommunications and computers. By the late 1970s, these needs could be met only by producing more-sophisticated memory devices like those that dominated the chip market in the United States—devices in which the US firms had a commanding lead—or by buying from American producers. Consistent with their infant-industry approach, the Japanese chose to develop their own.

By 1980 this choice had paid off. Although government support for the VLSI program was prematurely terminated in 1979, by that time the participating firms had developed one-micron device technology, submicron process technology, and 64K DRAMs. In essence, the program helped Japanese firms achieve technological parity with American firms in the production of the most sophisticated memory devices. Indeed, the Japanese firms were so convinced of the benefits of the VLSI program that they launched a private-sector extension to complete the research agenda without government help.[13]

The dramatic success of VLSI was partly a function of a temporary shortfall in American production capacity in 1976–77. This in turn was the result of the 1975 recession, during which American firms curtailed their capacity expansion plans. When the semiconductor market recovered in 1976–77, American companies were caught short, which forced their customers to search for other sources of supply and opened the door to new competitors. By that time the Japanese were ready to step in.

Not only was the timing of the VLSI program fortuitous, but the choice of DRAMs proved critical. DRAMs are the largest-volume commodity product of the semiconductor industry. They are a standardized good with almost perfect substitution capability among different manufacturers producing at the industry norm. Because they are standardized and require the least investment in support and distribution services, DRAMs are also one of the easiest product lines for newcomers to adopt. The only significant entry barriers are scale economies and the learning curve. Scale, in particular, became increasingly important after the mid-1970s. Whereas it cost only $3 million to build a fabrication facility in 1970, the price approached $75 million by 1980. In addition, intellectual property protection poses barriers to entry, but relatively weak ones because there are multiple ways to design a standard part. In the 1970s, moreover, intellectual property protection for semiconductors was still fairly weak.

Finally, since DRAMs are a commodity product, manufacturing costs have a significant effect on competitive outcomes. The best way to drive down the cost of production is to improve yields. Improving yields depends in turn on improving control over the manufacturing process—something that comes from experience; hence the significant learning curve effects. These links between

---

13. For more in-depth analyses of the VLSI program, see Flamm (1989), Borrus (1988), and Howell et al. (1988).

volume production, yields, and cost competitiveness played to the Japanese strength.

In particular, policies of promotion and protection helped the Japanese companies gain the scale and technical experience they needed to become formidable competitors in the DRAM market. Protection allowed Japanese producers to reach minimum scale; promotion reduced their risk in making the big capital investments necessary to enter.[14] Such policies would not have been successful had the Japanese initially tried to target other semiconductor products, such as microprocessors, where competition depends on proprietary design innovations, and where US companies had significant first-mover advantages because their products had already been adopted as the standards in important systems products. On the other hand, the targeting of DRAMs helped create knowledge in large-scale production process technology that had spillover benefits for Japanese companies in their efforts to break into other, less standardized product lines in the 1980s.

The effects of promotion and protection in the Japanese industry must also be understood in the context of the industrial structure in which they occurred. The Japanese semiconductor industry is dominated by six multidivisional, vertically integrated firms, which manufacture electronics systems serving end-markets in consumer electronics, computers, and telecommunications equipment. These six firms are NEC, Hitachi, Toshiba, Fujitsu, Mitsubishi, and Matsushita. Together these firms form an even more concentrated oligopoly structure than that which prevails in the American merchant market. In the mid-1970s, for example, these six firms controlled 79 percent of domestic sales in Japan (Steinmueller 1986).

Although all of these firms produce semiconductors for in-house purposes, a majority of their semiconductor sales are external. Only about 20 percent of their production is consumed internally, and in memory devices the figure is even lower. Thus, the Japanese firms are neither captive producers, as are IBM and AT&T, nor entirely merchant producers, as are Intel and National Semiconductor. Moreover, unlike the US merchant firms, the Japanese firms are large consumers of semiconductors, especially advanced integrated circuits. Together, they account for about 60 percent of total Japanese semiconductor consumption.

The internal structure of the Japanese companies and their close relationships with each another and with various parts of the Japanese government—especially MITI, MPT, and NTT—have been important barriers to American producers seeking to sell in the Japanese market. During the 1970s, American companies succeeded in penetrating the Japanese market primarily with advanced product innovations not yet produced by the Japanese firms. As Japanese suppliers became competent in the production of such devices, American suppliers experienced a decline in demand and saw their shares of the Japanese market level off or decline, even as Japanese demand grew.[15]

---

14. The policies of promotion and protection and their effects on Japanese producers were not unique to the semiconductor industry. For a general discussion and interpretation of Japanese industrial policy see Tyson and Zysman (1990). On Japan's promotion and protection of its electronics industry, see also Anchordoguy (1990).

15. This pattern has been observed in other Japanese industries and has been described

Through the middle to late 1970s, this pattern can be understood as the result of formal protectionism—through various trade, investment, and technology barriers, the Japanese government restricted imports to products not yet available from indigenous suppliers. After the liberalization of most of these barriers, however, the pattern persisted (and, significantly, preferential procurement through NTT remained in place).

The Japanese often claim that US companies failed to gain market share in Japan after liberalization because of a mismatch between Japanese demand and American supply. According to this explanation, American firms—whose products were heavily tailored to computer, industrial, and defense applications—did not offer the products required for Japan's consumer electronics applications. But this explanation is misleading. By the late 1970s Japan's market was about 50 percent data processing and communications, 40 percent consumer electronics, and 10 percent industrial and defense uses. Although it is certainly true that American firms were not offering products to supply many consumer electronics applications, they accounted for at most 20 percent to 25 percent of total Japanese demand. Commodity products such as DRAMS, EPROMS, and microcontrollers, which were supplied by all of the American producers, could be used in many other Japanese consumer goods. In addition, since US producers were competitive in supplying chips for data processing and communications, had they been able to obtain 60 percent of the Japanese market for these applications, as they did in Europe, they would have captured about 30 percent of the total Japanese market. Preferential procurement of Japanese chips for these applications was consistent with NTT's "Japan-only" procurement strategies—which persisted through the 1980s—and with Japan's infant-industry strategy in computers.[16]

There is a strong *prima facie* case that the incentives and business practices of the Japanese firms themselves also played a role in restricting the access of American producers once the Japanese government ceased to act as a formal gatekeeper. It is necessary to recall the Japanese companies' structure and the environment in which they functioned in order to understand why and how they acted in this way. Each of the six firms is part of a *keiretsu*—with preferential sales arrangements among member firms and restrictive arrangements that block access to distributional channels by nonmember companies. All six participated in cooperative research and production activities, sponsored by MITI, designed to encourage specialization and communication and to discourage competition between the companies. All of the companies were active participants in the Electronics Industries Association of Japan (EIAJ), a legal trade association with a long history of detailed exchanges of confidential information on cost, production, and company sales. Four of the six firms—Matsushita, Hitachi, Toshiba, and Mitsubishi—themselves had a long history of overt and clandestine methods for cartelizing the consumer electronics market in Japan and coordinating export

as a moving band of protection: protection lasts only as long as is necessary to develop competitive Japanese suppliers; once such suppliers appear, imports fall sharply. In contrast to other countries, Japan is distinctive for its very low level of intraindustry trade—in product lines where its producers are competitive, it imports very little. See Tyson and Zysman (1989) for elaboration.

16. For an in-depth examination of this strategy, see Anchordoguy (1989).

efforts abroad.[17] The two others—NEC and Fujitsu—were the beneficiaries of preferential NTT policies in the procurement of computers and telecommunications equipment.[18] Finally, all functioned in a lax antitrust environment in which there was no credible sanction against cooperative or collusive behavior.

The continued difficulties of American companies in accessing the Japanese market can be explained in either of two ways. One possibility is that the Japanese companies worked in undocumented and undetected ways to cartelize the Japanese marketplace at the expense of foreign companies. Similar efforts involving some or all of the same companies have been documented in the television and office computer industries (Yamamura and Vandenburg 1986). The structure of the Japanese industry was obviously more conducive to cartel-like behavior than that of the American industry. Such behavior was also made more likely by the exemption of the computer and semiconductor industries from Japan's Anti-Monopoly Law.

The alternative explanation is that the patterns of specialization, distribution, cooperation, and trust fostered by decades of protection and promotion and by the *keiretsu* system led Japanese companies to prefer buying from one another rather than from an outsider—even when that outsider was a new Japanese entrant, and especially when that outsider was a foreign company supplying competitor firms, like IBM, in lucrative downstream markets.[19]

So far as the effects on international trade and American producers are concerned, it does not really matter whether the cartel explanation, or what Ronald Dore (1986) calls the "relational handshake" explanation, of Japanese behavior is the correct one. In the end, access to the Japanese market by American companies continued to be effectively limited to products not currently offered by their Japanese competitors. And the Japanese authorities condoned, if they did not actually encourage, this behavior.

The structure of the Japanese industry had another behavioral effect that proved devastating for American companies. Because of their vertical integration and *keiretsu* linkages, the Japanese companies had very deep pockets: they had access to relatively cheap and patient capital to finance massive investment spending even during periods of market slowdown, and to incur sustained losses as part of an aggressive pricing strategy to increase their market shares. Only the two US merchants that were partly diversified, Texas Instruments and Motorola, could afford to invest countercyclically or sustain losses for long periods of time. The consequences of these differences in industrial structure were first apparent in the aftermath of the 1975 recession. While American firms, strapped for cash, cut capacity expansion during the downturn, Japanese firms cross-subsidized their investment, which gave them their first opportunity to gain market share in the United States. By 1983, the Japanese companies were out-investing the American companies—a trend that has persisted to the present day.

---

17. For more on this history see Yamamura (1986) and Choate (1990).

18. On the role of preferential procurement in the development of the Japanese computer industry, see Anchordoguy (1988).

19. This interpretation is consistent with the evidence on *keiretsu* links and their effects on import penetration cited in chapter 3.

The deep pockets of the Japanese companies also allowed them to wage an aggressive pricing war in the depressed market conditions of 1985–86.[20] This was one of the major factors behind the exit of seven out of nine American companies from the production of DRAMs by 1986 and the domination of the latest generation of DRAM chips by the Japanese. By the end of 1986, the Japanese firms had a virtual monopoly in a key input for all of the systems applications in which they were trying to become significant competitors.

Finally, Japan's successful thrust down the learning curve in DRAMs gave its companies another competitive advantage in the marketplace: by 1980, Japanese firms were delivering to their US and Japanese customers fewer defects per shipment, by an order of magnitude, than their American counterparts. Yet this should not be interpreted to mean that Japanese firms had simply become "better." The initial Japanese advantage was derived from targeting DRAMs: by concentrating their production on one major product line, Japanese firms achieved higher yields than the American merchants, which manufactured a wider array of products. By the mid-1980s, however, the Japanese quality advantage was no longer significant. American firms had responded to the competitive challenge, and their defect rates were not appreciably different.

The Stagnation of the European Industry

The European approach to the semiconductor industry, like the Japanese, used protection to support its national firms. European producers were protected in several ways: by a steep tariff of 17 percent, which survived both the Kennedy and the Tokyo rounds of tariff reductions under the General Agreement on Tariffs and Trade (GATT); by rules of origin that effectively blocked the use of imported semiconductors in European electronics manufactures crossing the EC–EFTA boundary; and by informal nontariff barriers, including preferential procurement practices, that encouraged European production by foreign producers to serve the European market. All of these practices stimulated substantial direct investment by American producers in European production facilities.[21]

Unlike the Japanese, the Europeans allowed—indeed, encouraged—such direct investment as a substitute for imports. The explicit objective of Japanese strategy was the creation of a Japanese industry, whereas the *de facto* objective of the European strategy gradually became the establishment of a European production base, regardless of ownership. The Japanese strategy closed the Japanese market to investment by US companies, thereby reserving domestic demand for Japanese companies, and forcing US firms to transfer technology to their Japanese competitors if they wanted to profit from growth in that market.

---

20. The Japanese pricing strategy was similar in many respects to the aggressive forward pricing strategy used by Texas Instruments in the 1970s to gain market share. What distinguished the Japanese strategy was the ability of the Japanese companies to sustain significant losses because of their vertical structures and deep pockets.

21. For more detailed discussions of the history of the European semiconductor industry see Borrus (1988, chapter 8), Flamm (1990), and Howell et al. (1992). A similar position on the detrimental effects of American foreign direct investment on the European semiconductor industry is taken by Ernst and O'Connor (1992, 78).

In contrast, the European strategy allowed American companies to earn a return by investing in European production facilities, without transferring their technological know-how to budding European competitors. Through such investment, American companies could preempt the developing European market for advanced products that European companies could not yet supply. Some observers believe that such investment was a key factor behind the failure of the European producers to gain a growing share of world markets.[22]

Another reason for the weakness of European producers was the fragmentation of the large European market into much smaller national markets, which eliminated the potential for European product specialization. Ironically, market fragmentation was encouraged by national policies that discouraged cooperation between companies from different European nations while at the same time encouraging them to cooperate with American firms. As a result, US companies were able to operate in most of the major European countries, capturing the benefits of scale that were denied to their European competitors.

Europe's difficulties in semiconductors were also aggravated by the failure of its promotional policies in the computer industry. European governments not only protected national computer markets through high tariffs but also promoted national champions by means of direct subsidies and preferential procurement. This strategy was a failure, and the European computer industry continued to lag well behind its US competitors.[23] In this respect the European situation was similar to the Japanese one. Like the Europeans, the Japanese had targeted the computer industry and had encouraged their producers into head-on competition with IBM. Both the European and the Japanese strategies failed initially, although the Japanese strategy has fared better over time. But whereas the Europeans continued to target the computer industry directly, with relatively modest support for the semiconductor industry, the Japanese developed policies to promote the semiconductor industry directly as a means of building strength in the computer industry. Only in the late 1980s, in response to the precipitous decline in the fortunes of the European semiconductor industry and to the mounting challenge of the Japanese, did the Europeans finally began to develop significant programs to support their semiconductor producers.

The weakness of the European computer industry meant that it had relatively little demand for the high-performance chips that drove technology development in the United States. Instead, European semiconductor companies focused on products for telecommunications and for industrial markets, where European producers remained strong. As a consequence, the European semiconductor companies produced mainly for European users and made only minimal sales to the rest of the world. Indeed, the largest integrated national champions promoted through national policies, for example France's Thomson and Germany's Siemens, mainly developed semiconductor capacities to serve their internal needs.

---

22. See, for example, the arguments by Dosi (1981).

23. Many reasons have been suggested for the failure of the European strategy in computers. For a comprehensive discussion, see Flamm (1988).

By concentrating production on specialized proprietary chips in this sheltered environment, the European companies failed to develop state-of-the-art manufacturing skills that were critical to competitive success in commodity memory products. As these products became the most rapidly growing segments of the global semiconductor market, the share of the European companies in this market fell precipitously, even within Europe itself. Flamm estimates that between 1975 and 1985 Europe's share of the global merchant semiconductor market fell by about 50 percent (Flamm 1990, 236). During this period the share of European companies in the European market declined from 50 percent to 35 percent (Borrus 1988, 196).

The Impact of Different Development Strategies on Trade Flows and Market Shares

The story of the spectacular rise in the world market share of the Japanese semiconductor industry and the offsetting fall in that of the American semiconductor industry is well known.[24] Seen in the light of the histories of manipulated trade told here, it is also understandable. Government policies shaped the domestic environments of US and Japanese firms and reversed the fortunes of once-dominant American companies and their Japanese followers.

In addition, a technical disjuncture in DRAM production occurred in the mid-1970s that ultimately benefited the Japanese. During the early 1970s the Japanese firms pioneered so-called CMOS technology, used in low-cost logic devices for such products as calculators and watches. In contrast, computer memory devices, particularly the DRAMs pioneered by Intel, were fabricated in the NMOS technology that had been used by most American producers since the 1960s. By 1983–84, as a result of an innovation in lithography equipment, the relative cost of CMOS fell below that of NMOS, which had previously been the low-cost technology. According to Ernst and O'Connor (1992, 37):

> U.S. memory producers had looked down on CMOS technology as . . . insufficient for the stringent requirements of computer memories. . . . All of a sudden, the long acquaintance of the Japanese with CMOS technology turned out to be an important competitive advantage. For the now predominant process technology, Japanese firms were in a better position than their American counterparts to improve yields and to deliver new memory generations.

Japan's growing strength in integrated circuit production was reflected in Japan's trade and in the share of Japanese firms in world markets. In the US

---

24. Following standard practice, all of the market share figures cited in the following discussion are based on dollar-denominated revenues for each country (based on the revenues of companies headquartered in that country) divided by total dollar-denominated industry revenues. This practice means that market share calculations for individual countries are sensitive to changes in exchange rates. For example, the increase in the dollar's value against the yen between 1981 and 1985 by itself tended to increase the US market share and decrease Japan's. This implies that the decline in the US share during this period would have been even greater than the observed decline, and the increase in Japan's share would have been even greater as well, had the dollar remained stable. The opposite is true for the 1985–89 period, when the fall in the dollar's value tended to decrease the US share and increase Japan's.

Table 4.3 Japan: trade in semiconductors, 1967–90 (millions of dollars)[a]

Year	Exports		Imports	
	Integrated circuits	Total	Integrated circuits	Total
1967	n.a.	16.6	0.0	12.0
1968	n.a.	18.7	0.0	15.5
1969	n.a.	27.1	21.8	47.7
1970	n.a.	27.2	57.4	92.5
1971	n.a.	27.9	69.6	89.8
1972	6.8	42.0	54.2	81.3
1973	9.5	84.3	122.5	181.8
1974	22.9	130.8	154.7	206.3
1975	45.5	140.8	134.9	182.9
1976	76.7	236.0	199.4	280.7
1977	117.9	309.4	207.6	291.7
1978	248.2	480.4	291.4	378.0
1979	494.5	753.8	449.6	556.2
1980	808.8	1,087.6	480.3	609.3
1981	904.9	1,236.5	517.8	686.7
1982	1,144.8	1,425.9	511.4	641.2
1983	1,784.2	2,150.0	642.4	785.9
1984	3,271.2	3,778.3	935.6	1,137.4
1985	2,439.7	2,920.9	693.8	836.3
1986	3,107.4	3,797.3	867.7	1,026.2
1987	4,096.6	5,005.4	1,125.4	1,307.6
1988	6,598.3	7,915.4	1,761.0	2,003.1
1989	8,313.0	9,681.1	2,246.9	2,547.0
1990	7,595.1	9,005.4	2,589.1	2,921.3

a. In 1965 and 1966 the Japanese exported only discrete semiconductor devices (DSDS); these included germanium transistors, silicon transistors, germanium diodes, silicon diodes, and silicon diodes for silicon rectifiers. Thus the data for this period do not include integrate circuits.
b. In the 1967–72 period the Japanese began exporting integrated circuits; however, the data available do not distinguish between these and DSDS.
Source: Japan Electronics Bureau; Japan External Trade Organization.

case, domestic firms retained leadership in integrated circuits through the early 1980s but suffered a growing trade deficit. This situation contrasted sharply with the Japanese experience: both government policies and firm export strategies produced increased market share for Japanese firms and significant trade surpluses in integrated circuits for Japan. Through 1978, Japan ran a net trade deficit in integrated circuits (table 4.3). Thereafter, as Japanese 64K DRAMs began to hit the market, integrated circuit exports expanded rapidly. Japan's trade surplus in these products grew from $44 million in 1979 to $2.3 billion by 1984. Imports from the United States more than doubled during this time, while exports to the United States grew 10-fold. Japanese firms focused their trade on the US market: chips destined for the United States went from 24 percent to 45 percent of Japanese exports.

In 1978, companies headquartered in the United States (excluding captives) produced 55 percent of global semiconductor revenues, while Japanese companies produced 28 percent. By 1986, US firms captured only about 40 percent

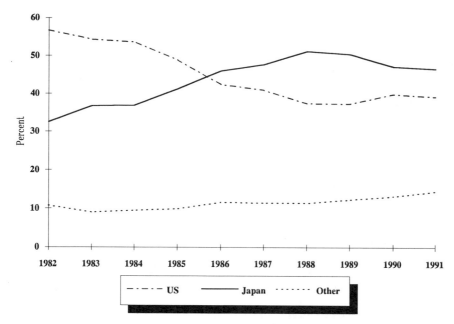

Figure 4.1 United States, Japan, and Europe: shares of the worldwide semiconductor market, 1981–90. *Source:* Dataquest. Data reproduced with permission.

of global revenues as Japanese companies claimed around 46 percent. In 1985 the famous crossover occurred: the global share of the Japanese companies jumped ahead of that of the US companies (figure 4.1). Rankings of individual US companies dropped accordingly.[25]

US companies lost market share to Japan in almost all product lines. But the Japanese gain in share was most extreme in the DRAM market. In less than a decade, American companies went from market dominance to a minor role, as the Japanese gained ascendance and then dominance in this critical product (figure 4.2). The crossover in DRAM market shares had already occurred by the end of 1981.

Slightly more than half of the overall decline in the US global market share in semiconductors between 1978 and 1985 was the result of faster growth in the Japanese market—a market that was served primarily by Japanese suppliers. The remainder of the decline resulted from the growing penetration of the US

---

25. These data include merchant producers. Since no reliable production or revenue estimates exist, wholly captive manufacturers, the largest and most significant being IBM and AT&T, are excluded. Including IBM and AT&T would change the absolute rankings (i.e., US shares of the world semiconductor market would probably be closer to those of Japan), but it would not alter the trend in the US–Japan comparison. The best estimates suggest that semiconductor production by IBM has been roughly equivalent to that of NEC, Japan's largest producer, and AT&T has roughly a quarter of that volume. Given the declining fortunes of both AT&T and IBM in their respective markets in the latter half of the 1980s, it is reasonable to assume that neither gained share over the time period.

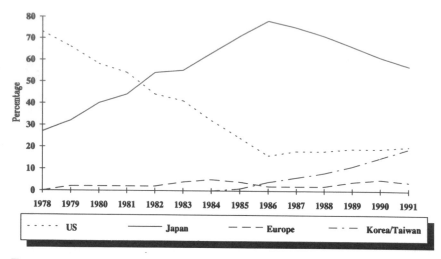

Figure 4.2 United States, Japan, and Europe: shares of the worldwide DRAM market, 1978–89. *Source:* Dataquest. Data reproduced with permission.

market by Japanese producers.[26] Between 1978 and 1985, semiconductor imports from Japan increased from less than 5 percent of total US semiconductor consumption to 17 percent. In contrast, sales by US companies as a share of total Japanese semiconductor consumption were more or less stagnant: 10 percent in 1978 and 9 percent in 1985.

From Manipulated to Managed Trade: The US–Japan Semiconductor Trade Agreement

Had governments withdrawn from active participation in semiconductor markets after 1985, Japanese firms would probably have moved from a position of rough parity to virtual dominance. The changing economic structure of the industry made it even more likely that Japan's huge, vertically integrated firms would capture greater shares of the world market in the late 1980s and 1990s. The primary reason was that rising economies of scale in production were making it almost impossible for small merchant firms to invest in new fabrication facilities.[27] By 1985 the cost of building a plant with minimum efficient scale was approaching $150 million; by 1991 the comparable figure was $500 million. Any firm without stable cash flows from nonsemiconductor businesses or a large-volume commodity integrated circuit business, such as DRAMs, would have difficulty keeping up with its larger, better-financed Japanese competitors.[28] Rising

---

26. *The Semiconductor Industry*, a report of a Federal Interagency Staff Working Group, Washington, 16 November 1987.

27. Charles Ferguson, a well-known critic of the US semiconductor industry, made this argument. In 1985, during visits to the Harvard Business School, he predicted that the US merchant industry would be bankrupt within three years (Ferguson 1988).

28. As the references cited in chapter 2 indicate, there is a growing economics literature confirming the influence of cash flow on enterprise investment capabilities.

barriers to entry for new players, and increasing barriers to mobility or reentry for existing players, made it likely that the industry would become more concentrated, and, barring a change in technology, that industry leaders (now in Japan) would gradually strengthen their hold on the market. Under this scenario, US and other firms might retreat to niches and survive, but they would have a declining impact on international trade and global supply.

This scenario did not emerge as quickly or as completely as it would have otherwise, because governments continued to shape the domestic environments and structure of international trade in semiconductors. As the title of this section suggests, trade in semiconductors is no longer simply manipulated; since 1986 it has been actively managed.

The history of this management begins with the formation by US semiconductor producers of the Semiconductor Industry Association (SIA) in 1977. Despite their fierce competition in the marketplace, American semiconductor firms had a variety of shared interests, especially concerning access to the Japanese market. Between 1979 and 1986, the SIA was highly successful in realizing many of its trade policy objectives (Yoffie 1988). It lobbied successfully for the elimination of all semiconductor duties in the United States and Japan and for the passage of the Semiconductor Chip Protection Act, which offered intellectual property protection to chip designs in the United States and encouraged foreign countries to reciprocate.[29]

Its members battered by unprecedented short-term revenue losses and continued long-term losses in global market shares, the SIA finally submitted a formal Section 301 petition against unfair trading practices of the Japanese companies in June 1985. The petition was filed only after large users of semiconductors, such as IBM and Hewlett-Packard, indicated that they would not stand in its way. Like the US merchant semiconductor firms, many of the major users of semiconductors had come to believe that there was a lack of fair market access in Japan that ultimately worked to the detriment of American producers and users alike.[30]

Although there was industry agreement about the wisdom of a 301 petition against the Japanese, there was less agreement about the wisdom of pursuing antidumping relief. Some US firms expressed interest in pursuing antidumping cases as early as 1982, but others worried that successful cases would increase semiconductor prices in the United States, thereby harming the industry's important users and weakening their support for a 301 petition. But concern over the price effects of an antidumping strategy quickly faded in the wake of aggressive pricing by the Japanese in the industry's cyclical downturn of 1985.

Consequently, shortly after the 301 petition was filed, Micron Technology, one of the members of the SIA, charged Japanese firms with dumping 64K DRAMs. Then, in late September 1985, Intel, Advanced Micro Devices (AMD), and Na-

---

29. There had been a long history of friction between the United States and Japan on the patent issue. Texas Instruments' applications for patents in Japan were not acknowledged by the Japanese until 1989. Since then Japanese firms have been paying Texas Instruments significant royalties on these patents.

30. When IBM was approached about the wisdom of a finding against the Japanese under the 301 petition, its position reportedly was, "Not only should you act, but you must act for the good of the nation" (Prestowitz 1988).

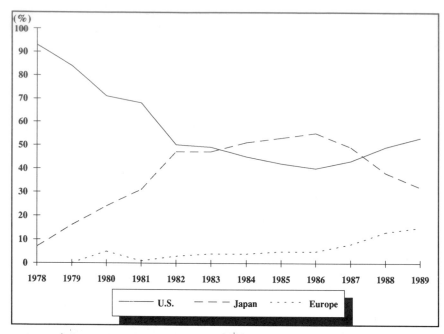

Figure 4.3 United States, Japan, and Europe: shares of the worldwide EPROM market, 1978–89. *Source:* SIA *Fourth Annual Report*, November 1990. Data reproduced with permission.

tional Semiconductor claimed that Japanese firms were dumping EPROMs, another memory device in which US producers still retained significant market shares (figure 4.3). Finally, in an unprecedented move, the US Department of Commerce "self-initiated" a case, charging Japanese firms with dumping 256K DRAMs and 1M (one-megabyte) DRAMs.[31]

The large American merchants chose to emphasize the dumping issue in EPROMs. In late 1985 these producers, squeezed by their Japanese competitors in previous generations of DRAM products, hoped to prevent a repeat performance in EPROMs. They were justifiably concerned about such a performance in the wake of Hitachi's threat to undercut the bids of other suppliers, including Intel and AMD.[32] Whereas a successful antidumping suit in 256K DRAMs was deemed to be too late to benefit most American companies, it was thought that a successful antidumping suit in EPROMs would be early enough to be preventive

---

31. Texas Instruments was the logical company to initiate a dumping suit in 256K DRAMs. The company, however, produced most of its DRAMs in Japan and as a matter of corporate policy did not take active positions on trade disputes. In fact, Texas Instruments had refused to join the SIA for almost a decade after it was formed. There are also unconfirmed reports that Texas Instruments encouraged the Department of Commerce to bring the antidumping suit in 256K DRAMs because the company did not want to jeopardize its relationships in Japan. According to a Department of Commerce official at the time, the government informed industry members of its intent to bring an antidumping suit in 256K DRAMs, and there was no opposition.

32. The Hitachi memo is cited in Semiconductor Industry Association (1990).

without being costly to EPROM users. This expectation proved to be correct on both counts.

Several months of negotiations between US and Japanese officials ensued in response to the 301 petition and the antidumping suits. Finally, the United States and Japan announced an accord on semiconductor trade in August 1986. The accord was a first in many respects. It was the first major US trade agreement in a high-technology, strategic industry, and the first one motivated by concerns about the loss of high-technology competitiveness rather than concerns about employment. It was the first US trade agreement dedicated to improving market access abroad rather than restricting it at home. Unlike previous bilateral trade deals, it attempted to regulate trade not only in the United States and Japan but in other global markets as well. It was the first time the US government threatened trade sanctions on Japan for failure to comply with the terms of a trade agreement. Finally, the agreement signalled several major shifts in US trade policy that were to characterize the rest of the decade—shifts toward aggressive unilateralism, conditional reciprocity, and managing trade by results as well as by rules.

The 1986 semiconductor trade agreement (SCTA) addressed both access to the Japanese market and dumping by Japanese firms in the US market.[33] According to its terms, the dumping suits and the Section 301 case against Japan were suspended in return for stipulated actions to improve market access for American companies and to terminate dumping by Japanese firms.

On the market access issue, the official agreement said that the government of Japan would provide sales assistance to US and other foreign companies selling in Japan and would encourage long-term relationships between Japanese users and foreign suppliers. It also said that both governments anticipated improved opportunities for foreign sales in Japan. In a confidential side letter to the official agreement, the Japanese government went further and stated that it "understood, welcomed, and would make efforts to assist foreign companies in reaching their goal of a 20 percent market share within five years."[34] The 20 percent figure meant an effective doubling of the foreign share of the Japanese market.[35]

On the dumping issue, the SCTA suspended the EPROM and DRAM investigations without the imposition of duties (despite an assessment of dumping margins of

---

33. According to one of the American company officials involved in the negotiations, at the eleventh hour the Japanese negotiators offered a solution involving Japanese "voluntary" restraints on exports, but the American negotiators refused the offer, since the intent of the American industry was to increase competition in the Japanese market, not to reduce competition in the US market.

34. According to comments made by a Motorola official at a December 1991 conference at the Harvard Business School, the market access provisions of the agreement grew out of a series of private bilateral talks between the Japanese and American suppliers, initiated by the Japanese. The five Japanese company participants at these talks initially agreed to a target of more than 20 percent, which amounted to about 13 percent of the total Japanese market. This offer was rejected as inadequate, but an overall figure of 20 percent of the market was later accepted by both sides.

35. Note that the SCTA set a share figure in terms of the nationality of suppliers, not where they were located. Thus, sales by American-owned firms from any production location, including Japan, were to count in the calculation of the US market share.

up to 188 percent for individual Japanese suppliers). The Department of Commerce instead established so-called foreign market values for each Japanese producer, based on cost information that it agreed to provide. A producer's foreign market value established an indicative cost-based price level; if sales occurred below that level, the producer would be presumed to be dumping in the sense of selling below average cost (plus an 8 percent profit margin allowable under US antidumping law).[36] Under these arrangements, a Japanese company was free to undercut the prices of its Japanese or American rivals, but only as long as its own prices did not fall below its foreign market value. To help enforce these pricing restrictions, MITI agreed to monitor the export prices of Japanese companies for several semiconductor products, including EPROMS, 256K DRAMS, 1M DRAMS, ASICS (application-specific integrated circuits), and 8-bit and 16-bit microprocessors.

Several distinctive features of the SCTA's antidumping provisions should be noted. First, the agreement required the monitoring of costs and prices on a wide range of products, including several that had not been the subject of the pending dumping investigations. This arrangement was meant to deter dumping of such products in the future. The American companies had long complained that, by the time a finding of dumping was made, they had already suffered substantial and irreparable harm. The SCTA tried to address this complaint by heading off dumping before it occurred.

Second, the agreement was structured to reflect the global nature of competition in the semiconductor industry. Because American and Japanese producers competed around the world, an agreement that simply halted dumping by Japanese producers in the US market would leave American producers exposed to unfair Japanese competition in third-country markets. If Japanese producers were able to offer more attractive prices in such markets, US and other consumers would switch their purchases there, and the United States would become what the industry called a "high-price island."

Third, the dumping provisions focused on the cost and pricing behavior of individual firms. The SIA, cognizant of the concerns of its US customers about higher semiconductor prices, explicitly opposed both an import quota and a price floor as mechanisms for responding to Japanese dumping. Because the evidence indicated that individual Japanese companies had significantly different costs, the agreement allowed low-cost Japanese producers to continue to compete on price with high-cost Japanese producers; as Japanese costs fell, so would the foreign market values. From the US perspective, this internal Japanese competition would have two beneficial effects: it would limit any price increases resulting from the enforcement of the agreement, and it would discourage further expansion of capacity by Japan's high-cost producers, thereby making it easier for lower-cost American producers to win a share of the Japanese market.

---

36. These pricing restrictions on the Japanese did not apply to their US production facilities. A similar exclusion was adopted by the Europeans in their pricing agreements with the Japanese in 1989 and 1990. The exclusion of local production facilities from the antidumping agreements was another factor encouraging the surge of Japanese investment in such facilities by the end of the decade.

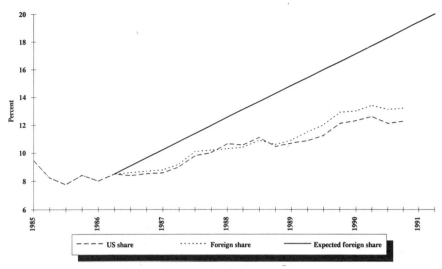

Figure 4.4 Japan: shares of the semiconductor market held by non-Japanese companies, 1985–91. *Source:* SIA *Fourth Annual Report*, November 1990. Data reproduced with permission.

The Effects of the Agreement on Trade and Pricing

Effects on Foreign Market Access in Japan

After 1986, Japanese firms had the benefit of the world's fastest-growing domestic chip market. Just as Japanese firms realized a larger share of world production, Japan's share of world consumption exceeded that of the United States after 1985, and the gap continued to widen through the rest of the decade (according to Dataquest data). In such a scale-sensitive business, limited access to the world's largest market (Japan) significantly disadvantaged American and other foreign suppliers.

But did the market access agreement have any impact on sales to Japan by US and other non-Japanese-affiliated firms? The quantitative evidence suggests that, after the US government retaliated against Japan in March 1987, the market share of non-Japanese firms started to rise (figure 4.4). Furthermore, according to industry officials, government pressure on Japanese firms was instrumental in improving the prospects for US sales. By the third quarter of 1991, the foreign share of the Japanese market was approximately 14.3 percent, up from 8.5 percent when the agreement was signed, and at its highest level ever. Although American companies accounted for most of this increase, European, Korean, and Taiwanese companies also saw their share of the Japanese market expand from 0.3 percent in 1986 to 1.4 percent by the end of 1991.

The increase in foreign market share was largely the result of concerted action by the Japanese semiconductor companies themselves to realize a 20 percent foreign share in their own purchases. (As of the summer of 1991, Hitachi, NEC,

Mitsubishi Electric, Oki Electric, and Toshiba had already done so, and Sony, Fujitsu, and Matsushita were planning to do so.) In late 1987, responding to American retaliation for failure to observe the SCTA, these companies joined with several other Japanese companies in the EIAJ to form the EIAJ Users Committee. Each of the 60 members of the committee adopted a market access plan of its own. In 1988 the Japan Automotive Parts Industry Association also began to explore ways to expand purchases of foreign semiconductors. These efforts by individual Japanese companies to increase their foreign semiconductor purchases mirrored a larger national effort in Japan to increase imports of all manufactured goods. The relevant Japanese authorities encouraged greater imports through beneficial tax treatment and jawboning, responding to relentless pressure from US trade officials.

After the SCTA took effect, American firms undertook a variety of initiatives to increase their sales in Japan. For example, between 1986 and 1990, US suppliers added 30 sales offices to the 42 offices already in place in Japan. They also opened more than 16 new design centers (a fourfold increase), 6 new testing and quality centers for a total of 18, and 4 new failure analysis centers for a total of 15. Overall, between 1986 and the end of 1990, expenditures by US companies for personnel in Japan had increased by 32 percent, capital expenditures by 162 percent, and sales expenses by 86 percent (SIA 1990b, 4–15).

Most American producers did not resort to direct investment in Japanese production facilities to increase their Japanese sales. Although many American producers have invested heavily in European production facilities, and despite the conventional wisdom in Japan that foreign producers will remain marginal players without such investment, only a handful have invested directly in Japanese facilities. These few include Texas Instruments, which operates three wafer fabrication, assembly, and test complexes; Motorola, which has a wholly owned integrated facility and also a joint venture with Toshiba; Analog Devices, which operates an assembly and test plant; and LSI Logic, which runs a front-end plant with Kawasaki Steel. The other major US merchant suppliers have apparently concluded that their near-term sales prospects in Japan do not justify the several hundred million dollars it would cost to build a front-end facility. Instead, most American suppliers have chosen the much less expensive option of bolstering their investment in facilities for design, testing, and sales.

Some American companies have complemented their investment strategies by forming alliances with Japanese firms. The most notable example is the alliance between Motorola and Toshiba. Although it was in the works before the signing of the SCTA, it was strengthened and expanded, in part as a result of the incentives set in motion by the trade agreement. The alliance involves a far-reaching exchange in which Motorola has leveraged its technological strength in microprocessors to obtain a strong foothold in the Japanese DRAM market. As a result, Motorola packages and markets DRAMS manufactured by Toshiba and has acquired memory technology to produce 256K, 1M, and 4M DRAMS and 256K and 1M SRAMS. In return, Toshiba has received 8-, 16-, and 32-bit microprocessor technology from Motorola. Using the technology acquired from Toshiba, Motorola is now manufacturing its own 1M DRAMS in Japan and Scotland and has transferred the process to its Arizona facilities. After withdrawing from the DRAM market in early 1985, Motorola used its alliance with Toshiba to rebuild its DRAM market share. DRAMS are now the company's largest-revenue-producing memory product. Nonetheless, despite this expansion, Motorola's share of the global DRAM market remains less than 5 percent.[37]

The 20 percent target for foreign market share established by the SCTA side letter could not be met solely through the sale of memory devices. Consequently, the target assured that, in addition to increased purchases of foreign memory devices, Japanese companies would have to design proprietary foreign devices into their electronics systems products. The market trend toward ASICs, a segment in which there are many leading-edge American companies, provided an opportunity for them to design their circuits into Japanese systems products. By the end of 1991, a large number of design-in relationships between American chip producers and Japanese systems producers had been established. Success stories include Japanese compact disc players incorporating US advanced digital signal processors; the design-in of American ASICs into Japanese camcorders and transmission equipment, and the decisions of Japanese automobile companies to develop custom integrated circuits with American suppliers and to increase their purchases of American and other foreign chips (SIA 1990b, Howell et al. 1992). Most American companies believe that they would not have had the opportunity to bid on such projects, let alone win them, without the pressure of the SCTA.

Finally, it is important to emphasize that sustained US pressure, backed by the threat of further trade action, played a critical role in the increase in the US share of the Japanese market that began in earnest in 1989. Until then, American firms had simply recaptured the roughly 10 percent of the Japanese market they had traditionally supplied before the 1985–86 slump. Tough talk by the Bush administration and SIA lobbying efforts in 1989 spurred Japanese manufacturers into action. Fears that the SIA might get the White House to make semiconductors a US trade priority under the Super 301 provision of the 1988 trade act led to a series of initiatives by Japanese companies to facilitate the development of long-term relationships with US suppliers. These initiatives, complemented by the efforts of American suppliers to expand their Japanese sales, paid off in a large increase in US market share between early 1989 and the end of 1990 (figure 4.4).

By 1990, the increased share of Japan's market meant annual additional sales of over $1 billion for American companies. Had the 20 percent target been achieved by then, they would have earned an additional $1.16 billion in sales that year. According to the SIA (1991), these additional revenues would have translated into $137 million in R&D, $130 million in capital investment, and 5,470 American jobs. Not surprisingly, the American government, encouraged by the American companies, continued to press Japan to realize the target and ultimately agreed to its extension in 1991, when the SCTA expired. (For more on the details of this extension, see the discussion below.)

Effects on Pricing

In the first few months after the conclusion of the SCTA, the prices of semiconductor exports from Japan jumped sharply. US customers reported that prices of 256K DRAMs rose anywhere from two to eight times the preagreement price.

---

37. In 1989, according to Dataquest estimates, Motorola was the ninth-largest producer of 1M DRAMs, accounting for 4.6 percent of the global market, based on units sold.

Shortly thereafter, the Commerce Department incorporated more up-to-date cost data in its calculation of foreign market values, and by early 1987 US customers were reporting that prices based on the revised foreign market values were not too far off what the market itself would have produced.

By March 1987, SIA members were convinced that the Japanese were violating the SCTA by selling below foreign market values in third markets and by failing to increase purchases from US producers. Evidence of the former came from documentation of sales at less than foreign market value by Japanese companies in the Far East (SIA 1990b, 60). Evidence of the latter came from the fact that there had been virtually no increase in the US share of the Japanese market since the signing of the agreement (figure 4.4).

In an unprecedented move, the US administration responded to the SIA's complaints by imposing sanctions on the Japanese producers. It did so in a highly charged atmosphere: both houses of Congress had voted to encourage the administration to apply sanctions, and the Defense Department had issued a study that pointed with alarm to declining US competitiveness in semiconductors and the semiconductor equipment industry.

The sanctions that were imposed on 17 April 1987 took the form of 100 percent tariffs on certain Japanese computers and electropneumatic hammers, products carefully chosen because there were alternative American suppliers. The prices of 256K DRAMs began an unprecedented increase in the second quarter of 1987 that lasted through the end of 1988 (table 4.4). Thereafter, although prices of these devices began to decline, they remained higher than their lowest 1986 level through the end of 1989. Prices of 1M DRAMs exhibited similar trends between 1986 and 1990. These prices abruptly reversed their downward slide during the last quarter of 1987 and increased through the third quarter of 1988. Thereafter they began to decline, finally falling below their lowest 1986 level by the third quarter of 1989. Through the end of 1990, however, the prices of 1M DRAMs exceeded reasonable estimates of their total average production costs by Japanese producers (see figure 4.6). Revealingly, although slightly higher than before the agreement, prices of both 256K DRAMs and 1M DRAMs in Japan were noticeably lower than they were in the United States, Europe, and East Asia through the middle of 1989 (figure 4.5).

The most dramatic DRAM price increases occurred in 1988, when spot prices for 256K DRAMs tripled over a four-month period, and American consumers reported significant difficulties in obtaining adequate supplies at any price.[38] Some American users even complained that they were being pressured by their Japanese suppliers to license their technology, buy unwanted specialized chips, or make long-term advance orders as a condition for purchasing the DRAM quantities they needed. In contrast, Japanese consumers grumbled about higher prices, but there were no reports that they had difficulty in obtaining the supplies they needed (Howell et al. 1992, 102). The price hikes and supply interruptions for several US system vendors caused them to ration memory shipments, delay new product introductions, and increase prices.[39] Since spot prices for DRAMs

---

38. For detailed price information, see Flamm (1992); for anecdotal evidence on these difficulties, see SIA (1990b) and Ferguson (1989).

39. Flamm (1992) reports that, as a result of the increases in semiconductor prices, computer prices were affected in 1988 and 1989.

Table 4.4 Average selling prices for 256-kilobyte and 1-megabyte DRAMS, 1984–92 (dollars per chip)

Year	Quarter	256K DRAMS	1M DRAMS
1984	1	31.00	
	2	23.50	
	3	17.50	
	4	14.00	
1985	1	9.50	150.00
	2	5.15	125.00
	3	3.00	110.00
	4	2.25	100.00
1986	1	2.25	48.00
	2	2.30	34.00
	3	2.50	45.00
	4	2.20	25.00
1987	1	2.25	20.00
	2	2.37	18.00
	3	2.50	15.50
	4	2.65	17.00
1988	1	2.90	18.00
	2	3.00	18.50
	3	3.35	19.00
	4	3.50	17.80
1989	1	3.40	16.25
	2	3.50	15.50
	3	3.00	13.95
	4	2.75	10.50
1990	1	2.15	7.25
	2	2.00	6.37
	3	1.85	5.97
	4	1.80	5.05
1991	1	1.77	4.55
	2	1.70	4.50
	3	1.65	4.33
	4	1.60	4.18
1992	1	1.55	3.80
	2	1.50	3.25

Source: Dataquest. Data reprinted with permission.

rose three to six times higher than long-term contract prices, the effective price paid by any consumer depended heavily on the percentage of demand it had to purchase on the spot market.

By early 1989 most major US consumers were reporting that they could obtain adequate supplies, and the gap between spot and large contract prices disappeared. By mid-1989 the regional price differentials had also disappeared—prices in Japan were roughly equal to prices in other major markets. In addition, both 256K and 1M DRAM prices were trending downward, partly in response to the introduction of the next-generation 4M DRAM device, whose price had fallen continuously since its appearance in the second half of 1988.[40]

40. A recent study argues that, by the end of 1989, the average price per bit for DRAMS was on its long-term trend, estimated by the 1974–84 relationship between the average price per bit and cumulative bit consumption. This estimated relationship in turn is in-

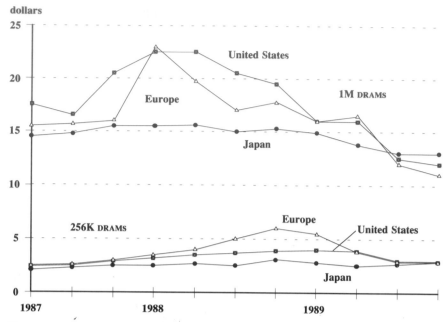

Figure 4.5 Prices for 256-kilobyte and 1-megabyte DRAMS, by country,1987–89.
Source: Dataquest. Data reproduced with permission.

But DRAM prices remained high enough to yield hefty profits for their Japanese producers at least through the end of 1990. Flamm (1991) estimates that higher prices meant $3 billion to $4 billion in additional annual profits on global semiconductor sales of $45 billion and global DRAM sales of approximately $10 billion by early 1989. Since the Japanese had the lion's share of the DRAM market, they earned the lion's share of these "bubble profits." The two remaining American DRAM producers, Texas Instruments and Micron Technology, also profited substantially from the price surge. According to one Wall Street semiconductor analyst, DRAM sales accounted for between 30 percent and 40 percent of Texas Instruments' semiconductor operating profit in 1987, and as much as 60 percent in 1988. Micron, which specialized in DRAM production, enjoyed a sixfold rise in revenues between 1986 and 1988 and became profitable that year for the first

---

terpreted as the "long-term learning curve" for DRAM production. The study also concludes that, compared with this relationship, prices were excessively low between the third quarter of 1984 and the second quarter of 1987, presumably because of dumping, and excessively high between the second quarter of 1987 and the third quarter of 1989, presumably because of the price effects of the trade agreement. Although these conclusions are provocative, they depend on the assumption that the estimated learning curve relationship for 1974–84 is the appropriate standard of comparison. Since the Japanese did not become a major competitive force in the industry until 1980, and since their learning curve gains were probably more dramatic than the American gains, it is not clear that the 1974–84 relationship is the appropriate standard by which to judge 1984–89 price trends. For more detail see Technecon Analytic Research (1991).

time in three years.[41] The bubble profits of the Japanese, in turn, were plowed back into R&D and investment. As a consequence, the gap between capital and R&D spending by Japanese companies and American companies expanded still further. By 1988 capital spending by Japanese semiconductor companies was nearly $2 billion more than that of American semiconductor companies, and the R&D spending of the top five Japanese companies exceeded that of the top five American merchant firms by about $1.5 billion (National Advisory Committee on Semiconductors 1989, 10–11). Thus, the bubble profits had the perverse result of strengthening the Japanese companies for future rounds of competition in new products.

Was the SCTA responsible for the dramatic price increases in DRAMS and the huge additional profits earned by the Japanese producers after the middle of 1987? Most critics of the agreement think so. However, there are four reasons for concluding that the chain of causality between the agreement and the ensuing price increases was neither as simple nor as direct as many observers believe. First, according to industry experts, higher DRAM prices after 1987 were partly the result of a cyclical upsurge in demand stemming from growth in the computer industry, and partly the result of unanticipated technical difficulties associated with bringing new 1M supply capacities into production (SIA 1990b).

Second, contrary to what many have asserted, the SCTA did not establish an overall price floor. Indeed, US negotiators had rejected an earlier Japanese offer to do so in return for withdrawal of the antidumping suits. The whole idea of calculating foreign market values for individual Japanese companies was to allow the more efficient among them to sell at lower prices, thereby encouraging competition among the Japanese suppliers and preventing an overall price floor. At least through the end of 1990, however, DRAM prices remained above the individual foreign market values of the Japanese firms, even those of high-cost producers such as Oki (figure 4.6).

Third, as demonstrated below, similar antidumping provisions for EPROMS in the SCTA did not have similar effects on world prices. And fourth, some evidence suggests that the Japanese producers began acting to stop the slide in DRAM prices in late 1985—*after* the exit of four major American DRAM producers (AMD, Intel, Motorola, and Mostek) and *well before* the signing of the SCTA.[42] In late 1985 the Japanese press began to report efforts by Japanese companies to cut DRAM production and raise prices. In December 1985 most Japanese producers announced across-the-board price increases of 20 percent on 64K and 256K DRAMS (*Nihon Keizai Shimbun,* 11 January 1986). At the same time, both NEC and Hitachi, which together accounted for about 55 percent of Japan's 256K DRAM shipments, announced that they were curtailing production. Japanese DRAM consumers were outraged by the price increases, and the Japanese press commented on the anomaly of price increases in a situation of swollen inventories and massive surplus capacity (*Nihon Keizai Shimbun,* 30 January 1986). The data in table 4.4

41. The rough calculations used to estimate these profit figures were derived from models constructed by Daniel L. Klesken, semiconductor analyst at Prudential-Bache.

42. I am grateful to comments from Thomas Howell for the arguments that appear in the next four paragraphs and for the evidence to support them, most of which is contained in Howell et al. (1992).

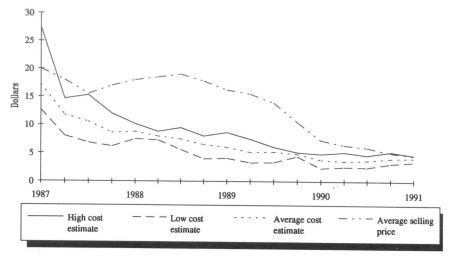

Figure 4.6 Cost estimates and average selling prices for 1-megabyte DRAMS, 1987–91. *Sources:* Cost data: SIA *Fourth Annual Report*, November 1990, 64; price data, Dataquest. Data reproduced with permission.

suggest that prices of 256K DRAMS indeed began to stabilize in the fourth quarter of 1985.

In April 1986, still several months before the conclusion of the SCTA, MITI disclosed that it would begin to implement a new system of regulating Japanese production and pricing "in order to break the deadlock in Japan–US semiconductor negotiations" (*Nihon Keizai Shimbun*, 24 April 1986). According to Japanese press accounts, under MITI's "guidepost" system, a committee established within MITI (including scholars and other experts) would meet with semiconductor producers to discuss their production plans for the coming quarter and to compile production guideposts to curb overproduction and stabilize domestic prices (*Nihon Keizai Shimbun*, 24 April 1986). This approach was identical to approaches used by MITI to handle the problem of "excessive competition" at other times in several other industries.

MITI began issuing its supply-demand guideposts on 30 September 1986, shortly after the signing of the SCTA. In addition, MITI gradually introduced a four-part program of export controls that included export allocations and an effective minimum price floor on DRAM exports to different regional markets.[43] In 1987 MITI announced a 10 percent revision of its production guidepost or forecast for 256K DRAMS for the first quarter of 1987 (MITI *Semiconductor Supply Demand Forecast*, 23 March 1988). In March 1987 it announced another 20 percent cut in production volume from the prior quarter, which amounted to a hefty 32 percent reduction from the fourth quarter of 1986. In addition, during the spring MITI began issuing guideposts for 1M DRAM production as well. The Japanese press reported that MITI allocated overall production cutbacks for both 256K and 1M

---

43. MITI's attempts to control investment, production, and exports are described in detail in Flamm (1989, 1992). A 1988 GATT panel ruling in response to a complaint by the European Community found MITI's system of production and export restrictions to be impermissible under GATT law, and it was formally terminated.

DRAMs between the individual Japanese producers, which led the more efficient ones, notably NEC, to complain that the controls prevented them from increasing their market share (*Asahi Shimbun*, 20 March 1987). Even when DRAM prices began to rise sharply during the last two quarters of 1987, the Japanese press reported that MITI not only was maintaining production controls but was also supervising company investment plans to avoid an "oversupply of product" (*Nihon Keizai Shimbun*, 10 October 1987).

The price increases and supply shortages that resulted from MITI's administrative guidance proved highly profitable for the Japanese semiconductor industry as a whole. MITI defended its measures as necessary to support the SCTA and mitigate trade friction with the United States. But this explanation lacks credibility. If MITI had been acting simply to enforce the provisions of the SCTA, it would not have needed to restrict production, investment, and exports to such an extent that prices would rise above the foreign market values of the highest-cost Japanese producers. Did MITI make a mistake in its forecasts, so that prices vastly overshot the levels required by the SCTA? This, too, is hard to believe, since MITI was making accurate forecasts of semiconductor production, investment, and domestic demand every three months.[44] In fact there is a more compelling explanation, which is also consistent with MITI's history of continuous involvement in the industry since its inception: MITI worked with the firms to encourage cartel-like behavior that would benefit all of them. And it did so in ways that were characteristic of its approach to industries experiencing losses: it stipulated production and investment cutbacks to remove "excessive competition" while allowing the weakest domestic firms to survive. Seen from this perspective, the SCTA was merely a convenient excuse for MITI to "stabilize" the market, something it would have tried to do anyway, once the Japanese firms had consolidated their hold, giving MITI the opportunity it needed to act.

Although MITI may have initiated actions to stabilize the Japanese market, the behavior of the Japanese producers indicates that they themselves came to see the attraction of greater cooperation to control supply and shore up prices. There were several signs of cooperative behavior by the Japanese producers in 1988 and 1989. In 1988 industry spokespersons began to assert that a new pricing rule prevailed in the semiconductor industry. DRAM prices for each previous generation of memory device had tended to decline asymptotically toward the $3 level, as mass production of that generation peaked—the so-called pi rule of pricing. In future generations of products, however, the Japanese contended that the so-called *bai* rule would apply, meaning that the price of every new generation of product would decline to a level about twice that of the previous generation.[45]

Other clues of cartel-like behavior in 1988 and 1989 include continued restraint on investment in 1988 despite huge inventory rundowns, higher prices, higher profits, and surging demand; and repeated comments by Japanese industry spokespersons about the value of cooperation and the desirability of avoiding the kind of "excessive competition" that had resulted in huge losses in 1985 and

---

44. Evidence on the accuracy of the MITI forecasts is presented in Flamm (1989) and Ferguson (1989).

45. For a discussion of these pricing rules of thumb, see *Japan Electronics Almanac* (1989).

1986. In product lines they dominated (they held 90 percent of the global market in 1M DRAMs), the Japanese producers behaved as though profitability mattered more than market share.[46] Throughout 1988 and 1989, they claimed to be pursuing a "prudent" approach to investment in 1M DRAM facilities, because they were "unwilling to risk a repetition of the global DRAM overcapacity of 3 to 4 years before, a situation that resulted in disastrous price cutting and large financial losses in many cases" (*Electronic News*, 22 August 1988, 22). According to the Japanese press, Japanese companies established a "coordination structure" among themselves to consolidate their production and maintain their prices in 1M DRAMs. As a result, they came to "enjoy the full benefits of market stabilization at a high price" (*Nihon Keizai Shimbun*, 16 May and 28 June 1989). Indeed, in sharp contrast to previous DRAM generations, the price of the 1M DRAM did not decline from its 1,900- to 2,000-yen level for a two-year period between mid-1987 and mid-1989 (table 4.4; Howell et al. 1992). Higher DRAM prices in turn meant sharply higher profits. In 1989, for example, half of Toshiba's total profits came from its semiconductor division.[47]

Probably the most telling evidence of cartel-like behavior occurred in September 1989 when, in response to weakening demand and prices, Toshiba—the acknowledged leader in 1M DRAM production, cost, and price—announced its decision to cut production, prompting similar announcements by all the other Japanese producers on the same day. According to the Japanese press, these production cutbacks were announced in an effort to stabilize prices as demand reached its peak (*Nihon Keizai Shimbun*, 14 September 1989). At the time of the announcements, DRAM prices still significantly exceeded total average production costs (and marginal production costs) for the major Japanese producers (figure 4.5). Yet rather than cut prices to sell more chips and gain market share at the expense of higher-cost producers, the low-cost producers chose to cut production—hardly the outcome one would expect in a competitive market.

It is important to emphasize that a price-cutting strategy was not ruled out by the SCTA, since the foreign market values for the low-cost producers were still lower than the prices they were charging. According to an estimate by Flamm, which is consistent with SIA data (figure 4.5), Toshiba's price of $9 for a 1M DRAM in December 1989 compared with an upper-bound estimate of $5 for Toshiba's foreign market value (Kenneth Flamm, Brookings Institution, personal communication, January 1990).

What, then, was the role of the SCTA in getting the Japanese companies to behave in more cooperative ways? Given their history and the environment in which they functioned, it is likely that even in the absence of the trade agreement these companies—under MITI's guidance—would have realized the extent of their market power and behaved more cooperatively after they had succeeded in driving out American competition. Certainly, their *keiretsu* structure, the absence of credible antitrust enforcement, a long history of cross-shareholding, shared R&D efforts, and other cooperative links between the Japanese firms in question, and the fact that they competed with one another in a variety of other downstream systems markets, made a cooperative outcome more likely. And

46. This argument is also made by Ferguson (1989).

47. Estimate reported by Hajime Karatsu to the National Research Council, Symposium on "Linking Trade and Technology Policies," Washington, 10–11 June 1991.

such an outcome was certainly more likely than it would have been had the tables been turned and a small number of American firms dominated DRAM production. In such a case, the responsible American government agencies would have actively discouraged cooperative behavior—in glaring contrast to the way the responsible Japanese government agencies behaved.

On the other hand, the timing of cooperative behavior on the part of the Japanese companies, following so closely upon the SCTA, suggests an alternative explanation. This explanation, which is consistent with the theoretical literature on the effects of trade restrictions in imperfectly competitive industries, sees the trade agreement as an external threat or prod that precipitated a change in industry behavior (see, e.g., Krishna 1989, Dixit 1988). A collusive arrangement is difficult to achieve even when it benefits all of the players in a concentrated industry. But external pressure may encourage or even necessitate such an arrangement on a temporary basis, and if the firms see the benefits to be had, they may continue to behave cohesively even after this pressure has been removed.

Market power was an essential precondition for a cooperative outcome in DRAMS. In EPROMS, a product in which American companies still retained a significant share of the world market at the time the SCTA was signed, the outcome was very different (see figure 4.3). Although MITI tried to use production and investment guideposts in EPROMS, its forecasts were far off the mark. Because American and European firms retained a market share of around 45 percent in EPROMS, it was virtually impossible for MITI to guide the Japanese producers to coordinated production restraint in the face of significant non-Japanese competition.[48] Second, according to some industry observers, Japanese firms became noticeably less aggressive in seeking market share in EPROMS after the agreement.[49] Third, after a brief increase between the second quarter of 1987 and the first quarter of 1988, the prices of 256K EPROMS were stable during most of 1988 and began to fall in 1989, while prices of 1M EPROMS fell throughout 1988 and 1989 (table 4.5; figure 4.7). During much of the period, EPROM prices in the United States and Europe were actually lower than they were in Japan (figure 4.8). According to industry experts, EPROM prices declined in a historically predictable pattern (Howell et al. 1992, 105). Finally, American and other buyers did not report shortages in EPROM supplies, and American EPROM suppliers such as Intel asserted that EPROM prices never significantly rose above their marginal costs because of competitive market conditions. According to an industry source, another American producer, AMD, lost money on EPROMS throughout 1987 and 1988.

The divergence of results in DRAMS and EPROMS helps to illustrate how government policy can affect trade in high-technology industries. It is especially

48. According to Howell et al. (1992, 105), in Japanese-dominated product areas such as DRAMS and SRAMS, Japanese production conformed closely to MITI's guideposts. In other product lines, such as EPROMS and microprocessors, it did not.

49. Personal communication with officials of an American company active in the EPROM market. It was further suggested that Hitachi, the number-two firm in EPROMS in 1985, dropped out of the market by the end of the decade partly because of a loss of face associated with its 1985 memo in which it advocated an aggressive pricing strategy. The memo was one of the pieces of evidence used by American companies in their EPROM antidumping action against the Japanese companies.

Table 4.5 Average selling prices for 256-kilobyte and 1-megabyte EPROMS, 1984–92 (dollars per chip)

Year	Quarter	256K EPROMS	1M EPROMS
1984	1	77.59	
	2	48.11	
	3	37.17	
	4	29.47	
1985	1	21.55	
	2	12.14	
	3	5.67	
	4	4.63	
1986	1	4.32	150.00
	2	4.71	73.13
	3	4.73	59.75
	4	4.47	55.78
1987	1	4.47	36.00
	2	4.59	30.40
	3	4.71	27.17
	4	4.73	25.69
1988	1	4.87	21.47
	2	4.83	20.31
	3	4.86	19.26
	4	4.89	18.46
1989	1	4.40	17.00
	2	3.64	16.65
	3	3.07	14.35
	4	2.70	11.25
1990	1	2.56	9.86
	2	2.38	8.62
	3	2.35	7.19
	4	2.35	5.36
1991	1	2.30	4.90
	2	2.28	4.82
	3	2.15	4.35
	4	1.95	3.95
1992	1	1.85	3.70
	2	1.65	3.45

Source: Dataquest. Data reproduced with permission.

important for understanding differences between national oligopolies and cross-national oligopolies. Because of significant internal economies and dynamic feedback effects in production, the semiconductor industry is inherently oligopolistic. Moreover, because technological and capital costs of entry have risen sharply over time,[50] the market power of incumbent firms has been increasing.

Whether market power is exercised, however, depends on the ability of individual firms to commit to a cooperative strategy. For a variety of reasons, such a strategy seems more likely to emerge when an industry is dominated by a small number of Japanese firms, as the semiconductor industry was in the mid-1980s. First, there is no credible threat of antitrust prosecution. Second, infor-

---

50. Dataquest has estimated that, by the early 1990s, output from a single new fabrication plant had to achieve a 6 percent world market share in order to warrant construction.

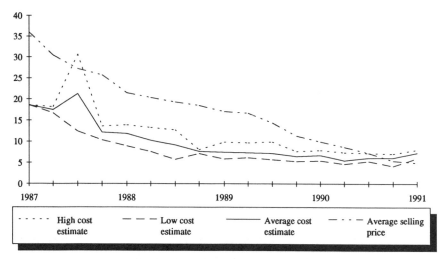

Figure 4.7 Cost estimates and average selling prices for 1-megabyte EPROMS, 1987–91. *Sources:* Cost data: SIA *Fourth Annual Report*, November 1990, 64; price data, Dataquest. Data reproduced with permission.

mation is regularly exchanged between firms through a number of publicly sanctioned channels, including industry associations, MITI panels, and government-organized and government-sponsored R&D projects. Third, because most large Japanese firms are members of large business groups, they compete with one another in a variety of product markets—and the greater the extent of multiproduct competition, the greater the long-run costs of deviating from a cooperative strategy in a particular product line. Fourth, because of their financial structure, Japanese firms can credibly threaten to sustain losses for a substantial period of time to deter the entry of new competitors into an industry they dominate. Thus, all other things being equal, a Japanese oligopoly is more likely to be cooperative than an oligopoly composed of American or other companies with different financial structures.

On the other hand, a collusive or cooperative arrangement in a Japanese oligopoly, like most such arrangements, is inherently unstable and can quickly dissolve under changing market conditions. By the second half of 1989, slumping demand, strong competition from Korean suppliers in 256K and 1M DRAM chips, and the jockeying for position in new 4M and 16M DRAM generations began to weaken the ability of the Japanese industry to sustain a cooperative outcome. Revealingly, just as the elimination of most non-Japanese suppliers appeared to precipitate collusive behavior among the Japanese companies after 1985, so the appearance of new non-Japanese suppliers, especially Samsung and Siemens, appeared to precipitate the breakdown of such behavior in late 1989. The development of the U.S. Memories Consortium, which looked like a reality at the time, may have also played a role in destabilizing the Japanese cartel. Since late 1989, slowing global demand and stiff competition from the Koreans, who now account for about 18 percent of global DRAM sales, have caused the prices of DRAM devices to continue their downward slide and have undermined the market

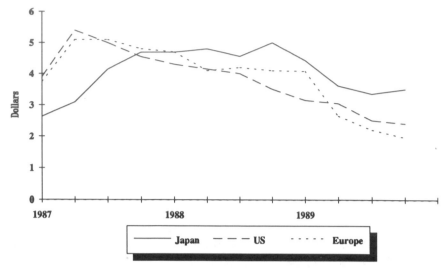

Figure 4.8 Prices for 256-kilobyte EPROMS, by country, 1987–89. *Source:* Dataquest. Data reproduced with permission.

power of the Japanese suppliers (see table 4.4). By 1991 prices for 4M DRAMS were reportedly too low to recoup the cost of building a new production line to make them.

Effects on Global Market Shares

Perhaps the most important gains of the SCTA for US producers have been achieved in the EPROM market, the very market that had mobilized them to take defensive trade action in the first place. Between 1978 and 1986, the US share of the global EPROM market declined by more than half.[51] After the SCTA took effect, this trend was dramatically reversed, and US producers gained back more than 10 percentage points of the global market, while their Japanese competitors lost more than 15 percentage points. In 1988 the US share of this market once again exceeded the Japanese share (see figure 4.3). By 1991, according to recent Dataquest estimates, American companies claimed about 64 percent of the North American market and about 25 percent of the Japanese market for EPROMS. For many American producers (especially AMD, National Semiconductor, and Texas Instruments), who view EPROMS as an important technology driver, the gains in the EPROM market are of great significance.

As an unanticipated consequence of the SCTA, the global EPROM market has also become more competitive. In 1987, three major non-Japanese producers—

---

51. In response to the claim that most of the decline in the global market shares of US producers during the 1980s was simply due to exchange rate changes, a recent study (Finan and Anderson 1991) examines what would have happened to these shares if exchange rates had remained unchanged. The study concludes that more than 70 percent of the decline in the global market share of US producers and more than 60 percent of the increase in the global market share of Japanese producers between 1982 and 1989 was the result of "real" changes in their competitive positions, not the result of calculating shares in terms of a declining dollar.

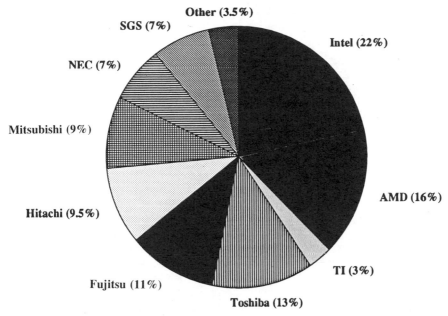

Figure 4.9 Shares of the worldwide 1-megabyte EPROM market, by company, 1990. Source: Dataquest. Data reproduced with permission.

National Semiconductor, SGS-Thomson, and Texas Instruments—entered or reentered EPROM production. As a consequence of greater competition, the market share of the top four firms in EPROMs declined from 59 percent in 1985 to 54 percent in 1990. More-intense competition is the main reason why EPROM prices never increased sharply in 1987 or 1988 despite the SCTA's antidumping provisions.[52]

Although the SCTA initially encouraged a less aggressive strategy by the Japanese companies in the EPROM market, they have recently focused their investment on the market's high-end products. They have largely withdrawn from lower-density EPROMs (256K and lower) and have become more aggressive in 1M EPROMs and in a new product called flash memory, which is likely to be one of the fastest-growing segments of the memory market in the 1990s. By the end of 1990, the Japanese companies claimed approximately 45 percent of the 1M EPROM market, compared with 41 percent for American producers (figure 4.9). Perhaps in an effort to head off renewed trade friction in the high-end memory market, in the summer of 1992 Fujitsu and AMD formed an alliance to build a Japanese production facility for EPROMs and flash memory.

The SCTA also abruptly halted the sharp decline in the American companies' share of the global DRAM market. In fact, they even managed to win a small increase in global market share, from 17.9 percent in 1987 to 19.8 percent by 1991 (see figure 4.2). Nonetheless, the share of the North American DRAM market

52. According to the manager of one of the leading EPROM manufacturers, firms were unlikely to break even in EPROMs in 1991 with less than 10 percent of the market. If this calculation was correct, only the top four firms were breaking even.

claimed by American producers continued to decline, albeit more slowly and erratically than it had before 1986. By 1991 this share had dropped to about 27 percent, from about 31 percent in 1987. During the same period, the Japanese share of the North American DRAM market also declined, from 61 percent to 52 percent, while the share of East Asian suppliers (primarily Korea) increased from about 7 percent to about 19 percent.

Despite higher prices and profits in the DRAM market between 1987 and 1989, Motorola was the only American company to reenter DRAM production, and it did so primarily as part of its alliance with Toshiba. Texas Instruments, which remained in the DRAM business prior to the SCTA, has also increased its DRAM production capacity since 1986, but mainly in foreign locations, including Japan, Taiwan, and Italy. Both the Taiwanese and the Italian governments have provided special incentives to attract Texas Instruments' investment. Except for Micron, an American DRAM producer that has invested solely in the United States, more than 80 percent of the DRAM capacity expansion projects undertaken by the American companies since the SCTA went into effect have occurred abroad, primarily in Japan.

Motorola licensed some of its key technology to Toshiba in order to obtain the DRAM technology necessary for its reentry; and Motorola now relies heavily on the joint venture for its DRAM production. Toshiba also made market access commitments to Motorola as part of this agreement. Since the SCTA was signed, Texas Instruments has expanded DRAM capacity in Japan, Taiwan, and Italy, in the latter two instances taking advantage of special government incentives.

On the basis of both industry structure variables and home-country characteristics such as factor endowments, Japanese firms should have maintained their oligopoly of the DRAM market. Even though DRAM prices bulged in 1987 and 1988, the barriers to entry for new firms were enormous. Minimum scale for a state-of-the-art facility was approaching a half-billion dollars; product life cycles had become shorter, leaving less time for late entrants to recoup investments; and with the significant experience advantage of the Japanese, new entrants would have to fear retaliation. Nonetheless, the Japanese share of the global DRAM market declined from about 80 percent to about 57 percent between 1986 and 1991, almost entirely as the result of a surge in share by the Koreans (see figure 4.2). Aided by their government's explicit targeting of the semiconductor industry and the generous subsidies that ensued, the Korean companies were not deterred by high barriers to entry in the memory market or by the credible threat of a preemptive price war waged by their Japanese rivals.[53] In addition, the Koreans were helped by higher DRAM prices in 1988 and 1989, which reversed their significant financial losses earlier in the decade.

Most American companies that considered reentering memory production after 1986—either individually or collectively as part of the abortive U.S. Memories Consortium—had none of the Koreans' advantages. The American merchant firms that gave up DRAM production in 1985–86 did so believing that the Japanese government was committed to maintaining the Japanese industry and that the Japanese companies, with government help and their own deep pockets, would be able to outlast them in a disastrous price war. Certainly, the methods

---

53. For a complete discussion of Korean promotional and protectionist policies in the semiconductor industry, see Howell et al. (1992). The decline in the Japanese share of the DRAM market reflects almost entirely a rise in the share of the Korean and Taiwanese suppliers.

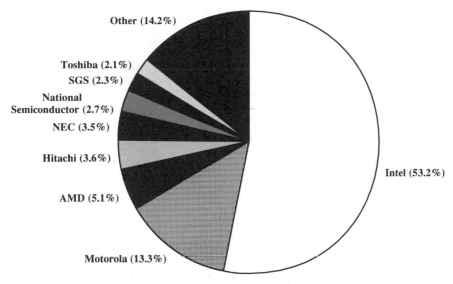

Figure 4.10 Shares of the worldwide microprocessor market, by company, 1990.
Source: Dataquest. Data used with permission.

used by MITI to enforce the trade agreement in ways that benefited even the weakest Japanese producers only strengthened this belief. Both the Japanese government and the Japanese companies were capable of making a credible commitment to deter the reentry of most American merchant companies into DRAM production, where the Japanese threat was strongest.

The Korean companies, which like their Japanese competitors had their government's backing, mounted the most significant challenge to the Japanese in the DRAM market. Aided by a publicly funded European research program, Siemens also emerged as a producer of 4M DRAMs in 1989. Although the Japanese continue to dominate the markets for both 4M and 16M DRAMs, which are the frontier-technology volume memory products as of this writing, by 1992 Samsung, the largest Korean producer, had emerged as the largest producer of 1M DRAMs and the fifth-largest producer of all memory chips in the world (*Business Week*, 3 February 1992, 44–45).

In 1990 the Japanese share of the global semiconductor market declined for the first time since 1982—from 50.4 percent in 1989 to 47.1 percent in 1990. This was followed by a further decline to 46.5 percent in 1991 (see figure 4.1). The two-year drop in Japan's global market share was the result of two factors: rapid growth in the microprocessor segment, which American firms continue to dominate (figure 4.10), and a sharp decline in prices and revenues in the memory segment, which Japanese firms continue to dominate (figure 4.2). The collapse of prices in the DRAM market, in turn, was partly the result of efforts by the Japanese companies to respond to the Korean challenge at the low end of the DRAM market.[54]

---

54. Indeed, aggressive price cutting by Samsung on 1M DRAMs forced the major Japanese

Effects on Trade Patterns in the United States and Japan

Although the SCTA is a trade agreement, its effects on underlying trade patterns between the United States and Japan have been relatively small compared with its effects on competitive dynamics, prices, and company shares in the world market. In addition, because of the global nature of the US semiconductor industry and the increasing globalization of the Japanese semiconductor industry as well, trade flows, which are calculated across national boundaries, are singularly misleading indicators of the competitive positions of companies with different national headquarters. As the following discussion demonstrates, sales by American companies are not the same thing as exports from the United States, nor do imports into the United States necessarily reflect sales by Japanese or other foreign countries.

Since 1986, imports as a percentage of US consumption have continued their somewhat erratic upward trend, increasing from about 50 percent of US consumption before the agreement to more than 62 percent by 1989 (table 4.6).[55] However, the foreign subsidiaries of US companies still account for some 65 percent to 70 percent of US semiconductor imports.

Thanks in part to rising DRAM prices, the share of Japanese imports in US consumption of semiconductors more than doubled between 1986 and 1989, from less than 10 percent to more than 20 percent. Since then, mainly as a result of declining DRAM prices, this share has stabilized, reaching about 22 percent in 1991 (calculations based on a comparison of total sales in the US market in that year reported by Dataquest and US imports from Japan reported in *U.S. Industrial Outlook*, 1992, chapter 16, 7). DRAMS continue to account for the lion's share of US semiconductor imports from Japan (about 40 percent in 1991; *U.S. Industrial Outlook*, 1992, chapter 16, 7).

US imports of all semiconductor products were about 84 percent higher in value terms in 1991 than they were in 1986. But the value of all US semiconductor exports increased even more dramatically, by approximately 180 percent, during the same period (see table 4.1). As a result, the US trade imbalance in semiconductors, which hit a high of $2.5 billion in 1986, had fallen to little more than $500 million by the end of 1991. Japan, however, has remained a relatively small market for US exports, accounting for only about 10 percent of total US exports in 1990 and 1991 (*U.S. Industrial Outlook*, 1992, chapter 16, 7). As a consequence of relatively small exports to Japan and relatively large imports, mainly of DRAMS, from Japan, the US trade imbalance in semiconductors with Japan was on the order of $1½ billion in 1990 and $700 million in 1991.

Imports have continued to claim a small share of Japan's domestic market for semiconductors. After shrinking to a low of about 6 percent in 1986, imports as a percentage of Japanese consumption rose to about 10 percent in 1989, but this was still below the 1982 level (table 4.7). Exhibiting a similar trend, imports as a fraction of total semiconductor sales in Japan increased from about 8 percent

---

producers to reduce their prices and production of this product and to move more aggressively into the new 4M DRAM technology.

55. There is no consistent US import series available to calculate this series through 1992.

Table 4.6 United States: semiconductor imports as a share of total semiconductor consumption, 1982–89
(percentages)

	1982	1983	1984	1985	1986	1987	1988	1989
Total imports	56.8	49.1	50.4	52.7	47.4	53.0	60.5	62.5
Imports from Japan	7.5	8.1	12.3	10.6	9.8	11.7	16.0	21.1

Source: Dataquest. Data reproduced with permission.

Table 4.7 Japan: semiconductor imports as a share of total semiconductor consumption, 1982–89 (percentages)

	1982	1983	1984	1985	1986	1987	1988	1989
Imports from United States	10.0	10.0	9.0	6.0	5.0	5.0	6.0	7.0
Imports from non-US sources	4.0	3.0	2.0	1.5	1.0	1.5	2.0	3.0
Total imports	14.0	13.0	11.0	7.5	6.0	6.5	8.0	10.0

Sources: Japan, Ministry of Finance; Dataquest (data reprinted with permission).

in 1986 to approximately 13 percent in 1990, but this represented virtually no change from the 1982 figure.[56]

Both Japan's exports and its trade surplus in semiconductors also continued to increase through 1989, significantly boosted by higher DRAM prices. In 1990, however, both indicators fell, as DRAM prices softened and microprocessor imports increased (see table 4.3). Although Japan's imports of semiconductors from the United States increased after 1986, both absolutely and as a share of Japanese consumption, the bulk of sales to the Japanese market by American companies— approximately 75 percent in 1989—does not originate from US locations (table 4.8). Three American companies—Motorola, Intel, and Texas Instruments— account for approximately 60 percent of all sales by American companies to Japan. Two of these companies, Motorola and Intel, gained disproportionately during the SCTA's first two years, enjoying a 260 percent increase in their sales in Japan, compared with a doubling of overall sales of American companies in Japan. Undoubtedly, a good portion of the incremental Japanese sales of these two companies originates from their offshore locations: Intel's and Motorola's assembly operations in Southeast Asia and the Philippines and Motorola's Japanese subsidiary. Texas Instruments also supplies the Japanese market mainly from its Japanese facilities.

The New Semiconductor Trade Agreement: The Story Continues

The SCTA was a five-year agreement, scheduled to expire on 31 July 1991. By the first quarter of 1990, however, two things were already evident. First, any effort to extend the SCTA's antidumping provisions would be strongly opposed by the computer industry, which had been harmed by the sharp runup in DRAM prices between 1987 and 1989. And second, the market access target of 20 percent would not be met by the SCTA's deadline. By the first quarter of 1991, the foreign share of the Japanese market had climbed to about 14.0 percent, but growth had leveled off.

Working cooperatively with representatives of the American computer industry, representatives of the American semiconductor industry lobbied for a

---

56. These shares are based on figures for total sales in Japan provided by Dataquest and Japan's import figures in table 4.3.

Table 4.8   Japan: semiconductor imports from the United States and semiconductor sales by US companies in Japan, 1984–89 (millions of dollars)

	1984	1985	1986	1987	1988	1989
Imports from the United States	278	149	169	256	371	543
Sales by US companies	965	695	948	1,255	1,956	2,147

Sources: Constructed by the authors from Japanese Ministry of Finance and Dataquest data (reproduced with permission).

new agreement with Japan that would curtail and modify the SCTA's antidumping provisions and extend its market access provisions. Following protracted negotiations with the Japanese, a new five-year accord was reached in the summer of 1991. As part of the negotiations, the United States agreed to suspend the remaining sanctions against the Japanese producers for SCTA violations. (Half of the sanctions had been removed in 1987 after the Commerce Department determined that dumping had ceased.)

In contrast to the SCTA, the new semiconductor agreement (NSCTA) includes explicit mention of the 20 percent target for market access, which both governments agreed should be realized by the end of 1992, in effect extending the SCTA's market access provisions for 17 months. At Japan's insistence, however, the deal's language explicitly notes that the target is neither a guarantee, nor a ceiling, nor a floor on foreign market share. Nonetheless, American negotiators have made it clear that they view at least substantial progress toward realization of the target a commitment. At the time the new agreement was signed, Linn Williams, the Deputy US Trade Representative and chief negotiator, stated that reimposition of sanctions was a possibility should the United States not get the "substantial market access we think we should" (SIA 1991).

The NSCTA's antidumping provisions represent a compromise between the semiconductor industry and its customers in the computer industry. Under the NSCTA's terms, the US government no longer collects cost and price data from Japanese companies and no longer sets foreign market values for DRAMs and EPROMs. Instead, the Japanese firms are required to collect the data that would be needed in the event of an antidumping investigation and to provide such information within 14 days of a request by the US government. This arrangement is designed to faciliate the implementation of fast-track antidumping investigations—a goal supported by many high-technology companies, not just those in the semiconductor industry. Overall, the NSCTA leaves open the possibility of continued conflict between the United States and Japan in the semiconductor industry. If American companies decide to pursue antidumping actions, their efforts will be facilitated by the terms of the agreement, which in turn may act to deter aggressive price reductions by the Japanese companies. In addition, if the market access target of 20 percent is not reached by the end of 1992, which as of this writing is almost a certainty, the United States will have to decide how to respond.

The Japanese cite sluggish growth in Japan as the major reason why the foreign share of Japan's market stagnated between 14.0 percent and 15.0 percent after the NSCTA was signed. The Japanese also point to a number of market access initiatives undertaken by MITI during 1991 and 1992 as a sign of good faith. But the sluggish market explanation of the slowdown in foreign sales proferred by the Japanese rings hollow, because until recently they often cited rapid growth of their market as the reason for their inability to increase the share of foreign suppliers. One begins to wonder at what point in the industry cycle conditions *would* be favorable for an expansion of foreign market share. In addition, the experience of the SCTA, as well as those of Cray and Motorola, indicate that sustained US pressure—backed by a credible commitment to sanctions—is often necessary to secure Japan's adherence to a formal trade agreement that threatens the interests of powerful Japanese companies.

Thus, it is not surprising that, shortly after a US government interagency panel chided Japan for insufficient progress on market access, the foreign share of Japan's semiconductor market climbed to 16 percent in the second quarter of 1992, compared with 14.6 percent in the preceding quarter. This represented the largest quarterly increase since 1986, and followed an announcement by American computer companies offering their support for the NSCTA. Apparently warnings by the US government that it would take additional actions as necessary to fulfill the terms of the agreement by year's end, and a united front comprised of American semiconductor and computer manufacturers, propelled the Japanese into action.

Whether the United States should impose sanctions on the Japanese if the 20 percent target is not met by the end of 1992 requires an assessment of whether the Japanese have made bona fide efforts to increase market opportunities for American and other non-Japanese companies during the preceding 18 months, as they explicitly committed themselves to do. If US trade negotiators are not convinced that the Japanese have honored the commitment, some kind of sanction is warranted, both as a prod to further Japanese efforts and as a signal that the United States remains committed to its longstanding market access goal. Ultimately, however, the NSCTA's success should be judged on the basis of whether substantial new market opportunities have been provided, not on the basis of whether the 20 percent target is realized within a specific period of time.

An Overall Assessment of the SCTA

The conventional wisdom among economists is that the SCTA was an unmitigated failure. But the evidence presented here suggests that a more nuanced conclusion is closer to the mark. The SCTA was a qualified success with respect to some of its objectives: the US share of the global DRAM market stabilized; the precipitous decline in the US share of the global EPROM market was reversed; and the share of American and other foreign companies in the Japanese market reached new highs.

Nor did the SCTA reduce competition in the United States, Japan, or the world. Indeed, the SCTA, combined with other policy measures taken in the United States, Europe, and East Asia, has resulted in a more competitive market than would have prevailed if the growing market power of the Japanese firms had been left unchecked. Competition in the EPROM market has been stimulated by the growing shares of American and European producers, at the expense of their Japanese counterparts. Although initially dampened between 1986 and 1989, as the Japanese producers consolidated their market dominance, competition in the DRAM market has been reignited by several factors, including an increase in production by American companies such as Motorola and Texas Instruments; IBM's deal with Siemens to co-develop and co-produce next-generation DRAMS; the growing strength of the Korean suppliers, promoted by their government and attracted by the hefty profits earned by the Japanese; and the expansion of production capacity in Europe, encouraged in part by European policies to develop a regional supply base in semiconductors in the wake of supply shortages and higher prices between 1986 and 1989. Moreover, if the improved access of foreign producers in Japan permanently weakens the market power of the *keiretsu* firms, as the SCTA intended, then Japanese users of semiconductors will benefit from greater competition. On this note, the rising share of non-Japanese suppliers in DRAM sales in Japan from less than 5 percent in 1987 to almost 15 percent in 1991 is a promising sign (calculations based on Dataquest estimates).

To argue that the SCTA has realized at least some of its underlying objectives, however, is not to argue that it was the best means for realizing them. Like any policy measure, trade or otherwise, the SCTA's merits can be evaluated only by comparing its costs with its benefits and by comparing it with policy alternatives. These are the tasks of the remainder of this chapter, which analyzes the SCTA's lessons for US trade and industrial policy for the semiconductor industry.

Lessons for U.S. Trade Policy from the Semiconductor Experience

Managed Trade as a Second-Best Policy Alternative

Support for free trade and opposition to managed trade are among the few things that unite economists from different theoretical and political traditions. But, as we have seen, trade in the semiconductor industry has never been free in the traditional sense. The appropriate standard of comparison for evaluating some form of managed trade in this industry—as in the other technology-intensive industries examined in this book—is not free trade but manipulated trade, in which multifaceted government interventions on both sides of the trading relationship affect competitive outcomes.

Although managed trade is nowhere clearly defined, it is commonly understood to encompass any trade agreement that establishes quantitative targets on trade flows. Managed trade thus lies at one end of a continuum between regulating trade flows through fixed rules and regulating them through fixed quantities or targets.

According to this definition, the market access provisions of both the SCTA and the NSCTA are examples of managed trade because they specify a quantitative target for the minimum share of the Japanese market to be supplied by foreign producers. To use a terminology suggested by Bhagwati (1988, 83), both agreements are examples of a particular form of managed trade, called a "voluntary import expansion" (VIE) agreement. Such an agreement establishes a minimum target for the share of a country's market to be satisfied by imports or foreign producers. In contrast, another kind of managed trade agreement, of which there are many more examples, is the "voluntary export restraint" (VER). A VER establishes a quantitative limit on a country's exports to one or more of its trading partners and thus implicitly establishes a quantitative limit on their imports from that country.

VERS are designed to restrict trade and competition, and, as the evidence in the next chapter confirms, they usually have that effect. VIEs, in contrast, are designed to increase trade and foreign sales in economies in which policies or structural impediments limit access for foreign suppliers. The intent of a VIE is to stimulate competition where it is effectively excluded or managed, not to reduce it.

Despite this critical analytical distinction, economists tend to oppose VERS and VIEs with equal vigor. Opposition to VIEs rests on three *a priori* arguments: that VIEs result in the cartelization of markets; that they increase prices by limiting competition; and that, by violating the nondiscrimination principle of the GATT, they undermine the world trading regime. All three of these arguments are subject to qualification on analytical grounds alone. None of them are confirmed by the actual experience of the SCTA or NSCTA.

When a country establishes a minimum import or sales target for the companies of one or more of its trading partners, it is hardly setting up an industry cartel. Indeed, if the target applies to an industry in which there is ample evidence of market closure—an essential precondition for the appropriate imposition of a VIE—and if the target applies broadly to sales from all foreign suppliers rather than to a single supplier, then the VIE may actually increase competition. From a static perspective, the target may indeed look like nothing more than the creation of a buyers' cartel, with the government of the importing nation orchestrating minimum sales of foreign products to unwilling domestic customers. But from a dynamic perspective, the target and orchestrated sales may stimulate changes in supply and demand behavior that increase competition, both in the importing country and in the world market.[57]

Many critics of the SCTA's market access provisions question the existence of barriers to the Japanese semiconductor marketplace in the first place. As noted earlier, most overt barriers, with the significant exception of preferential procurement by NTT and later by MPT, were formally abolished by 1978. Nor is there any documented evidence that clandestine government barriers substituted for formal ones thereafter. Why, then, did the share of American producers in Japan's market remain unchanged?

For the reasons noted earlier, the preferred Japanese explanation—a mismatch between American products and Japanese demand—is inadequate. The alternative explanation offered by the US industry, and supported here, is that preferential arrangements both within and between the Japanese suppliers and their *keiretsu* partners acted as an opaque but nonetheless powerful barrier to foreign suppliers. The structure of the Japanese firms producing semiconductors, the incentive environment in which they functioned, and their history of co-

---

57. These procompetitive effects are also apparent in the aftermath of the 1979 managed trade arrangement for third-party radio systems in Japan, as discussed in chapter 3.

operative and collusive actions in other electronics markets provide a strong *prima facie* case in support of this explanation. Subsequent econometric analysis by Lawrence—which demonstrates that *keiretsu* links are barriers, although not impenetrable ones, to foreign sales—also lends credence to this interpretation.

Another criticism of the SCTA's market access provisions focuses on the "arbitrary" nature of the 20 percent target. There is greater merit to this line of attack. According to available accounts, American negotiators did not make a systematic effort to develop a measure of what the foreign share of the Japanese market would have been in the mid-1980s, absent *keiretsu* barriers and earlier Japanese policies restricting trade and direct investment. Rather, the 20 percent figure, which meant a doubling of the US share of the Japanese market, represented a lower-limit "best guess" by the US industry based primarily on its much higher share of other global markets.[58] Clearly, there was a large degree of arbitrariness in the choice of this figure, and this is one of the chief shortcomings of the VIE approach in this case.

As the SCTA example indicates, the specification of a VIE's quantitative target will always be a controversial, imprecise, and ultimately arbitrary exercise. VIEs are therefore always second-best policy remedies: they are inferior to the first-best approach of unimpeded market competition, but they may sometimes prove superior to doing nothing when such competition is constrained by structural impediments and foreign trading practices.

Developments in the Japanese semiconductor market show evidence of the procompetitive, dynamic effects of the SCTA's market access provisions. On the supply side, several American producers, anticipating at least a minimum share of the lucrative Japanese market, have increased their investments in sales, distribution, technical support facilities, and production capabilities in Japan. Because the SCTA establishes a VIE for all foreign suppliers, both Korean and European companies have also been able to increase their presence in the Japanese market.[59] As noted earlier, the credible long-term threat of the Korean suppliers was one of several factors that weakened cooperative pricing practices by Japanese producers in DRAMs by 1990.

On the demand side, Japanese users of semiconductors have increased their purchases from foreign suppliers, and the share of these suppliers in the Japanese marketplace has increased, especially since 1989. Even more important to the long-run dynamics of the market, Japanese users are now more willing to entertain bids and to design-in products from American suppliers. Several American companies have reported winning contracts that they could not have bid upon without the pressure of the SCTA. As an illustration, in 1991 the EIAJ announced that there had been a 40 percent increase in the number of design wins by US semiconductor companies to Japanese customers in 1990. American

---

58. As noted earlier, if American producers had been able to supply the same fraction of demand for semiconductors for telecommunications and computer products in Japan as they did in Europe, their share of the Japanese market would have been at least 30 percent. The American firms supplied on the order of 40 percent of the European market—the other major global market for semiconductors—and 66 percent of the total world market, excluding Japan, in 1986.

59. Because the VIE was specified for all foreign suppliers, it was not inconsistent with the GATT's nondiscrimination principle.

producers believe that most of these bids would not have been possible without the 1986 agreement and the US government's commitment to see that it was honored (SIA 1991).

According to American companies, the VIE provisions of the SCTA have partially countered the effects of *keiretsu* impediments to the Japanese market. At a minimum, these provisions mean that a bigger share of the cartelized domestic marketplace in Japan has been opened to competition from foreign suppliers. At a maximum, the resulting competition may finally destabilize these cartelized arrangements altogether. If the minimum outcome prevails, the benefits of the VIE will be limited mainly to foreign suppliers able to increase their sales in Japan.[60] If the maximum outcome prevails, the benefits of the VIE will certainly be greater and will be shared by consumers and producers around the world.

There is no denying that the SCTA's market access provisions are being "managed" or implemented by the active involvement of the Japanese government. MITI officials communicate regularly with Japanese company officials to encourage them to increase their semiconductor purchases from American suppliers. At the same time, there is no denying that there is intense competition among American suppliers to increase their shares of these purchases. Even more important for the long run, there is substantial learning by both American and Japanese companies about one another's product needs and capabilities.

Finally, it is important to emphasize how critical US government pressure has been in realizing progress on the SCTA's market access goal. Even after the imposition of sanctions in 1987, the share of US producers in the Japanese market increased slowly; by mid-1989 it had recaptured only the roughly 10 percent level reached before the 1985–86 slump. Thereafter, tough talk by the Bush administration and the SIA's lobbying efforts to get semiconductors on the Super 301 agenda led to active Japanese efforts to increase market opportunities for American companies. The result was a more rapid increase in the US share in 1989 and 1990. Once again the lesson that emerges is the extent to which US pressure—backed by a credible commitment to sanctions—is necessary when a bilateral trade agreement threatens the interests of powerful Japanese companies.

Lessons About Antidumping Remedies

The SCTA's antidumping provisions are much harder to justify than its market access provisions.[61] According to US antidumping laws, the Japanese companies were guilty of dumping both DRAMs and EPROMs, and the dumping margins were substantial. In this industry, as in most other high-technology industries in which antidumping measures have been applied, dumping was defined and

---

60. According to the SIA (1991), the 5-percentage-point increase in the share of American producers in the Japanese market realized during the course of the 1986 agreement meant an additional $1 billion in annual sales. Of that amount, roughly $120 million was invested in capital equipment and another $120 million in R&D.

61. The following discussion assumes that the market access provisions can be separated from the antidumping provisions. Analytically, this is correct. Politically, however, it may be unrealistic. Without the pressure of antidumping suits, the Japanese producers might have been unwilling to negotiate, and without the antidumping provisions, which ultimately proved beneficial to them, they might have been less willing to implement the market access provisions.

measured as selling below a constructed measure of average total costs adjusted by an arbitrary 8 percent profit markup. Unfortunately, this definition suffers from serious shortcomings as it relates to high-technology industries such as semiconductors.

Even in perfectly competitive markets, profit-maximizing firms with no significant market power may find it rational to price below average total cost under some conditions. In other words, there is nothing in such pricing behavior to suggest market power, unfair practices, or predatory malice. In contrast, pricing below marginal cost or average variable cost may be a sign either of predatory behavior, designed to encourage other firms to exit the market, or of preemptive behavior, designed to deter other firms from entering the market (see, e.g., Milgrom 1987, Milgrom and Roberts 1982, Tirole 1988). Consequently, as Flamm (1991) argues, "the economic problem with cost-based definitions of dumping is not necessarily their existence, but their use of the wrong cost concept as the prima facie trigger for consideration of possible intervention." Especially in high-technology industries where the temptation to discourage entry is large, and the costs of curtailed entry are even larger, the possibility of predatory pricing should not be discounted (Milgrom 1987).

When domestic suppliers are involved in predatory practices, domestic antitrust laws are the appropriate channel for redress. When foreign suppliers are involved, however, these laws are often not applicable or enforceable. As a result, most countries employ specific trade laws, including antidumping laws allowable under the GATT to restrict the anticompetitive practices of foreign firms.

A second deficiency of cost-based definitions of dumping—even those that are restricted to measures of marginal or average variable cost—is that they can generate misleading conclusions about the motives of foreign producers in high-technology industries. Because of significant scale and learning economies in production in these industries, both domestic and foreign companies have a strong incentive to set their current prices in anticipation of realizing lower costs as they increase their volume. Setting current prices on the basis of future expected costs rather than contemporaneous actual costs, be they average or marginal, is called forward pricing, a practice that was pioneered in the semiconductor industry by Texas Instruments. The same production conditions that make a forward pricing strategy attractive are also likely to make a predatory pricing strategy attractive. Consequently, under such conditions, a simple comparison of current prices and costs cannot distinguish truly predatory pricing from forward pricing; to establish a presumption in favor of the former, additional evidence is required.

The American dumping cases brought against Japanese semiconductor producers in 1985 did not attempt to measure the divergence between their marginal or average variable costs and their prices, but did allege predatory behavior. As evidence, American producers pointed to the infamous Hitachi memo instructing distributors of Hitachi EPROMs to quote their price at 10 percent below the price bids of any competitor, Japanese or American. Challenging the claim of predatory behavior, representatives of the US Federal Trade Commission argued before the US International Trade Commission that the memory market was characterized by competitive rather than predatory pricing. However, the written testimony submitted by the Federal Trade Commission conceded that "in a market characterized by predation, one would predict both a tendency for existing non-Japanese to exit the market and a distinct absence of new entrants."[62] Both conditions were satisfied in the DRAM and the EPROM markets in the mid-1980s. In addition, the US industry emphasized the predatory capabilities of the Japanese industry, concentrating on its *keiretsu* structure and the supportive policies of the Japanese government.[63] Given the history of government and business practices in the Japanese industry, there was indeed a strong *prima facie* case that the Japanese companies had both predatory capabilities and intent, as they slashed prices in the early 1980s to wrest market share from their American competitors.

The real error in the application of US antidumping laws to the semiconductor case was not the finding itself but the chosen remedy. The SCTA's pricing provisions amounted to what the Europeans call a "price undertaking." Japanese producers agreed to guidelines requiring them to increase their prices, not only in the United States but in all other markets including their own. In return, the US government and US companies dropped their dumping charges, and no dumping duties were levied on Japanese imports. Without this agreement, once dumping had been established, American law required the automatic imposition of duties for as long as the Japanese companies continued to sell below their foreign market values. If, instead, they had increased their selling prices to levels that covered these values—as they usually do when a dumping finding has been made—no duties would have been imposed.

In either case, the United States would have become a "high-price island," hurting American computer companies (many of which had been silent allies during the negotiations) and forcing them to offshore production in search of cheaper components. The SCTA's pricing provisions were designed to prevent this outcome by requiring the Japanese to raise their prices wherever they sold.

In a conscious effort to limit the price increases that would inevitably result from a termination of dumping, the SCTA's architects also tailored its pricing provisions on a company-by-company basis. Japanese companies with lower costs could charge lower prices than their higher-priced Japanese competitors and still honor the agreement. The intent was to allow competition among the Japanese suppliers, as the imposition of dumping duties would have allowed.

With reason, the American negotiators argued that their approach did not establish an overall price floor on semiconductor imports. But it did establish a price floor for individual Japanese suppliers. What the Americans overlooked was the likelihood that these suppliers, with the help and encouragement of their government supporters, would choose to cooperate rather than compete if they could. In fact, their overwhelming dominance in the global DRAM market allowed a cooperative outcome—the establishment of a temporary price floor benefiting all Japanese suppliers. In the EPROM market, in contrast, where non-Japanese suppliers still held 40 percent of the global market as of 1986, there is no pricing or anecdotal evidence to suggest effective cooperation among the Japanese suppliers.

---

62. Sarah J. Goodfriend, "Analysis of the DRAM Market," appendix to the 11 April 1986 FTC submission, cited in SIA (1990b).

63. For reasons elaborated in chapter 7, a condition requiring demonstration of predatory capabilities is a more realistic approach to improving the nation's dumping laws than a condition requiring demonstration of predatory intent.

The contrast between developments in the DRAM and EPROM markets reveals the importance of timing in formulating and applying antidumping remedies. The SCTA's pricing provisions were not as deleterious in EPROMs as they were in DRAMs because in the former market they were applied early enough to deter dumping and encourage competition, while in the latter market they had distinctly anticompetitive effects because of their timing. As it turned out, these effects worked to the advantage of the dumping firms. It seems ironic, then, that it was the US government that brought the dumping case in 256K DRAMs.[64] Most of the US suppliers recognized the danger of an antidumping action in this product and preferred to concentrate on EPROMs, where they believed they could satisfy their customers' demand without major price increases.

The SCTA approach allowed—and to some extent required—the Japanese companies under MITI's leadership to increase their DRAM prices and earn the lion's share of the bubble profits generated in the global DRAM market between 1987 and the end of 1990.[65] These profits in turn were plowed back into investment and R&D in DRAMs, in other parts of the semiconductor market, and in upstream and downstream electronics products. In contrast, the imposition of company-specific antidumping duties might have encouraged continued price competition among the Japanese companies as they fought to gain share from one another in the American market. Profits would then have been lower than they turned out to be once MITI–orchestrated controls were enacted under the ruse of enforcing the SCTA's pricing provisions. Finally, a traditional antidumping remedy would have included the imposition of antidumping duties; to the extent these duties were actually collected, the increased revenues from higher Japanese DRAM prices in the US market would have accrued to the American government rather than to the Japanese producers.

Even more desirable than a traditional antidumping remedy, with its inevitable price and third-country island effects, would have been a countervailing subsidy to offset the injury to domestic DRAM producers resulting from Japanese dumping. By 1986 the global DRAM market had become increasingly concentrated in the hands of a few vertically integrated Japanese suppliers. This concentration of a market for a basic input in the electronics industry was cause for concern, especially given the increasing flows of proprietary information between input suppliers and users that was made necessary by technological developments in downstream products. The distinctive characteristics of the Japanese suppliers— in particular, their vertical integration into systems production, their *keiretsu* links, and their ties to the Japanese government—made the concentration of the

---

64. There is no explanation of why the government took the unprecedented action of initiating its own antidumping action against the Japanese companies in 256K DRAMs. There are unconfirmed rumors in the industry that the government may have been encouraged to do so by Texas Instruments, the major American supplier of this product at the time. Because a significant share of Texas Instruments' DRAM production was located in Japan, the company might not have thought it wise to initiate an antidumping action against its Japanese competitors. In any event, the government suit was an important prod to get the Japanese to negotiate an agreement.

65. In hindsight, both producers and users of semiconductors in the United States recognized the disadvantages of the SCTA pricing provisions. Under pressure from users, the producers explicitly disavowed the use of price floors of any kind in the negotiation of the 1991 semiconductor trade agreement with Japan.

DRAM market in their hands particularly troublesome.[66] Moreover, given their vertically integrated structure, Japanese suppliers controlling the price of an input such as DRAMs are naturally tempted to maximize profits over time by integrating further into user industries that purchase this input (Vernon and Graham 1971).

Under these circumstances, in 1986 a reasonable case could have been made for a US subsidy either to deter the exit or to encourage the reentry of US DRAM suppliers with the objective of containing the developing market dominance of the Japanese.[67] Over time, such an approach might have generated social returns for the users of DRAMs—principally America's computer manufacturers—in excess of the private returns earned by any one of them. Flamm has called such a subsidy the equivalent of providing "anticartel" insurance. Such an approach would have also signaled a US commitment to support domestic DRAM producers against a predatory attack by the Japanese, thereby discouraging future attacks.

Despite its strengths, however, a countervailing subsidy was a nonstarter in the ideological and budgetary climate prevailing in the United States in 1986. Instead, the US government negotiated an antidumping agreement giving the Japanese government the excuse it needed to encourage cooperative behavior between Japanese suppliers at the expense of American users. Moreover, even later, when some American producers and users explored the possibility of cooperative reentry into DRAM production through the proposed U.S. Memories Consortium, the US government steadfastly refused to provide financial assistance or even to grant an antitrust waiver to encourage their efforts. According to some industry participants, the consortium was derailed at least in part by strategic price reductions by the Japanese. When US government officials were questioned about their unwillingness to support the U.S. Memories initiative, they replied that if the initiative were worthwhile the market would support it. But this assertion was beside the point: it overlooked the fact that a loss-making DRAM production capability, although not privately profitable in the short run, would have generated social returns in the form of a more competitive global DRAM market.

As it happened, the SCTA unwittingly encouraged this outcome over the medium run, in part by motivating the reentry of some American suppliers and in part by motivating the expansion of Korean, Taiwanese, and European suppliers in response to higher prices and market shortages. In the short run, however, the SCTA's pricing provisions played into the hands of the Japanese companies that dominated global DRAM production and were able to charge substantially higher prices and earn huge bubble profits at the expense of their customers, many of whom were American computer companies. The estimates presented earlier suggest that in 1988 alone these profits may have represented a transfer

---

66. As the Japanese would be quick to point out, some other segments of the semiconductor market, especially the lucrative microprocessor market, are dominated by a few American companies. But as ongoing litigation and competition between AMD and Intel in microprocessors demonstrates, antitrust enforcement in the United States acts to blunt excessive market power in a timely and credible way. The same cannot be said of Japan.

67. This argument has also been made by Flamm (1989) and is elaborated formally in his article on the European semiconductor industry (Flamm 1990, 257–63).

of as much as $4 billion from the users of DRAMs to their producers, who were primarily Japanese.

This experience illustrates both the dangers of market concentration in an essential high-technology input industry like semiconductors and the shortcomings of trade policy to mitigate such dangers. Indeed, if anything, the SCTA's antidumping provisions in DRAMs actually made matters worse, strengthening the tendency toward cooperative behavior already gaining momentum among Japanese producers in late 1985. If the goal of American policy had been, as it should have been, the preservation of a competitive global DRAM market, a temporary US subsidy to deter the exit of at least some American suppliers in 1986, or to encourage their reentry in 1987 or 1988, would have been a more effective remedy than the SCTA's price undertaking in DRAMs. For considerably less than the $4 billion ultimately transferred to the Japanese companies in the form of bubble profits, the United States might have been able to secure more competitive DRAM conditions between 1987 and 1990 and maintain a strong domestic DRAM capacity at the same time.

Recently, many of the concerns about the dependence of US computer producers on Japanese DRAM suppliers have been echoed with respect to Japanese dominance in liquid crystal displays (LCDs). Indeed, the dependence in the LCD case is even more dramatic. By mid-1990, Japanese electronics companies supplied nearly 90 percent of the world's LCD market, almost exclusively through exports from Japan. Ten leading Japanese companies, most of them vertically integrated producers of electronic components and systems, now control over 80 percent of this market. No US company except IBM can match the technological position of the Japanese companies, and IBM's facilities are located in Japan (Ernst and O'Connor 1991, 91).

LCDs are an essential input in and account for an increasing share of the total value added of many electronic products, in particular laptop computers.[68] LCDs are also an input in many technologically advanced weapons systems. Under current market conditions, US producers of both commercial and military systems that need LCDs depend on a small group of Japanese suppliers operating almost entirely from Japanese locations. The market is concentrated both geographically and structurally. As a consequence, US users of LCDs are vulnerable to potential strategic behavior by their Japanese suppliers in a variety of forms, including unfavorable prices and delayed or erratic deliveries of the latest devices. In addition, the small US producers of LCDs are vulnerable to strategic behavior to deter their expansion or force their exit. The Advanced Display Manufacturers of America (ADMA), an industry group that brought a successful antidumping action against Japanese display manufacturers in 1990, cites evidence of such behavior in its antidumping petition (Hart 1992). Without attempting to judge the merits of this case, it is easy to conclude that the dominance of the Japanese suppliers in the LCD industry gives them both the incentive and the capability to engage in such behavior.

In July 1991 the ADMA won its antidumping suit against the Japanese, and stiff antidumping duties of nearly 63 percent were imposed on active-matrix

---

68. For the next generation of personal computers and workstations, now being designed, semiconductors and displays alone are estimated to account for more than half of the total hardware cost, and this trend is likely to continue (Ernst and O'Connor 1991, 43).

LCDs, a product line in which the Japanese currently account for over 90 percent of the world market. This decision was strongly criticized by the US computer manufacturers, especially Apple and IBM, which are the largest users of Japanese imports of these displays for their laptop and notebook computers. Since the imposition of duties applied only to imports, and since there was no attempt to control Japanese prices in other markets (as there was in the SCTA), the effect of the decision has been to make the United States a high-price island, and to encourage American computer makers to move their production facilities off-shore. In the wake of the decision's announcement, they immediately threatened to do so.[69]

The use of the antidumping remedy in the LCD case, although understandable from the American industry's point of view, is a mistake from the national point of view. Its negative consequences are easily predictable. Higher prices on Jap-anese imports will not save the US LCD industry and will harm US industries using LCDs as inputs, encouraging them to migrate to lower-cost production locations abroad. In this sense, the decision is a kind of reverse (or perverse) industrial policy, pitting the interests of the successful American computer in-dustry against the interests of the fledgling but doomed American display in-dustry. Most US LCD companies—including all of the companies involved in the antidumping petition—are small specialty producers and cannot compete with their much larger, vertically integrated Japanese rivals on costs or access to capital. Indeed, some American producers have found it difficult to raise capital precisely because the US capital market sees the LCD industry as a Japanese monopoly, meaning that strategic behavior on the part of Japanese suppliers precludes the profitable long-term expansion of American competitors (National Advisory Committee on Semiconductors 1991, Hart 1992).

If the United States decides that it is important to have a global LCD industry that is less concentrated both structurally and geographically than it is today, something other than an antidumping remedy will be required. So far, the American users of LCDs who stand to lose the most from strategic behavior by their Japanese suppliers seem unconcerned about the risks, or are seeking private solutions, such as IBM's formation of a cooperative production facility in Japan. Only the US Defense Department has expressed misgivings about the situation, and the Defense Advanced Research Projects Agency (DARPA) has provided funds to support research projects by American producers on advanced display technologies with military applications.

Ultimately, if the United States decides that broader measures are required, two policy options deserve consideration (see Borrus and Hart 1992): policies, such as the relaxation of antitrust regulations or the provision of public funds for generic R&D, to encourage greater cooperation or vertical integration be-tween American suppliers and American users; and policies to promote domestic high-volume production, perhaps through encouraging foreign direct invest-ment by Japanese suppliers. In a promising development in August 1992, DARPA

---

69. An IBM executive called the ITC decision an eviction notice from the US government to the fastest-growing segment of the American computer industry (*The New Republic*, 9 December 1991, 18). The Japanese computer producers that had located assembly facilities for laptops in the United States also threatened to relocate back to Japan. Ironically, their threatened decision was made easier by the elimination of tariffs on imports of Japanese laptops as part of the negotiations for the 1991 semiconductor trade agreement.

announced a plan to establish and fund a consortium of US companies to refine manufacturing techniques for next-generation displays. The consortium is to be funded by both DARPA and industry participants and is to concentrate on innovations in process technologies that have the potential to benefit both producers and users of displays. The proposed DARPA initiative bears striking similarities to Sematech, another DARPA–financed project that has helped to reinvigorate the American semiconductor and semiconductor equipment industries. (Sematech is described in greater detail at the end of this chapter.)

Active-matrix LCD technology was an American invention. The fact that the Japanese are the dominant producers of this technology cannot be explained by Japanese trade practices. Market access barriers in Japan have not been a significant issue in this industry. Nor need one attribute predatory intentions to the pricing strategies of the Japanese companies, which can afford to undercut their American competitors on the basis of lower costs and deeper pockets. The ADMA's antidumping petition cited an interview with a Toshiba executive who claimed that his company was prepared to accept red ink for five to six years in order to participate in the display industry (Hart 1992, 9). But this claim was not necessarily predatory, although it doubtlessly reflected Toshiba's deep pockets. Weaknesses in manufacturing capabilities and shortfalls in the availability of long-term capital have been the major sources of the competitive difficulties of American producers (Florida and Browdy 1991). No trade policy response can solve these problems.

Lessons About Foreign Investment as a Substitute for Trade

Ironically, in the long run the SCTA's greatest benefit for the United States as a production location—but not necessarily for the structure of the global semiconductor industry, and certainly not for US–owned semiconductor companies—may be substantial direct investment by the Japanese firms. Although Japanese semiconductor managers believe that it is preferable to produce in Japan—in terms of costs, management of engineers, and control of production—they are resigned to shifting more of their operations to the United States and Europe to avoid future trade friction.[70] As table 4.9 indicates, between 1986 and 1994 the share of offshore production in total production by Japanese semiconductor companies is projected to rise from 6 percent to 28 percent.

By the end of 1990 there were five Japanese fabrication facilities for semiconductors in the United States, four of them established after the SCTA went into effect. Four of the five produced memory chips. The five facilities are owned by Mitsubishi (1989), NEC (1984 and 1987), Hitachi (1989), and Fujitsu (1988). By the end of 1990, only Sony and Toshiba among the major Japanese suppliers did not have American fabrication facilities, and both had plans to build them by the mid-1990s. According to intentions announced to date, the Japanese companies will construct 11 new fabrication facilities in the United States during the 1990s.

In addition to new greenfield investments in such facilities, the Japanese semiconductor companies and their suppliers have spearheaded a wave of ac-

---

70. This observation is based on interviews with managers of Japanese firms in December 1989.

Table 4.9 Shares of production of integrated circuits produced offshore, by home country of parent, 1980–94
(percentages)

Home country or region	1980	1981	1982	1983	1984	1985	1986	1987	1988	1989	1990	1991	1992	1993[a]	1994[a]
Japan	0	0	0	0	3	4	6	8	10	15	20	22	25	27	28
United States	50	65	74	71	66	70	67	66	67	65	64	63	62	61	61
Europe	50	35	25	27	30	25	29	28	26	25	24	21	20	20	19
Asia and Pacific	0	0	0	0	0	0	0	0	0	0	3	5	5	5	6

a. Projected.
Source: Dataquest. Data reproduced with permission.

quisitions of American producers of semiconductors and semiconductor equipment and materials. According to a new study, of the 60 foreign acquisitions of American companies in the semiconductor industry between October 1988 and April 1992, 51 were by Japanese companies. The Japanese also accounted for 30 out of a total of 39 foreign acquisitions of American semiconductor equipment producers during this period (Spencer 1992). Growing Japanese ownership of the American semiconductor equipment industry has occurred in the context of a growing Japanese share of the global industry. Between 1982 and 1990 the world market share of US equipment makers fell from 70 percent to 45 percent; by contrast, the share of Japanese companies increased from 25 percent to 49 percent (according to numbers provided by Sematech). In particular product segments, the US decline was even sharper. For example, in lithography equipment, which is used to transfer integrated circuit patterns onto silicon wafers, the share of US companies plummeted from 71 percent in 1983 to 29 percent in 1988 (US General Accounting Office, National Security and International Affairs Division 1991). The decline in the US share of the industry producing semiconductor materials has been equally precipitous. MITI's designation of this industry as a priority sector touched off a stampede of investment by Japanese companies that contributed to overcapacity, lower prices, and the withdrawal of American competitors. Consequently, the Japanese share of the materials market rose from 21 percent in 1980 to 73 percent in 1990, while the share of US suppliers declined accordingly.[71]

The surge of Japanese investment in the US semiconductor industry and in other high-technology industries has sparked a heated policy controversy. On one side are those who argue that foreign direct investment brings substantial benefits in the form of jobs, capital, technological know-how, and local community externalities. Indeed, as noted in chapter 2, a growing body of empirical evidence on foreign direct investment in the United States supports this argument.

Proponents of foreign direct investment also maintain that foreign affiliates bring special technological or organizational skills that allow them to compete in the United States despite initial cost and marketing disadvantages against more entrenched American companies. In other words, direct investment makes economic sense only when the foreign investor has unique, company-specific advantages that more than offset the often-substantial cost disadvantages of setting up operations away from headquarters. Consumers in the host country— in this case the United States—benefit as a result of the greater competition these advantages engender in the domestic marketplace.

On the other side of the controversy are those who emphasize three possible disadvantages of foreign direct investment. First, it may actually displace or deter the entry or expansion of US–owned companies, which still locate much more of their production, quality jobs, and R&D in the United States than foreign companies do.[72]

Second, foreign direct investment may reduce market competition. If, for example, foreign investment knocks out one or more domestic competitors,

---

71. For an up-to-date, detailed survey of trends in the equipment and materials industries, see US International Trade Commission (1991).

72. For evidence on this point and a more complete discussion of some of the possible disadvantages of foreign direct investment, see Tyson (1991).

either by buying them out directly or by squeezing them out gradually, the result may be a more concentrated industry both nationally and globally, with the remaining firms able to exercise significant market power. Most of the empirical studies of foreign direct investment fail to analyze its effects on industry structure and long-run competitive dynamics. Does a foreign acquisition result in the exit of a competitor, and will the resulting concentration in an industry deter the entry of future competitors? These questions are rarely posed, let alone answered.

Third, foreign direct investment could threaten national security by transferring control over key military technologies to foreign firms or investors in concentrated industries. As a result of their market power, these firms in turn could place conditions or restrictions on the sale of such technologies to American users.

Concern over foreign direct investment in the US semiconductor industry since 1986 has focused on its possible adverse effects on both market competition and national security. Because semiconductors are a indispensable input throughout the electronics complex, strategic control over their supply by a concentrated Japanese oligopoly poses a threat to downstream producers throughout the world. It also poses a threat to American military capabilities that rely on high-technology electronics.

The growing concentration of the global semiconductor equipment and materials industries by a handful of Japanese companies poses a similar strategic threat to both commercial and defense interests. The commercial threat has already had observable consequences. According to a 1990 study by the Defense Science Board, Nikon, one of only two Japanese suppliers of certain kinds of semiconductor manufacturing equipment, withheld its latest models from foreign customers for up to 24 months after making them available to Japanese customers.[73] In another recent study, the Department of Commerce warned that one factor contributing to the loss of US technological and industrial leadership in the semiconductor industry is the "high level of foreign acquisitions throughout the semiconductor supply chain" (US Department of Commerce, Bureau of Export Administration, Office of Industrial Resource Administration 1991). Most of these acquisitions have been by the Japanese companies that are themselves the major suppliers and/or *keiretsu* associates of the Japanese semiconductor companies.

Some of these acquisitions have had dramatic effects on industry structure. As an illustration, Sony's acquisition of Materials Research Corporation, a major US manufacturer of semiconductor equipment, caused the share of the world market for so-called sputtering equipment supplied by US–owned companies to drop from 60 percent to 2 percent. By acquiring Semi-Gas Systems, which accounted for 38 percent of the American market for gas cabinets, Nippon Sanso raised its share of this market from 2 percent to 40 percent.

In principle, when a foreign investment or acquisition in the United States has potentially significant anticompetitive effects on market structure, it can be investigated and blocked by the Justice Department, but this has rarely been done. Perhaps signaling a new willingness to monitor these effects, the Justice Department investigated and filed suit against the sale of Semi-Gas Systems to

---

73. Defense Science Board Task Force, *Foreign Ownership and Control of US Industry*, released by the office of Congressman Mel Levine (D-CA), 13 May 1991.

Nippon Sanso, even after the interagency Committee on Foreign Investment in the United States (CFIUS) had approved the takeover on national security grounds. Ultimately a US district court ruled that there were no antitrust grounds for preventing the sale, and it was completed.

Review by the Justice Department of the consequences of foreign direct investment for both national and global industry structure is especially important in vital input industries such as semiconductors, and in cases in which there is a presumption that the foreign investor has engaged in or is likely to engage in anticompetitive behavior against American companies either at home or abroad. For example, it makes little sense not to screen the acquisitions of American semiconductor and semiconductor equipment manufacturers by the Japanese companies that engaged in dumping and cooperative pricing and investment behavior between 1986 and 1990. Yet neither the Justice Department nor any other government agency has regularly undertaken such monitoring.

In principle, foreign acquisitions of American semiconductor and semiconductor equipment manufacturers, like all foreign acquisitions in defense-related industries, can be monitored for their possible adverse effects on national security in accordance with the Exon-Florio amendment to the 1988 trade act. In practice, however, the CFIUS, the interagency panel to which the President has delegated this authority, has been remarkably passive. Between October 1988 and the summer of 1992, the CFIUS received notification of 700 proposed investments. During this time period, according to a data base developed by the Economic Strategy Institute (Spencer 1992), there were at least 600 foreign acquisitions of American high-technology companies. Of these investments, 60 were related to semiconductors, 30 to semiconductor equipment, and 63 to advanced materials. Nonetheless, the CFIUS chose to investigate only 14 of the 700 cases of which it received advance notification, and it ultimately chose to block only one: the proposed acquisition of an aerospace components manufacturer by a Chinese company. In three other cases, the proposed acquisition was restructured and finally cleared by CFIUS. Only one of these three involved the acquisition of a semiconductor equipment supplier, and the foreign company involved was German, not Japanese. As already noted, the CFIUS reviewed and approved without change Nippon Sanso's proposed acquisition of Semi-Gas on national security grounds (Spencer 1991).

A prudent policy toward foreign direct investment when it involves a product or industry deemed critical to national security should follow two basic principles. First, it should use requirements for national ownership or local production by foreign suppliers to enhance national control over suppliers regardless of their nationality. Second, it should seek a diversity of suppliers to maintain a competitive global supply base (Moran 1990). The first principle motivated the CFIUS's decision to require that the German firm Hüls A.G., as part of its acquisition of Monsanto, keep production and development of Monsanto's eight-inch silicon chip in the United States.[74] Both principles motivated the departments of Defense and Commerce to cooperate with IBM and other American companies to find a domestic buyer for Perkin-Elmer—the only American semiconductor manufacturer working in the photolithography area—to prevent its

---

74. In addition, Hüls agreed not to transfer this technology abroad for five years and to make its output of silicon chips available to Sematech.

acquisition by Nikon, its major Japanese competitor and the dominant global supplier. As a result of these cooperative efforts, Perkin-Elmer ultimately sold its photolithography business to Silicon Valley Group, a California startup company, and with the help of Sematech (see below) has since developed a new lithography technology to challenge Nikon's virtual monopoly of this product niche.[75]

The CFIUS's record to date indicates that neither of the two national security principles suggested here has been accorded much significance. The CFIUS has no authority to impose performance requirements on foreign investors. In the Hüls case, the company voluntarily offered during its CFIUS review to commit itself to continued US production of Monsanto's eight-inch chip. Recently, however, a Treasury Department representative on the CFIUS recommended against voluntary performance conditions, stating that the government opposes such conditions in principle.[76]

Nor, as the Semi-Gas Systems example illustrates, has the CFIUS addressed the issue of an acquisition's effect on the number or the diversity of suppliers. Certainly, there is no evidence suggesting that the CFIUS has ever considered the health of domestically owned producers, the current level of foreign ownership in an industry, or possible anticompetitive behavior by the acquiring company. Indeed, in 1990 the panel approved a pending acquisition by a Japanese company of the last remaining American producer of ultrahigh polysilicon, an advanced material developed on an Air Force contract for the Strategic Defense Initiative project; and it did so despite the fact that there was a pending antitrust case by the American company against the Japanese acquiring company and six other Japanese firms for allegedly forming a cartel to manipulate world polysilicon prices (Spencer 1991). In like manner the CFIUS has failed to review most of the acquisitions of American producers of semiconductors and semiconductor equipment by Japanese companies; and it has done so despite evidence of their anticompetitive behavior vis-à-vis American companies, despite their dominant shares in the world market, and despite the fact that some of the targeted American companies are participants in Sematech.

The actions of the CFIUS to date indicate that it is not seriously concerned about the potential national security threat, let alone the strategic economic threat, posed by Japanese control over the semiconductor industry and its major equipment and materials suppliers. This book's evidence about the business practices of the large, vertically integrated Japanese companies that dominate the semiconductor industry challenges the wisdom of the CFIUS position. As D. Allan Bromley, the President's science and technology adviser, recently noted, a "coherent purchasing program" organized by another nation could gradually

---

75. For more on this deal, see US International Trade Commission (1991, 4–10, 4–11).

76. For example, Nippon Sanso offered to separate itself through a so-called confidentiality agreement from Sematech-led research to which Semi-Gas employees were privy, but the Treasury Department gave its approval to the deal even though there was no follow-up on the confidentiality offer, and no agreement has as yet been signed. The United States, meanwhile, is leading the charge against performance requirements on foreign direct investment in the Uruguay Round discussions.

"nibble away" US control over its strategic technologies (quoted in Spencer 1991, 3).

To argue that foreign acquisitions of high-technology companies should be monitored more thoroughly for their effects on global competition and national security does not mean that such acquisitions should be actively discouraged. The majority of them are likely to be beneficial, and when necessary they can be modified to address legitimate concerns, as was done in the Hüls case. In other cases, a credible screening process may motivate private-sector actors to devise a purchase plan to deter a foreign acquisition that has dubious ramifications for market structure or national security. The Perkin-Elmer experience provides a precedent for such an approach. In such cases the government can play a constructive initiating or supporting role. For example, the Defense Science Board (1991) recommends that for national security reasons the Defense Department should sometimes use such instruments as loans and purchase guarantees, R&D credits, and procurement to motivate US companies to purchase a domestic firm targeted for foreign acquisition.

Ultimately, foreign direct investment, whether by acquisition or by the establishment of greenfield operations, must be evaluated against its counterfactual: what would be the result if the investment did not take place? Such investment is likely to be preferable when the alternative is increasing dependence on imports or the failure to develop a new technology because of limited domestic capital or manufacturing capabilities. In such cases, investment by domestically owned companies may be the first-best outcome over the long run, but it may not be an available option. Under these circumstances, foreign investment is a second-best alternative.

Lessons About the Pitfalls of Unilateralism

By design, the SCTA and the NSCTA have worldwide ramifications. Their market access provisions apply to all "foreign-capital affiliated" firms, not just to American suppliers. In other words, market access is defined in multilateral, not bilateral terms. And the SCTA's antidumping provisions were designed to control the pricing behavior of the Japanese companies wherever they sold. But the rest of the world was not included in the negotiation of either part of the agreement. When chip prices soared and supplies became scarce around the world in 1987 and 1988, foreign governments scrambled to promote their own interests.

In the wake of these troubling trends, the Europeans took a number of measures to strengthen their flagging producers. These measures included the initiation of dumping investigations against Japanese producers of DRAMs and EPROMs, which resulted in price undertaking agreements in 1989; the clarification of European dumping rules to identify fabrication as the rule of origin for semiconductors; and the development of JESSI, a pan-European R&D program in semiconductor technology with a planned budget of about 4 billion ecu (about $5½ billion) over a six-year period from 1989 to 1996.

Together these new policy initiatives, along with the 14 percent European tariff on semiconductor imports, touched off a boom in direct investment in Europe by both American and Japanese semiconductor producers. By the summer of 1990, most of the major producers from both countries were either building or had announced plans to build new European fabrication facilities. In some cases these substituted for similar production capacities elsewhere. For example, LSI Logic, citing overcapacity, closed a semiconductor facility in California while opening a comparable facility in Europe to avoid being shut out of the European market (Howell et al. 1992, 303). Japanese producers, however, dominated the direct investment boom in the European semiconductor industry, posing a long-term threat to American producers, who supplied 44 percent of the European semiconductor market in 1991 through both exports and local European production.

European policy initiatives to strengthen European semiconductor producers have been motivated mainly by the Japanese challenge. Nonetheless, these initiatives have produced spillover frictions between the United States and Europe. For example, Europe has interpreted the antiscrewdriver regulations of its antidumping law in ways that have encouraged Japanese companies to choose semiconductor chips produced by European companies instead of chips produced by their American competitors. (Europe's antidumping laws are discussed in greater detail in chapter 6.) Only after a US protest did the Europeans postpone a value-added proposal for printed circuit boards requiring that at least 45 percent of a board's components be of EC origin, a condition that had this effect on Japanese sourcing practices.[77]

The Americans and the Europeans have also run into disagreements about eligibility requirements for membership in JESSI and Sematech. IBM was especially eager to join JESSI, but its initial inquiries were rebuffed because Sematech was organized to rule out foreign participants. Ultimately, IBM was admitted to JESSI, even though no European participants were admitted to Sematech. But IBM is a special case: it has substantial European R&D operations, it is involved in a major cooperative research and production venture with Siemens (a JESSI member) for next-generation memory chips, and it has world-class semiconductor process and product technologies.

Europe and the United States share common interests in the semiconductor industry. American suppliers currently hold a larger share of the European market than either the European or the Japanese producers. Both European and American suppliers and users of semiconductors want to avoid the strategic threats posed by the market power of their Japanese competitors. Privately, American and European companies are working together on a variety of cooperative ventures to address these threats.

At the company level, the most ambitious joint venture is the one between IBM and Siemens. Both companies were initially motivated to participate in a joint R&D effort on DRAM process technologies in response to their common concerns about excessive dependence on Japanese chip suppliers. Since then the two companies have extended their joint venture to production of 4M DRAMS in Europe. Recently, both companies have announced plans to join with Toshiba in a new R&D joint venture for 16M DRAMs, which are likely to become the mainstay of computers by the end of the decade. European semiconductor producers have also participated in a number of cooperative development efforts with other American companies. For example, several European companies are

---

77. For a more complete discussion of the printed circuit board conflict between the United States and Europe, see Flamm (1990).

involved in the ACE consortium, initiated by a number of American computer manufacturers, including Microsoft, Compaq, and MIPPS, to merge the DOS and the UNIX operating systems. This consortium is partly a response by some American computer companies to the competitive challenges posed by recently announced cooperative development efforts between IBM and Apple. But it is also a response to the Japanese computer strategy of developing systems that depend on sophisticated hardware components rather than on proprietary software operating systems.

There are also cooperative efforts between American and European semiconductor companies at the industry level. The SIA and the European Electronic Components Association (EECA), for example, have been holding regular talks to develop common positions on trade policy issues. Not surprisingly, their greatest success to date has been in developing common proposals on questions of dumping—in particular, how to construct costs to measure dumping, how to speed up the dumping remedy process, and what kinds of remedies to impose. In some areas, however, trade conflicts continue to divide American and European producers. For example, American producers would like to see the elimination of European tariffs, while European producers would not. In addition, the Europeans have lobbied for balanced regional trade in semiconductors, proposing what would amount to a regional managed trade arrangement. But American companies, committed to improved market access rather than managed trade, have rejected such proposals.

The semiconductor industry is a global oligopoly in which a relatively small number of firms, headquartered primarily in the United States, Europe, Japan, and Korea, produce, invest, and sell throughout the world. It is also an industry in which trade outcomes are manipulated by government policies, and in which bilateral trade barriers and trade deals have proliferated during the last decade, with spillover effects on other nations. The global nature of the industry and the ever-present hand of government policy make it an ideal candidate for a plurilateral agreement between interested governments to achieve deeper integration not only on trade issues, such as tariffs and dumping regulations, but also on related policy issues such as R&D support, procurement, foreign direct investment, and business practices. To be successful, such an agreement requires credible monitoring and enforcement capabilities. Recently, the European Commission has called for a special consultative forum on semiconductor trade within the Organization for Economic Cooperation and Development. The United States should support the European proposal, since the development of such a forum could serve as the first step in the development of a sectoral agreement along the lines suggested here. In a global industry like semiconductors, deeper regional integration at the aggregate level is not an effective substitute for deeper plurilateral integration at the sectoral level.

Lessons About Domestic Policies

If the United States wants to maintain a domestically based, domestically owned semiconductor industry, either as anticartel insurance or because of the industry's strategic significance in both the military and the economic sense, it must foster a supportive policy environment at home. Some important actions have already been taken, including the easing of antitrust restrictions on cooperative

R&D projects and reductions in the cost of capital attributable to a change in the monetary and fiscal mix. Other general policy measures that would contribute to the health of the semiconductor industry are a permanent increase in the R&D tax credit,[78] the easing of antitrust restrictions on cooperative production projects, and increased support for engineering education. All of these measures are currently under consideration and should be adopted.

In addition to these economy-wide measures, the government should continue its support for Sematech, the cooperative R&D project involving several American companies to develop and disseminate advanced semiconductor process technologies.[79] Sematech grew out of industry and government concern that the Japanese semiconductor companies were outspending and outperforming their American competitors in manufacturing process R&D and capital equipment. Fueling this concern was a study (National Science Foundation, National Materials Advisory Board 1986) that asserted that the Japanese suppliers had moved ahead in optical lithography and in several areas of emerging technological importance such as x-ray lithography. The study also found that the level of R&D work under way in at least 10 Japanese firms was matched by only two American firms. Many American semiconductor users, including IBM, lobbied for Sematech's creation because of their interests in ensuring that the semiconductor chips available from American producers were technologically equivalent and price-competitive with those available from Japanese producers. By 1988, when Sematech began, these interests were sorely threatened by the market power of the Japanese DRAM suppliers and the contraction of the American industry for semiconductor equipment. Indeed, by that time American producers had little alternative but to turn to Nikon for certain kinds of essential chipmaking machines.

Sematech is a five-year project, scheduled to end in 1993. It is budgeted at approximately $200 million a year, half of which is to be supplied by the industry participants and half by federal, state, and local governments. In fact, the Department of Defense, through DARPA, has supplied the bulk of public funds, in the amount of about $100 million per year during the last four years.

The Defense Department has always supplied R&D support for the semiconductor industry, but over the years its research projects have concentrated on narrow military applications. According to one estimate, in recent years as much as 70 percent of Defense Department R&D support for the semiconductor industry has concentrated on developing hardened chip technology capable of withstanding a direct nuclear hit (see Yager 1991). Sematech is therefore an important break with past trends in Defense Department R&D support, and one that reflects an awareness of new realities in the semiconductor industry. During

---

78. The tax treatment of depreciation is also an issue for the American semiconductor industry. Eighty-eight percent of the acquisition of semiconductor equipment can be written off by Japanese companies during the first year, compared with only 20 percent for American companies, who must wait four years to accumulate the deductions captured by Japanese firms in the first year.

79. Sematech includes 14 American semiconductor companies, among them IBM, AT&T, and all of the major merchant suppliers. In addition, 80 percent of the American semiconductor equipment manufacturers are members. Membership for American companies is voluntary and depends on their willingness to contribute to the project's financing and to agree to its terms about licensing research results and the like.

the course of the 1980s, the commercial sector, not the military sector, was responsible for the major technical advances in semiconductor process and product technology. Whereas in the past innovations developed for the military produced commercial spinoffs, in the decade of the 1980s the reverse was true: innovations developed for commercial use produced military "spin-ons." This has led some decision makers within the Defense Department to conclude that it should focus more of its research support on commercial technologies with "dual-use" applications (i.e., both civilian and military). Sematech fits the bill, while at the same time addressing the Defense Department's desire to preserve domestic semiconductor production capabilities for national security purposes.

Even Sematech's most ardent supporters do not predict that it will give American producers of either semiconductors or semiconductor equipment the power to recapture their lost market share from their Japanese or other foreign competitors. A fair assessment of Sematech should focus instead on its specific objectives: the development and dissemination of frontier process technology for American semiconductor companies; and the survival of competitive American producers of semiconductor equipment to guarantee a competitive structure for the global industry. Sematech's results to date indicate success on both scores. As a result of the dissemination of new manufacturing processes developed by Sematech, American chip manufacturers are likely to reach parity in process technologies with the best of their Japanese competitors by the end of 1992, thereby eliminating an earlier Japanese advantage.

Equally noteworthy, Sematech has revitalized some segments of the American semiconductor equipment industry. For example, as a result of its cooperation with domestic equipment companies in Sematech, Motorola has switched from Japanese to American suppliers for a large portion (75 percent to 90 percent) of its equipment purchases for its new American fabrication facility. Intel, too, has increased its equipment purchases from American suppliers. Perhaps most dramatically, in 1991, after a decade of decline even greater than that which occurred in the semiconductor industry, the share of American producers in the global market for semiconductor equipment increased by 3 percentage points, from 44 percent to 47 percent, according to data provided by VLSI Research.

According to its participants, Sematech has fostered these gains in part by improving communication between the American semiconductor industry and the American semiconductor equipment industry, which has traditionally been fragmented, disputatious, and undercapitalized, especially in comparison with its Japanese counterpart. In addition, Sematech, in conjunction with the coordinated buyout of Perkin-Elmer's lithography business by SVG, has been instrumental in the development of a new lithography technology, Micrascan, that is a competitive alternative to lithography technology available from the Japanese. IBM's access to Micrascan is one reason why Toshiba and Siemens were attracted to participate in a joint venture with IBM for R&D in 16M DRAMS.

Sematech is defended by its proponents as a generic research project whose results will benefit all participating firms without determining market outcomes, but will be near enough to market competition to have practical significance. For many economists, however, the generic nature of Sematech research is not enough to justify its use of public funds. According to traditional economic analysis, the government should assist a particular firm or industry only when such assistance will clearly provide public benefits beyond those realized by the firm or industry in question. From this perspective, the fact that Sematech merely benefits all of its participants is beside the point.

Ultimately, the justification for government support for Sematech depends on the national benefits resulting from securing more-competitive structures for the global semiconductor and semiconductor equipment industries and from maintaining American technological and production capabilities in both of them. Some of these benefits are related to national security narrowly defined; some are related to the commercial interests of the users of semiconductors; and some are related to the local technological insights and learning nurtured by domestic producers and fostered by Sematech's ongoing research programs.[80] Because none of these benefits can be precisely specified or measured, some observers question their very existence. But to conclude that such benefits do not exist is just as much a matter of faith and judgment as to conclude that they do.

In light of the obvious military significance of the semiconductor industry, the strong *prima facie* case for its economic significance, and the compelling evidence from the 1986–90 period of the dangers of Japanese market domination, it is more prudent to err in the direction of supporting industry-specific programs, like Sematech, when they are not needed than in the direction of opposing them when they are needed. The latter error is likely to be considerably more costly in terms of forgone security and economic benefits.

To reiterate a theme that resonates throughout this book, in the semiconductor and semiconductor equipment industries, as in most high-technology industries, a defensive trade policy cannot substitute for supportive domestic policies. And given the heavy hand of government intervention around the world, the inexorable trends in underlying production conditions, and the current market dominance of Japanese producers, economy-wide measures of support, although necessary, are not sufficient. Despite its pitfalls, an industrial policy approach is also required. If the United States fails to choose the semiconductor industry as a winner, American producers may well become long-run losers in the rigged game of international competition.

---

80. Sematech is directly providing some funds to support ongoing semiconductor research and training at a number of universities.

5

Industrial Policy and Trade Management in the Commercial Aircraft Industry

Historical Decisions in a Strategic Industry

Economics of the Industry

History of the Industry

The Economic Analysis of Government Intervention in the Commercial Aircraft Industry: The Case of Airbus

Trade Friction in the Aircraft Industry

Challenges Facing the American Commercial Aircraft Industry

Conclusions

Historical Decisions in a Strategic Industry

"Judged against almost any criterion of performance—growth in output, exports, productivity, or innovation—the civilian aircraft industry must be considered a star performer in the [postwar] U.S. economy" (Mowery and Rosenberg 1982, 101–02). The industry is the country's largest exporter, running a net trade surplus of $17.8 billion in 1991. American producers account for almost 80 percent of the world's commercial aircraft fleet (excluding the former Soviet Union). Not surprisingly, the commercial aircraft industry is a symbol of America's technological and market dominance. But today American producers face two critical challenges: an internal challenge resulting from cutbacks in defense procurement and indirect military subsidies, and an external challenge resulting from the growing competitive strength of the European aircraft consortium, Airbus Industrie. Continued American success depends on how American companies and the American government respond to these two challenges.

Airbus is a government-backed consortium of companies from France (Aérospatiale), Great Britain (British Aerospace), Germany (Deutsche Airbus), and Spain (CASA). After two decades of massive government support, Airbus has developed a family of competitive aircraft models and by 1991 had captured about one-third of the world market for large commercial jets. It has achieved technological parity with Boeing and replaced McDonnell Douglas as the second-

This chapter was coauthored with Pei-Hsiung Chin, a Ph.D. candidate in economics at the University of California, Berkeley.

largest producer in the world. Since 1990 the Europeans have been debating when to subsidize and launch the A350, a 600-seat jumbo jet about one-and-one-half times the size of the Boeing 747. A successful launch of the A350 would pose a major competitive threat to Boeing, the leading American producer, which claimed an average of about 55 percent of the global market during the last five years (table 5.1).[1]

Meanwhile McDonnell Douglas, the United States' second-largest commercial producer and its largest military contractor, is facing possible bankruptcy in its commercial operations. Its most recent commercial model, the MD-11, has not delivered either its promised flight range or the revenues required to develop a complete family of aircraft for future rounds of competition. Substantial reductions in military procurement, with more to come, threaten McDonnell Douglas's military operations as well. Even under the most optimistic scenarios, further contractions in these operations seem inevitable. At the end of 1991, the company sought relief from the financial crunch in its commercial operations through the proposed sale of 40 percent of its equity to Taiwan Aerospace Company. Although this deal was attractive for McDonnell Douglas, it presented several drawbacks for the American aircraft industry as a whole and for its American suppliers. As of this writing, it looks as if the deal has fallen through, and the company's fate as a commercial aircraft producer remains uncertain.

How should the United States respond to the internal and external challenges confronting the American commercial aircraft industry? What trade and industrial policies should be adopted to ensure that the nation continues to benefit from the jobs, profits, and export earnings that industry leadership would guarantee? This chapter seeks to answer these questions through a historical analysis of global competition in the industry during the postwar period.

Informed policymaking in the commercial aircraft industry requires an understanding of its unique economics, which are described in the next section of this chapter. Immense technological risk and huge upfront development costs, as well as economies of scale, scope, and learning, drive the industry toward a natural monopoly with a single producer dominating the global market. Such an outcome is desirable for production efficiency, but this is not the only criterion for evaluating the welfare consequences of the industry's structure. Another criterion is dynamic efficiency—the extent and pace of technological change and product differentiation, both of which are of critical importance to the downstream air carrier industry. Since the launch of a new aircraft always involves substantial risk, and since the cost advantages of staying with a proven model are enormous, there is an understandable incentive for the incumbent producer to postpone innovation. In other words, the industry's economics give rise to an inherent tension between static production efficiency and dynamic efficiencies, and between the welfare of the producer and that of its customers.

In fact, as the evidence in the third part of this chapter indicates, persistent government intervention both at home and abroad has prevented a natural

---

1. In 1990, Boeing's share of market deliveries was 45 percent, compared with Airbus's share of 34 percent and McDonnell Douglas's share of 21 percent. *Collision Course in Commercial Aircraft: Boeing-Airbus-McDonnell Douglas, 1991,* Case No. 9-391-106, Harvard Business School, Exhibit 5, 1991.

monopoly outcome. Moreover, in keeping with the analysis suggested here, this intervention has had the effect of encouraging product differentiation and technological change, to the benefit of the air carrier industry.

Throughout much of its history, the American aircraft industry has benefited from a makeshift but nonetheless effective industrial policy. Although the goals of this policy have been primarily military in nature, it has had unintended and unavoidable spillovers on the commercial marketplace. For reasons that are discussed below, indirect industrial policy support for the commercial aircraft industry is no longer nearly as important as it was even fifteen years ago. Nonetheless, because of the industry's economics, the effects of past support are long-lived. Both Boeing's monopoly of the wide-body, long-range market and its consequent position in the global industry have their roots in engine technologies and design competitions funded by the US military. Similarly, McDonnell Douglas's current difficulties can be traced to its head-on competition with Lockheed during the 1960s and 1970s for the wide-body, medium-range market—a mutually destructive competition made possible by the "life pre-servers" provided to both companies by their substantial military operations.

In contrast to American industrial policy support, European industrial policy support for Airbus has had avowedly commercial objectives, although such intervention has often been defended on dual-use grounds (i.e., that technol-ogies developed under this support will have military as well as civilian appli-cations).[2] Given the industry's economics, Airbus would not have stood a chance against American producers without massive development, production, and marketing support during its first 25 years. Because of scale, scope, and learning economies, a potential entrant to the industry faces much higher production costs than do incumbent firms. It takes years of losses for a new firm to develop a family of aircraft and to produce them on a large enough scale to realize economies comparable to those enjoyed by existing firms. Moreover, the upfront development costs and technological risk associated with launching such a family are enormous. Together these conditions pose insurmountable barriers to the entry of new competitors through market means. The visible hand of govern-ment was behind the new European entrant and will be behind any potential new entrants such as Taiwan Aerospace or Mitsubishi in the future.

But why would governments be willing to assume the huge financial costs and risks of promoting a commercial aircraft industry? The answer lies in the industry's "strategic" military and economic significance. Commercial aircraft production is strategic in the conventional military sense because of spillovers between commercial and military operations. Scope economies and technological innovations spill from one side of the industry to the other. All commercial airframe producers are also major military contractors (table 5.2), and the two sides of the industry share an overlapping pool of subcontractors and component suppliers. The synergies between the military's emphasis on performance and flexibility and the commercial sector's emphasis on cost and reliability have been

---

2. The Europeans often justify their subsidies to Airbus on the grounds that a commercial aerospace industry is essential to preserve the technology base required for national se-curity needs. This justification is strikingly similar to the argument the United States has used to justify its federal support for the semiconductor consortium Sematech. A similar observation is made by Moran and Mowery (1991).

Table 5.1 Orders of narrow- and wide-body commercial aircraft, by company and model (units in backlog)

Type of aircraft	1975	1976	1977	1978	1979	1980	1981	1982	1983	1984	1985	1986	1987	1988	1989	1990
Boeing																
Narrow-body aircraft																
707	16	11	17	10	5	23	21	18	25	17	14	16	18	18	13	20
727	66	117	184	196	170	106	39	18	8	0	0	0	0	0	0	0
737	23	21	34	139	138	150	167	134	121	187	353	423	441	615	932	916
757	0	0	0	40	40	112	136	121	113	94	101	79	83	196	372	392
Total narrow-body	105	149	235	385	353	391	363	291	267	298	468	518	542	829	1,317	1,328
Wide-body aircraft																
747	33	20	42	93	101	76	46	29	31	37	54	102	146	173	196	298
767	0	0	0	84	135	156	173	157	118	84	59	55	75	103	191	183
777	0	0	0	0	0	0	0	0	0	0	0	0	0	0	0	49
Total wide-body	33	20	42	177	236	232	219	186	149	121	113	157	221	276	387	530
Total	138	169	277	562	589	635	582	477	416	419	581	675	765	1,105	1,704	1,858
McDonnell Douglas																
Narrow-body aircraft[a]	51	26	55	99	109	106	45	50	61	131	180	203	213	346	423	400
Wide-body aircraft																
DC-10	18	15	30	57	53	25	9	3	0	5	8	6	7	1	0	0
MD-11	0	0	0	0	0	0	0	0	0	0	0	0	29	88	126	175
Total wide-body	18	15	30	57	53	25	9	3	0	5	8	6	36	89	126	175
Total	69	41	85	156	162	131	54	53	61	136	188	209	249	435	549	575

Total by US manufacturers	207	210	362	718	751	766	636	530	477	555	769	884	1,014	1,540	2,253	2,433
Airbus Industrie																
Narrow-body aircraft[b]	0	0	0	0	0	0	25	25	47	51	90	236	294	404	445	663
Wide-body aircraft																
A300	0	0	0	0	104	108	98	44	21	3	17	14	34	34	66	78
A310	0	0	0	0	61	76	88	102	91	72	45	38	45	40	48	70
A330													12	12	110	138
A340													68	71	84	89
Total wide-body	0	0	0	0	165	184	186	146	112	75	62	52	159	157	308	375
Total	0	0	0	0	165	184	211	171	159	126	152	288	453	561	753	1,038
Total by US and European manufacturers	207	210	362	718	916	950	847	701	636	681	921	1,172	1,467	2,101	3,006	3,471

a. Discrepancies between totals and sums of individual items are in the original source.
b. Narrow-body aircraft produced by McDonnell Douglas include the DC-9 and the MD80. Figures for Airbus Industrie from before 1979 are unavailable, but the quantities involved were minor. Narrow-body aircraft produced by Airbus Industrie include the A320 and the A321.
Source: Seidler Amdec Securities, Inc. Data used with permission.

Table 5.2   Aircraft company revenues from military aircraft and related sales, 1989

Company	Millions of dollars	Percentages of total
MBB	783	47.0
Aérospatiale	1,355	33.5
British Aerospace	3,470	53.6
Total Airbus	5,588	46.1
Boeing	4,361	23.4
McDonnell Douglas	5,919	55.5

Source: Office of Technology Assessment, *Competing Economies: America, Europe, and the Pacific Rim* (Washington: Government Printing Office), October 1991.

central to aircraft technology and innovation. A competitive commercial aircraft industry thus contributes to a nation's military prowess.

Complementarity between military and civilian operations also exists because both have recurrent but usually asynchronized business cycles. Without a civilian aircraft industry to keep aerospace engineers and workers actively occupied, the cost of maintaining an independent military aerospace capability with surge capacity would be prohibitive. It is no accident that the countries that boast the major commercial aircraft producers are also the biggest arms-selling democracies. Security concerns alone dictate that both the United States and Europe will continue to produce commercial aircraft. But future defense cuts and conversion ensure that a larger portion of the American aerospace capability will have to rely on the civilian sector than in the past.

The commercial aircraft industry is also strategic in the economic sense. As the evidence in chapter 2 indicates, the industry has made major contributions to the American economy in the form of high-wage and high-skill jobs, R&D support, and exports throughout the postwar period. Some of this evidence is consistent with the proposition that the aircraft industry is "strategic" in the theoretical sense that it generates "excess rents" or higher returns to factors of production than they could earn elsewhere in the economy. Indeed, the industry is widely regarded as the best example of an industry in which strategic, beggar-thy-neighbor, rent-shifting policies may improve national economic welfare. Europe's determined effort to grab a share of the lucrative global market for commercial aircraft from the United States is often understood in terms of such a rent-shifting objective.

How should the United States respond to the challenges now before its commercial aircraft industry in light of its obvious strategic significance? Unfortunately, there are no simple answers to this question. Tired nostrums based on free market ideology are strikingly irrelevant, since they are based on assumptions of perfect competition fundamentally at odds with the industry's production conditions. They are also at odds with political reality given the industry's dual-use features. Government intervention in the industry, both at home and abroad, is likely to be a mainstay of the future just as it has been a persistent feature of the past.

There is no textbook theory of optimal policy choice to guide intervention in a global dual-use industry such as the aircraft industry, in which a monopoly outcome holds the promise of static production efficiencies and substantial rents for the producer but threatens the price and pace of innovation and product differentiation for users. Moreover, the task of striking the appropriate balance between static and dynamic efficiencies and between the interests of producers and consumers is vastly complicated by national boundaries. In a single-supplier world, industry rents would accrue disproportionately to a single nation, although cross-national subcontracting arrangements might provide a mechanism for their broader distribution across a number of countries. Indeed, the proliferation of such arrangements during the postwar period, often the result of intense government arm-twisting, can be understood in just such terms. Even in a single-supplier world, however, the government of the supplying nation would have to weigh the interests of its own producer against those of its consumers—a complicated task in its own right. From a global welfare standpoint, the task is even more daunting since it requires weighing the interests of users in other nations as well.

The characteristics of the aircraft industry are such that neither the simple textbook presumption that foreign subsidies are a gift nor the popular political presumption that they harm domestic economic welfare can be accepted at face value. As strategic trade theory demonstrates, subsidies can shift rents from one country to another. In the aircraft case, by undermining a natural monopoly outcome, subsidies can also reduce global production efficiencies, thereby dissipating as well as shifting global rents. Depending on how subsidies affect the terms of competition, rents can be further dissipated by aggressive price competition or by costly, duplicative rounds of product innovation. But while domestic producers may be harmed, domestic users may be helped by foreign subsidies, especially those aimed at promoting product innovation and differentiation.

Under these circumstances, a prudent response to foreign government intervention in the aircraft industry must balance its possible adverse effects on production efficiency, producer rents, national wage and employment opportunities, national R&D and its associated local spillovers, and national security against its possible beneficial effects on users through enhanced competition on the basis of price, product differentiation, and product innovation. In short, no simple economic theory or political platitude can substitute for a detailed analysis of a particular foreign intervention and the proposed policy response. The last four sections of this chapter provide such an analysis to evaluate the US response to past European subsidies for Airbus, and to suggest appropriate policy reactions to future European subsidies and to possible joint ventures between American producers and foreign suppliers, such as the deal between McDonnell Douglas and Taiwan Aerospace.

Economics of the Industry

Since its inception, the commercial jet airframe industry has been highly concentrated. In 1953, when Boeing was bringing the US industry into the jet age, John McDonald, a leading industry analyst, wrote, "It is pretty clear that all three builders cannot stay in this market; perhaps not even two can make money on jets in the next ten years. The first question is which of the three, Douglas,

Lockheed, or Boeing, is going to drop out" (McDonald 1953, 217). Four decades later, this still describes the industry rather accurately, with Airbus in place of Lockheed and McDonnell Douglas the most vulnerable. Underlying this tendency toward a natural monopoly, first and foremost, is the technology of airframe manufacturing. Airframe technology and innovation limit the number of potential entrants, compel them to compete across whole product families, and shape their strategic interactions in successive product launches, which are ruinously risky. Each product family, as the embodiment of a common set of technology, defines a firm's position in the market. Each successive launch, as an act of innovation, restructures the market. The enormous cost and forbidding risk of new product launches crucially affect market conduct and performance. Analyses that do not take the central importance of innovation into account are inadequate and misleading.

Airframe Technology

Airframe producers integrate numerous technologies and systems, originating from various fields and industries, into ever more efficient and capable means of air transport. A modern jet aircraft consists of millions of components, incorporating a wide range of seemingly unrelated technologies: materials, propulsion, electronics, hydraulics, and aerodynamics, to mention a few. Each of the many constituent systems of a jet aircraft is extremely complex. The $4 billion to $6 billion in upfront R&D expenditure required to develop a new commercial jet is spent mostly on integrating these complex components rather than on their separate development: prototype aircraft development consistently ranks first in research expenditures, followed by expenditures on avionics, propulsion, and aerodynamics (Mowery and Rosenberg 1982, 135).

Airframe technology has two other related features central to the functioning of the industry. One is the importance of technology and innovation exogenous to the industry. As Mowery and Rosenberg (1982, 103) point out, "The aircraft industry is unusual in the extent to which it has benefited from the interindustry flow of innovations that typifies the modern economy . . . reflect[ing] . . . the high degree of systemic complexity embodied in its products." As a whole, outside industries such as metallurgy, petroleum, and electronics have provided a steady stream of innovations that have substantially improved aircraft performance. Another major source of innovations outside the commercial aircraft industry proper is the military sector. With its emphasis on performance and its tolerance of cost, the military side of the industry has generated many technologies with dramatic commercial applications, including the jet engine itself.

Technological uncertainty is the other central feature of the commercial aircraft industry. The interactions of the many individually complex systems in a large aircraft and the resulting overall performance are exceptionally difficult to anticipate from design and engineering data. Unexpected but crucial, even fatal, defects or deficiencies are frequently acknowledged only after test flights. This uncertainty reflects both the complex nature of high-performance system integration and the still-modest state of scientific theory regarding the behavior of key components such as materials (Mowery and Rosenberg 1982).

These technological features of the aircraft industry have important economic consequences. Aircraft manufacturing as complex system integration implies a

Table 5.3 Costs to develop selected commercial aircraft

Aircraft	Year entered service	Development costs		
		Millions of current dollars	Millions of 1991 dollars	Millions of 1991 dollars per seat
McDonnell Douglas DC-3	1936	0.3	3	0.1
McDonnell Douglas DC-6	1947	14	90	1.7
McDonnell Douglas DC-8	1959	112	600	3.8
Boeing 747	1970	1,200	3,300	7.3
Boeing 777		5,000[a]	4,300[a]	14.0[a]

a. Estimated.

Source: Office of Technology Assessment, *Competing Economies: America, Europe, and the Pacific Rim.*

certain cost structure. Technological uncertainty constitutes a major part of the tremendous risk that distinguishes the business. Cost and risk together explain much of the tendency toward concentration. Counteracting this tendency, however, is the fact that the exogenous stream of innovation meanders, sometimes benefiting potential entrants more than incumbents.

Cost Structure and Market Concentration

The cost structure of the commercial aircraft industry is distinguished by unparalleled increasing returns to scale. Scale economies, resulting mainly from huge development costs and strong learning effects, are significant both within a single product and across products, which are differentiated mainly by size and range. As we have seen, the difficulty of systems integration entails huge development expenditures, which represent about two-thirds of fixed cost (table 5.3). In addition, the complex production process results in dramatic learning effects. According to Klepper (1990, 777):

> An essential part of learning appears in the assembly of aircraft. Craftsmanship and timing of thousands of activities are required. Such experience is embodied in the workforce and accumulates with the number of aircraft that have been produced. There is worldwide consensus that aircraft production exhibits a learning elasticity of 0.2—i.e., production costs decrease by 20 percent with a doubling of output.

Aircraft production exhibits substantial scope as well as scale economies. Because some production stages are not unique to a particular type of aircraft, the learning effects realized in the production of one kind of aircraft can influence the marginal cost of producing another (Klepper 1990, 777–78). This cross-learning effect gives rise to a "commonality game" in aircraft design. It is standard practice to spread development costs across products by using common features and parts (figure 5.1 illustrates this commonality for the Airbus family). If a firm wants to exploit scope economies and commonalities, it must develop a family of products sharing technologies and parts.

But a product family provides the firm with more than just cost advantages. It also provides external benefits to its customers. As long as an airline carrier sticks to one basic airframe supplier—or one product family—it can realize

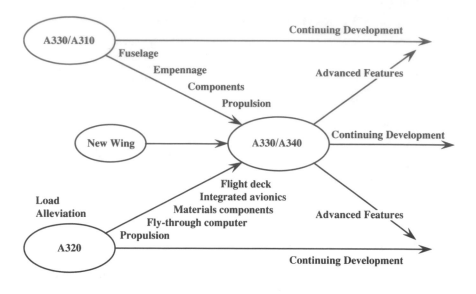

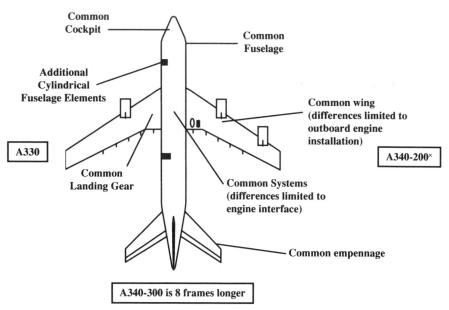

Figure 5.1 Commonality of components among Airbus models. *Source:* Airbus Industrie.

substantial savings in personnel training, maintenance, and inventory. Pilots, for example, have to be certified for particular types of airplanes and require additional training to switch from one type to another (*The Economist*, 1 June 1985, 8). The more similar a new aircraft is to those a pilot has already flown, the less new training is required.

Technological uncertainty and exogeneity are also behind the phenomenon of product families. The more technologically innovative a new aircraft is, the greater the risk that design and manufacturing flaws will frustrate its launch. But the steady stream of exogenous innovations also means that there are always opportunities to make a significantly better aircraft soon after a new design is developed. Cost and risk dictate that firms introduce new products only over an extended period. Both new technological opportunities and competition can motivate a firm to modify its older products for better performance or a different market niche, leading to the phenomenon of "derivatives," or improvements within a particular product line.[3]

Incremental modifications within a product family, although not technologically "interesting," can be economically important. Learning by doing extends beyond the design and production phases into the actual use of a aircraft. Through extended use the performance characteristics of an aircraft design and its elaborately differentiated but interdependent parts become better understood. This allows the full exploitation of the model's potential through incremental improvements.[4]

Scale and scope economies are significant in many industries, but the commercial aircraft industry is special in that it is truly global. Development costs, learning by doing, commonality of design within families, derivatives, and learning by using add up to a cost structure whose potential efficiency scale[5] dwarfs the total world market. Dynamic scale economies do not limit the number of both products and producers so strongly in any other sector. A firm has to sell roughly 600 units of a new airplane just to break even. This usually takes at least eight years—twelve if development time is included. At the beginning of the jet age, 600 aircraft could easily amount to half of the total market (hence McDonald's contemporary estimate, cited above, that at most two firms could survive in the market of the 1950s). Although the world market has grown

---

3. Stretching the fuselage of an existing aircraft is the most common form of derivative production: "The carrying capacity of the airplane depends, first of all, on the capacity of the engines. As engine performance is improved, exploitation of the potential requires redesign or modification of the airframe. The simplest response, as improved engines become available, is merely to stretch the fuselage and add more seats. Indeed, as this phenomenon came to be better understood, most airplanes were deliberately designed in order to facilitate subsequent stretching" (Mowery and Rosenberg 1982, 124).

4. According to Mowery and Rosenberg (1982, 122–23), "In the DC-8 we have an aircraft that has experienced a more than 50 percent reduction in operating energy costs over its life span on a per-seat-mile basis, as well as a [two-fold] increase in productivity . . . although the basic configuration has been largely unchanged and the modifications have been relatively unsophisticated compared to differences between aircraft types."

5. The more conventional term, "minimum efficiency scale," or the scale required to exhaust increasing returns, is not applicable here for reasons discussed in the ensuing sections.

rapidly since then, making room for the efficient production of additional products, the scope economies embodied in a product family continue to exceed the size of the global market. In other words, the production level required to exhaust the scale and scope economies associated with a single product family still exceeds total global demand. Judged solely on the criterion of production efficiency, therefore, the large jet aircraft industry tends toward a natural monopoly.

Product Differentiation and Launch Risk

Production efficiency, however, is only one consideration necessary for evaluating the welfare consequences of a given market structure in this industry. Another is the structure's effects on efficiency in the downstream air carrier industry. A complete analysis of economic efficiency and welfare in the air transport industry must include both the industry that produces commercial aircraft and the industry that uses them to provide air transport services. The productivity and quality of service in the latter industry depend on the production efficiency, product differentiation, and technological progress of the former.[6]

There are, however, underlying conflicts or trade-offs between the efficiency needs of the two sides of this beneficial market partnership. In particular, dynamic scale and scope economies in the aircraft industry limit the incentives of producers to vary the size and range of their products (horizontal differentiation) and their overall quality (vertical differentiation). But limiting horizontal differentiation also restricts the ability of air carriers to realize so-called deployment efficiency in servicing the demands of different routes, while limiting vertical differentiation restricts their ability to choose an optimal trade-off between capital costs and operating costs.

To some extent, market bargaining between air carriers and aircraft producers serves to resolve these conflicts. In particular, the incentives for product differentiation by the producers are affected by the demands and terms offered by the air carriers. Bargaining between the producers, who are trying to exploit the scale and scope economies of a particular product family, and air carriers, who are looking for greater variety, results in compromises on both sides. But this market process is highly imperfect, both because of the concentrated nature of the industry and because of the tremendous risk and uncertainty associated with the entry of a new product or new product family.

The innovations required for the launch of a new aircraft entail huge upfront capital costs, which are recouped slowly and only with a considerable lag. It usually takes four to five years to develop, test, and certify a new airplane. In part the delay is the result of technological complications and uncertainties. But economic considerations also play a role. Limited and discontinuous product differentiation means that an aircraft producer always confronts a diverse set of demands from air carriers when it introduces a new model. To accommodate as many of these demands as possible, the producer traditionally experiments with dozens of "paper airplanes" before choosing a specific design for devel-

---

6. As a result of technical progress in the commercial aircraft industry, the air carrier industry has registered one of the highest rates of productivity growth of all US industries both before and since World War II (Mowery and Rosenberg 1982, endnote 1).

opment (Mowery and Rosenberg 1989, 171). During this experimental phase, the aircraft company works with a large number of air carriers, not just the few that are likely to become the launch customers.

The capital requirements associated with the launch of a new product are another source of tremendous risk for the aircraft producer.[7] The enormous size of these burdens can be best appreciated by comparing them with the producer's net worth. As an illustration, the development costs of the Boeing 747 were estimated at $1.2 billion— more than triple Boeing's total capitalization at that time. Similarly, the development costs of the DC-10 were estimated at three times the capitalization of Douglas (figures from Office of Technology Assessment 1991, 15–16).

Nor does a producer quickly earn net revenues sufficient to offset these huge upfront costs. In general, planes are priced on the basis of average expected cost for an initial production batch of 400 to 600 units. The first units are sold at a loss because the producer has not yet moved very far down its learning curve. According to one estimate, a new aircraft continues to produce negative cash flow until about the 70th unit (Office of Technology Assessment 1991, 26), and then turns profitable only if the new product turns out to be a market success.

There is always a high probability that a producer will never recover the upfront investment of a new product launch. To launch a new aircraft, a producer needs to target a hole in the market—that is, an area of growing demand not well served in terms of aircraft size and range by existing products. However, the demand for aircraft is highly cyclical in volume and volatile in structure; at the initial product development stage, it is very difficult to predict what the market will be like when the product is finally ready for delivery several years later. During the production run, the market will change even further. In addition, technological inconstancies may prevent a producer, after a huge initial investment, from developing a model of the promised size and range, at the promised cost, and with the promised safety performance. Unforeseen structural fatigue caused the market failure of the first commercial jet, the de Havilland Comet, produced in Great Britain in the early 1950s. The MD-11, developed by McDonnell Douglas, is the most recent example of a new product that has failed to meet its predicted specifications. As has been the case before, the failure of the engine supplier to deliver on expected performance was the source of this aircraft's difficulties.[8]

Another uncertainty in the launch decision for a new aircraft arises from trade-offs between its price and its performance. A producer must decide which currently available technologies to integrate into a new model. Because they entail higher development and production costs, more-innovative models carry higher price tags, but they are also likely to have lower operating costs as a

---

7. Development costs amount to about 40 percent of the upfront capital costs, with an additional 20 percent going to tooling and facilities, and the remainder going to finance work in progress.

8. General Electric, the engine supplier, had promised to deliver an engine capable of powering 300 passengers across 7,000 nautical miles, but it proved unable to meet this commitment. As a result, Singapore Airlines canceled its $2 billion order for the MD-11 and turned to the Airbus A340 (*New York Times*, 3 August 1991).

result of greater fuel efficiency and reduced pilot requirements. In addition, if no other model incorporates the new features and they prove to be popular, there are monopoly profits to be had by the innovating producer.

For the air carrier there is a major trade-off between capital and operating costs. Fuel accounts for an estimated 56 percent of an aircraft's cost over its lifetime, whereas the aircraft itself accounts for only 14 percent, with the remainder incurred for maintenance, financing, and other direct operating expenses (Boeing Commercial Airplane Company 1982, 13). This trade-off hinges on fuel prices and interest rates—two factors that are very difficult to predict at the time work begins on a new model.

Finally, in selecting available technologies to incorporate into any new model, the producer must choose between marginal improvements on existing technologies and truly revolutionary technological opportunities. As an example, the Airbus A320 introduced the so-called fly-by-wire system as a vertical differentiation strategy. This system was a marginal innovation on existing technologies. For that reason, Boeing urged air carriers not to buy the A320 but to wait for new models based on the revolutionary new "unducted fan" engine technology. Unfortunately, this technology was not ready as early as Boeing anticipated, and the A320 found a product niche, largely at Boeing's expense. Had Boeing's prediction been correct, the A320 would have been a market failure.

Development and production costs represent another important trade-off in product launch. If a firm allows itself ample time and investment to develop a new plane—thereby incurring the risk that others will introduce new models first—it can devise a significantly better manufacturing process and lower its production costs. On the other hand, if a firm succeeds in beginning delivery of a new model faster than its competitors—thereby winning a bigger share of initial orders—the resulting dynamic scale economies also provide an important cost advantage. Since the market for any particular type of aircraft is small, a first-mover advantage often means the difference between success and failure. Consequently, a successful first move for a particular model has a strong deterrent effect on the entry of competing models, as has been the case with Boeing's 747 and Airbus's A320.

Industry Organization and Multiple Sourcing

Because of the tremendous risks, the launch of a new commercial aircraft entails "betting the company." Hence there is always an understandable incentive to postpone the introduction of a new model. Working against this incentive, however, is the fear that excessive caution could mean surrendering market position to more-intrepid competitors. How do aircraft producers handle these competing incentives and the risks they confront?

In other industries, highly risky and expensive new types of investment are often handled through vertical integration or joint ventures (Carrol 1975, 164). Indeed, vertical integration among air carriers, engine producers, and aircraft producers was orchestrated in US industry by the government prior to the New Deal. During this phase of the industry's development, the US market was dominated by three vertically integrated, transcontinental operators, including one operator built on the consolidation of United Airlines, Boeing, and Pratt &

Whitney. The New Deal, however, broke up these three operators and outlawed vertical mergers (Mowery and Rosenberg 1982, 104–05, endnote 2, 24).

Contemporary aircraft and major air carrier companies are simply too global in their operations and too influenced by national governments to make significant vertical integration a feasible alternative. Aircraft producers therefore use joint ventures to diffuse their launch risks. Successful bids for contracts by both engine suppliers and parts subcontractors usually involve significant risk-sharing arrangements. Air carriers also take on risk by placing substantial advance orders and making advance payment for new models. Advance launch orders, however, have never been large enough to guarantee that an aircraft producer would break even (Milner and Yoffie 1989). Even with varied joint venture arrangements, the launching aircraft company cannot shed the enormous risks involved.

Before the mid-1970s, when foreign air transport markets and foreign aircraft producers were of minor importance to American companies, US air carriers repeatedly chose not to pool their orders and guarantee the success of a single aircraft company, even though they were well aware of the cost advantages of single sourcing. According to Carrol (1975, 158/59):

> Regardless of how reasonable the natural monopoly scenario may seem, it is not the one which has actually appeared for commercial aircraft. Indeed, almost invariably at least two quite similar competing aircraft have actually been produced. Examples are . . . the DC-8, 707 and 880; the DC-10 and L-1011; and the DC-9 and 737. . . . In each generation of competition there has been a distinct winner (or least loser) who produced a large number of planes while the other producer absorbed substantial losses. Thus, not only was one producer usually able to take advantage of its learning curve, but also the price of aircraft reflected its costs (both fixed and variable) and not some markup over the average of all producers' cost.

Government Involvement and Market Contestability

The historical record indicates that the United States has had a makeshift, unintentional, but nonetheless effective industrial policy toward its commercial aircraft industry. Indeed, as Moran and Mowery (1991, 5) argue, the US domestic policy framework provided important support for the civilian aerospace industry in its infancy; that support resembled the kind that Japan more recently provided to its infant semiconductor industry. Government support for the American civilian aircraft industry has taken several forms, including preferential procurement of aircraft for military purposes, support for both defense and civilian R&D in aerospace, loan guarantees, and airline regulation that fostered competition through the provision of new aircraft rather than through price.

All of the nation's commercial aircraft producers have been major defense contractors, at least at critical moments in their development. The enormous flow of federal government contracts has provided profits (and even in some cases covered tooling costs) that could be applied to the development of commercial aircraft. During the first twenty years of its existence, for example, Boeing ran losses on its commercial operations, just as Airbus did during its first twenty years (Office of Technology Assessment 1991b). Boeing was able to sustain these losses only because of its military operations. At least through the 1960s, endemic market volatility and subcompetitive returns in the commercial aircraft market were offset by market security and often supercompetitive returns in the military market.[9] Operations in the latter market provided an implicit subsidy for operations in the former.

At certain critical moments, government contracts provided the safety net to catch a plummeting commercial airframe company. Large backlogs of these contracts furnished steady income during periods when commercial activities were depressed. Even as late as the early 1980s, for example, the US Air Force bought 60 KC-10s, an airplane that was virtually identical to the DC-10 (except for the addition of in-flight refueling equipment). Without this purchase, McDonnell Douglas would not have been able to keep its DC-10 production line open until the market improved in the late 1980s, allowing development of its derivative MD-11.[10]

A second source of government support for the commercial aircraft industry has been the provision of public funds for both defense and civilian R&D programs. In 1915 a National Advisory Committee on Aeronautics (NACA) was established to fund research in generic civilian and military technologies. The National Aeronautics and Space Administration (NASA) absorbed NACA in 1958 but continued its mission. The NASA R&D budget paled in comparison with the explosion of federal funds for defense R&D in aerospace during the postwar period, but NASA continued to play an important role through its research installations and its participation in several collaborative R&D projects (Moran and Mowery 1991, 5).

Postwar support for defense R&D provided much of the technology and even some of the plant used by the commercial aircraft industry at critical points in its development.[11] For example, according to Carrol (1975, 148):

> the Boeing 707 in its tanker version sold several hundred planes, and the 707 itself was built in a plant leased from the government. Lockheed sold commercial versions of its C-130, C-141 and C-5A. [The Lockheed L-1011 and the DC-10] and Boeing 747 were all spawned by technical advances on the engines used for the C-5A. In short, every generation of new civilian air transport has relied heavily on technology developed for the military.

In the words of a recent Harvard Business School case on the aircraft industry, "by absorbing the heavy research and development costs for jet engines, jumbo airframes and wings, and advanced avionics, federal military grants allowed Boeing [and McDonnell Douglas] to move down the learning curve on commercial planes with far smaller investments of their own capital."[12]

Although US policy has not been designed to guarantee successful performance in the commercial operations of American aircraft producers, R&D sup-

---

9. Carrol (1972), using a model to impute sales and profits to either government or commercial operations for the American aircraft producers, found such a pattern of sub- and supercompetitive profits.

10. "The Big Six: a Survey of the World's Aircraft Industry," by J. Andrews, *The Economist*, Vol. 295: Special Survey, June 1, 1985, p. 10 (Office of Technology Assessment 1991b, 40).

11. Of course, the benefits of new technologies financed by the Department of Defense were not restricted to American producers but were ultimately available to the European producers as well. However, the American producers enjoyed substantial first-mover advantages in both the design and the use of these technologies.

12. *Collision Course in Commercial Aircraft: Boeing-Airbus-McDonnell Douglas, 1991*, Case No. 9-391-106, Harvard Business School, 1991.

port, large backlogs of "safe" military contracts, and the government's unwillingness to allow a huge defense contractor to fail completely "whatever its commercial sins" (Carrol 1975, 162) have emboldened American producers to undertake risky commercial ventures and have helped them raise the considerable financial wherewithal required to do so. When a military contractor has been threatened with bankruptcy, the government has usually stepped in with a rescue operation. For example, federal loan guarantees and a favorable antitrust review encouraged the "arranged" wedding between the McDonnell and Douglas aircraft companies in 1967. Somewhat later, in 1971, Lockheed was rescued from the brink of bankruptcy by a $250 million loan guarantee. If this history is any guide to the future, and if the substantial military operations of McDonnell Douglas are ultimately threatened by its current commercial difficulties, the US government is likely to arrange some kind of rescue mission.[13]

Finally, federal regulation of the airline industry through 1980 proved to be an indirect, unintentional, but significant source of public support for the postwar development of the civilian aircraft industry. As a result of regulatory restrictions on entry and price competition, American airline carriers competed with one another on service and quality, both of which could be enhanced by procurement of new generations of aircraft models. Thus, the regulated, large domestic market provided a strong base of demand for technological innovation by the aircraft producers. In the words of Moran and Mowery (1991, 5), "regulated air transportation in the U.S. market served as a kind of springboard for exports in a fashion similar to what strategic trade theory recommends or what Japan has practiced in other export sectors."

Overall, US government policy in the form of R&D support, procurement, loan guarantees, and airline regulation enhanced competition and demand in the aircraft industry. American producers did not have to bet their entire future to introduce new products; instead, they had to bet only the commercial and sometimes less profitable parts of their operations. Of course, given underlying industry economics, greater competition reduced production efficiency. All other things being equal, multiple sourcing kept production costs higher on average than they would have been with single sourcing. Moreover, to the extent that aircraft producers excessively duplicated each other's R&D efforts, resources were misallocated. But air carriers enjoyed offsetting benefits in the form of greater horizontal, vertical, and temporal product differentiation, with spillover benefits for their customers.

As a result of the dismantling of airline regulation in the 1980s, stagnant real aggregate expenditures for aeronautics research by both NASA and the Department of Defense, and an apparent reduction in commercial spillovers from military aerospace technologies,[14] American industrial policy support for its commercial aircraft industry is no longer nearly as important as it was even 15 years ago. Nonetheless, given the production and competitive dynamics of the industry, history matters, and current market outcomes cannot be divorced from past policy intervention. For example, although military sales have become steadily

---

13. For more on the current difficulties of McDonnell Douglas and possible US policy responses, see the concluding section of this chapter.

14. Moran and Mowery (1991, 8) note, however, that high-performance avionics technologies developed for military purposes may have commercial spillovers.

less important for Boeing over time, its monopoly in long-range jumbo jets with its 747 aircraft and its consequent dominant position in the industry grew out of engine technologies and design competition funded by the US military. As the evidence below indicates, Boeing did bet its commercial operations on the risky 747 project, but it did so secure in the belief that its military operations—at the time a much more significant fraction of the company's total operations—would not be seriously jeopardized.

Even in its heyday, however, American industrial policy in the aircraft sector was motivated primarily by military objectives, and its spillover effects on commercial aircraft capabilities have been largely unintended. As the Lockheed case discussed below demonstrates, the US government has not prevented the bankruptcy and exit of its military suppliers from commercial operations. Nor, as a rule, has the US government provided direct financial assistance for the development and production of commercial aircraft. The only exception was the government-financed supersonic transport (SST) program, which was initiated in response to cooperative efforts between France and Great Britain to build a supersonic passenger plane in the 1960s. When environmental concerns caused supersonic flight to be limited to overwater routes, the estimated market became so small that the US government terminated SST funding. By that time, according to the Office of Technology Assessment, approximately $1 billion had been spent. With additional appropriations from NASA, the Department of Transportation, and the Federal Aviation Administration, 10 of the most promising SST technologies were adapted for subsonic commercial applications, many of which found their way into the Boeing 757 and 767 models (Office of Technology Assessment 1991a, 90).

In contrast, European intervention in the aircraft industry has been motivated primarily by commercial objectives, although these objectives have been defended on dual-use grounds. Like the American commercial aircraft producers, all of the members of the Airbus consortium are also substantial suppliers of military aircraft. In Europe, as in the United States, there have been synergies and beneficial spillovers between the military and the commercial operations of these companies, and many of the technological breakthroughs in one area have found a second use in the other.

Dual-use considerations, however, are not the determining factor behind government support of the Airbus program; commercial considerations are. Important differences in the form of policy intervention reflect the difference in European and American goals. Direct financial support has been the principal mechanism used by the European governments in the Airbus program. This support has been provided in a variety of ways, including government contracts, loans, loan guarantees on favorable terms, guarantees against exchange rate losses, equity infusions (each of the Airbus members has been or is at least partially government-owned), tax breaks, debt forgiveness, and bailouts.[15] Current widely cited estimates suggest total Airbus subsidies on the order of $25 billion to $26 billion over 20 years.[16]

---

15. For example, over $1 billion in loans to develop the A300 and the A310 were forgiven the German Airbus partner by the German government in 1988.

16. This includes a substantial amount of unpaid interest on government loans at sub-

The very different experiences of Lockheed with the L-1011 and Airbus with the A300 and A310 vividly demonstrate the significance for industry outcomes of direct financial support of Airbus. These experiences are described in a recent report by the Office of Technology Assessment (1991a, 196) as follows:

> Lockheed was a company with a strong military business and experience pro-
> ducing commercial transports and had learned many of the skills needed to
> make wide-bodied aircraft in the military C-5 transport program. Airbus was a
> newly formed organization drawing on the technical skills of members none of
> which had previously designed or produced a wide-body transport. Lockheed
> sold 73 L-1011s during the first year it was offered. The A300 took 7 years to
> sell that many. During some of this period, Airbus was producing planes for
> inventory and financing costs. During the first ten years of production, deliveries
> of the A300 and A310 (a derivative of the A300 requiring additional investment)
> combined were almost the same as those of the L-1011. The L-1011 lost roughly
> $4 billion. No one knows what Airbus lost during this period, but it would be
> reasonable to expect the losses were at least as great as Lockheed's. Even so,
> Airbus shortly brought out four new models and two derivatives while Lockheed
> was forced to exit the commercial aircraft business. . . . The difference between
> Lockheed's fate and that of Airbus is largely attributable to the direct financial
> supports the members received from their governments.

Most of this support has come in the form of launch aid or low-interest loans with long repayment periods (table 5.4). By the end of 1990, the governments of France, Great Britain, and Germany had provided $5.6 billion in launch aid, of which only $500 million had been repaid, and an additional $2.3 billion had been pledged for the future A330 and A340 models. The German government pledged an additional $3 billion as part of the merger between Daimler and MBB, the German member of the Airbus consortium. These pledges total almost 75 percent of the development funds used in Airbus models to date.[17]

In principle, the launch aid provided by the European governments is repay-able, but only if the products developed with such aid are profitable. The com-panies that receive the aid are not required to pay back the funds from their other, non-Airbus business activities. As a result of this arrangement, govern-ment money, not company money, has borne the significant risks of product launch. Companies have not been bet—public funds have. Public insurance against company risk has encouraged the Airbus consortium to be aggressive in the launch of new models, to exploit new markets and new technological opportunities. Indeed, as noted below, during the 1980s Airbus was more ag-gressive in introducing a number of new technologies than was either McDonnell Douglas or Boeing.

Airbus, like the American commercial aircraft producers, has also benefited from government assistance in export sales. US assistance to its producers has

---

sidized rates (testimony of J. Michael Farren, Under Secretary of Commerce for Interna-tional Trade, before the Joint Economic Committee, 27 February 1992). The European governments have steadfastly argued that the appropriate cost of capital to be used in the measurement of its subsidies to Airbus be the cost of government funds, while the United States has argued that it should be the commercial interest rate. The latter is the rate used by the Department of Commerce to reach its estimate of $25.9 billion. According to Boeing officials, total European subsidies of $26 billion amount to $8 million per Airbus sold.

17. Office of Technology Assessment (1991a, 197). This estimate is based on US calcula-tions, but according to Department of Commerce officials, the Europeans widely agree that it is in the ballpark.

Table 5.4   Public launch aid for Airbus Industrie, by country and aircraft model, through 1988[a] (billions of dollars)

	A300 and A310				A320[d]				A330 and A340				Totals by country			
	France	Great Britain	Germany	Total	France	Great Britain	Germany	Total	France	Great Britain	Germany	Total	France	Great Britain	Germany	Total Airbus
Commitments	1.2	0.1	3.0	4.3	0.7	0.4	0.9	2.0	0.8	0.7	1.6	3.2	2.7	1.2	5.5	9.5
Disbursements	1.1	0.1	1.5	2.7	0.7	0.4	1.0	2.1	0.3	0.3	0.3	0.8	2.1	0.8	2.8	5.6
Value at government borrowing rate[b]	3.3	0.3	3.1	6.7	1.2	0.6	1.1	2.6	0.3	0.4	0.3	1.1	4.8	1.3	4.7	10.7
Value at corporate borrowing rate[c]	7.5	0.3	5.7	13.3	1.8	0.7	1.2	3.7	0.4	0.4	0.3	1.0	9.6	1.3	7.1	18.0

a. These figures represent all launch aid and include funds allotted to non-Airbus aircraft projects such as the French ATR 42 and 72. Officials in France, Germany, and Great Britain have stated that the numbers are accurate. Neither firms nor governments in Europe discuss public supports at a level more detailed than those used here, so it is impossible to tell by how much the table overestimates Airbus aid. Since Airbus is by far the largest aircraft venture currently receiving public financing in Europe, it is likely that these figures overestimate Airbus launch aid by only a little.
b. Value of disbursed funds as of 31 December 1988, including interest accrued assuming government rates (10-year treasury bills). The effects of staggered disbursements and loan repayments during the course of the programs have been factored in, and end-of-1988 exchange rates used.
c. Value of disbursed funds as of 31 December 1988, including interest accrued assuming corporate prime rates. The effects of staggered disbursements and loan repayments during the course of the programs have been factored in, and end-of-1988 exchange rates used.
d. The development costs of Airbus's launch of the stretched version of the A320 designated the A321 were financed without government assistance, with a line of credit from the Euro Investment Bank. The financing was not project based but rather based on Airbus's credit standing as backed by the liability of the members.

Source: Office of Technology Assessment, *Competing Economies: America, Europe, and the Pacific Rim* (Washington: Government Printing Office, October 1991) from US Department of Commerce data.

174

come primarily in the form of export financing provided by the US Export-Import Bank. During periods of weak domestic demand, when the commercial operations of US producers have been threatened, such financing has sometimes been substantial.[18] The Europeans also have export credit agencies whose mission is to equal or beat the terms offered by their trading competitors. In the late 1970s, when Airbus was struggling to break into the US market, the United States and Europe engaged in a flurry of competitive and costly export financing. To prevent this from recurring, they worked out a bilateral agreement in 1981 that was formalized in the Organization for Economic Cooperation and Development in 1985.[19] This agreement established maximum time periods and minimum allowable interest rates that governments could offer on loans for the purchase of large commercial aircraft. Since that time, in part because of the agreement and in part because of developments in the financial market that have changed the way aircraft purchases are made, export financing has become a less important policy tool.

The European governments have also used a variety of inducements to support foreign sales by Airbus. European landing rights or additional landing slots have often been offered to foreign air carriers purchasing Airbus aircraft. But more exotic inducements in the form of elaborate countertrade and barter deals have also been offered, especially by France (for examples, see Office of Technology Assessment 1991a, 227). The US government has occasionally offered inducements, more often for military than for commercial aircraft sales, although the two are often related.[20] Since inducements are by their nature difficult to document, much less quantify, it is impossible to determine whether they have been of greater significance in the foreign sales of European or American aircraft. About all that can be said with certainty is that neither the European nor the American government has been entirely innocent of offering inducements. However, both sides have recently desisted from such offers under an informal bilateral agreement reached in 1986 (see discussion below).

Finally, although there are no explicit procurement regulations requiring European airlines to buy Airbus products over their American competitors, informal pressure working through a variety of channels, including partial or complete state ownership of the relevant national airlines throughout much of the 1980s, appears to have had some effect. Undeniably, Airbus has done significantly better with European airlines than with American airlines, but this is at least partly the result of the willingness of Airbus to design its products with the special features of the European market in mind. Indeed, the A300 was targeted precisely at the high-density, short-haul European routes. Yet both Air France and Lufthansa have only Airbus products, even in those product categories with direct American competition—for example, from the Boeing 757. On the other hand, it is difficult to believe that European procurement preferences pose an

---

18. Between 1967 and 1977 the Eximbank provided $5.8 billion in loans on $12.8 billion in export sales of commercial jet aircraft (Office of Technology Assessment 1991a, 98).

19. The Large Aircraft Sector Understanding (LASU) allows for loans of 10 to 12 years at rates based on the US Treasury bond yield.

20. It is probably not a coincidence, given the extent of US–Israel military cooperation, that the fleet of El Al, the national air carrier of Israel, consists entirely of American commercial aircraft.

impenetrable access barrier to American products. In 1988, for example, about 1,000 Boeing aircraft were in operation in Europe, compared with only 56 Airbus aircraft in operation in the United States (*Business Week*, 9 July 1990, 46–50).

As the preceding discussion suggests, competition in the global aircraft industry during the postwar period has been influenced by the very visible hand of government manipulating a number of policy tools. The following section presents a brief history of this competition with two objectives: first, to demonstrate the effects of various industrial policies on market conduct and performance; and second, to show the long shadow of the history of government intervention in industries with huge, dynamic scale economies. In particular, the historical record reveals how an implicit US industrial policy contributed to the ascendance of US firms in the world market in the 1950s and 1960s and to the beginning of their fall from dominance thereafter. It also shows the effects of explicit European industrial policies, especially launch aid, on the technological choices made by Airbus, and how these choices influenced the pace of innovation in the industry in the 1970s and 1980s. When these two stories of industrial policy are juxtaposed, what stands out is the pervasive influence of government intervention in the commercial aircraft industry.

History of the Industry

The history of the commercial jet aircraft industry can be divided into two parts and four stages (tables 5.5 and 5.6). During the first part (1952–72), modern air transport was developed in two stages, each of which was predicated on a breakthrough in engine technology. In the 1950s the turbojet engine introduced the jet age with planes like the Boeing 707 and the DC-8. In the 1960s the turbofan engine made possible long-range aircraft such as the Boeing 747 and the DC-10. These models were called wide bodies to distinguish them from the single-aisle, narrow-body jets developed during the first stage. Both the turbojet and the turbofan engines were drastic innovations that totally changed the economics of aircraft manufacturing, reversing the market positions of competing American firms and establishing American dominance in the world industry.

No such drastic technological innovations occurred during the second half of commercial jet history, which began in 1978. Instead, firms and countries competed to replace first-generation aircraft with more efficient and differentiated products for the rapidly expanding global market. New narrow bodies were first delivered in the 1980s, and new wide bodies are to be delivered in the 1990s.

There was, however, one major change in the global aircraft industry after 1978, namely, the unmistakable emergence of Airbus as a serious economic competitor. As noted earlier, as a result of Europe's market-oriented industrial policy, Airbus achieved technological leadership in the development of commercial aircraft and determined the pace of new product launch during the 1980s. The competitive challenge posed by Airbus was felt in both the narrow-body and the wide-body markets.

National Differences, Home Market Effects, and the "Jet Lag" Reversal: 1952–66

Jet technology was a European invention. In fact, Europe gave the world its first commercial jet engine, its first jet transport, and its first supersonic transport.

Before Airbus, however, European technological leadership did not translate into commercial success. Instead, the Europeans found themselves buying cheaper and better planes from moderately protected and heavily subsidized American firms. The anxiety many Americans now feel about Japanese dominance in electronics is comparable to the anxiety many Europeans felt about American dominance in the commercial aircraft industry before the launch of Airbus.

Jet technology was revolutionary in a double sense. First, it represented a breakthrough beyond the existing technological traditions based on piston engines and propellers. Before World War II the United States had lagged behind Europe in both theoretical aerodynamics and provision of high-speed research facilities, the advances that made jet technology possible. Instead, the United States devoted its efforts almost exclusively to development-oriented problems. Edward Constant, in his book on the subject, attributes "the failure of American engineers to originate the concept of the jet to American ignorance of the theoretical knowledge underpinning aeronautical design" (Constant 1980, 241–46; see also Mowery and Rosenberg 1982, 130).

Second, as a result of jet technology, the cost of aircraft development and manufacturing skyrocketed, causing revolutionary changes in firm size and market structure within and across national boundaries. Jet technology was economical only in a large, integrated market that allowed both scale economies and competitive discipline. Before World War II, through heavy government involvement[21] the United States had developed the world's best commercial transports and the world's best and largest commercial aviation system (Constant 1980, 244). When jet technology arrived, this large home market gave American producers an overwhelming cost advantage over the established European firms, which served much smaller national markets. By the early 1960s the pressures of scale-dominated international competition finally drove several independent European nations to see their common future in "the creation of a European aircraft industry, with Europe as its basic market."[22] In this way, Airbus was born as a response to the scale advantages of the American producers.

The world's first commercial jet aircraft was the de Havilland Comet developed in Great Britain. Work on the Comet started in 1946, indicating that the basic technologies existed well before American commercial efforts began. The plane first flew in 1949 and entered service in 1952, more than six years before the first US commercial jet, the Boeing 707. "Orders by international carriers were heavy. In a sense, the subsequent role of Boeing as well as Douglas in this

---

21. Mowery and Rosenberg (1982, 141) describe Civil Aeronautics Board (CAB) regulations and their impacts on airframe innovation: "Continued congressional dissatisfaction with passenger safety and regulatory policy in general within air transportation led to the establishment of the Civil Aeronautics Board in 1938. Through its issuance of operating certificates and its overseeing of airline fares, the board effectively controlled pricing policies of airlines, as well as entry into or exit from air transportation, during the 1938–1978 period. These powers were used throughout the postwar period to prevent entry into scheduled trunkline air transportation and to prevent price competition. The CAB also controlled the award of routes to airlines; in general, multiple carriers were allowed to operate in 'major' city-pair markets, while less important routes often were allowed to be monopolized by a single carrier."

22. *Report of the Committee of Inquiry into the Aircraft Industry*, cmnd. 2538, London, 1971 (the Plowden Report).

Table 5.5 Production of narrow-body commercial jet aircraft, by model, 1952–90 (quantities delivered except where noted)

	Turbojet models							Turbofan models				
	British Comet	French Caravelle	Boeing 707	Douglas DC-8	Convair 880/990	Boeing 720	British Trident	Boeing 727-100	Boeing 727-200	British BAC1-11	Douglas DC-9	Boeing 737-100
Design features												
No. of engines	4	2	4	4	4	4	3	3	3	2	2	2
No. of seats	104	80	165	189	121	165	100	94	145	79	85	103
Range (miles)	2,800	2,400	5,800	6,000				2,500	2,200	2,100	1,300	1,300
1952	11											
1953	9											
1956	6											
1957	8											
1958	7		8									
1959	18	18	77	21								
1960	20	39	67	91	14	24						
1961	14	39	12	42	33	68						
1962	13	35	38	22	33	30						
1963	2	23	28	19	16	6						
1964	2	22	32	20	4	6	12	6				
1965	1	18	52	31	2	9	10	95		34	5	
1966		18	77	32		6	11	135		46	69	
1967	1	20	113	41		5	1	148	7	20	152	4

1968		15	111	102			11	46	114	26	203	105
1969		11	59	85			9	9	106	40	121	114
1970		9	19	33			2	10	44	22	53	37
1971		4	10	13			13	9	24	12	45	29
1972		5	4	4			11	2	39	7	32	22
1973		3	11				7		92	2	29	23
1974			21				4		91	4	48	55
1975			7				6		91	2	42	51
1976			9				9		61	6	50	41
1977			8				7		67	3	22	25
1978			13				4		118		22	40
1979			6						136	3	39	77
1980			3						131	2	18	92
1981			2						94	2	16	108
1982			8						26	1	10	95
1983			8						11	2		82
1984			8						8	2		60
1985			3									32
1986			4									21
1987			9									24
1988												7
1989			5									
1990			4									
Total	112	279	836	556	102	154	117	571	1,260	240	976	1,144
Backlog in 1991		20										

Sources: Seidler Amdec Securities (delivery and backlog); Aviation Week and Space Technology, 16 March 1992 (design specifications). Data used with permission.

179

Table 5.6 Production of wide-body commercial jet aircraft, by model, 1969–90 (quantities delivered except where noted)

	Turbojet models						Turbofan models			
	Boeing 747	McDonnell Douglas DC-10	Lockheed L-1011	Airbus A300	Boeing 767	Airbus A310	McDonnell Douglas MD-80	Boeing 757	Boeing 737-300	Airbus A320
Design features										
No. of engines	4	3	3	2	2	2	2	2	2	2
No. of seats	452	250-380	250-400	220-345	174-290	210-280	155	186-220	141	179
Range (miles)	5,000	4,100	4,000	2,800	4,600	5,000	2,600	4,600	2,700	3,900
1969	4									
1970	92									
1971	69	13								
1972	30	52	17							
1973	30	57	39							
1974	22	47	41	4						

Year										
1975	21	43	25	9						
1976	27	19	16	13						
1977	20	14	11	16						
1978	32	18	8	15						
1979	67	36	14	24						
1980	73	40	24	39			5			
1981	53	25	28	38			62			
1982	25	11	14	46	20		33	2		
1983	23	12	6	19	55	17	51	25		
1984	16	10	4	19	29	29	44	18	7	
1985	24	11	2	16	25	26	71	36	83	
1986	35	17		10	27	19	85	35	120	
1987	23	10		11	37	21	94	40	137	
1988	24	10		17	53	28	120	48	158	16
1989	45	1		24	37	23	117	51	146	58
1990	70			19	60	18	139	77	174	58
Total	825	446	249	339	343	181	821	332	825	132
Backlog in 1991	296			78	184	64	400	371	916	663

Sources: Seidler Amdec Securities (delivery and backlog); *Aviation Week and Space Technology,* 16 March 1992 (design specifications). Data used with permission.

market was saved only by the structural fatigue which the first Comet suffered" (Philips 1971, 124).

The entry of Comet provided an immediate impetus to American firms. In the decade before World War II, Douglas had dominated the American market thanks to the efficient operating characteristics of its DC-3. Other airframe producers survived mainly on military contracts. The war strengthened the relative positions of these producers, but Douglas remained dominant. By the 1950s, only four US firms had the technical and financial resources to contemplate manufacturing civilian jet aircraft: Boeing, Convair, Douglas, and Lockheed. Their conduct and fortunes during this period demonstrate the importance of scale economies and government involvement in the jet age.

When Boeing started developing its 707 in 1952, it had been largely out of the commercial market for two decades. In 1949 it had tried to enter the market with the Stratocruiser. Although the plane was the fastest and most luxurious airliner available at the time, it was also a costly defeat. In contrast, Boeing's all-jet bombers, the B-47 and the B-52, were huge successes, giving the company a lead in jet technologies over the other US firms. With such a background, Boeing "made a move in the jet-transport field that is at once daring and cautious. The move is daring in its aim of getting to the market first . . . and cautious in being embodied in a dual civil-military basic transport design, which can be developed in either or both directions" (McDonald 1953, 217).

In contrast to Boeing, Lockheed and Douglas—the market incumbents in existing commercial technologies—decided to delay the introduction of the new jet technology:

> After careful study of the prospects, [Lockheed] concluded that [it] could undertake either long-range jets or medium-range turboprops, but not both. Because of the British lead in jet transports, R. E. Gross [Lockheed's owner] believed the American industry would need help from the government to catch up, and when Boeing secured its advantageous position in jet bombers and tankers, the Lockheed planners decided not to compete. (Rae 1968, 211)

In 1952, many considered turboprops commercially more promising than jets on the grounds of relative fuel consumption. C. R. Smith, president of American Airlines, later explained why his prediction had been wrong:

> I don't think anybody could have anticipated, at the time I made all the speeches about fuel consumption, that we'd get the problem cured as readily as we did. And we would not have gotten it cured had it not been a military necessity, because the military necessity brought about a tremendous expenditure of funds for that purpose. (quoted in Rae 1968, 207)

Also in 1952, Douglas undertook its first serious study of the desirability of introducing jet technology. Its corporate annual report revealed the uncertain nature of market demand in an innovative industry:

> Operational experience and cost data on the use and maintenance of engines of the size required for jet transports of the future are meager or non-existent. These cost figures will play a deciding part in the desire or ability of the airlines to absorb the jet transport into the existing traffic patterns of their individual operations and earn sufficient additional income to pay for the new equipment. (Douglas Aircraft Co. annual report, cited in Rae 1968, 206)

Douglas decided in 1953 not to compete with Boeing in the first jet transport market. As the entrenched firm in the existing technology, Douglas wanted to keep the current equilibrium as long as possible before launching into the expensive and technologically uncertain field of jet transport.[23] Douglas intended "to be 'late' and better, the later the better if the customers will hold. Their sales strategy is to make a paper jet and make no investment until they have enough orders to justify the cost of tooling . . ." (McDonald 1953).

But the customers did not hold for long. Between 1938 and 1978, trunkline air transport entry and pricing in the United States were effectively controlled by the government. Unable to compete on price, carriers considered the rapid introduction of state-of-the-art aircraft as an important marketing strategy. When one airline purchased new aircraft promising a service-quality advantage, rival carriers would not wait long in ordering new planes, since only with timely delivery of comparable aircraft could they match the challenge in nonprice competition. Thus, despite its original preference for turboprops, in 1955 American Airlines decided to borrow heavily and order 30 Boeing 707s, which had been launched by its archrival, Pan American World Airways.

This loss of a long-standing customer to Boeing in 1955 ended Douglas's waiting. In the words of Donald Douglas, "Our hand had been forced. We had to go into the building of the DC-8 as a jet transport or else give up building airplanes" (quoted in Rae 1968, 208). Douglas's entrenched position made the huge capital and risk required for their catch up effort manageable. It is indicative of the strength of its original customer base that, when Douglas announced the DC-8 in 1955, 10 major airlines immediately placed orders. The project was financed by the profits of the DC-6 and the DC-7 series, by borrowing, and by customer advance payments (Rae 1968, 208).

American air carriers chose to have closely competing aircraft in each category. In the medium range, Pan Am actually divided its order, the largest in the industry until then, between the Boeing 707 and the DC-8. In the shorter ranges, the competing jet models were the Convair and the Boeing 720, and in the shortest range the Boeing 737 and the DC-9. The air carriers benefited from fierce price competition among the producers on these models—competition that would have bankrupted at least some of them if not for their military business.

Convair was the last American firm to launch a commercial jet aircraft during the first round of competition. When its 880/990 entered service in 1960, the market was already preempted by Boeing and Douglas. Unable to recover its high development costs, Convair suffered monumental losses and retreated to its military business (Rae 1968, 210). Douglas did not do much better. Price cutting below costs to promote sales of the DC-8 and the DC-9 overstretched the company financially. In 1967 Douglas was forced to merge with McDonnell Aircraft, a major military contractor, as part of a marriage arranged by the federal government and supported by a federal loan guarantee. Douglas's largely civilian product line was thus complemented by McDonnell's military contracts (Mowery and Rosenberg 1982, 133; *The Economist*, 1 June 1985, 7).

Thus, even the huge US market proved unable to support two profitable firms in the new commercial jet business without government R&D support, military

---

23. Note the similarity between Douglas's reluctance to adopt a technological innovation when it was the incumbent firm, and Boeing's later reluctance to adopt a technological innovation when it was the incumbent firm and Airbus was the entrant.

procurement, and a dose of government-led company rationalization. The pressure toward a natural monopoly outcome in the absence of such help was inexorable. Because of their smaller economic size and smaller defense budgets, the individual European countries could not withstand the pressure. For example, Great Britain, the second-largest producer of commercial aircraft, rationalized its industry into two firms, but the pressure of work-sharing seriously hindered competition between them (Heyward 1989, 83). Although British planes had good basic designs, their costs were much higher because of small production runs, and they lacked the numerous small details that made American planes more satisfactory for passenger service (Rae 1968, 212).

Trade, of course, is a way to expand relevant market size. Some have argued that the European producers were hurt because they were effectively denied access to the crucial US market by the protection afforded US manufacturers by the "Buy America Act" (Todd and Simpson 1986, 194–95). Industry economics, however, probably mattered more than the 5 percent tariff. The launch of a jet aircraft required close collaboration in design and heavy financial commitments between a producer and its airline customers. Domestic producers thus had a natural advantage over foreign producers in forming launch partnerships with domestic airlines. A larger home market allowed a larger launch order, which then generated self-reinforcing cost advantages. Jet aircraft is a classic case in which a country's comparative advantage in international trade derives initially from production for the home market.

In the early 1960s the aircraft industries of the individual European countries were in crisis. Even in Great Britain, the two commercial aircraft firms depended on the government for their very survival. But the British government simply could not maintain its massive support levels. The Plowden Report of 1965 confirmed that the aircraft industry, being high-value-added, skill-based, and capital intensive, was "exactly the sort of business activity on which Britain should concentrate." The fundamental need was to increase efficiency, to achieve competitive scale economies, and to reduce development costs. The solution, the report argued, was comprehensive European collaboration: "a European aircraft industry, with Europe as its basic market." The report "saw no realistic prospect" of collaboration with American firms, for they had no overriding need for cooperation. On the other hand, the national aircraft industries of Europe all suffered from the same basic problem and could not survive individually. Although the report was prophetic, it took another 13 years for the Europeans to form a binding partnership.

Drastic Innovation, Implicit Industrial Policy, and Wide-Body Competition: 1966–1978

Developments in engine technology rather than airframe innovations have been the most important factors behind the evolution of the aircraft industry. A decade after the first jet transport, the original turbojet engine was superseded by the turbofan engine, leading to a new generation of aircraft. Like the original turbojet, the turbofan was a British invention, and it was first produced by Rolls-Royce. Fan engines, by pulling as well as pushing air, had the potential to generate much greater thrust than the basic turbojet. Adding huge fans, however, caused intimidating heat, weight, and aerodynamic problems, which initially severely limited their commercial application. Again, it was US military initiative and resources that solved these problems and made the turbofan a drastic innovation on which aircraft-producing firms and countries came to depend.

The Pentagon wanted a new transport jet for personnel and weaponry. Boeing, Douglas, and Lockheed proposed modified versions of their existing jets. But the military pushed for a behemoth more than twice as big. With substantial defense support, General Electric finally succeeded in developing a turbofan three times more powerful than existing engines. As a result, market competition in the commercial aircraft industry was unsettled and ultimately redefined. At the time General Electric introduced its new engine design, the three American airframe companies were engaged in two US government design competitions: competition for a new military transport, the C-5A, and competition for the SST, a supersonic transport project introduced in response to the English-French Concorde project. All three companies put together skilled design teams to compete on these projects, and all three benefited from government-funded R&D experience. Both the winners and the losers of the C-5A competition ultimately used their design teams and government-funded technological breakthroughs to enter a new round of competition in commercial jet aircraft.

In this second stage of competition, product differentiation decisions proved more important than company differences in innovation incentives. In contrast to the first stage of competition, all three remaining American companies plunged headlong into the business of making new wide-body jets. All three competitors correctly believed that success or failure in this round of launch competition would determine their long-term market position. Moreover, each team was already on its way to developing a wide-body jet as a result of participation in the government-funded C-5A and SST projects. Unfortunately, what appeared to be an economically rational decision for each individual company was not an economically rational decision for the industry. Even at the time, it was clear that world market demand for aircraft, although growing rapidly, could not profitably accommodate three new wide-body jets.

According to John Newhouse, who authored the most comprehensive study of the wide-body competition, a medium-range, medium-size, two-engine plane advocated by American Airlines was what the market needed the most. Pushing the limits of available technology, Boeing leapfrogged this option, introducing the four-engine jumbo 747. Lockheed and McDonnell Douglas then chose to compete head-on by introducing simultaneously two long-range trijets. According to Newhouse (1982, 123), "The consequences of these [launch] decisions . . . injured each of the three suppliers but left in their wake an opportunity for European companies to become something they had never been—a competitive threat to the Americans."

The Boeing 747 proved to be the most profitable commercial aircraft ever made. Indeed, mainly as a result of its monopoly position in the long-range 747 market, Boeing has been the only profitable commercial aircraft producer during the last twenty years. Today, according to one estimate, Boeing makes $45 million on each 747 it sells for an estimated $150 million apiece.[24]

---

24. *Collision Course in Commercial Aircraft: Boeing-Airbus-McDonnell Douglas, 1991,* Case No. 9-391-106, Harvard Business School, 1991, 1–2.

Although, with the benefit of hindsight, the launch of the 747 looks like a brilliant business decision, by the normal business standards of its time it looked like a fatal mistake. Boeing launched the 747 without a prior detailed market analysis. Instead, the plane was a response to a surge in exogenous technology that grew out of military specifications (Newhouse 1982, 171). On the day it lost the C-5A competition to Lockheed, Boeing started developing the commercial version that became the 747, even though a commercial equivalent of the C-5A was, in 1966, simply too big for the route structures of most civilian airlines. According to Newhouse (1982, 123):

> Usually, a new airplane reflects the needs of the market; thus, it is a compromise—not an ideal fit for any one of the big airlines but close enough to what they think they need to be generally acceptable. The 747 was not a compromise; the only American carrier that wanted an airplane that large was Pan Am, and it is unlikely that the major foreign airlines desired it either. But rightly or wrongly—wrongly in retrospect—they all felt that they had no alternative. The big foreign carriers were unwilling to concede Pan Am a major marketing advantage.

The fact that product choice was dominated by the strategic decision of the biggest buyer reflected a major market imperfection in the air transport industry. Because of the importance of a launch order, a launch customer's power over product choice can be disproportional to its actual share of the total order or to the scale of an efficient production run. Pan Am bet its future on the 747 in the hope of achieving a competitive advantage; the gamble nearly bankrupted both Pan Am and Boeing. Between 1969 and 1972, Boeing did not receive a single order for the 747 from domestic airlines. In 1968 Boeing had 101,000 employees in Seattle. Three years later the number had dropped to around 37,000 (Newhouse 1982, 169–70). Boeing survived this disaster by drawing on revenues from its successful 727—a plane with no close competitor at the cluster point of demands for narrow-body aircraft—and income from its military contracts, and by restructuring to reduce redundancy and inefficiency. Boeing became much more market-oriented as a result of its initial 747 experience and gained a lasting productivity advantage over other its competitors.

The injuries that Lockheed and McDonnell Douglas inflicted upon themselves in the wide-body competition proved much more disastrous over the long run. In 1966 American Airlines initiated the wide-body aircraft proposal that eventually led to the decisions by Lockheed and McDonnell Douglas to develop wide-body airplanes. Based on its forecast of growth in passenger traffic, American considered a wide-body, double-engine aircraft capable of carrying 250 passengers across 2,100 miles the best fit for market needs. Lockheed started working on the wide-body jet when it received American's proposal. After losing the SST competition to Boeing at the end of that year, Lockheed put its best engineers on American's project, intending to use its SST and military aircraft experience to develop the most advanced commercial jet. Engineers from six major carriers worked as a group with Lockheed to develop exact specifications for the new wide-body jet. Whereas both American and Eastern Airlines wanted a twin-engine, midrange aircraft, Trans World Airlines (TWA) insisted on a wide-body design capable of crossing the country nonstop, even though it had already ordered several 747s for its longer routes. TWA prevailed, for reasons unclear even to the other participating airlines (Newhouse 1982, 143):

In acting as they did, the big carriers . . . tied themselves to another airplane for which there was no particular need, if only because it wasn't sufficiently different from the 747, which they all had ordered. . . . Each of the big carriers would have been helped more and harmed less by a smaller, shorter-range airplane; this was especially true when the price of fuel began to shoot up. But even in the late 1960s . . . it was clear that the larger part of the exuberant growth in the airline traffic was in the middle- and shorter-range routes.

After Douglas merged with McDonnell in early 1967, it plunged into the wide-body competition. Developed according to a common set of specifications encouraged by a common group of carriers, the McDonnell Douglas DC-10 and the Lockheed L-1011 became all but indistinguishable in their basic design. For the carriers, "Lockheed had the more attractive airplane, but McDonnell-Douglas inspired greater confidence as a company" (Newhouse 1982, 147). All of the carriers stood to benefit by making a common choice. They knew that if they split their orders, neither aircraft would succeed and higher costs would be unavoidable. "In a divided market, some part of which would have to be shared with Boeing's 747, the less successful of the two competitors would eventually drop out, leaving its customers in the worst kind of trouble" (Newhouse 1982, 155–56). This is exactly what happened.

Against their common best interests, strategic interactions among carriers, producers, engine suppliers, and the government led to a divided market. As in other classic prisoners' dilemmas, each participant would have been better off with a coordinated decision, but in the absence of a coordinating mechanism each chose to act in its own private interest, with negative results for everyone. The outcome was probably the most critical blow to the US commercial aircraft industry in its entire history.

Neither Lockheed nor McDonnell-Douglas could have survived, let alone dared to undertake, head-on competition in their wide-body designs without their military operations. "Sales competition between the MD DC-10 and the Lockheed L-1011, the bankruptcy of Rolls-Royce (sole engine supplier for the L-1011), and the C-5A contract nearly bankrupted [Lockheed]. The collapse of Lockheed was averted in 1971 only by a federal loan guarantee of $250 million" (Mowery 1987, 39). But the reprieve was temporary—in 1981, Lockheed exited the commercial market for good.

As noted earlier, McDonnell Douglas was provided a life vest in the form of military procurement of the KC-10, a slightly disguised version of the DC-10. But the damaging effects of its decision to compete head-on with Lockheed on a trijet wide-body persist to this day. Jackson McGowen, who was in charge of Douglas's aircraft operations, "particularly regrets the DC-10/L-1011 competition, which he feels should not have occurred and should not have been allowed to occur" (Newhouse 1982, 136):

McDonnell Douglas would have done itself and the other parties a great favor had it withdrawn the DC-10. . . . But the company's management judged, wrongly, that yielding the market for big trijets to a competitor would amount to a long step out of the commercial business. McDonnell Douglas had also been considering a second airplane—a wide-body twin. And that was the airplane to have developed. Europe's Airbus program was indefinitely shelved at precisely this moment—the spring of 1968. Had McDonnell Douglas gone forward with its twin, the Europeans would not have revived their Airbus. In an elegiac tone, Douglas's president . . . says: 'We missed the big twin, and that's not the only thing we missed.' (Newhouse 1982, 159)

Thereafter, McDonnell Douglas watched its world market share in commercial aircraft gradually erode, and with it the base on which to fund new generations of aircraft.

As noted earlier, the wide-body competition between Lockheed and McDonnell Douglas was a classic prisoners' dilemma. All the participants—the producers themselves, the airline companies, and the government—would have been better off with a coordinated decision to develop a single new aircraft designed to meet the demands of most of the airline companies. Moreover, this was realized at the time. The problem was not one of market information; it was one of market coordination in the presence of risk and imperfectly competitive conditions on both sides of the market.

Ultimately, the outcome in this situation was a reflection of the particular industrial policy context in which it occurred. By its actions, the government influenced who the competitors were, what they competed on, and how they competed. First—through loan guarantees to Lockheed, an arranged merger between McDonnell and Douglas, and indirect assistance channelled through military R&D proposals and procurement—the government determined who the competitors would be. Second, through its regulation of fare and route structures and through its development support for the new engine technology embodied in the design of both the L-1011 and the DC-10, the government influenced the terms of competition for both the carriers and the producers. Third, the government influenced the incentives of both Lockheed and McDonnell Douglas to engage in mutually destructive head-on competition in their commercial activities, by providing a life preserver in their military activities. Without it, strong market incentives would have contained such competition. As it was, both companies were emboldened to bet their commercial operations on a highly risky venture, secure in the expectation that at least their substantial military operations would survive. Their links to the military indulged their willingness to take on risk in a way that the discipline of the market, even one that was highly imperfect, would not have allowed. Whatever its intent, the defense industrial policy of the US government had a significant influence on corporate conduct in the commercial aircraft industry at this critical moment in its history.

Despite its pervasive and varied influence, however, the US government forswore the role of market coordinator. And in the absence of such coordination the American firms embarked on a mutually destructive competition that provided a critical opening for a successful and intentional industrial policy by the Europeans. Because of their accumulated production, the American companies could have produced almost any aircraft at a lower cost than the Europeans, but they unintentionally left a market gap between the narrow bodies and the jumbos to Airbus, which introduced a differentiated product and initially achieved not a cost or technology but an availability advantage (Majumdar 1987).

Ironically, American Airlines' proposal became one of the significant inputs in the design of the first Airbus model—the A300B, a smaller version of the A300—which was officially launched in 1969 by Germany and France.[25] Unfortunately, the plane's delivery hit the 1973–74 recession. However, reflecting the

---

25. Great Britain had withdrawn from the cooperative European venture in 1968 in pursuit of alliances with American producers.

strength of the European commitment to the Airbus project, the company was able to weather the recession by producing "whitetails"—aircraft that no airline had yet ordered (hence with no airline logo appearing on their tailfins) but were instead financed with public funds. When the European economies recovered in 1975, Airbus had an inventory lead over its American competitors. Its sales in that year exceeded those of the DC-10 and the L-1011 combined (Heyward 1989, 53–55). The Airbus was off and flying as a real competitive threat to the American commercial aircraft industry.

Technological Uncertainties, Market Position, and the New Narrow Bodies: 1979–1984

Boeing responded to the challenge of the A300 by simultaneously introducing two aircraft: a new jumbo twinjet, the 767, to compete directly with the Franco-German A300B; and the 757, a derivative of the 737, to be produced in cooperation with Great Britain to lure the British away from the European consortium. For the British, an alliance with Boeing was very tempting. Boeing was a major customer of the British firm Rolls-Royce, which supplied engines for the 747, and the main supplier of aircraft to British Airways, the largest British airline company. A production alliance with Boeing would mean common rather than competitive interests for Britain's airline, aircraft, and engine makers. Ultimately, however, the British declined to accept Boeing's terms because they amounted to a subcontracting relationship rather than a real partnership. France also expressed hesitations on the Airbus project during this period and flirted with both Boeing and McDonnell Douglas, but no alliances materialized for the same reason.

As a vehicle to bring the British back into the Airbus consortium, the A310, a derivative of the A300B, was launched in 1979, and the work was redivided among Great Britain, France, and Germany. The real competition between the now-consolidated European and American producers concerned the replacement of old narrow bodies:

> Following the launch of the A310, there was a debate within Airbus about the choice of the next project with which to extend further the Airbus 'family'. There was some interest . . . in a four-engined, long-range aircraft. However, market surveys indicated that a 150 seat, '727' replacement would offer the best prospect. . . . MDD [McDonnell Douglas] and Boeing were also considering new projects to meet this demand, but in the event, both preferred to produce derivatives of existing aircraft as interim contestants pending the emergence of new technologies. Early in 1981, Boeing launched the 737-300, and MDD followed with a variant of the DC9, the MD80. Airbus Industrie decided it had to attack this market with a new, advanced technology A320. (Heyward 1989, 58)

In 1980, reflecting US dominance of the world civil jet aircraft industry, American producers accounted for approximately 85 percent of the world's operational commercial jet transports (Piper 1980). Far down on their learning curve, and with the prospect of a propfan engine offering dramatic performance enhancement over the turbofan, Boeing and McDonnell Douglas chose to develop a derivative product in the interim. In contrast, Airbus chose to innovate, introducing several new technologies into its A320, including variable-camber wings, active controls, fly-by-wire technology, digital autoflight systems, sidestick controllers, and composite materials. Of these the most important was the fly-by-wire system, which, although unproven and risky, could considerably reduce both fuel consumption and personnel requirements.[26] Boeing urged air carriers not to buy the A320 but to wait for new models based on the radical propfan innovation. Ultimately, however, this revolutionary engine technology did not materialize as the American producers had anticipated.

Airbus was the first to introduce several technological innovations in the 1980s, not because McDonnell Douglas and Boeing lacked the requisite technological knowledge, but because their market positions generated different competitive incentives. Boeing, as the incumbent producer, had a natural tendency to exploit dynamic scale economies on its existing product families. For McDonnell Douglas, the pace of technological innovation was constrained by the lack of profitability—between 1969 and 1989 it lost more than $1 billion. Its financial difficulties stemmed from its head-to-head fight with Lockheed for the wide-bodied jet market in the 1970s. It was a fight from which McDonnell Douglas has never fully recovered.

In contrast to Boeing and McDonnell Douglas, Airbus had both the incentive to compete on new models, to neutralize Boeing's cost and price advantages on existing models, and the funds to do so, provided by the European governments.[27] Without their substantial launch aid, Airbus would not have been able to leapfrog both Boeing and McDonnell Douglas in technology, thereby gaining industry control over the pace of new product launch in the 1980s.

Innovation Incentives, Demand Fluctuations, and the New Wide Bodies: 1985–1991

A similar pattern of differential launch behavior was apparent in the late 1980s, when American and European commercial airline manufacturers competed to replace the former wide-body aircraft. All three companies believed that the airlines would want to replace their DC-10s, L-1011s, and some older 747s with new aircraft during the 1990s (*Business Week*, 13 August 1990, 55–56). McDonnell Douglas had been waiting for several years for the right market situation to launch an upgraded derivative of the DC-10 , during which time its wide-body production capacity was kept open only with orders from the US military (*Wall Street Journal*, 8 May 1985, 12). In 1986 it launched the MD-11, a three-engine, wide-body jet derivative of the DC-10 technology it was designed to replace.

Backed by the European governments, the Airbus consortium had a more ambitious plan. In 1987, it launched the A330/340 program. These big new Airbuses shared the same basic airframe. The A330 had two engines to fly 330

---

26. The A320 suffered several early crashes, but the underlying problems were corrected before its market had vanished.

27. For Airbus the problem was to persuade its government sponsors to spend another $1.5 billion while the A300 and A310 were still repaying their launch costs. The French were dedicated to an early launch and declared their support for the A320 in mid-1981. Initially, the British and German governments would not commit to an "industrial launch" of the A320. However, in 1984, when the A320 had managed to accumulate more than 90 orders, the British and Germans were finally persuaded that the market was ready, and were willing to contribute the necessary funds to launch the aircraft, which subsequently became the best-selling Airbus model.

passengers across 4,800 miles; the A340, equipped with four engines, had fewer seats but could fly over 7,000 miles.

Both McDonnell Douglas and Airbus doubted that there was enough demand for all of their proposed new planes to be profitable. Therefore, between 1988 and 1990 they held serious discussions to study the possibility of an AM300, an integration of their proposed new wide-body designs. A joint venture between McDonnell Douglas and Airbus would have rivaled Boeing for global market share. Even more important, the integrated model under negotiation had the potential to become the first real competitor to the 747; it would fly the same distance as the 747 but with one fewer engine.

Although a partnership between McDonnell Douglas and Airbus made both commercial and trade-political sense, no private agreement emerged despite two years of negotiations. Allegedly, negotiations broke down after the two sides failed to agree on who would build the cockpit, a critical portion of the aircraft. But alternate technological trajectories lay behind this disagreement. For each company, the negative cost-structure effects of departing from or shrinking its original product family exceeded the scale-economy benefits of merging with another product family to produce a hybrid.

The world aircraft market started a steep upturn in 1987, and interest in and orders for both the MD-11 and the A330/340 intensified. McDonnell Douglas hoped that the MD-11 would strengthen its financial and market position, and initial signs were promising. By March 1991, 377 MD-11s had been ordered, selling out the company's production capabilities through 1995. Unfortunately, however, the MD-11 has been plagued by both technical and engineering problems. The first planes were delivered months late, with several engineering deficiencies. As a consequence, the plane has not been able to achieve its maximum flight ranges when filled to capacity. American Airlines, the main launch customer of the MD-11, expressed great disappointment when the plane proved unable to complete its inaugural voyage in January 1991. American used the performance shortfall of the MD-11 as an excuse to refuse delivery of its full launch order at a time when the airline industry was experiencing a cyclical decline.

Thus, contrary to expectation, the MD-11 has not solved the financial difficulties of McDonnell Douglas's commercial operations. By the middle of 1991, squeezed by Airbus competition in the commercial market and battered by huge cutbacks in its military operations, McDonnell Douglas's survival as a commercial aircraft producer was at stake, and there was growing speculation that it would exit the industry. Its only viable alternative was to launch a new aircraft to compete directly with the Boeing 747. But the company lacked access to the necessary funds. An infusion of private capital was not forthcoming: McDonnell Douglas stock was taking a beating, and traditional customers such as American Airlines were dissatisfied with the company's performance. The only option was an infusion of public funds. The question was: from whom?

Meanwhile, in 1988 Boeing reacted to the launches of the A330/340 and the MD-11 by proposing a stretch model of the 767-300 wide body with a 747-like hump. But its major airline customers showed scant interest in this derivative. A year later, Boeing devised an entirely new design, slightly larger than the competition's, with two big engines for efficiency and flexibility. Boeing brought together eight prime customers with "design-build teams" to make decisions on features such as wings and avionics for its new 777 model. In addition, Boeing engaged three major Japanese companies to build 20 percent of the airframe for the 777. As part of this deal, the Japanese Aircraft Development Corporation (a subsidiary of MITI) agreed to fund a portion of the development costs of the project. Through this arrangement, Boeing was able to at least partially offset the development subsidy advantages provided to Airbus by the European governments and to fortify its position as the dominant supplier of commercial aircraft to Japan. Boeing's strategy is also understandable as an effort to preempt a possible alliance between the Japanese and either Airbus or McDonnell Douglas, both of which have courted them.[28] In early 1991 Boeing took the risk of launching the 777 for production by 1995; at the time of this decision, only United Airlines had ordered the 777, as part of a $22 billion deal that included other Boeing aircraft as well.

The Government's Hand in Commercial Aircraft Competition

The foregoing brief history of postwar competition in the commercial aircraft industry shows the ever-present role of government. Competition in the industry has been greater than it would have been if market forces alone had prevailed and pushed the industry toward a natural monopoly outcome. Both the American and the European governments have directly or indirectly determined both the players and their strategies in various rounds of competition. The Europeans have done this deliberately to build a world-class European firm. They have succeeded. The Americans have done this inadvertently with the intent of creating a technologically advanced defense-aerospace complex. Unintentionally, but nonetheless effectively, they have at the same time supported the development of a competitive commercial aerospace complex. Nonetheless, the unwillingness of the American government to intervene in the industry for commercial objectives has taken a toll. Most dramatically, if the US government had worked with industry representatives to head off the trijet confrontation between Lockheed and McDonnell Douglas, the disastrous competition that destroyed one, severely weakened the other, and left the market opening critical to Airbus's first success could have been avoided. But the US government steadfastly refused to take on the role of coordinator, even in a market where the players and their competitive strategies were a creation of public policy choices.

The Economic Analysis of Government Intervention in the Commercial Aircraft Industry: The Case of Airbus

As noted repeatedly throughout this book, industrial policy intervention in a particular industry can be effective in the sense of achieving its objectives, or

---

28. The preemptive motive behind Boeing's alliance with the Japanese on the 777 project is clearly suggested in the words of Boeing's commercial airplane president Dean Thornton, who has argued that the Japanese "are going to become involved in a commercial jet program one way or another. We sure don't want them to get involved with Airbus." Meanwhile, Airbus managing partner Jean Pierson has stated that Airbus might bring the Japanese in on its 350 project during the second half of the 1990s.

effective in the simple sense of influencing market outcomes without necessarily being welfare-enhancing. The question of the welfare effects of industrial policy has been raised in the context of European subsidies to promote Airbus. This question has attracted attention both because of the conflict between the United States and Europe over aircraft subsidies and because, under the peculiar market and production conditions of the industry, they can have potentially dramatic effects on national economic welfare, shifting rents from one set of national players to another.

Two major economic analyses of the welfare effects of European subsidies to promote the entry of Airbus exist: one by Richard Baldwin and Paul Krugman (1988b) and the other by Gernot Klepper (1990). Baldwin and Krugman concentrate on market competition between a single pair of products: the Airbus A300 and the Boeing 767. They compare three hypothetical scenarios with different market structures: an Airbus monopoly in which the A300 is the only medium-size, medium-range plane available; a duopoly in which the 767 follows the A300 into this market; and a Boeing monopoly in the absence of the Airbus entry. They assume that the European governments granted an implicit subsidy to the development of the A300 in the form of a required rate of return on investment lower than that facing Boeing.[29] They estimate that this subsidy amounted to about $1.5 billion of European taxpayers' money at 1974 prices.

According to Baldwin and Krugman's simulation model, which rests on a number of highly restrictive and questionable assumptions,[30] European subsidies to promote the entry of the A300 had the following welfare effects: the rest of the world gained unambiguously from an increase in consumer surplus attributable to lower aircraft prices and lower airfares; the United States lost unambiguously because reductions in Boeing's producer surplus outweighed the gains enjoyed by American consumers; and the welfare effects for the Europeans were ambiguous—sometimes positive and sometimes negative, depending on the parameter values used. Despite these mixed results, Baldwin and Krugman (1988, 68–69) conclude that "the A300 project constituted both a beggar-thy-neighbor policy and a beggar-thyself policy for Europe."

This conclusion is stronger than is warranted by the questionable assumptions on which it rests.[31] In particular, Baldwin and Krugman assume away an essential characteristic of commercial aircraft production: economies of scope between one aircraft model and a whole product family. The A300 was only the first of

---

29. This assumption is questionable because there is no reason to assume that the cost of capital to Boeing and to Airbus would have been the same in the absence of government intervention. American companies tended to pay a higher cost for investment funds than many European companies throughout the 1970s and 1980s, even in industries where government intervention was not an issue.

30. Other questionable assumptions of the Baldwin and Krugman analysis include the absence of any linkage between competition in the A300 and the Boeing 767 markets and the markets for other aircraft produced by Airbus and Boeing; the exclusion of McDonnell Douglas as a potential competitor; and the assumption that market conduct can be modeled as a Cournot competition between producers of a homogeneous product.

31. Baldwin and Krugman qualify their conclusion in the following way: "Given the degree of simplification necessary to produce a tractable model, it is difficult to base policy conclusions on our results." However, their more provocative statement is commonly cited by others without qualification.

a family of Airbus products and technological breakthroughs that would not have been possible without the subsidized entry of Airbus. Any complete analysis of the economic viability of this strategy requires a full accounting of the costs and benefits of the A300 and of the entire family of products and learning it spawned.

A more recent and more sophisticated study of economic rationality in the aircraft industry, by Gernot Klepper (1990), attempts to remedy the shortcomings of the Baldwin-Krugman study by incorporating scope economies. Like that of Baldwin and Krugman, Klepper's modeling approach suggests that any assessment of the wisdom of government policy in an inherently concentrated industry requires an assessment of its effects on competition. Klepper models competition among three product families in the markets for short-, medium-, and long-range aircraft. He compares the three scenarios with different possible market structures: a Boeing monopoly, a Boeing–McDonnell Douglas duopoly, and a Boeing-Airbus duopoly. The calculated welfare effects of European subsidies to Airbus differ considerably depending on which of the two no-Airbus scenarios is chosen as the benchmark. Klepper concludes that the government-supported entry of Airbus as an antimonopoly policy increased consumer welfare but reduced overall welfare because of large offsetting losses in producer surplus. In other words, the Airbus entry benefited consumers by lowering prices, but hurt producers by reducing their production scale and increasing their costs. The bottom line is the same as that in the Baldwin-Krugman study: under most scenarios European subsidies to promote the entry of Airbus were not welfare-improving and hence not economically rational for Europe. And they were *unequivocally harmful* to the United States.

The Baldwin-Krugman and Klepper studies share two shortcomings: the first concerns the question they pose, and the second their methodologies. First, the question of whether policies to promote the entry of Airbus increased static economic welfare for Europe is moot. Whether economically rational in this narrow sense or not, these policies cannot be reversed. The entry question has been decided, and on political, military, and technological as well as economic grounds.

Second, these researchers' methodology is inadequate even for the welfare question they pose. Neither study, for example, estimates the welfare effects of the high-wage job opportunites created in Europe and destroyed in the United States as a result of the substantial shift in global aircraft production occasioned by European subsidies. A study by Katz and Summers (1989, 256–58) concludes that when such effects are included in the balance, these subsidies had strongly positive effects on European welfare and strongly negative effects on American welfare. A study by Dickens reaches the same conclusion, using a somewhat different and more conservative method for estimating the labor-market effects of European subsidies (Dickens, 1992, 24).

Both the Baldwin-Krugman and the Klepper studies also fail to assess the effects of European subsidies on the pace and direction of innovation in the aircraft industry and the resulting benefits for air carriers and their passengers. The brief history told in the previous section indicates that these effects have been substantial.[32]

---

32. Moran and Mowery (1991) also argue that sales competition among the aircraft pro-

Once these labor-market and innovation effects are added to the picture, it becomes much more difficult to assess the overall impact of European subsidies on American economic welfare. On the one hand, the United States lost high-wage jobs and producer surplus as production shifted toward Europe; on the other hand, US air travelers benefited from lower prices, and US air carriers benefited from lower prices and a larger choice of products, embodying technological innovations that might otherwise not have been available at the time.

Even before Airbus became a serious market contender, competition between McDonnell Douglas, Lockheed, and Boeing was possible only with substantial US government support for each of them. Overall, government subsidies in the United States and in Europe have increased competition and accelerated innovation in the aircraft industry. In the absence of a more formal modeling effort, it is impossible to conclude that the overall welfare effects of such subsidies have been positive. But there should be no presumption that they have been negative either.

Trade Friction in the Aircraft Industry

The 1979 GATT Agreement on Civil Aircraft

Huge scale and scope economies make exports critical for US commercial aircraft companies.[33] Even before the 1970s, about one-third of all the commercial aircraft produced in the United States were sold to foreign buyers, and trade has become steadily more important since then. Trade has also been critical to the success of European efforts to build a competitive commercial aircraft capability. The European governments and companies cooperating in the Airbus venture recognized from the outset that exports were essential to realizing the global scale required to cover production costs. Of particular importance were exports to the large American air transport market, the base of American competition (tables 5.7 through 5.10 present data on trade in aircraft and engines from 1977 to 1987).

In addition to their common interest in unfettered access to one another's markets, American and European producers share a common interest in removing barriers to joint ventures, subcontracting, and offshore procurement of components. Again, this interest is rooted in the special features of the aircraft industry. The links between commercial aircraft companies and national defense establishments, as well as economies of scale, rule out significant foreign direct investment as a substitute for trade. However, cross-border production arrangements, which stop short of foreign direct investment but instead take the form of elaborate joint ventures and subcontracting deals, have become increasingly attractive to producers as ways of improving access to foreign markets and

ducers, spurred by the technological innovation strategy of Airbus, has produced sustained R&D races in the industry. According to them, rivalry between the Airbus A300 and the Boeing 767 led to vigorous investment in R&D to gear up for the subsequent round of competition among the A330/A340, the MD-12, and the Boeing 777.

33. The author would like to express their appreciation to Sally Bath, Director, Office of Aerospace International Trade Administration, Department of Commerce, for her invaluable insights and assistance on this section on "Trade Friction in the Aircraft Industry." She does not, however, necessarily share the views expressed there.

Table 5.7   Geographical composition of world imports of aircraft
engines, 1977–87

Country	1977	1979	1981	1983	1985	1987
Millions of dollars						
World[a]	3,057	4,789	7,662	7,751	9,417	13,315
United States	174	609	1,548	1,176	2,456	2,960
European Community	1,628	2,502	3,947	3,843	4,042	5,900
Germany	225	336	509	513	648	930
Great Britain	633	883	1,600	1,431	1,502	2,110
France	329	608	768	908	973	1,433
Asia	596	723	1,023	1,780	1,862	2,937
Japan	191	236	348	477	722	893
Canada	200	275	161	247	177	170
Percentages of total						
World[a]	100.0	100.0	100.0	100.0	100.0	100.0
United States	5.7	12.7	20.2	15.2	26.1	22.2
European Community	53.3	52.2	51.5	49.6	42.9	44.3
Germany	7.4	7.0	6.6	6.6	6.9	7.0
Great Britain	20.7	18.4	20.9	18.5	15.9	15.8
France	10.8	12.7	10.0	11.7	10.3	10.8
Asia	19.5	15.1	13.4	23.0	19.8	22.1
Japan	6.2	4.9	4.5	6.2	7.7	6.7
Canada	6.5	5.7	2.1	3.2	1.9	1.3

a. Market economies only.
Source: United Nations, Statistical Yearbook of International Trade, various issues.

cooperating with would-be competitors.[34] Foreign sourcing of components also offers traditional cost advantages. In addition, as the development costs and technological challenges of launching new aircraft mount, producers have scrambled to find foreign partners to provide some of the development capital and to share both the financial and the technological risks.

The shared interests of both the American producers and the emerging European producers in freer trade proved to be a stimulus to the successful negotiation of the 1979 GATT Agreement on Trade in Civil Aircraft. But conflicting rather than shared interests motivated the lobbying efforts of the US producers to get such an agreement.

By the early 1970s, the American companies were already expressing concern about the fact that the Europeans, with direct government backing and assistance, had achieved high levels of sophisticated production capability. By 1978 concern had turned to alarm as a result of Airbus sales in East Asia, the Middle East, and the United States itself. Airbus successfully penetrated the domestic monopoly of the American producers by offering Eastern Airlines an extremely attractive deal, which included a six-month free trial period, an operating cost

---

34. According to Moran and Mowery (1991, 27), the rationale for development and production "alliances" in both military and civilian aerospace contains a large element of deliberate constituency building to gain political as well as commercial backing from industrial and labor actors in the target market. For example, the high (albeit declining) American content of Airbus aircraft aids the European consortium in its efforts to penetrate US markets. Similarly, Boeing's choice of a European engine producer (Rolls-Royce) or a Japanese partner (Mitsubishi) yields benefits in foreign market access.

Table 5.8 Geographical composition of world exports of aircraft engines, 1977–87

Country	1977	1979	1981	1983	1985	1987
Millions of dollars						
World[a]	3,910	6,034	8,469	8,668	9,738	14,224
United States	1,070	1,934	3,077	3,423	3,695	4,773
European Community	2,154	3,093	3,949	3,903	4,429	6,927
Germany	443	493	385	552	696	1,205
Great Britain	1,070	1,519	2,465	1,772	2,109	3,086
France	379	550	336	618	816	1,334
Asia	237	229	317	358	506	967
Japan	145	99	137	81	133	177
Canada	272	475	759	565	683	889
Percentages of total						
World[a]	100.0	100.0	100.0	100.0	100.0	100.0
United States	27.4	32.1	36.3	39.5	37.9	33.6
European Community	55.1	51.3	46.6	45.0	45.5	48.7
Germany	11.3	8.2	4.5	6.4	7.1	8.5
Great Britain	27.4	25.2	29.1	20.4	21.7	21.7
France	9.7	9.1	4.0	7.1	8.4	9.4
Asia	6.1	3.8	3.7	4.1	5.2	6.8
Japan	3.7	1.6	1.6	0.9	1.4	1.2
Canada	7.0	7.9	9.0	6.5	7.0	6.3

a. Market economies only.
Source: United Nations, *Statistical Yearbook of International Trade*, various issues.

guarantee, and favorable export credit terms. The risk to Airbus from this deal was substantial. Should the A300 fail to satisfy Eastern, the airline could return the aircraft, with damaging and possibly fatal harm for Airbus's reputation. But the benefits of a successful deal were equally substantial: a foothold in the heretofore impenetrable American market. As the American producers were quick to point out, the financial costs of the deal to Airbus were covered by European subsidies.

At the time of the Airbus offer to Eastern, C. Fred Bergsten, then an official at the US Treasury Department, proposed to then-Secretary W. Michael Blumenthal a countervailing duty (CVD) to offset the subsidies offered by the Europeans. A large duty, speedily introduced, might have been a serious deterrent to future European efforts to subsidize Airbus sales. In addition, the Europeans were still heavily dependent on American commercial aircraft, and thus the risk that significant retaliation could harm American producers was relatively low. In short, the conditions for using the US CVD law both as a remedy and as a deterrent were relatively auspicious in 1978. Subsequently, as Airbus became a more important competitor, the threat of European retaliation to CVD relief intensified, and American producers became reluctant to propose its use.

Ultimately, the use of CVD relief in 1978 was blocked not by the aircraft producers but by Eastern Airlines, which appealed to Secretary Blumenthal to reverse his decision. Eastern's chief executive Frank Borman made the request directly, arguing that Eastern and other American air carriers stood to benefit from Airbus's aggressive selling tactics (C. Fred Bergsten, personal communication). This was undoubtedly true, but an informed policy judgment required

Table 5.9　Geographical composition of world imports of aircraft, 1977–87

Country	1977	1979	1981	1983	1985	1987
Millions of dollars						
World[a]	6,902	14,802	22,776	19,600	21,320	26,057
United States	604	1,126	2,827	2,100	3,600	4,519
European Community	3,006	7,208	9,064	8,803	8,614	9,922
Germany	1,230	2,322	4,312	4,392	3,613	4,670
Great Britain	655	2,429	1,432	1,445	2,082	998
France	474	1,018	1,166	881	572	1,198
Asia	1,473	3,000	5,001	4,035	5,034	5,884
Japan	201	750	1,347	1,490	1,497	1,755
Canada	264	906	1,524	1,071	1,490	1,435
Percentages of total						
World[a]	100.0	100.0	100.0	100.0	100.0	100.0
United States	8.8	7.6	12.4	10.7	16.9	17.3
European Community	43.6	48.7	39.8	44.9	40.4	38.1
Germany	17.8	15.7	18.9	22.4	16.9	17.9
Great Britain	9.5	16.4	6.3	7.4	9.8	3.8
France	6.9	6.9	5.1	4.5	2.7	4.6
Asia	21.3	20.3	22.0	20.6	23.6	22.6
Japan	2.9	5.1	5.9	7.6	7.0	6.7
Canada	3.8	6.1	6.7	5.5	7.0	5.5

a. Market economies only.
Source: United Nations, *Statistical Yearbook of International Trade*, various issues.

that these benefits be weighed against the costs to US producers and the forgone benefits of deterring future Airbus subsidies. No such judgment was made, and a promising opportunity to moderate these subsidies was lost.

Meanwhile, American producers became more vocal about the ominous and unfair nature of European export subsidies and called for a halt to "predatory export financing." Gradually these complaints broadened to include multifaceted industrial policy supports for Airbus and their adverse consequences for Europe's trading partners. Rather than requesting protection as a remedy, the American companies requested R&D support, tax credits, and more Eximbank financing to match the sales terms offered by the European governments. At the same time, working through the US aerospace advisory committee for the Tokyo Round discussions, the American producers called for a sectoral GATT agreement to address the specific issues underlying trade conflict in the aircraft industry.

Negotiations toward such an agreement were begun in Geneva in May 1978. The American objective, in the words of its negotiating representative, was to have a "unique sectoral agreement establish[ing] a free trade framework" (Piper 1980). This meant an agreement that would effectively constrain European support for Airbus. What the Americans wanted was not only a "free trade" agreement that eliminated traditional trade barriers, but also a "free market" agreement that constrained European industrial policy support. The United States won the first point but lost the second.

The 1979 GATT Agreement on Trade in Civil Aircraft is summarized in box 5.1. Because of their common interests in freer trade, the Americans and the Eu-

Table 5.10 Geographical composition of world exports of aircraft, 1977–87

Country	1977	1979	1981	1983	1985	1987
Millions of dollars						
World[a]	10,188	19,240	27,870	25,287	28,806	33,227
United States	5,893	9,779	14,877	12,323	14,497	18,133
European Community	3,460	7,592	10,114	10,381	10,822	11,346
Germany	916	1,735	3,359	3,382	3,342	3,605
Great Britain	878	2,693	2,687	2,888	3,120	2,313
France	1,000	2,133	2,021	2,226	2,430	3,107
Asia	222	755	1,011	977	1,422	1,031
Japan	21	72	119	151	118	224
Canada	303	576	1,031	995	1,254	1,550
Percentages of total						
World[a]	100.0	100.0	100.0	100.0	100.0	100.0
United States	57.8	50.8	53.4	48.7	50.3	54.6
European Community	34.0	39.5	36.3	41.1	37.6	34.1
Germany	9.0	9.0	12.1	13.4	11.6	10.8
Great Britain	8.6	14.0	9.6	11.4	10.8	7.0
France	9.8	11.1	7.3	8.8	8.4	9.4
Asia	2.2	3.9	3.6	3.9	4.9	3.1
Japan	0.2	0.4	0.4	0.6	0.4	0.7
Canada	3.0	3.0	3.7	3.9	4.4	4.7

a. Market economies only.
Source: United Nations, *Statistical Yearbook of International Trade*, various issues.

ropeans were able to concur on eliminating a wide range of border and nonborder trade barriers, including tariffs, quotas, preferential technical standards, closed procurement arrangements, mandatory subcontracting arrangements, and export subsidies.[35] A Committee on Trade in Civil Aircraft was established for continuing consultation among the signatories to ensure the agreement's implementation.

The 1979 GATT agreement successfully eliminated most traditional trade impediments and substantially liberalized aircraft trade. As a result, cross-national subcontracting and sourcing of components exploded in the following years, changing the organization of the global aircraft industry forever. According to Mowery and Rosenberg (1989, 186), "U.S. exports of aircraft parts and components grew rapidly after the signing of the agreement. Exports of components and other parts grew at an average annual rate of 36 percent from 1977 to 1982, from roughly $2 billion to roughly $4 billion. Exports of aircraft engines increased from slightly more than $200 million to more than $800 million during the same period." In response to the growing European threat, American producers also made greater use of international cooperative production arrangements, which

---

35. Because the OECD had been concerned with aircraft export financing for some years and was negotiating an agreement toward that end, the GATT agreement did not address this issue. As noted earlier, a companion agreement on export financing, first between the United States and Europe and later within the OECD, significantly reduced trade friction and the prospect of mutually destructive export subsidies.

were rendered considerably more attractive by the elimination of trade barriers.[36] Overall, the US Department of Commerce estimates that, through the end of 1991, the 1979 agreement saved American companies in the aircraft and parts industries as much as $1 billion in tariffs and other duties (personal communication from Sally Bath, Director, Office of Aerospace, International Trade Administration, Department of Commerce, October 1991).

Why, then, did the 1979 GATT agreement fail to head off worsening friction between the United States and Europe in commercial aircraft? The answer is simple: it failed to address the competing industrial priorities and policies behind this friction. International rules can moderate trade conflict when the parties to the conflict can find common ground or mutual interest, but they cannot eliminate conflict when the interests of the parties are fundamentally antagonistic. Both the Europeans and the Americans stood to benefit from reducing barriers to trade in aircraft, but their interests were at odds over the question of industrial policy support for Airbus. The Europeans were fervently committed to such support, the Americans adamantly opposed. Given this conflict, any compro-

---

36. It is extremely unlikely that any large jet aircraft will ever be designed or built solely within national boundaries again. According to the MIT Commission on Industrial Productivity (1989), Boeing has stated flatly that it will no longer consider such huge undertakings without foreign partners.

mise agreement on the question would necessarily be vague, imprecise, and ultimately unenforceable.

In the negotiations leading up to this compromise, the Europeans emphasized the concept of "managed competitive balance." They sought rules that would allow subsidies to the extent required to produce aircraft that would be technically and economically competitive with US products. For its part, although the United States endorsed the concept of "equal competitive opportunities" for both American and European producers, it would not condone government intervention aimed at establishing competitive balance. Government policy, according to American negotiators, should establish an open competitive environment, but should not arrange competition so as to influence its outcome (Piper 1980, 233). This high-minded principle conveniently overlooked the effects of previous American policies on the competitive position of American producers at that time.

Despite intense American pressure, the Europeans were only willing to agree to rules on government support that were limited in scope, vague in stipulation, and weak in enforcement. Moreover, even in those instances in which the Europeans bowed to US pressure for more precise language, the United States won a victory in words only, not intent. For example, although the Europeans had lobbied for a vague statement that the "the signatories to the Agreement have the firm intention to avoid attaching inducements" to aircraft sales, they ultimately agreed to the US–sponsored statement that "signatories agree to avoid attaching inducements of any kind." But the American negotiator, mindful of the European attitude concerning inducements, warned, "If future practice follows past, the U.S. government may well want to review its 'hands-off' policy regarding civil aircraft marketing efforts in export markets" (Piper 1980, 238).

The issue of industrial policy was even more controversial. The Europeans insisted on language that reflected their position as a condition for signing the agreement. Box 5.1 reveals the ultimate hollowness of the commitments the Europeans were willing to make. According to the agreement's preamble, many of its signatories (read the Europeans) view the aircraft sector as a particularly important component of industrial policy, and while they will seek to eliminate the adverse effects on trade resulting from government support in civil aircraft development, production, and marketing, they recognize that such support, of itself, would not be deemed a distortion of trade. This language is in fundamental disagreement with the US philosophical position on subsidies.

Article 6 of the agreement, which deals explicitly with government support to the industry, is likewise a vague compromise that conforms to Europe's underlying position. According to this article, the signatories affirm that in their participation in, or support of, civil aircraft they shall *seek to avoid* adverse effects on trade in civil aircraft[37] (in the sense of articles 8.3 and 8.4 of the 1979 GATT Agreement on Subsidies and Countervailing Measures), but they recognize the presence of widespread government support in the aircraft industry and the desire of producers in all signatories to participate in the expansion of world

---

37. The adverse effects on trade identified by the agreement include injury to the domestic industry of another signatory; nullification or impairment of the benefits accruing directly or indirectly to another signatory under the GATT; and serious prejudice, including the threat of it, to the interests of another signatory.

civil aircraft markets. The agreement also recognizes the principle that "aircraft pricing should be based on a reasonable expectation of recoupment of all costs, including nonrecurring program costs and identifiable and prorated costs of military research and development on aircraft," but there is no explicit or enforceable ban on pricing that violates this principle. In short, the agreement accepts the legitimacy of national industrial policies in the aircraft industry and establishes no precise or enforceable restrictions on either the kinds or the extent of such policies. Nor did the signatories to the agreement disavow the use of such policies; rather they committed only to "seek to avoid" their adverse effects on trade.[38]

Bilateral Friction Between the United States and Europe: 1979–1991

If the American producers left Geneva with enthusiasm for the 1979 agreement, their enthusiasm was quickly dashed by the growing success of the Airbus A300 in the global market for wide-bodied aircraft between 1981 and 1985. During this period, sales of the A300 exceeded sales of both the DC-10 and the L-1011—in some years the A300 captured 50 percent of all orders for wide-bodied jet aircraft. As McDonnell Douglas and Lockheed landed devastating blows upon one another in their head-on competition between the DC-10 and the L-1011—a competition that clearly violated the pricing principles of the 1979 aircraft agreement—the A300 gained market share at the expense of both. Ultimately, a much-weakened Lockheed exited commercial aircraft production altogether in 1981.

The global slowdown in the market for commercial aircraft in the early to mid-1980s sharpened the conflict between the American and the European producers. With US exports of civil aircraft down by as much as 50 percent in 1982–84 from their 1979–80 peak, US producers complained bitterly about the unfair pricing strategies of Airbus and the unfair government subsidies that made them feasible. Even Boeing, which successfully parried the competitive challenge of the A300 by launching the 757 and 767 models, circulated a report alleging that Airbus was not covering its costs and was benefiting from massive government subsidies.

Boeing's concerns mounted when Airbus realized its second successful penetration of the American market with a major sale to Pan Am in 1984. This sale was of great symbolic significance since Pan Am was a key Boeing customer and had a reputation as the foremost launcher of new aircraft in the American air transport industry. As if these inroads by the A300 were not enough, in 1984 Airbus announced its decision to launch the A320, with the help of its supporting member governments. Unlike the A300, which was built on existing American technologies, the A320 embodied significant technological innovations that made it a serious competitive challenge for Boeing. It was one thing to watch smaller American producers lose market share as a result of a wise European decision

---

38. The agreement recognized that these adverse effects could arise through the effects of subsidized imports in the domestic market of the importing signatory; the effects of the subsidy in displacing or impeding imports of similar aircraft into the market of the subsidizing country; or the effects of subsidized exports in displacing the exports of similar aircraft of another signatory from a market in a third country.

on the size and range of the A300, but it was quite another to watch Airbus challenge Boeing with a new technology. The announcement of the A320 was also significant because it confirmed a commitment among the European governments—including the British government, which had earlier withdrawn from the A300 project—to continue collaboration in commercial aircraft for the foreseeable future.

Friction between the United States and Europe over the A320 accelerated in 1984 and 1985 as Boeing and Airbus competed for a large contract with Air India.[39] In June 1984, Air India signed a letter of intent to buy twelve 757 aircraft from Boeing, with the option to purchase an additional 13. But Airbus managed to reopen the negotiations, offering to deliver its new A320 at a substantial price discount by 1989 and to lease Boeing 737s and Airbus A300s to Air India in the meantime. In toto, Airbus offered financing to cover an estimated 85 percent of the cost of the purchase, an amount permissible under the OECD export financing agreement. Airbus eventually won the bid in September 1985.

Boeing and US officials were outraged. Airbus was accused of violating Article 6 of the 1979 agreement, which required pricing on a reasonable expectation of recoupment of costs. In addition, the Europeans were accused of violating the agreement's ban on inducements. This accusation was based on rumors that as part of the Airbus deal the French government had promised technical assistance to clean up the Ganges River, support for India's efforts to secure additional World Bank loans, and faster delivery of French Mirage fighter jets. These rumors were based on the fact that French officials had made several high-level "multiple-purpose sales calls" in the months prior to the announcement of the Airbus contract (Yoffie 1990, 338).

This announcement of the deal between Airbus and Air India occurred in the context of growing congressional and business pressure in the United States for a tougher unilateral trade policy to confront "unfair" foreign trading practices. On 23 September 1985, President Ronald Reagan delivered a much-publicized speech on trade policy in which he defined the US objective as "fair trade" and announced his support for using Section 301 in unilateral pursuit of this objective. In a follow-up press conference, the president delineated various alleged violations of trade agreements by the nation's trading partners. Airbus was number three on the list.

Meanwhile, Boeing openly accused the European governments of subsidizing Airbus to the tune of $10 billion and lobbied Washington to obtain a full disclosure of the extent of their subsidies and the financial results of the Airbus consortium. Although Boeing urged prompt negotiations with Europe, Boeing officials stopped short of asking the president to file a 301 action.[40] Europe represented Boeing's largest foreign market, and Boeing was unwilling to risk retaliation by the European governments in the event of a formal 301 complaint.[41]

---

39. The following two paragraphs on the Air India deal are based on Yoffie (1985, 332–53).

40. Boeing's President Dean D. Thornton also stated publicly that "I don't support any form of subsidy for us, even if Airbus continues to receive subsidies and political support" (quoted in *Aviation Week and Space Technology*, 16 December 1985).

41. The contrast between Boeing's unwillingness to file a 301 petition against Airbus and

American air carrier companies, fearing the effects of a virtual Boeing monopoly in commercial aircraft, likewise did not favor protectionist measures against Airbus. If credible action was to be taken to convince the Europeans to desist from subsidies and unfair inducements for Airbus, it would have to be initiated by the US government. Moreover, given the politics of trade policymaking in the United States, any such action would have to be acceptable to the American producers.

But the government itself was divided on the issue of what to do. The State Department argued against any action because it might upset broader geopolitical relations with the Europeans and jeopardize national security interests.[42] According to Prestowitz (1989), other government officials argued against doing anything on the grounds that European subsidies for Airbus were a gift for the American airlines buying their aircraft. Still other officials argued that the US aircraft producers should file antidumping suits on their own behalf—their fears of retaliation notwithstanding. Ultimately, President Reagan's strike force to combat unfair foreign trading practices declined to act against Airbus. In this case, the "aggressive unilateralism" of the United States and its ability to bully its trading partners proved to be more talk than action throughout the 1980s. But tough talk rather than tough action was all the American industry was willing to tolerate.

After 1986 the United States and Europe held intermittent bilateral talks on their aircraft dispute. During these on-again, off-again negotiations, which lasted through early 1992, the US government repeatedly considered initiating 301 action or CVD relief against Airbus subsidies, but the American producers routinely opposed such actions. They preferred to work toward a bilateral deal to extend the 1979 aircraft code. This approach also served Europe's desire to avoid a formal GATT review of its subsidy practices, a review that would have involved the disclosure of sensitive national information.[43]

The US government, too, preferred a bilateral solution to a formal GATT panel, in part because it was not obvious that a complaint against European subsidies in the context of the vaguely worded 1979 aircraft code would have been successful.[44] Europe repeatedly expressed the view that, if the United States were

---

the Semiconductor Industry Association's willingness to file a 301 petition against the Japanese semiconductor companies is instructive. Boeing's dependence on the European market militated against a 301 action, whereas the American semiconductor industry was not dependent on the Japanese market because of the very access barriers that were at the heart of the American industry's 301 arguments.

42. The State Department's role is described by Prestowitz (1989, 405): "In the fall of 1985, when the President created the strike force to act against unfair trade, it declined to act against Airbus. Secretary of State [George P.] Shultz usually did not attend the strike force meeting, but he did attend the one on the Airbus in December 1985. Any action against the Airbus, he said, would upset our relations with the Europeans and most especially with the French. This would harm our national security and therefore should not be considered."

43. Under Airbus consortium rules, complete information about the amounts, terms, and conditions of member-government support is not regularly exchanged among the four partners. Indeed, the lack of information has been a formidable impediment to the progress of the bilateral talks between the United States and Europe.

44. According to the Europeans, even if the United States had brought a complaint against

to lodge a formal GATT complaint, it would be laughed out of court for two reasons. First, because their subsidies were in principle repayable, the Europeans believed them to be GATT-consistent.[45] Second, the 1979 agreement required only that each side seek to avoid government support that has "adverse effects" on trade. Given the continued dominance of Boeing in the global marketplace, the Europeans believed that it would be difficult to demonstrate such effects. On these two grounds, the Europeans steadfastly maintained that their development subsidies did not violate the 1979 GATT agreement.

The bilateral talks between the United States and Europe revealed the major points of disagreement between them, often in a heated atmosphere of charges and countercharges. Many of them revolved around technical questions such as how to determine the boundary line between the development phase and the production phase of a new aircraft model, and which interest rate to use to calculate the subsidy component of a European loan to Airbus. But the most important point of disagreement concerned the extent of allowable public launch aid. In earlier rounds of talks, both sides agreed to informal bans on inducements and production subsidies. Neither ban covered launch aid, however, which has been the largest component of European support for Airbus. According to American estimates, which the Europeans do not dispute, public funds covered 100 percent of the launch costs of the A300 and approximately 75 percent of the launch costs of the A320, and a comparable level is committed for the A330/340 program currently in operation (personal communication with Sally Bath, October 1991).

Over the course of the 1986–91 negotiations, both sides gradually narrowed their differences over the launch aid question. The initial American position that European subsidies were unfair and should be terminated gave way to a more realistic position that such subsidies should be reduced and capped, but need not be eliminated altogether. American negotiators gradually accepted the validity of the European argument that past subsidies were defensible on infant-industry or "competitive inequity" grounds. The US negotiating goal became one of establishing new rules for government intervention in an industry of "mature adults," including a rule on the overall extent of public launch aid.

The first real signs of a possible compromise on a cap for launch aid occurred in 1990, after the United States had filed a formal GATT complaint against an exchange rate guarantee program for Airbus initiated by the German government. The program itself reflected growing European concern over the budgetary toll of the Airbus program. In response to this concern, in 1988 the German government decided to sell MBB, the German state-owned member of the Airbus consortium, to Daimler-Benz. As part of the terms, the German government made several major concessions to Daimler-Benz, including paying off MBB's outstanding loans for Airbus production, rescheduling the repayment of MBB's outstanding Airbus launch aid, offering an additional $1.6 billion in launch aid

Airbus subsidies to the GATT in 1986, before the global market took off, it would have been unsuccessful. In that year, Boeing, with over 1,000 aircraft in service in Europe compared with only 56 Airbuses operating in the United States, made record profits and sales (*The Economist*, 5 July 1986, 62).

45. According to Commerce Under Secretary J. Michael Farren, however, it is extremely unlikely that any of the past subsidies to Airbus will ever be repaid. Certainly there has been no evidence of repayment so far.

for the A330/340, and guaranteeing MBB against most potential losses that might result from a rising deutsche mark and a falling dollar.[46] The last of these concessions amounted to a guarantee against losses on export sales resulting from exchange rate changes. Such an arrangement appeared to be an explicit violation of general GATT restrictions on export subsidies.

Daimler-Benz's request for an exchange rate guarantee reflected the very serious risk caused by exchange rate fluctuations in an industry in which global sales are denominated in a single currency. In the aircraft industry, that currency is the dollar, and major fluctuations in its value relative to the European currencies can have big effects on the price competitiveness of American and European producers. Of course, if currency fluctuations are the equilibrating mechanism for national trade imbalances, then these effects should be viewed simply as part of the natural equilibration process.[47] In 1988, the United States still had a huge trade deficit and Germany a huge trade surplus, so the dollar's drop and its competitive effects on German and American producers were precisely what was necessary for correcting macroeconomic imbalances. Indeed, since 1985 the United States had been working with Germany and the rest of the G-7 nations to bring the dollar down for this purpose. But macroeconomic imbalances were hardly paramount in the minds of the German officials and Daimler executives who negotiated the terms of the MBB sale.

They were, however, paramount in the minds of US officials, who vigorously attacked the exchange rate guarantee program. USTR Carla A. Hills called it "the most reprehensible type of subsidy. Much, much worse than the usual production subsidies. Once you subsidize currency fluctuations you're destroying the balance wheel that makes the trade mechanism work" (*Journal of Commerce and Commercialization*, 2 October 1989, 1). The United States was particularly concerned that the Daimler example would serve as a model for the use of exchange rate guarantees in other countries to offset the effects of the dollar's decline on the price competitiveness of their exports.

In late 1989 the United States filed a formal GATT complaint against the German exchange rate guarantee program as a violation of GATT Article VI on export subsidies. At the request of the German government, the United States put the complaint on hold, agreeing to discuss the program in bilateral negotiations covering all aspects of the aircraft dispute.

During 1990, some progress toward a compromise was achieved. The United States proposed that subsidies be cut from about 75 percent to about 25 percent of the total development cost of a new model. This proposal was defended on the grounds that it would "level the playing field" between the American producers and Airbus, because the former were thought to have an estimated 25 percent cost advantage over the latter (Sally Bath, personal communication,

---

46. The maximum liability of the German government for the guarantees through 1996 was $1.3 billion, with another $863 million for the period 1997–2000 (Office of Technology Assessment 1991a, 205–07).

47. On the other hand, when currency markets fluctuate wildly, with large effects on trade as happened in the 1980s, trade frictions inevitably result. This example demonstrates that the global economy ultimately faces a choice between managed trade and managed exchange rates.

October 1991). The Europeans instead offered to cap launch aid at 45 percent of total development cost.

Despite a number of promising contextual factors, including the growing market share of Airbus, the budgetary constraints of its supporting governments, and the more aggressive antisubsidy stance of the European Commission, neither the Americans nor the Europeans were willing to compromise much further, and the talks broke down in early 1991. The United States then reactivated its GATT complaint against the German exchange rate guarantee and lodged a second complaint against other Airbus subsidies as a violation of the 1979 aircraft code. In early 1992 a GATT panel finally ruled in favor of the United States in the former case.[48]

The 1992 US–EC Bilateral Agreement

Under the pressure of this decision and the other pending GATT case, bilateral talks between the two sides resumed. Surprisingly, these talks finally produced a bilateral agreement that addressed all of the major points of contention. Box 5.2 contains a summary description of the 1992 agreement, which applies to all future government involvement in the development of commercial aircraft of 100 seats or larger in both countries.

The agreement has several remarkable features. First, it establishes specific quantitative limits on both direct and indirect (military) subsidies for the development of new aircraft. The maximum allowable direct subsidy rate of 33 percent for the development cost of a new aircraft is clearly a compromise. Identifiable benefits from indirect subsidies are also restricted to 4 percent of the value of each firm's annual sales. In light of earlier European charges that American producers had benefited from huge indirect subsidies, this limit appears low, but it reflects the fact that such subsidies are likely to be considerably less important in the future than they have been in the past.

Second, the agreement resolves the dispute over which interest rate should apply to the repayment of launch aid. Although the Europeans prevailed in their choice of the government cost of borrowing over the commercial interest rate, the Americans won terms that accelerate the repayment of such aid, thereby reducing the value of lower borrowing costs. The United States also won another major victory on the highly contentious question of transparency. The agreement contains detailed reporting requirements that are essential to its enforcement. Ironically, these requirements should also prove useful to the Europeans in their ongoing efforts to increase the efficiency of the Airbus consortium.

Third, the agreement mandates at least two annual meetings a year for the purpose of monitoring its implementation, with additional meetings required at the request of either side. Coupled with the transparency requirements, these meeting requirements establish a framework for settling disputes.

Finally, the agreement explicitly proposes that its new disciplines be incorporated into the 1979 GATT agreement on civil aircraft and be adopted by all of

---

48. In July 1992, as part of the terms of a deal to complete the full privatization of Deutsche Airbus, the exchange rate guarantee was officially terminated (*New York Times*, 20 July 1992, C5).

Aircraft covered
All aircraft of 100 seats or larger are subject to the provisions of the agreement.

Direct support levels
Funds advanced by governments for aircraft development may not exceed 33 percent of total development costs and are to be provided only to programs in which there is a reasonable expectation of recoupment within 17 years.

Interest rates
Airbus will repay the first 25 percent of total development costs at the government cost of borrowing (GCOB) within 17 years of first disbursement; the remaining 8 percent will repaid at the GCOB plus 1 percent within 17 years of first disbursement.[1]

Repayment conditions
Airbus will make repayments on a royalty or per-plane basis and in a specified manner that limits backloading. Under previous practices, the terms and conditions on government launch aid to Airbus had allowed it to delay payment until late in the repayment cycle, thereby increasing the value of low-cost support.

Prior commitments
The agreement does not apply to any prior or outstanding government support committed to large civil aircraft programs.

Indirect supports
Both sides agree that indirect (i.e., military) supports should neither confer unfair advantage on manufacturers of civil aircraft nor lead to distortions in international trade in such aircraft.

Identifiable benefits from indirect support are limited to 3 percent of the value of industry-wide turnover in each signatory and 4 percent of the value of each firm's annual sales. Benefits will primarily be calculated as cost reductions in the development of a civil aircraft program realized from technology acquired through government R&D programs.

Transparency
Both sides agree to exchange, on a regular and systematic basis, information on the total amount of government support for new development projects and its share in total development costs; the terms and conditions of such support; aggregate data on disbursements and repayments relating to direct government support; and aggregate amounts of identifiable indirect support. In addition, both sides agree to provide a complete list of prior disbursements and commitments, including information on the type of repayment obligation and the planned repayment period.

Inducements and offsets
By clarifying rules on inducements in the 1979 GATT agreement, the 1992 agreement strengthens the prohibition on governments conferring special favors in exchange for aircraft purchases. Both sides agree that such inducements include foreign military or economic aid and landing rights.

Escape clause on emergency aid
Either side may temporarily derogate from the agreement, *with the exception of the development support provisions*, if the survival and financial viability of an aircraft manufacturer are in jeopardy. Any such withdrawal would require consultations with representatives of the other side, full disclosure of information to justify the withdrawal, and full explanation of the remedy to be used.

Production supports
No further production subsidies are allowed.

Equity infusions

Equity infusions are excluded from the agreement. However, both sides commit themselves not to provide equity in such a manner as to undermine the effectiveness of the agreement.

Dispute settlement mechanisms

Both sides will consult at least twice a year to ensure the functioning of the agreement. Either side may request consultations related to the agreement at any time. Such consultations must be held no later than 30 days after they are requested.

---

1. The United States had wanted commercial interest rates to apply but finally accepted the European position.

Source: Adapted from "Agreement Concerning the Application of the GATT Agreement on Trade in Civil Aircraft."

its signatories. In fact, the Europeans had hoped to get them to participate in the new agreement from the beginning, but this strategy was seen as a delaying tactic by the Americans, who suggested multilateralizing the bilateral agreement at a later date. The United States prevailed on this point, but both sides have wasted no time in recommending the extension of their bilateral deal to other interested GATT members.

Despite its specificity on some bitterly contested issues, the 1992 agreement does contain some important loopholes. An emergency escape clause allows either side to derogate temporarily from its terms—with the exception of those covering direct development supports—if the survival and financial viability of an aircraft manufacturer are jeopardized. Such a withdrawal requires prior consultations and the disclosure of full information for justification. In the event of a withdrawal, the agreement's prohibitions on production subsidies, inducements, equity transfusions, and other forms of government assistance could be temporarily relaxed. Given the highly cyclical nature of the market for global aircraft, both sides saw an escape clause as a necessary condition for accepting the agreement.

The agreement also explicitly allows the use of national trade laws to address all conflicts other than those relating to the magnitude and terms of direct and indirect government supports. This means that trade actions involving such issues as dumping, intellectual property protection, and business practices are not precluded.

Finally, the agreement can be terminated by either side at the end of one year. Thereafter, unilateral withdrawal from the agreement can only take effect 12 months after prior notification of an intent to withdraw.

Overall, the 1992 agreement is a noteworthy accomplishment for both sides and a major improvement over the 1979 aircraft agreement. Although it has been criticized by some US observers (but not by the American producers, who support it) because it allows the Europeans to continue to subsidize Airbus, this criticism overlooks a crucial point: because of the industry's underlying economics, government support for the development of new aircraft cannot and should not be ruled out altogether. Rather the challenge is to specify parsimonious and precise rules that permit subsidies for beneficial innovation and competition while precluding rent-shifting subsidies that injure all parties. The 1992 agreement meets this challenge by proscribing certain kinds of beggar-thy-neighbor and efficency-reducing subsidies, such as inducements and production subsidies, while controlling potentially beneficial development subsidies through specific rules and enforcement mechanisms.

Why were the United States and the European Community finally able to agree in some detail on issues they had been debating for years? The growing competitive success of Airbus was a major consideration on both sides. By 1992 Europe had realized its long-term goal of building a European producer that was Boeing's competitive equal. As Airbus's share of the market grew, its need for public development assistance diminished, and some of its European supporters seized upon the opportunity to economize on their future commitments. It also seems likely that, having realized their goal, the Europeans wanted to secure Airbus's place in the global industry by deterring the entry of new subsidized foreign competitors in the future. In this respect, the proposed deal between McDonnell Douglas and Taiwan Aerospace (discussed below) may have been a factor encouraging the Europeans to compromise, in the expectation that a bilateral deal with the United States would cover the possible provision of subsidies by Taiwan and other Asian governments to McDonnell Douglas.

The success of Airbus also motivated the American producers, especially Boeing, to accept a compromise. By the end of 1991, their patience with the Europeans was wearing thin. Infant-industry subsidies to level the playing field were one thing; generous beggar-thy-neighbor subsidies to grab market share were quite another. Even Boeing, which had previously counseled patience, was beginning to argue that unilateral American action would soon be required if bilateral negotiations continued to fail.[49] Clearly, however, a bilateral agreement was preferable as long as it imposed enforceable limits on European subsidies that left the playing field relatively level for the development of future aircraft models.

Finally, both Europe and the United States may have been moved to compromise because of excess capacity conditions in the global market[50] and the growing danger of a trade or subsidy war that would dissipate rents for both sides.

Challenges Facing the American Commercial Aircraft Industry

The 1992 agreement contains but by no means eliminates the external challenge to the American aircraft industry posed by continued European support for Airbus. And it does nothing to reverse the damage done by past support. Boeing

---

49. Boeing is understandably intent on trying to reach some "level-playing-field" agreement on the launch subsidy question before Airbus makes good on its intention to launch the 350, which would pose a major competitive alternative to the Boeing 747. In a January 1992 speech before the Council on Foreign Relations, Boeing Chief Executive Officer Frank A. Shrontz argued that "enough is enough" and expressed his opinion that Boeing had a strong case for retaliatory action against Europe under US trade law.

50. According to Wall Street projections, with which Boeing officials largely concur, total annual demand for new aircraft deliveries is not likely to exceed 600 airplanes per year for the next decade, whereas current industry production capacity is 1,000 airplanes per year and climbing.

already faces stiff competition from Airbus even in the American market. Revealing just how intense this competition has become, United Airlines, long the most loyal and biggest Boeing customer, recently signed a deal to lease 50 A320s from Airbus, with an option for 50 more. And the competition is likely to intensify further when the Airbus consortium finally decides to launch the A350, which will threaten if not terminate Boeing's monopoly in the market for long-range, wide-bodied aircraft.

McDonnell Douglas, too, has already been harmed by Airbus. Contrary to what some American observers have suggested, however, the company's woes are not simply the result of European subsidies to Airbus, although it is Airbus that has cut most deeply into its market share. Rather, its commercial problems can be traced to more than two decades of undercapitalization and stagnant technology, brought on by its earlier competition with Lockheed. In addition, as noted earlier, the company has encountered unexpected technical and cost problems with its new MD-11 aircraft.

Both American producers also confront internal challenges resulting from sustained cutbacks in defense procurement and indirect military subsidies. (Table 5.2) Such cutbacks have already inflicted severe damage on McDonnell Douglas, the nation's largest military contractor. Indeed, in 1991 the company was forced to defer payment on a $1.35 billion debt to the Department of Defense and to request an advance of $1 billion. Meanwhile, as Pentagon officials worried about how to save the company's military operations, a growing number of analysts speculated about whether it would be forced to exit the commercial aircraft industry.

To meet the internal and external challenges confronting American producers during this decade, the United States will have to replace its outmoded and expensive military industrial policy with a civilian industrial policy. Rather than hope that foreign intervention in the industry will cease, the United States will have to respond with offsetting interventions at home. Rather than assume that dependence on foreign suppliers does not matter, it will have to recognize the dangers of excessive dependence on such suppliers for critical component technologies, such as advanced avionics.[51] Rather than hope that the market will solve the problem of military conversion, it will have to fashion a domestic strategy to speed the process and reduce its costs.

Does the United States have the will and the capability to address these challenges? The response of domestic policymakers to the serious difficulties of McDonnell Douglas during the last two years is not cause for optimism. After struggling to find private and public sources of capital in the United States to support its commercial operations, in November 1991 McDonnell Douglas struck a tentative deal with Taiwan Aerospace Corporation, a public-private company established to develop an aerospace industry for Taiwan. According to the initial terms of the deal, McDonnell Douglas would sell a 40 percent share of its private operations to Taiwan Aerospace for $2 billion, at least 29 percent of which was to be provided by the Taiwanese government. In return, Taiwan Aerospace, as an equity shareholder, would participate in the manufacturing and marketing of all McDonnell Douglas aircraft, including the new MD-12, which the company

---

51. Moran and Mowery (1991, 49/50) emphasize the dangers of a potential foreign stranglehold over the provision of critical component technologies in the aircraft industry.

hoped to launch with the infusion of Taiwanese capital. According to some reports, as much as 60 percent of the work on the MD-12 was to be done in Taiwan.

As of this writing, the deal's fate is uncertain. After studying it carefully, the Taiwanese government and private investors want to negotiate better terms. But even if they finally agree to a deal, would it serve the interests of the United States? A disturbingly small number of American policymakers have even asked the question.[52] While the Taiwanese government sponsored a three-month study to assess the merits of the deal, the American government paid scant attention to it.

Behind the American attitude is the presumption that what is good for a private company like McDonnell Douglas is good for the nation. But McDonnell Douglas is no ordinary private company—it is, as noted above, the nation's largest military contractor and the guardian of some of its most sensitive military technologies. And the proposed deal with Taiwan Aerospace is no ordinary market transaction—it involves the active participation of the Taiwanese government.

Many American observers, however, see the deal as simply an extension of the globalization trend apparent in the aircraft industry for decades (Mowery 1991). Moreover, the overall assessment of this trend is a positive one: globalization, in this view, has simply enhanced efficiency, improved market access, and bolstered competition (Moran and Mowery 1991, 29–34). Some American policymakers have expressed concern over the possible transfer of military technologies to McDonnell Douglas's foreign partners, but the company has promised to structure its deal to prevent this.[53] And if a deal is finally negotiated, its effects on national security will be assessed by the Committee on Foreign Investment in the United States, which can then recommend to the president whether to approve or block the deal. The agency's record to date (see chapter 4) strongly suggests that it would be approved on national security grounds without conditions.

Meanwhile, there has been no attempt by the American government to influence the terms of the deal on commercial grounds, despite the active participation of the Taiwanese government on the other side of the bargaining table. At the very least, one might have imagined an effort by the American government to work with McDonnell Douglas and representatives of its subtier supplier firms to bargain for greater employment and subcontracting opportunities.[54]

---

52. Two congressional committees did hold hearings on the deal in December 1991 and March 1992. The following discussion draws on testimony by the authors of this chapter at the March 1992 hearings.

53. In written testimony before the Joint Economic Committee on 27 February 1992, John Wolf, executive vice president at McDonnell Douglas, described how the company would structure the deal to avoid national security risks (US Congress, Joint Economic Committee 1992).

54. One might argue that, if the US government becomes involved in negotiating the subcontracting terms of the deal, it will encourage other countries to do the same in deals involving American companies. But other countries already do this, and lack of action by the US government has failed to deter them. The real question is whether the US government should take a more active role in negotiating deals when other governments are already participants, not whether the United States can block their participation by setting a good example of hands-off policy.

These suppliers and others in the industry have already been harmed by earlier subcontracting deals involving McDonnell Douglas and Boeing in Europe, Japan, and elsewhere.[55] Often these deals are offset arrangements linking sales by these companies in particular markets to their purchases from local suppliers. Such offset deals are best understood as a mechanism for distributing the rents from aicraft production around the world. As foreign nations actively negotiate to grab some of these rents from the United States, American policymakers have been largely oblivious to their efforts.

The American government also appears to have been oblivious to the possibility that a deal between McDonnell Douglas and Taiwan Aerospace would lead to future violations of the GATT subsidy code, the 1979 GATT civil aircraft code, the 1985 OECD agreement on export financing, or the 1992 bilateral agreement with the Europeans. Although McDonnell Douglas has assiduously denied that any subsidies from the Taiwanese government would be involved in the deal, the claim is hard to believe. Industry estimates indicate that anywhere from $5 billion to $10 billion would be needed to launch the MD-12.[56] Where would this money come from? The Taiwanese government is the most likely source. Indeed, its recognition of this fact—a fact that seems to have escaped many American observers—is the main reason why the deal is now floundering.

Finally, the American government has not asked the hardest question of all about a possible deal between McDonnell Douglas and Taiwan Aerospace to develop the MD-12. Would the entry of this new aircraft into a global market already suffering from substantial excess capacity be in the national interest? As the history of international aircraft competition presented in this chapter indicates, the correct answer to this question requires a balancing of consumer and producer interests and of static and dynamic efficiencies. On the one hand, the entry of a new aircraft, especially under conditions of global excess capacity, is likely to reduce prices, benefiting airline companies and their passengers. Depending on its design, a new aircraft might provide additional consumer benefits in the form of greater product choice and enhanced product capabilities. On the other hand, greater competition is likely to reduce economies of scale for each producer and raise industry costs. Higher costs, combined with lower prices, are likely to reduce industry rents, making all producers worse off. Boeing, as the only "unsubsidized" producer, would be likely to feel the pinch the hardest.

---

55. According to International Trade Administration estimates by Michael Farren in his written testimony before the Joint Economic Committee on 27 February 1992, foreign products (excluding the engines) installed on the Boeing 767 probably represent close to 15 percent of the total, and the share on the 777 may be as high as 30 percent. For McDonnell Douglas, foreign products (excluding the engines) range from 15 percent to 20 percent of the aircraft value of the MD-11 and the MD-80/90, up significantly from the foreign content of the older DC-9 and DC-10.

56. McDonnell Douglas (testimony by Larry Clarkson, vice president of Boeing, before the Joint Economic Committee, 27 February 1992) reports estimates of the total investment cost for the MD-12 program in the range of $4.0 billion to $5.4 billion. Boeing believes that the actual amounts will be much higher, in the $7.0 billion to $10.0 billion range, including upfront investment costs as well as cumulative negative cash flow during the first years of production. Moreover, Boeing believes that this is a lower estimate based on the assumption that the MD-12 will ultimately be a market success. Now that McDonnell Douglas is considering an all-new aircraft, the actual number is likely to be closer to Boeing's estimate.

Reduced profits in turn would hamper Boeing's ability to meet the challenge of a subsidized A350 entry later in the decade.

All of these possible effects depend in part on the features of the product in question—in this case, the MD-12. If it offers little in the way of new technology or product differentiation, as the first trijet design proposed by McDonnell Douglas did, then it is more likely to be simply rent-dissipating.[57] The history of the industry, especially the episode of mutually destructive competition between McDonnell Douglas and Lockheed, highlights the dangers of duplicative competition.

Even if the MD-12 model finally chosen entails real product innovation, as the more recent four-engine, double-deck, 600-passenger superjumbo design proposed by McDonnell Douglas did (*Aviation Week and Space Technology*, 16 March 1992), it would still have rent-dissipating effects. Indeed, these effects might be even more severe, if, as seems likely, Boeing and/or Airbus should decide to accelerate entry into the superjumbo market to prevent McDonnell Douglas from gaining a first-mover advantage. As long as the global industry suffers from significant excess supply, a subsidized three-way race for the superjumbo market would reduce prices, increase costs, and intensify trade friction between the producing nations.

Without an institutional mechanism for analyzing the dynamics of current competition in the aircraft industry and for projecting its future directions, the American government is simply incapable of posing, let alone answering, the complicated questions suggested by the proposed deal between McDonnell Douglas and Taiwan Aerospace. And without such a capability, the nation will continue to suffer from a woeful lack of strategic vision about what is arguably its most strategic industry. The McDonnell Douglas case clearly demonstrates that a civilian industrial policy is sorely needed to guide the American aircraft industry through the difficult days of conversion, restructuring, and intensified foreign competition that lie ahead.

Conclusions

Several conclusions emerge from this history of competition in the global commercial aircraft industry. First, if one accepts recurrent government intervention in the industry as a given, as we do, then the relevant policy challenge at the international level is the design of multilateral rules that proscribe the most harmful forms of intervention while allowing those that encourage innovation and competition. The 1992 bilateral agreement between Europe and the United States is a major step toward meeting this challenge.

Second, the policy remedies available in the nation's trading laws are not adequate to the task of responding to foreign targeting programs in the aircraft industry. A recent influential book by Clyde V. Prestowitz, Jr. (1989), cites the

---

57. The trijet design for the MD-12 first proposed in the deal with Taiwan Aerospace was a stretch version of the MD-11, which itself is a derivative of the DC-10. With a new wing and larger engines, the trijet MD-12 would have been able to fly an estimated 8,000 nautical miles. As a McDonnell Douglas official admitted, this version of the MD-12 would not "offer customers anything they couldn't get anyplace else" *Aviation Week and Space Technology*, 16 March 1992, 14/15).

industry as "a prime example of how the interplay of American trade theory, trade laws, and security works to the disadvantage of American industry and ultimately of the American economy." Prestowitz (1989, 404) also argues that the American position in the aircraft industry is eroding, "not because others produce better or cheaper airplanes, but because of the American approach to trade." The implication is that, if the United States had used its trade laws— primarily its antidumping and countervailing duty laws and its Section 301 relief provisions—more aggressively to deter European subsidies to Airbus, the American industry and the American economy would have been better off. But this chapter raises serious questions about that conclusion.

First, European subsidies to Airbus may have harmed American producers, but they have also benefited American airline companies and their passengers by encouraging competition and innovation. The historical record of competition outlined in this chapter suggests that these user benefits have been substantial. Second, even if one assumes that past European subsidies reduced American economic welfare, the evidence presented here indicates that a protectionist US response to deter such subsidies would have made matters worse. Third, partly in recognition of this fact, the American producers have steadfastly opposed unilateral trade policy measures that would have invited European retaliation. Their opposition, rather than concerns about the national security costs of possible trade friction with Europe, has precluded such unilateral measures. Aggressive unilateralism on the part of the United States in the aircraft industry has taken the form of words rather than actions, because this has been the preference of the American producers themselves.[58] Finally, it seems unlikely that a unilateral trade policy action by the United States would have deterred European efforts to realize what has been their remarkably consistent long-term goal of building a competitive European aircraft producer.

A third basic conclusion of this chapter is that the real error of American policy has been that of a haphazard defense industrial policy, not that of an ineffectual trade policy. Both the persistent financial weakness of McDonnell Douglas during the last twenty years and the initial market opening for Airbus are the consequence of a disastrous and ill-advised competition between the American producers in launching the first wide-body commercial jets in the late 1960s. This competition was a reflection of the particular policy environment in which it occurred—the government's defense-oriented industrial policies influenced who the competitors were and how they competed. Since all of the American producers were major military contractors at the time, the safety net provided by their military operations and the technological breakthroughs funded by the military encouraged them to take risky decisions that the discipline of the market, even one that was highly imperfect, would not have allowed.

Rather than intervening to head off these decisions and to coordinate the industry at this critical juncture, the US government adopted a hands-off position, letting "market forces" determine the outcome, even though these forces

---

58. In recent testimony before Congress, Commerce Under Secretary J. Michael Farren, who has long been involved in the aircraft dispute with Europe, stated that the American negotiating position with Airbus has never fundamentally diverged from the position of the American industry. Moreover, throughout these negotiations there has been substantial agreement between Boeing and McDonnell Douglas. On some occasions, the American government has taken a harder line than that supported by the American producers.

were heavily tainted by the government's defense links with the industry. Ironically, while the European governments were working to rationalize their national aircraft producers into a coordinated pan-European venture and to target a promising niche in the commercial industry, the American government was inadvertently encouraging its producers to embark on an unsustainable, mutually destructive competitive strategy.

The American industry in the early 1990s is once again at a critical juncture, confronting intensified competition abroad and cutbacks in military procurement and indirect subsidies at home. To address these challenges in ways that serve the national interest, the United States needs a civilian industrial policy. It can no longer afford the expensive, defense-oriented industrial policy of the past. Nor can it afford to cling to the soothing but irrelevant belief that market forces alone will determine industry outcomes in the future.

6

Managing Trade and Investment: Europe's Evolving Strategy in the Electronics Industry

Videocassette Recorders: From Managed Trade to Managing Investment

High-Definition Television: The Strategy to Create European Champions

Understanding Europe's Evolving Strategy Toward the Electronics Industry

Lessons for US Trade and Industrial Policy

The creation of a unified market in Europe is one of the most important developments in the global electronics industry in recent history. The countries that comprise this market account for one-third of global GNP and one-third of global consumption of electronics output (Commission of the European Communities 1991). Yet despite their size and influence, the European countries lag in electronics technology and production. Europe runs a distant third after the United States and Japan in the production of computers and semiconductors, and a distant second after Japan in the production of consumer electronics products. In many electronics markets, including computers and semiconductors, Europe's share of global production has been declining. Only in the telecommunications field are European companies relatively strong, largely because of past preferential procurement practices linking national producers to protected national markets.

Reflecting the relative weakness of European producers, Europe's annual trade imbalance in electronics doubled between 1986 and 1990. In 1989, Europe's trade deficit in electronics hit 31.0 billion ecu (about $35 billion at then-current exchange rates; table 6.1); of that deficit, about 52 percent was in computer hardware and software and another 30 percent in consumer electronics (table 6.2). Europe's weakened position in electronics is also evident in world trade shares. Since 1970, the EC countries have suffered significant reductions in their global trade shares and increasing trade deficits in data processing systems, electronic equipment, and electronic components, primarily with Japan and, to a lesser extent, with the East Asian newly industrializing countries.[1]

The author is appreciative of helpful research assistance on this chapter by Michael Santoro. Funding for this assistance was provided in part by a grant from the Division of Research of the Harvard Business School.

1. See table 2.6 in chapter 2. These results are based on Guerrieri (1991).

Table 6.1 Trade balances in information technology and telecommunications, by region, 1986–89 (billions of dollars)

	1986	1987	1988	1989
Europe	−14.3	−21.8	−33.1	−35.0
United States	−7.5	−7.3	−5.2	−7.7
Japan	49.5	54.2	66.2	62.8
Rest of world	−27.6	−25.3	−24.2	−20.7

Source: Commission of the European Communities, The European Electronics and Information Technology Industry: States of Play, Issues at Stake and Proposals for Action, 1991.

Concerns over the competitiveness of the European electronics industry have not escaped the architects of the Europe 1992 strategy. Indeed, such concerns have been a major impetus to this strategy (see, e.g., Sharp 1991). Not surprisingly, many of the trade, procurement, and technology policies on the 1992 agenda have been fashioned to help European producers compete more vigorously in the electronics industry.

Seen in this context, the advent of a unified European market poses both opportunities and perils for American companies. On the one hand, depending on their form, policies to advantage European producers may actively disadvantage foreign producers. On the other hand, unification will bring significant efficiencies in the ability of all companies, foreign and domestic, to manufacture, sell, and distribute products for the European market. It is not simply duty-free movement of goods that will enhance the attractiveness of the European market; equally significant will be the harmonization of standards, which exert a strong influence on competitive outcomes in electronics. Electronics producers seeking to market in Europe will no longer face a bewildering array of national standards requiring customized production and distribution channels for relatively small national markets. Instead, common European standards will allow producers to realize cost savings and marketing advantages.

The European goal of restoring the competitiveness of its electronics industry raises several important questions for US producers and policymakers. Will European integration foster greater protectionism and greater discrimination in favor of European producers—in other words, as it has become fashionable to ask, will 1992 create a "Fortress Europe" in the electronics industry? Certainly, there are significant protectionist straws in the wind, such as the recent application of new, Community-wide rules of origin (described below) in conjunction with tougher European antidumping laws. Or will Europe pursue a somewhat more benign policy, not to protect European producers but to encourage European production regardless of the ownership or national origin of the companies that do the producing? Such a policy stance would be a "fortress" against imports but not against foreign direct investment. Global American companies might not be hurt, but both domestic American companies that wish to export and America as a production location would. Or, finally, will Europe disavow "fortress" policies of all kinds, instead relying on greater competition and broad-based promotional policies, such as greater R&D support for precompetitive technologies, to realize its goal of a stronger electronics industry?

Table 6.2 European Community: trade deficit in electronics, 1988 and 1989 (billions of dollars)

	1988	1989
Components		
Active	4.3	4.8
Passive	0.7	1.3
Computers		
Hardware	16.9	16.9
Software	1.2	1.4
Consumer electronics	11.2	10.6

Source: Commission of the European Communities, *The European Electronics and Information Technology Industry: States of Play, Issues at Stake and Proposals for Action, 1991.*

This chapter seeks to answer these questions by examining Europe's evolving strategy in two electronics products: videocassette recorders (VCRs) and high-definition television (HDTV). Europe's policies in these segments of the electronics industry have not been as well documented as its policies in other parts of the industry, such as semiconductors and telecommunications equipment.[2] The VCR case history begins with an explicit voluntary restraint agreement (VRA)—the first ever negotiated by the European Community—with Japan. This managed trade approach was followed by a progression of implicit and explicit policy maneuvers to encourage Japanese and later Korean producers to substitute European production for exports into Europe. Overall, the VCR case confirms the usual drawbacks of VRAS as a method of protection and supports the hypothesis that Europe's strategy is evolving toward a fortress against imports and a magnet for foreign direct investment. The HDTV case iillustrates two other facets of European policy, namely, the harmonization of standards and the provision of public support for R&D programs in electronics. In this case, more clearly than in the VCR case, Europe's strategy to date exhibits a preference for European producers and a willingness to use both nontariff barriers, such as technical standards, and exclusionary infant-industry programs to support European producers at the expense of their foreign competitors.

In both the VCR and HDTV cases, Japanese rather than American producers have been the direct and explicit target of European strategy. Indeed, US–Europe trade friction in electronics has been remarkably rare, and when it has occurred, it has been triggered by either US–Japan or Europe-Japan friction, as in the case of semiconductors.[3] Nonetheless, Europe's strategy of encouraging European production by Japanese companies to substitute for imports of VCRs has a clear precedent in its earlier strategy of encouraging European production by American companies to substitute for imports of computers. The two strategies have had similar effects: in 1990, American companies controlled 58 percent of Eu-

---

2. For insightful analyses of Europe's evolving strategy in the semiconductor and telecommunications industries, see Flamm (1990) and Cowhey (1990). Portions of the VCR and the telecommunications case histories are also told in Cawson et al. (1990).

3. See chapter 4 of this book and Flamm (1990) for a discussion of spillover trade frictions between the United States and Europe resulting from their actions toward Japan in the semiconductor industry.

ropean computer production, and Japanese companies about 50 percent of European VCR production.[4]

In these two product areas, as in the semiconductor industry, European policies have varied over time, but their ultimate effect has been to act as a magnet for foreign investment. The results of this strategy are apparent in a variety of indicators. For example, although Europe as a region accounted for 24 percent of global electronics production in 1990, European-owned firms accounted for only 19 percent. In contrast to Japan and the United States, where domestically based producers control (respectively) 94 percent and 92 percent of domestic electronics production, in Europe domestically based producers control only 79 percent of domestic production, with US–based companies accounting for 21 percent and Japanese producers for another 5 percent (according to data provided by the American Electronics Association).

Videocassette Recorders: From Managed Trade to Managing Investment

The Initial Japanese Challenge and the Protectionist European Response

It is interesting to note that neither Japanese nor European but American companies were the first to develop the basic technology for VCRs. Ampex developed VCR technology in the early 1950s and sold a small number of large machines, mainly to the television broadcast industry. Ampex attempted to develop a consumer product, but failed because it could not develop sources to manufacture large volumes efficiently. When the company was sold, its new owners decided to focus on the broadcast market rather than the consumer market. RCA, which licensed the original technology from Ampex, made the same decision. Only in the late 1970s, after the potential of the consumer market became clearer, did both Ampex and RCA make a late, futile, and (in the case of RCA) expensive effort to develop a consumer product. Thus, despite an initial American technological advantage, there has been virtually no VCR production in the United States by either domestic or foreign-owned companies.[5]

In contrast, three Japanese companies—Sony, Matsushita, and JVC—grasped the future significance of the consumer market in the early 1960s and mounted long-term efforts to develop a low-cost, home-use product.[6] In 1975, Sony's Betamax became the first such product to be brought to market. In the fall of

---

4. The computer share is based on figures in Commission of the European Communities (1991, appendix tables). The VCR share is based on numbers provided to the author by the French electronics firm Thomson.

5. For a complete discussion of the demise of the consumer electronics industry in the United States, see MIT Commission on Industrial Productivity(1989).

6. In VCRs, as in numerous other products, the Japanese built on original American and European basic research to perfect consumer applications and commercialize the results. The most recent example of this strategy is in the production of advanced computer displays, where the Japanese have captured the market for a product based on original American research.

1976, JVC, a member of the Matsushita group, introduced an alternative system called VHS. Among the factors contributing to the ultimate success of the Japanese companies were the following: fierce competition in the areas of technical development, standards, and price; patient capital and stable corporate ownership, which made a long-term research strategy possible; capable, technically knowledgeable leadership; modest subsidies from the Ministry of International Trade and Industry (MITI) in the early years of product development; and a strengthening technological base in microelectronic inputs (Rosenbloom and Cusamano 1987). In addition, the Japanese companies benefited from a sheltered home market in televisions as a result of distribution *keiretsu* and price-fixing arrangements, both of which have been well documented (Yamamura 1986; Choate 1990, chapter 6). These arrangements effectively precluded the entry of new firms of any nationality and allowed the Japanese television producers—Matsushita, Sony, Sanyo, Hitachi, Mitsubishi, Toshiba, and Sharp—to charge higher prices in Japan than those charged for virtually identical goods on the world market. The cushion of a high-volume home market in this related technology provided a sanctuary that reduced the risks involved in increasing VCR capacity to meet future demand growth.

Unlike Japanese firms in the semiconductor and computer industries, which had to struggle to catch up to their American rivals, Japanese firms in the VCR industry were the technological and efficiency leaders almost from the industry's inception. Moreover, because of their dominant position, they controlled 94 percent of global production as early as 1982, exercising substantial market power abroad and undisputed market power at home. But market power did not translate into collusive behavior, at least at this point in the industry's development. Instead, competition between the Japanese producers was fierce both at home and abroad. At stake was the issue of which standard—Sony's Beta standard or the Matsushita–JVC VHS standard—would ultimately carry the market.

Because most of their production was exported, competition among the Japanese companies was especially strong in foreign markets. By the early 1980s, more than 77 percent of Japanese production was exported, with Europe accounting for nearly 40 percent of the total and the United States another 30 percent (figures based on data in *Japan Electronics Almanac* 1990).

But there was an important distinction between the American and the European markets. In the United States there were no domestic VCR producers, in part because of the earlier demise of the American television industry at the hands of the same Japanese companies.[7] In contrast, the European countries had used a variety of policies—including national standards, national quotas, and explicit local content rules in conjunction with Community antidumping laws—to allow European producers to retain a major share of the European color television industry.[8] And one of these producers, Philips, had developed a third VCR standard, called V2000, which was being sold by both Philips and Grundig, a German company in which Philips then had a 25 percent interest.

---

7. For the story of the demise of the television industry in the United States see MIT Commission on Industrial Productivity (1989). For a political interpretation of America's policy and Japanese influence on it see Choate (1990, chapter 6).

8. For more detail on Europe's television strategy, see the case study of the HDTV industry below.

In addition, Philips was lobbying to have other European suppliers adopt its VCR standard over the competing Japanese standards.

Philips, like Matsushita, was one of the world's largest electrical appliance manufacturers, and it had actually launched the first VCR machine aimed at the consumer market in 1971, four years before Sony introduced its model. By the early 1980s, however, it was already clear that in an unrestricted market Philips and Grundig could not survive against the Japanese. In 1982, V2000 systems were selling for DM1,800, while the average price of a Japanese model was DM995. Some Japanese sets were selling for as low as DM800 as a result of massive competitive price cuts by the Japanese companies, which had dropped their prices on the European market by 60 percent in the course of a year.[9] In the face of such competition, Philips managed to gain only 20 percent of the German and the Dutch markets, with almost no market penetration elsewhere.[10] Even more disturbing for Philips, Thomson of France, Thorn-EMI of Great Britain, and AEG-Telefunken of Germany had negotiated joint ventures with JVC to manufacture and distribute VCRs using the VHS standard.

The impending demise of the fledgling European VCR industry startled both the European producers and the European governments into action. The French government reacted first, in 1982, even though no French firm was then producing VCRs. Indeed, Thomson was importing and distributing Japanese products under its own label, and Thomson officials had recently announced intentions to form a joint venture with JVC. Nonetheless the French government supported the goal of a "European solution" in the VCR market. Consistent with this goal, the French government in late 1982 forced all VCR imports to be cleared through the customs post at Poitiers (located about 75 miles inland and 175 miles from Paris) and inspected to ensure that all instruction books were in French. This action was clearly designed to block imports or at the very least to delay them until a supplementary tax on VCRs came into effect in January 1983. The Poitiers restrictions quickly became an embarrassment to the European Commission, and their elimination became a bargaining chip in negotiations between the Europeans over how best to respond to the surge in VCR imports from Japan.

At the same time that the French government unilaterally restricted Japanese imports, it also encouraged a Thomson initiative to merge with Grundig. Philips supported Thomson's proposed purchase, hoping that Thomson would then align itself with the Philips-Grundig V2000 standard. The French effort to create a European champion in VCRs through the merger of existing national champions from different European countries foreshadowed the dramatic mergers and consolidations that have since swept the European electronics industry in preparation for 1992. As a result of this restructuring, only two or three European multinationals now compete in most of the major segments of the electronics market.[11] In consumer electronics, not surprisingly, the dominant European

9. This price information is based on data cited by Yoffie (1986a). Yoffie's numbers are based on interviews with Japanese and European producers. See also "The World VCR Industry" in Yoffie (1990, 68–85).

10. Nomura Management School (1986, table 1, p. 3). The Nomura Management School documents were provided to the author by David B. Yoffie of the Harvard Business School.

11. At present, the three major European players in the consumer electronics markets are

players are now Philips and Thomson, the same two firms that the French government had hoped to tie together through the Grundig deal in vCRs. In 1983, however, the German antitrust authorities still looked askance at the formation of European industrial giants, and they blocked the merger between Thomson and Grundig on the grounds that it would capture a 55 percent share of the German market in consumer electronics.[12]

While these merger negotiations were proceeding, however, Philips and Grundig mounted a successful effort with the European Commission to win temporary protection. Initially they threatened an antidumping suit, which probably would have been successful under the EC antidumping law (discussed further below), and sought a tariff increase as an alternative. Their campaign for protection was waged through the European and national trade associations, the EC member governments, and the Commission itself.

The four main arguments on which Philips and Grundig based their campaign recall arguments used today to defend policies aimed at strengthening the European electronics industry.[13] The first argument stressed the unfairness of Japan's trading and industrial policy practices, in particular that of industrial targeting or "laser-beaming," that is, the development of enormous production capacities and the flooding of world markets in particular sectors. Although industrial targeting did not play a role in the emerging strength of the Japanese vCR industry, protectionist barriers and the cartelization of the Japanese market for consumer electronics did. In this sense the first argument of the European producers—which the American television manufacturers had used in vain in appeals to their own government—had some merit.

The second argument—which, given Europe's serious unemployment problems, carried the most weight with government officials—stressed the imminent consequences of the Japanese export offensive for employment in the European consumer electronics industry. In Europe, as in the United States, the possible loss of jobs from import competition was the traditional defense of protectionist policies, even though the evidence usually indicated that the cost of saving jobs through such policies was high and the effects were short-lived.[14] In the relatively labor-intensive consumer electronics industry, the employment defense, however misguided, was politically powerful. It had already proved effective at winning protection for the color television industry, whose major European producers were again Philips-Grundig and Thomson.

The third argument emphasized the potential loss of R&D capacity and the growing danger of European dependence on imported technologies. Variants of this argument, which identifies the electronics industry as "strategic" in the economic sense defined in chapter 2—or which identifies electronic technologies

---

Philips, which now controls Grundig; Thomson, which took over Telefunken, Nordmende, and Ferguson; and Nokia, a Finnish company, which bought the ITT subsidiary in Germany and Oceanic in France.

12. In addition, there have been industry rumors to the effect that the Grundig deal was blocked partly because one of Grundig's major semiconductor sources would have switched from Siemens to Thomson.

13. These four arguments are identified and discussed in Cawson et al. (1990, 310).

14. For empirical evidence on the effects of protectionist measures in a variety of US industries, see Hufbauer et al. (1986).

as providing "enabling" inputs for the rest of the economy—have won a growing number of converts in European policy circles.

Finally, Philips and Grundig emphasized the possible implications of the decline of the European consumer electronics industry for the maintenance of an independent European semiconductor industry.[15] By 1982 the Japanese had mounted a serious global offensive in semiconductors, and the share of European companies in the world semiconductor market was declining, for the reasons noted in chapter 4. Since European producers sold their semiconductor production almost entirely to European users, the fate of the former depended in large measure on the fate of the latter.

In response to mounting political pressures within Europe and from the Japanese government, which had been mobilized by the Japanese producers to avoid an antidumping case, the Community negotiated its first-ever VRA. As part of this agreement, the Japanese promised that exports to the Community would be limited to a maximum of 4.55 million sets in 1983 (compared with 4.9 million in 1982), 3.95 million in 1984, and 3.25 million in 1985.[16] The 1983 figure included quotas on VCR kits to be supplied by JVC for assembly at its British and German factories. In 1984 and 1985, separate restraints were negotiated for exports of completed products from Japan and exports of unfinished products to be assembled in Europe.[17] The restriction on VCR kits amounted to a local content provision, since it limited the ability of Japanese suppliers to circumvent quotas by increasing "screwdriver" assembly operations in Europe.

But the VRA did not stop at establishing quantitative limits on imports, as managed trade arrangements of this type usually do. In addition, the Japanese agreed to align the prices of their products with European levels, so that the price of Japanese VCRs in Europe after customs (including a tariff rate of 8 percent) would be the same as the Philips-Grundig factory prices. In effect, this agreement set a floor price for VCRs in Europe on the basis of Philips-Grundig's production costs for their V2000 model. These costs were estimated to be some 30 percent higher than equivalent Japanese costs (Nomura Management School 1986, Yoffie 1986b). Even in the absence of such a price agreement, quantitative restrictions on imports alone would have exerted upward pressure on prices. The agreement simply specified the minimum price increase the European producers would find acceptable. European consumers, of course, were not consulted.

The Effects of the VCR Agreement

Agreements of the type negotiated by the Europeans and the Japanese in the VCR industry have certain predictable effects. Such managed trade arrangements

15. In both Europe and the United States, the case for promotional policies to develop indigenous producers of HDTV was also based in part on the fact that the HDTV industry would be an important source of demand for indigenous semiconductor producers. For an analysis and criticism of the US argument see Hart and Tyson (1989). For more on European HDTV strategy see the case study below, and for a clear exposition of the "semiconductor" rationale for an HDTV policy in Europe see Samuel (1990).

16. For more details on the trade conflict leading up to the VRA see Yoffie (1986b).

17. In 1984 exports of unfinished kits were limited to 1.1 million units. This was in addition to the export quota of 3.95 million units for finished VCRs.

usually reduce import volumes and increase prices of both imports and domestic goods. In this case these effects were guaranteed because during the duration of the agreement there were no alternative foreign suppliers[18] and because the deal contained an explicit price floor.

Table 6.3 shows the agreement's effects on trade. VCR exports to the European Community from Japan declined by a total of 34 percent between 1982 and 1985. Since exports from Europe were insignificant, the decline in imports was matched by a decline in Europe's VCR trade imbalance (table 6.4).

The VRA's effect on prices is harder to determine with precision. The VRA cost consumers the excess between the price that was charged after it was imposed and the price they would have paid in its absence.[19] But there is no precise way to measure this excess, nor is any data series on VCR prices in Europe before and after the agreement available. According to official EC reports, VCR prices continued to decrease at a rate of 5 percent to 10 percent per year through 1985 (*Official Journal of the European Commission*, L240, 31 August 1988, 13).

VCR prices were influenced by a variety of factors between 1982 and 1985. First, the yen appreciated against many of the EC currencies during this period; this by itself might have increased the local-currency prices of Japanese VCR imports. On the other hand, the yen cost of VCR production continued to fall by an estimated 11 percent per year during this period (Nomura Management School 1986); this by itself might have reduced the local-currency prices of Japanese VCR imports. As the data in table 6.3 indicate, the yen price of Japanese VCR exports to Europe did in fact decline despite the VRA. Prices were also influenced by demand factors: in particular, the European VCR market grew more slowly in 1983–84 than it had during the previous three years. On the supply side, two major factors also affected prices. First, after Philips adopted the VHS standard at the end of 1984, the pressures for aggressive price competition between the Japanese companies moderated. Second, in 1985 Korean producers with licensed Japanese technology began to compete at the low end of the market, and the Japanese responded by introducing new high-end products. These competitive changes meant lower prices on some products and higher prices on others.

Given all the factors influencing VCR prices between 1982 and 1985, what can be said about the effects of the VRA on prices? As long as the VRA price floor was binding, which was probably the case at least until Philips sold off its V2000 stocks and switched to VHS (at the end of 1983), local-currency prices were probably at least 30 percent higher than they would have been otherwise (since Philips' costs were approximately 30 percent above the costs of producing an equivalent Japanese machine).

Some indirect evidence on the price effects of the VRA appears in a widening premium between the yen price of Japanese VCR exports to the European Community and the yen price of Japanese VCR exports to the rest of the world between

18. The Korean suppliers were prevented from mounting an export surge to Europe until 1986, after the expiration of restrictive clauses on exporting included in their technology license agreements with Japanese companies.

19. Moreover, there was considerable national variation in the effect of the VRA on prices. Prices were highest in France, which had lobbied for a small national share of the overall VRA quota, and lowest in Great Britain (Cawson and Holmes 1991).

Table 6.3 Costs of protection in videocassette recorders

| | Japanese exports to: | | | | | | | | |
| | European Community | | | Rest of world | | | EC premium (percentages) | European consumption (thousands of units) | Total premium (millions of yen) |
Year	Volume (thousands of units)	Value (millions of yen)	Price (thousands of yen)	Volume (thousands of units)	Value (millions of yen)	Price (thousands of yen)			
Before restraints									
1980	1,320	169,994	129,000	2,124	273,633	129,000	0		
1981	2,855	331,292	116,000	4,500	522,213	116,000	0		
1982	4,946	501,239	101,000	5,706	578,172	101,000	0		
During restraints									
1983	4,646	384,386	83,000	10,591	876,378	83,000	0	5,868	
1984	3,755	291,111	78,000	18,316	1,329,557	73,000	6.8	5,801	28,636
1985	3,252	221,713	68,000	22,223	1,359,392	61,000	11.5	6,262	43,877
After restraints									
1986	3,021	171,819	57,000	24,668	1,077,383	44,000	29.5	7,241	95,578
1987	2,889	139,451	48,000	19,912	719,276	36,000	33.3	9,700	117,825

Sources: Author's calculations based on data from the Japanese Ministry of Finance as reported in Japan Electronics Almanac, 1987 and 1989; EC consumption figures from Consumer Europe 1989/90.

Table 6.4   Europe: trade deficit in videocassette recorders, 1980–88 (millions of dollars)

	1980	1981	1982	1983	1984	1985	1986	1987	1988
Imports	884	1,621	2,400	2,350	1,823	2,064	2,871	3,327	2,086
Exports	135	151	153	155	182	231	305	338	140
Trade balance	749	1,470	2,247	2,195	1,641	1,833	2,566	2,999	1,946

Source: United Nations Trade Data Book.

227

1982 and 1985 (table 6.3). By 1985 this premium was 11.5 percent of the yen world price. Calculations based on this estimate indicate that between 1983 and 1985 European consumers paid a total premium of 62.5 billion yen or 323.8 million ecu on Japanese VCR imports.[20]

Whatever its effects on local-currency prices, the VRA certainly encouraged an increase in European production. By this standard, the agreement must be judged a qualified success relative to the goal of maintaining a "European" VCR industry. During the course of the VRA, VCR production in Europe expanded rapidly. In 1982 it was about 400,000 units, or about 11 percent of the total European market, with the remainder supplied largely by Japanese imports. Local production by Japanese companies was insignificant. But with the VRA this situation soon changed. The VRA encouraged the Japanese companies to move production facilities to Europe to get around the quantitative restrictions on their sales through imports.[21] According to some accounts, the specter of ongoing friction in VCRs also stimulated the Japanese companies to form joint ventures with their European competitors.[22] As a result of both of these trends, Japanese VCR production in Europe increased dramatically. By 1986, one year after the VRA's expiration, Japanese firms were responsible for about 40 percent of European VCR production in terms of units, while the Europeans held the remaining 60 percent, a substantial fraction of which were produced in joint ventures with the Japanese, and all of which involved the licensing of Japanese technology (Cawson et al. 1990, 222). In the same year, Japanese firms held 63 percent of the total European market—22 percent from European production and 41 percent from imports—while the total European share (joint ventures included) amounted to only 36 percent (table 6.5).

Although the VRA helped secure a European production or supply base in VCRs, it did not secure a distinctive European technology as many had hoped. Philips retired its V2000 technology by the end of 1983, when it began to manufacture under license from Matsushita. Thereafter, all the European producers used proprietary Japanese technology, and product innovation continued to emanate from Japan. Even today, most VCR production by European companies is pursuant to license agreements with the Japanese companies.[23]

Nor did the VRA by itself attract so-called high-quality investment by these companies. Initially the Japanese limited their investment to "screwdriver" operations. To some extent this tactic was restricted by separate quotas on subassembled kits in 1984 and 1985. In addition, the Japanese were under continuous subtle and not-so-subtle pressure from the European authorities to increase the local content of their European operations. Indeed, according to a document on

---

20. Based on an average exchange rate of 193 yen to the ecu between 1983 and 1985.

21. As is traditional, the application of the VRA quotas among the Japanese producers was based on their prequota market shares, so any attempt to gain share required foreign direct investment.

22. This argument was suggested in Nomura Management School (1987). Thomson officials also assert that trade friction had the effect of making the Japanese companies more willing to establish joint ventures with European companies. See *Business Week*, 15 May 1989, 28–32, and 23 October 1989, 146.

23. Thomson now has its own VCR technology and is phasing out production based on its licensing of Japanese technology.

Table 6.5   Japanese share of the European videocassette recorder market, 1986

	Thousands of units	Percentage of total European consumption
European consumption	7,241	100
European production by European companies	2,605	36
European production by Japanese companies	1,595	22
European imports from Japan	3,021	41

Sources: Consumption, see table 6.3; production, Alan Cawson et al., *Hostile Brothers* (Oxford: Clarendon Press, 1990), 222; imports, see table 6.3.

the VCR industry prepared by the Nomura Management School (1986), during the negotiations for the 1984 quotas the Europeans specified value-added rules similar to existing ones for televisions and audio tape recorders. According to these rules, only Japanese VCRs produced in Europe with local content of more than 25 percent were exempt from the 1984 quotas; for 1985 the comparable local-content figure was 45 percent.

Informal Pressures, Antidumping Threats, and Creeping Local Content Requirements

After the VRA formally expired at the end of 1985, the Europeans maintained pressure on the Japanese to expand and upgrade their European VCR production facilities.[24] The increase in the European tariff on VCR imports from 8 percent to 14 percent as of January 1986 provided a direct incentive for them to do so. The tariff increase was primarily targeted at the Korean firms, whose exports to Europe were increasing rapidly. Between 1986 and 1987 the Korean firms increased their VCR market share in Europe from 6 percent to 16 percent. The tariff was also preferred to a possible extension of the VRA by members of the European industry who felt that the quotas had worked to the advantage of the Japanese. Ironically, Japanese producers stood to benefit from the tariff, which of course protected their European operations. And European consumers continued to pay a mounting premium on their purchases of VCR imports from Japan (table 6.3). Nonetheless, average VCR prices within the Community declined by an estimated 20 percent a year in 1986 and 1987, largely in response to aggressive price cutting at the low end of the market by Korean firms (*Official Journal of the European Communities* L240, 31 August 1988, 13).

As early as 1986, the European companies were leveling antidumping threats against the Korean producers, were charging the Japanese screwdriver opera-

---

24. After the formal quotas expired, MITI worked with the Japanese producers to maintain informal quantitative controls on VCR exports to Europe through what the Japanese call the "observation manner" (Nomura Management School 1987). According to a report by the General Agreement on Tariffs and Trade (1991, 171), Japan still continues to monitor its exports of VCRs to Europe.

tions with "disguised dumping," and were lobbying for a tariff on electronic components imported from Japan for assembly in European VCR plants. The allegations of disguised dumping in the VCR industry were one of several factors motivating the adoption of new, tougher antidumping regulations by the European Commission in June 1987. According to these regulations, if the Commission applies an antidumping duty to a particular finished good, and if that good is produced locally using components imported from the offending country that total more than 60 percent of the good's value added, then the duty will be applied to the imported components as well.[25]

These new regulations, however, provided ample room for official discretion. In principle, the regulations did not amount to a 40 percent local content rule, but only specified that at least 40 percent of the content of a product not come from the country whose producers were found to be dumping that product. For example, if a Japanese producer were found to be dumping VCRs in Europe, but more than 40 percent of the value of the VCRs came from American or Korean inputs, the screwdriver regulations should not apply. In practice, however, these regulations have often been interpreted and administered as a *de facto* European local content rule. This practice follows a long tradition among European customs officials of assigning the origin of a product to the country with the largest single share of components in either number or value or, more simply, of classifying a product as "European" if 45 percent or more of its content is produced within the Community.[26] Indeed, Flamm (1990, 275) reports that this 45 percent rule of thumb has been used in the VCR industry, which explains why Japanese producers have often stated that they operate under a 45 percent local content rule in Europe, even though the Community has never formally legislated any such rule for VCRs as it did for televisions and audio tape recorders.[27]

Administrative discretion in the application of the screwdriver regulations has also been built into the "undertaking" process by which many European antidumping suits are resolved. Undertakings are confidential settlements whereby the party charged with an antidumping violation agrees to some action in return for which the charge is dropped. Undertakings have been more usual in antidumping cases than the imposition of actual duties by a factor of roughly two

25. According to these regulations, duties could be extended to products produced or assembled within the Community using imported inputs, under the following conditions: the party must be related to or associated with a producer whose imports are subject to an antidumping duty; the operation must have been started or substantially increased after the opening of the investigation; and the value of inputs used from the country of exportation must exceed 60 percent of the product's value added.

26. This traditional approach in conjunction with the screwdriver regulations is an obvious source of potential trade friction between the United States and Europe if, for example, Japanese producers are led to use European inputs over American inputs in order to meet an implicit 40 percent minimum European content condition. A variant of this problem arose in 1989 in a European antidumping suit against Japanese producers of computer printers. American semiconductor producers alleged that the Japanese producers substituted chips produced by European companies for chips produced by American companies in order to meet the *de facto* 40 percent European content rule on printed circuit boards, a key input in printers. For more detail on this dispute see Flamm (1990, 273–74).

27. According to Cawson et al. (1990), Philips and Grundig lobbied European trade officials for a minimum local content of 60 percent by Japanese VCR producers.

to one.[28] Although such agreements have usually taken the form of a promise by foreign suppliers to raise their prices by an agreed amount, in some cases they have consisted of a commitment by foreign suppliers to increase the European content of their product by an agreed amount.[29] In VCRs and other electronics products, the 45 percent rule has apparently become a standard feature in such agreements. Even this rule of thumb, however, can be overruled in practice. For example, the screwdriver conditions explicitly note that, if an electronics product falls short of a *de jure* 40 percent content rule, such considerations as the capital expenditures, research expenditures, and relevant technologies that are essential for assembly or manufacturing operations in the Community may be taken into account. In other words, in practice "technological complexity" might be a substitute for the simpler measure of local value added.

In the VCR case, European antidumping regulations and practices first became an explicit issue in March 1987, when the Commission received a dumping complaint filed by the European Association of Consumer Electronics Manufacturers against imports of VCRs originating in Korea (mainly from Daewoo, Goldstar, and Samsung) and imports from two Japanese companies (Funai and Orion). One of the companies participating in the complaint was J2T, a 50-50 joint venture between Thomson and JVC; the others were wholly European-owned companies. In the case of the Korean imports the dumping charge was based on a comparison of domestic and export prices, whereas in the case of the Japanese imports the charge was based on a comparison of estimated production costs and prices.

Based on the evidence in the complaint, the Commission initiated a formal antidumping investigation. The Commission's own report on this investigation at no point mentions any attempt to ascertain whether the pricing policies pursued by the alleged dumpers involved restrictive or anticompetitive business practices or were unfair in any way.[30] Instead, the Commission directed its attention to demonstrating that dumping existed and that it caused injury to the profits and production of "community producers." Given the substantial European production by Japanese companies not named in the dumping complaint, the challenge for the Commission was how to define what it meant by "community producers." The way it addressed this challenge would send a powerful message to foreign suppliers about the value of European production as a safeguard against Community antidumping actions.

In its investigation, the Commission drew an explicit distinction among four types of European production facilities: facilities that were fully owned by Eu-

---

28. GATT (1991). Recently, however, in lieu of undertakings, the Community appears to be moving toward greater use of actual antidumping duties. Moreover, a new EC ruling stipulates that, unless the price of a dumped foreign product increases by the full amount of the duty, the European companies may file an additional suit. This ruling clearly overlooks the role of supply and demand in the formation of prices. If applied, it would mean a further toughening of Europe's antidumping procedures.

29. For example, Howell et al. (1992, 304) report part of a confidential letter from the EC staff requesting that a Japanese company whose products were subject to an ongoing EC antidumping action show that it had achieved 40 percent non-Japanese value of parts in its weighted-average production and that it had achieved an increase of EC value in parts.

30. The following discussion of the Community's investigation and actions is based on the report presented in *Official Journal of the European Communities*, L240, 31 August 1988.

ropean companies; facilities that were joint ventures between European and Japanese companies; facilities that were fully owned by Japanese companies not included in the complaint; and facilities owned by the foreign companies under investigation. The first two were explicitly recognized by the Commission as "community producers," the first on the basis of ownership alone and the second on the basis of their "high level of local content . . . and their long-term commitment to investment and employment in the Community."[31] The Commission explicitly left open the question of whether fully Japanese-owned companies with substantial manufacturing facilities in Europe should be considered "community producers," while explicitly arguing that the companies named in the dumping complaint could not be so viewed despite local assembly operations by some of them.

The exclusion from the 1987 dumping complaint of all of the big Japanese companies with significant operations in Europe is noteworthy, since it suggests that they were not a source of serious price competition for the European companies, as they had been before the VRA was imposed and before they substituted local European production for exports from Japan. Revealingly, most of the wholly Japanese-owned companies in Europe indicated to the Commission that they supported the antidumping complaint—a position that makes sense if they too were harmed by aggressive price competition from the companies named in the complaint. Indeed, the Commission itself noted that the market share of some of the Japanese companies producing in Europe had declined as a result of import competition from the companies mentioned in the complaint.

The Commission's ambiguous position on whether the European facilities of the big Japanese companies qualified them as "community producers" or as "merely carrying out simple assembly operations" left open the possibility of further antidumping actions against those firms in the future.[32] In the 1987 investigations these facilities were scrutinized much more carefully than were the joint venture operations between Japanese and European companies. All of this maneuvering by the Commission sent a powerful message to foreign producers about the extent to which "substantial local content" could be an important defense against possible antidumping cases by the Community—a message reinforced by the anticircumvention provision in the antidumping law.

Following its preliminary investigation, in August 1988 the Commission imposed provisional antidumping duties on the companies named in the 1987 complaint. These duties were substantial, ranging from 29.2 percent on Daewoo to 18.0 percent on Orion and Funai. Finally, in February 1989, definitive duties were imposed. In keeping with European practice, however, definitive duties were not imposed on Daewoo, Samsung, Goldstar, and Funai, because they offered acceptable price undertakings. In short, they agreed to raise their prices enough to satisfy the European producers—or, in the words of the Commission, enough to allow "'community producers' to cover their costs of production and to provide them with an adequate profit" (*Official Journal of the European Com-*

---

31. Commission Regulation no. 2684/88 of 26 August 1988 (*Official Journal of the European Communities*, L 240, 5, 31 August 1988).

32. In July 1989 the Commission began an antidumping investigation of VCRs assembled by Japanese producers in Europe in accordance with the anticircumvention provision of the Community's antidumping laws.

munities, L 240, 5, 31 August 1988). As a result of these undertaking agreements, the final definitive duties applied only to imports from Korea not produced by Daewoo, Samsung, and Goldstar and to imports from the recalcitrant Orion.

Although the Commission noted that the imposition of duties and price undertakings might result in "possible limited disadvantage to consumers with respect to the higher prices of VCRS," it argued that "this disadvantage will be outweighed by the benefits of safeguarding employment and maintaining a foothold in this important technological sector." But these benefits were by no means forgone conclusions. The price undertakings benefited the targeted foreign suppliers as much as or more than their "community competitors," especially their wholly European ones. Whether Europe as a production location garnered additional employment and technological know-how depended to a large extent on whether these suppliers decided to forgo the harassment of future antidumping actions by following the example of the big Japanese companies that had moved production facilities to Europe earlier. The evidence indicates that they did. In the years that followed, the three major Korean producers named in the 1987 complaint significantly increased their European operations (Cawson and Holmes 1991, 171). A VRA limiting exports of VCRS from Korea to the European Community between 1987 and 1989 was also a factor motivating their decisions.

Another incentive for both Japanese and Korean suppliers to increase their investment in European VCR production facilities was the provision of state subsidies sometimes available for such investment.[33] For example, during the 1984–86 period, the British government was actively involved in a campaign to attract Japanese VCR investment. The British offered lavish subsidies, allowable under EC rules in the form of aid for less developed regions within Community states. Largely as a result, by the end of 1988 Great Britain had 12 foreign VCR production facilities—more than any other EC country. One of these facilities—the Sharp VCR plant in Wales—was the single biggest recipient of regional aid of any of the Japanese operations in Great Britain (Cawson et al. 1990, 254–59). According to a Thomson executive, state subsidies have sometimes reached 30 percent of the capital involved in a Japanese VCR investment in Europe.[34]

The various pressures encouraging Japanese—and, somewhat later, Korean—direct investment in European VCR production facilities produced results.[35] Individual Japanese suppliers gradually took measures to increase the local content of their existing facilities and to begin new ones. As an illustration, in 1986 Matsushita established a parts manufacturing company in Germany, called Mat-

---

33. State subsidies have also been available for other kinds of investments in electronics by foreign companies. For example, the Italian government put up $700 million for a proposed $1.2 billion package of spending on DRAM manufacturing and R&D by Texas Instruments in the depressed region around Avezzano, east of Rome. Similarly, Mitsubishi obtained $4 million from the German government to help build its $350 million DRAM plant in a depressed coal-mining region.

34. Interview and written information provided by a representative of Thomson Consumer Electronics, May 1990.

35. Japanese firms regularly rank trade friction as the primary reason for their investment in electronics production facilities in Europe. MITI has also actively advised these firms to increase such investment to avoid trade conflicts. See Moritani (1989) and Industrial Bank of Japan (1989).

sushita Video Manufacturing, to serve its assembly production facilities. Matsushita also licensed its technology in video machinery and related parts to Grundig so that the German firm could serve as a local supplier. JVC also succeeded in establishing integrated European production facilities in VCRs in its J2T joint venture by purchasing part of Thomson's facilities for production of VCR parts, including drums and cylinders. JVC, Sony, and Matsushita all encouraged their main Japanese parts suppliers to establish operations in Europe in order to "secure a stable European supply of VCR parts." And Sony has announced its goal of achieving complete localization of its European production facilities, including both components production and R&D (Micossi and Viesti 1990). The Japanese companies estimate that the costs of local production in Europe initially exceed the costs of production in Japan by 10 percent to 15 percent, but once production stabilizes at appropriate capacity levels, the European facilities run in the black.[36]

By 1988, as a result of Japanese foreign investment, 42 percent of European production of VCRs occurred in Japanese transplants, while European producers accounted for 57 percent.[37] In that year, European producers supplied approximately 17 percent to 18 percent of the total European market, while Japanese producers supplied approximately 73 percent (almost 50 percent from their European production facilities and 24 percent from exports from Japan; table 6.6).[38] According to a Thomson representative, moreover, no VCRs manufactured by European companies in Europe are manufactured from start to finish in Europe; rather, the typical pattern is for European companies to buy parts from Japanese firms and assemble them in Europe for sale in Europe. Nor do the European companies export VCRs from their European locations. In order to manufacture products that are competitively priced with Japanese VCRs on world markets, the European companies have moved much of their manufacturing offshore to take advantage of cheaper labor costs in East Asia. Thomson, for example, sells VCRs under the RCA label in the United States from its production facilities in East Asia. Thus it is possible—although not demonstrable with available information—that the local content of Japanese VCR production facilities in Europe exceeds the local content of European VCR production facilities in Europe.

What the available information does demonstrate is that Japanese companies have made considerable investments in European VCR production facilities and that these investments have displaced VCR exports from Japan. The ratio of local

---

36. Most of the evidence in the preceding paragraph is based on analysis in Nomura Management School (1987).

37. These figures are based on production numbers provided to the author by Thomson, May 1990.

38. These 1989 figures on market shares are approximate because they are based on 1988 figures and half-year 1989 estimates. The figures, which are based on data in *Electronics Industry Association of Japan Almanac* (1990), represent a big shift from the 1986 numbers reported above. Part of the difference between the 1986 and the 1989 numbers may be a result of differences in how the Japanese and the Europeans count joint venture production: the Europeans count it as production by European producers, and the Japanese as production by Japanese producers. For example, the Japanese estimate that European production by Japanese companies accounted for 44 percent of total European supply of VCRs in 1986, whereas the European estimates in table 6.5 indicate a much lower share of 22 percent. For the Japanese estimates see Industrial Bank of Japan (1989, 18).

Table 6.6 Market shares in videocassette recorders, by country, 1988 (percentages)

Source of product	United States	European Community	Japan	Other	World
Japanese firms					
Japanese operations	73.8	23.7	98.1	72.1	66.3
Offshore operations	6.0	0.4	0.0	10.2	16.3
US operations	1.9	0.0	0.0	0.0	0.0
EC operations	0.0	49.5	0.0	0.0	0.0
Non-Japanese suppliers in:					
Korea	17.5	9.1	1.9	13.4	12.2
Taiwan	0.8	0.0	0.0	2.5	0.8
United States	0.0	0.0	0.0	0.0	0.0
European Community	0.0	17.3	0.0	1.8	4.3
Total	100.0	100.0	100.0	100.0	100.0

Source: Japan Electronics Almanac 1989.

Japanese production to total Japanese supply in Europe is much higher in VCRs than in other electronics products: the fraction of total Japanese sales in Europe accounted for by local European production is now about 50 percent in VCRs, compared with only about 16 percent for all manufactured products sold by Japanese companies in Europe.[39] Japan's VCR exports to Europe peaked in 1982 and declined thereafter, as a result of which Europe's share in Japan's VCR exports plummeted (table 6.7).[40] In stark contrast, in all of their other major markets, including the United States, Japanese VCR producers sell mainly from their Japanese production facilities (table 6.6). Although there is an ongoing debate about whether foreign investment by Japanese companies will displace Japanese exports of manufactured goods more generally, in the VCR case there is little doubt that this has occurred in Europe and that it has been a response to ongoing trade friction.

Whether consciously or unconsciously, European policies have amounted to a disguised creep toward regional content requirements. And this creep has worked to foster substantial European production by Japanese suppliers in the VCR industry.[41] Flamm (1990) reached a similar conclusion in his study of evolving European policies toward the semiconductor industry.[42] Perhaps as a result of

---

39. Most American companies supply an even greater share of their European sales from European production facilities. According to Micossi and Viesti (1990, 4), local production accounts for 79 percent of the total sales of American firms in Europe.

40. According to a recent GATT report (GATT 1991, 172), the European Community continues to exercise import surveillance over Japanese VCRs, and France continues to restrict VCR imports from Japan through an industry-to-industry arrangement.

41. According to Ernst and O'Connor (1992), Europe's disguised creep toward local content in electronic typewriters, color televisions, VCRs, and computer printers has encouraged a similar approach in other countries, including some of the newly industrializing countries.

42. Flamm concludes that Europe's creep toward local content represents an attempt to build a regional supply base in critical input industries, where disruptions in supply or

Table 6.7 Japan: exports of videocassette recorders, 1981–88

Year	Total (thousands of units)	Percentages of total		
		United States	European Community	Others
1981	7,355	32.0	38.8	28.9
1982	10,652	24.0	46.4	30.1
1983	15,237	35.7	30.5	33.8
1984	22,071	53.9	17.0	29.1
1985	25,475	62.5	12.8	24.7
1986	27,689	65.0	10.9	24.1
1987	22,801	54.3	12.7	33.0
1988	22,039	43.4	15.1	41.5

Source: Japan Electronics Almanac 1989, citing Ministry of Finance data.

Europe's local content efforts, the subsidiaries of Japanese electronics companies procure a greater fraction of their inputs from locally based suppliers in the European Community than they do in the United States.[43] The US subsidiaries of Japanese electronics companies depend more on procurement of inputs from Japan than do Japanese operations anywhere else in the world.[44]

For many European policymakers, the first-best solution in electronics and other key industries such as automobiles is European production by European companies for the European market. But when the first-best solution proves unattainable (at least at acceptable political and economic cost), a second-best solution has gained support, namely, European production by foreign companies for the European market.

Local production is preferable to imports in a variety of ways: it provides jobs and opportunities for skill acquisition for local workers; it provides better access to foreign technologies; it provides an increased tax base and spillover benefits for regional development; and it may allow more effective control of anticompetitive behavior through the application of domestic competition policy.[45] Per-

oligopolistic control over supply by foreign firms can have significant effects in a wide range of downstream user industries. The VCR case, however, suggests that the European preference for local production over imports extends beyond input industries and is motivated by broader concerns than supply uncertainties in such industries.

43. According to MITI data provided to the author by the American Electronics Association office in Japan, Japanese electronics companies in the United States procure 23 percent of their inputs locally and 74 percent from Japan, with the remainder originating from third-country locations. In contrast, Japanese electronics companies in the European Community procure 35 percent of their inputs locally and 59 percent from Japan.

44. On average, according to data provided by the American Electronics Association, imports from Japan account for 61 percent of worldwide procurements by the subsidiaries of Japanese electronics companies. The comparable figure for the United States is 74 percent.

45. These effects have been identified and analyzed in other studies. For some recent evidence on the effects of foreign direct investment in Europe, see Micossi and Viesti (1990), Thomson and Nicolaides (1992), and Dunning (1990a). The effects of foreign investment on the trade balance are more difficult to predict than its other effects. Such investment may reduce imports directly, as in the case of VCRs, but may increase imports indirectly through imports of components used in the final product. At an aggregate level,

haps most significantly, local production fosters greater competition as more-efficient foreign producers meet their local counterparts in their own home market. Many Europeans agree that the greatest single source of benefit from Japanese foreign direct investment stems not from the performance of the Japanese companies themselves but from the stimulus to improve competitiveness that their presence gives to local competitors (Micossi and Viesti 1990, 23).

True, all of these benefits of foreign direct investment come at a price. As the VCR evidence indicates, initially the European facilities of Japanese companies operated at higher costs than their domestic facilities, although that is no longer the case.[46] European consumers have undoubtedly paid higher prices for Japanese VCRs than they would have if imports from Japan had not been blocked by a variety of policies (see table 6.3). But against the costs of protection must be weighed the benefits of the foreign direct investment it has triggered. Such benefits are rarely mentioned, let alone estimated, in empirical studies of the effects of trade protection. Yet they may be far more significant than higher prices for long-run welfare.

Despite the benefits of foreign direct investment, many European policymakers clearly view European production by European-owned companies as a superior option. The remainder of this chapter examines how the Europeans are using policy to achieve this outcome in high-definition television (HDTV), which promises to become a major consumer electronics market in the 1990s and one in which competition between American, European, and Japanese companies could be intense.

High-Definition Television: The Strategy to Create European Champions

HDTV is a new broadcasting technology that will offer cinema-quality pictures on a television screen. The key to higher picture resolution is the fact that HDTV television sets will transmit images containing over 1,000 horizontal lines as opposed to the current standards of 525 lines in the United States and Japan and 625 lines in Europe. HDTV is widely regarded by experts to be the next major growth segment of the consumer electronics industry, replacing VCRs, which constituted the most important segment in the 1980s.

The Europeans are determined not to lose the HDTV market to the Japanese as they did the VCR market. Since 1986 the Europeans have pursued a two-pronged strategy toward the goal of developing indigenous technological and production capabilities in HDTV. The first part of the strategy involves standards; the second involves the provision of public support for cooperative R&D programs to develop HDTV.[47]

There is widespread agreement within the Community that Europe should design its own HDTV transmission and production standards. In products with

studies of Japanese foreign direct investment in both Europe and the United States show that Japanese subsidiaries tend to import more per unit of output than their local counterparts, but that the gap tends to decline over time. In VCRs, this decline probably occurred more rapidly in Europe because of creeping local content requirements.

46. According to Cawson and Holmes (1991, 174), total unit production costs in Europe and Japan are now approximately equal in most consumer electronics products.

47. For more on the European strategy see Beltz (1991) and Hazard and Daems (1992).

purely consumer applications, standards setting has largely been left to market competition among the producers, with the most successful product emerging as the *de facto* standard. This was the case in VCRs. The setting of broadcasting standards, in contrast, always involves governments and public broadcasting organizations as well as manufacturers. The CCIR (the French acronym for International Radio Consultative Committee), a voluntary standards-setting body of the United Nations comprising the representatives of national governments, has the responsibility for setting standards for broadcast television.

The emphasis on distinctive European HDTV standards has its historical precedent in the European television industry, whose dominant PAL standard is different from the NTSC standard operating in both the United States and Japan. In 1965 the CCIR, faced with competing color television systems proposed by Germany, France, and the United States, decided to permit three incompatible standards—PAL, SECAM, and NTSC—to coexist. Following this decision, each Community member chose its own standard. This time around, however, the Europeans are committed to a Community-wide standard to avoid the fragmentation and inefficiencies associated with different national television standards.

The other element of Europe's evolving HDTV strategy is public funding to support research and development. Historically, the consumer electronics industry has not been considered "strategic" enough (or, as Cawson et al. 1990 put it, "noble" enough) to warrant state aid beyond the implicit aid resulting from protectionist trade policies. Philips and Thomson, for example, have been significant beneficiaries of state aid, but mainly in their defense and telecommunications activities, not in their consumer electronics activities.[48] HDTV, however, has won public financial support, in part because of a belief that HDTV breakthroughs in component and display technologies may have significant spillover effects on semiconductors, computers, and defense. Another factor motivating such support has been the goal of beating the Japanese in the next round of competition in the consumer electronics industry.

The technical challenges of making HDTV a reality are twofold: developing the technology to produce and transmit HDTV signals over satellite systems or over the more limited terrestrial bands available to conventional television systems; and developing and making a cost-effective monitor to receive such signals. The first challenge involves the development of a transmission standard, and the second the development of a production standard.[49]

The National Broadcasting Company of Japan (NHK), a quasi-public company, began to work on both parts of the technological puzzle in 1970. Since then it has spent over $500 million on HDTV research, and it has freely transferred all of its technological findings to Japanese companies. In addition, these companies—among them Sony, Toshiba, Hitachi, and Matsushita—have spent over $400 million on HDTV research,[50] encouraged in part by tax incentives and various

48. For an analysis of European promotional policies in telecommunications, see Cawson et al. (1990, chapters 4 through 8). For a discussion of how preferential procurement and defense contracting led to a sheltered European environment for the major European electronics firms, see Derian (1990).

49. For a good, brief introduction to HDTV technology see Hazard and Daems (1992).

50. These figures include expenditures through 1989. The public funding estimate does

forms of promotional support from the Ministry of Posts and Telecommunications and the Long-Term Credit Bank of Japan.

The Japanese effort has resulted in a satellite-based HDTV system called MUSE (Multiple Sub-Nyquist Encoding), which combines transmission and production standards in a single delivery system. The MUSE system requires that existing television sets be replaced by new sets designed to receive the MUSE transmission signal. Under the MUSE system, no existing sets in Japan, Europe, or the United States would be capable of providing HDTV. Thus, if MUSE became the HDTV standard, all television monitors would have to be replaced—presumably by Japanese products—in order to receive HDTV transmissions.

In May 1986 the Japanese producers proposed the MUSE standard for HDTV at a CCIR meeting in Dubrovnik, Yugoslavia. The American participants at the meeting supported their proposal, but the Europeans rejected it and lobbied for postponing a decision on HDTV standards until 1990.

Shortly after the meeting, Thomson and Philips announced plans for a joint venture in HDTV and sought public funding from the Eureka program. Unlike ESPRIT, which is an EC program providing Community funds to support cooperative, precompetitive R&D projects, the Eureka program functions primarily as a matchmaking body. The Community does, however, support the Eureka concept of encouraging cooperative cross-national European research and tries to coordinate its own projects with Eureka projects. Projects approved by the Eureka secretariat qualify for national R&D support, the terms of which vary from country to country.

In the case of HDTV, Eureka approved a cooperative R&D project proposed by Philips, Thomson, Bosch, and Thorn-EMI, to be called the Eureka EU95 HDTV Project. Although Eureka-95 (as it came to be called) was not a Community project, Directorate-General XIII, the Commission directorate responsible for telecommunications, agreed to play a coordinating role. The project includes all the leading European-owned companies in the television industry, backed by the national broadcasting organizations of the major countries. More than 20 business organizations from nine countries are participants in this effort. According to the terms of the project, the various national governments involved are expected to pay 50 percent of the costs, with the remainder to be paid by the industry participants.[51] The project was budgeted at 400 million ecu through 1989. Since its inception approximately 1,700 engineers, technicians, and support personnel have been involved full time in the project.

Eureka-95 was intended to establish an alternative HDTV system based on a European transmission and production standard called MAC (Multiplexed Analog Components). In 1986 an EC directive made the MAC standard mandatory for all satellite broadcasters except telecommunications satellite transmissions. The MAC standard called for 1,250 lines on an HDTV monitor, or twice the 625 lines of the PAL standard. The MAC-based HDTV transmission and reception equipment to be developed under the Eureka-95 project would enable existing television

---

not include the implicit subsidy provided by the national television research laboratories in which HDTV research has been carried out. Undoubtedly much more has been spent both by NHK and by the private companies on HDTV development since then.

51. Great Britain at first refused to allocate extra money to the Eureka-95 project, and Thorn-EMI eventually dropped out of the project (Cawson et al. 1990, 335–36).

sets to receive HDTV signals, albeit with no improvement in reception. The European alternative, like the Japanese system, was to be based on satellite transmission. Thus the choice of the MAC standard was consistent with an earlier decision by the European governments to adopt a direct broadcast satellite (DBS) delivery system for public broadcasting. Public broadcasting interests and the desires of the European governments to maintain control over programming on public broadcasting have been important factors in the evolution of Europe's HDTV policies. The goal of the Eureka-95 project was to achieve a working MAC–based transmission system for HDTV by the time of the next CCIR session. In fact, such a system was successfully demonstrated by 1988. When the CCIR met in 1990, the Europeans were once again successful in blocking MUSE, and the committee delayed a final decision on HDTV standards until 1994. Meanwhile, however, the MAC standard itself began to encounter resistance among European broadcasters and consumers. Although the standard was mandatory for satellite broadcasters, when Sky TV, a new private broadcasting channel, was launched in 1989, MAC–based equipment was not yet available, so Sky opted for PAL–based transmissions from a low-power transmissions satellite exempted from the MAC directive. British Satellite Broadcasting, which instead chose to wait for MAC equipment, fell behind Sky in the race for viewers and ultimately collapsed. Then, in the early 1990s, both Philips and Thomson introduced new, improved MAC–based sets. Their strategy was to get producers and broadcasters to offer programming in the MAC standard to increase consumer interest in these sets. But because of their very high prices and the unimpressive quality of available programming, they proved unpopular with both consumers and private broadcasters, who preferred cheaper sets based on the older PAL standard.

As Cawson and Holmes (1991, 177) argue, "while the manufacturers have every interest in introducing a new [standard] and especially one which would act as a form of passive protection against the Japanese, consumers have so far shown relatively little interest." In addition, there has been growing concern in Europe that a MAC–based analog standard might be rendered obsolete, even before it is put to any significant use, by an alternative, digital HDTV system under development in the United States (see below).

In July 1991, responding to pressure from European producers and broadcasters with a vested interest in MAC–based systems but meeting consumer and broadcaster resistance, the European Community announced a compromise position on standards. PAL would continue to be used for existing services, but the Community would provide 500 million ecu over five years to broadcasters willing to simulcast in MAC and PAL. In addition, all new broadcasters would be required to use only the MAC standard. Furthermore, from the beginning of 1993, all domestic television sets sold in Europe with diagonal screen widths of more than 22 inches—about one-third of the EC market—would have to incorporate equipment for receiving MAC–based broadcasts, and all satellite receivers would also have to be capable of receiving MAC–based transmissions.

But this compromise deal was itself short-lived. Despite intense lobbying by France, at the end of 1991 it was replaced by a still weaker one, allowing all broadcasters to choose their own standards but increasing the subsidies available to those who chose D2MAC to a total of 1 billion ecu over the next five years. These subsidies in turn complement ongoing financial support for the MAC standard from national governments through Eureka-95, the second phase of which commenced in 1990 at an estimated price tag of $500 million over three years (Samuel 1990, 22).

Europe's official strategy in HDTV bears a strong resemblance to Europe's *de facto* strategy in color television in some respects. Distinctive European standards—bolstered by restrictive licensing arrangements, successful antidumping suits against foreign suppliers, an explicit local content rule requiring 45 percent local value added, and strict import quotas in France and Italy—offered several European producers a temporary but significant degree of protection in color TVs. As a consequence, European companies were able to retain a large share of the European color TV market despite intense Japanese and Korean competition. About 80 percent of the color sets sold in Europe are still manufactured by European companies. In particular, the two largest European consumer electronics producers—Philips and Thomson—hold over 50 percent of the European market.[52] In contrast, all of the American color TV producers with the exception of Zenith were driven out of production by European and East Asian competition. Currently, Zenith accounts for less than 15 percent of the American color TV market (Hart and Tyson 1989), and the company recently announced that it would close all its television production facilities in the United States.

According to the terms of the 1992 Single European Act, protection in the form of distinctive national standards and national import quotas is slated to disappear. Barring a breakdown in the 1992 process, therefore, these components of the European color TV strategy will not be repeated. In their stead, however, the Europeans are using Community rather than national standards and promotional subsidies to encourage Community rather than national champions in HDTV. The would-be Community champions favored by this strategy are Philips and Thomson, the main European survivors of competition in color televisions.

These firms have staked their future on the HDTV struggle and have used their strong ties with national governments, Community officials, and European trade associations to shape Europe's HDTV policy. Critical to this policy is a distinctive European standard, which, according to one corporate official, "will give us a tremendous advantage."[53] And a primary motivation for such a standard from the corporate point of view is to gain this advantage at the expense of the Japanese. As another corporate official noted, "by having to go into a technology they didn't invent . . . the Japanese won't be able to test it on their home market. That is the fundamental keystone of our strategy."[54]

Producer rather than consumer interests have been the main force shaping Europe's HDTV policies. Even from the vantage point of producer interests, however, these policies may prove flawed. They may succeed in supporting a distinctive European standard, but fail in retaining the European market for European producers. The Europeans have blocked the MUSE standard, and this has certainly reduced the returns that Japanese firms might have realized from

---

52. Over time, as a result of increasing foreign investment, the share of European color TVs produced by the European subsidiaries of Japanese firms has increased, reaching 25 percent by 1987 (Cawson and Holmes 1991, 170).

53. Jean Camillot, Senior Vice President of Thomson International, quoted in *International Management*, March 1991, 37.

54. Thomson Vice President quoted in *Financial Times*, 17 July 1990, 12.

their substantial investment in this technology. In this sense, the European HDTV strategy has been an effective "spoiler" strategy against the Japanese.

Yet although Japanese producers may have been injured by the European strategy, they are hardly defeated. Instead, they are planning to manufacture HDTV equipment in whatever standard emerges in both Europe and the United States. As one Sony official put it, "We're manufacturers. If there is sufficient demand, we'll build anything."[55] Of course, the plans of the Japanese companies rest on the assumption that they will be able to license the European technology. However, this is not a forgone conclusion: in contrast to the United States, the European Community does not require producers to license proprietary technology as part of the standards-approval process. But the European producers did license their earlier PAL technologies to the Japanese, subject to some restrictions, and they may decide to do the same with their MAC technologies, especially through joint ventures or strategic alliances.[56] If this happens, the Japanese producers, who already have significant production, marketing, and distribution footholds in the European consumer electronics markets, may emerge as the major producers of HDTV equipment produced to the European standard. This outcome will be reminiscent of similar outcomes in other consumer electronics products including compact audio cassettes, PAL color TV systems, teletext, stereo TV sound, and compact discs. Unfortunately for the European producers, technological innovation has too rarely been translated into profitable product launches (Cawson and Holmes 1991, 177).

The VCR experience suggests that if the Japanese emerge victorious in the production of HDTV systems to European standards, there will be political pressure in Europe to revert to a second-best approach: the use of antidumping policy, rules of origin, and less overt forms of pressure to encourage Japanese companies to supply the European market through both local production and alliances with European-owned companies. This time around, however, the Japanese producers will undoubtedly find it more attractive to bow to European pressure, since they already have substantial complementary operations in Europe, and since a more unified European market offers a more attractive business opportunity. Under these circumstances, the European regional champions will not disappear, but they may not dominate the European HDTV market either.

From the vantage point of European consumers, Europe's current HDTV strategy poses yet another potential problem. Digital technological solutions for HDTV currently under development in the United States may make both the MAC and the MUSE standards obsolete. The danger for consumers in Europe is that the substantial financial commitment of both European governments and European producers to the MAC standard will impede the substitution of a superior tech-

---

55. Quoted in *International Management*, March 1991, 39. A Matsushita official was similarly quoted as saying, "If Europe has its own standard, we will manufacture to that standard" (*Financial Times*, 3 December 1990, 6).

56. PAL licenses were initially refused top Japanese producers by Telefunken and Thorn, but when the Japanese threatened to disrupt the market by exporting very low cost, inferior sets, Telefunken conceded and allowed licenses to the Japanese, but only for smaller-screen sets and only subject to restrictions in the volume of exports to Europe (Cawson et al. 1990, 224).

nological alternative.[57] On the one hand, the lack of competition among the European producers in the development of Europe's HDTV strategy makes such an outcome more likely. Philips, Thomson, and the other significant European consumer electronics companies are cooperatively engaged in the development of MAC technologies, and they share a strong common interest in fostering them. On the other hand, both Philips and Thomson are actively and cooperatively engaged in developing a digital HDTV transmission standard to submit to the Federal Communications Commission (FCC) for approval in the United States. As a result of substantial direct investment, these companies are among the three largest producers of color TVs in the United States, and together they account for more than 30 percent of the American color TV industry (Jeffrey Hart, Indiana University, personal communication, 17 October 1991).

The competitive environment for HDTV development in the United States, however, is very different from the competitive environment for HDTV development in Europe. The United States has not yet chosen an HDTV standard. Instead, the FCC has requested proposals from the private sector for a standard that would be compatible with existing American television receivers. The 1988 FCC ruling on compatibility effectively ruled out both the MUSE and the MAC standards for the American marketplace, and required a terrestrial rather than a satellite transmission standard. The ruling reflected the interests of consumers and broadcasters, not producers and their political allies.[58]

Several private groups have responded to the FCC ruling with research efforts to develop an HDTV standard that meets the FCC compatibility constraint. Several alliances, including those between General Instrument and the Massachusetts Institute of Technology, between Thomson and Philips,[59] and between Zenith and AT&T have proposed alternative, all-digital systems for the American market. In contrast to analog-based systems, these digital systems are designed to fit a full-blown HDTV signal into a terrestrial bandwidth, thereby meeting the FCC condition of compatibility with existing sets. The efforts of Thomson and Philips to meet the demands of the more competitive American market may ultimately have spillover benefits for the European market as well.[60]

Indeed, the problem of the possible obsolescence of the MAC technology may not be as great as it first seemed. For the medium term, Europe may be locked into MAC, but a digital standard will probably not be fully operational for another

---

57. A much smaller Eureka project, Eureka-256, is now under way on digital HDTV research. The British have been especially vocal about the need to explore digital broadcasting.

58. One interpretation of the FCC ruling was that, by blocking the MUSE and the MAC standards, it allowed time for American producers, especially Zenith, to come up with a standard of its own. But the FCC decision can be more simply interpreted as a natural extension of its earlier color TV ruling: new television systems for the United States must be based on terrestrial transmissions, in keeping with the principle of egalitarian access to television transmission for all potential viewers.

59. In 1990 NBC, the David Sarnoff Research Center, Thomson Consumer Electronics, and Philips North America initiated a cooperative research alliance to develop HDTV for the US market.

60. According to Cawson and Holmes (1991, 180), both Thomson and Philips are developing improved-definition televisions for the US market, and much of the technology under development will have applications for Europe.

several years. By that time the conversion from MAC to an all-digital standard may be a relatively easy task, especially for European producers, such as Thomson and Philips, who are working on both technological trajectories.

As of this writing the future competitive dynamics of the HDTV industry in Europe remain uncertain. What seems certain, however, is that at least for the foreseeable future there will be three different HDTV standards: one for Europe, one for Japan, and one for the United States. Incompatible standards, in turn, will reduce the potential economies of scale and learning in HDTV production, thereby reducing potential profits and increasing consumer costs. An irony of this situation is that different standards will offer at best temporary protection to individual producers. A European standard will not provide its European producers with much of an advantage in a world of global companies and sophisticated components capable of converting the same television set from one transmission standard to another. Standards are more likely to affect technological trajectories than to determine competitive outcomes among global companies like Sony, Philips, and Zenith. In this sense, the FCC compatibility ruling may be the most important standards decision of all: it initiated the research for a digital trajectory that may ultimately prove to be the superior one.

A second lesson that emerges from the HDTV story is the value of competition. In Europe, competition between private broadcasters and satellite transmission companies on the one hand, and between public broadcasters and consumer electronics producers on the other, motivated the recent Community compromise allowing consumers to continue to choose between the PAL and the MAC standards for the foreseeable future. In the United States, competition between producers to meet a technological constraint imposed in the interests of consumers may yield a superior technological outcome. In designing a strategy that favors Community champions over foreign competitors, Europe runs the risk of underestimating the value of competition by ceding too much market power to a small number of European producers.

Finally, the HDTV story also highlights the role of global companies in diffusing the effects of national policies across national borders. The benefits provided to Thomson and Philips by European policies in the color TV and the HDTV industries are enjoyed to some extent by American communities, workers, and consumers. Similarly, the benefits provided to Sony and Matsushita in their home electronics markets are enjoyed to some extent by both American and European communities, workers, and consumers. In a world of global companies, industrial policies and other measures to promote national producers have far-flung spillover effects.

Understanding Europe's Evolving Strategy Toward the Electronics Industry

Since the 1960s, the electronics industry has been accorded special significance in the industrial strategies and policies of the major European countries. The telecommunications and computer segments of the industry have been supported by the French, German, and British governments. In all three countries, lucrative public-sector contracts in data processing and telecommunications have been channeled toward national champions. In France and Great Britain, as in the United States, the defense industry has also been a major buyer of electronic equipment from domestic suppliers. In consumer electronics, domestic suppliers have been supported through protectionist measures in the form of quotas, local content requirements, antidumping enforcement, and restrictive standards.

National European policies to promote indigenous national champions in electronics are widely regarded as unsuccessful.[61] In both computers and semiconductors, European companies have lost world market share to the Japanese and the Americans; in consumer electronics, the losses have been to the Japanese. Only in telecommunications have European companies emerged as market leaders, but few would dispute the role of heretofore protected national markets and preferential procurement policies in this outcome.

As noted in the introduction to this chapter, concern over the failing fortunes of Europe's electronics giants was a major factor behind efforts to create a more unified European market by 1992. Indeed, discussions between Etienne Davignon, EC Commissioner for Industry between 1977 and 1985, and the heads of Europe's leading electronics companies provided both inspiration and growing corporate support for such efforts.

As Europe moves toward completing its internal market, its approach to the electronics industry is changing. The industry is still accorded priority in European development, as evidenced by the fact that the industry still has its own Community Directorate (Directorate-General XIII) to formulate and coordinate European policy. But there is growing debate about the goals of that policy and about the appropriate means to be used. As Margaret Sharp (1991, 149) has recently argued, "Community policies for advanced technology are currently proceeding along a twin track." On the one hand, Community-wide and Europe-wide support programs, such as ESPRIT and Eureka, have been developed to revitalize the European electronics industry. Because of their cooperative and cross-national features, these programs have also promoted and encouraged the substantial concentration that has swept the industry. National champions have been transformed into European multinationals or Community champions whose size and global affiliations put them well beyond the control of national authorities—and perhaps of Community-level authorities as well.

If cooperation and concentration are the first track of Community policies toward the electronics industry, deregulation and liberalization are the second. A unified European market that eliminates impediments to intra-European trade will be a more competitive market, exerting pressure on individual firms to be more responsive to market forces. The competitive pressures unleashed within Europe by the 1992 process are undeniable.

Within European policy circles, the debate continues about the relative weight to be accorded to these two tracks.[62] Those who favor greater government intervention to promote indigenous European technological and production capabilities in the electronics industry emphasize the first track, while those who extol the benefits of market competition emphasize the second, even if it means

---

61. See Sharp (1991) and Derian (1990) for a complete assessment.

62. According to Sharp (1991, 177), the twin tracks of the 1992 process echo the tension, implicit within the Community since its founding, between the minimalists who saw competition policy as the only necessary tool of industrial policy, and the maximalists who from the start argued for more interventionist supply-side powers.

that the challenges of the European market are mastered by participants other than the Europeans themselves.[63]

The ongoing debate between the interventionists and the liberalizers concerning the electronics industry is best reflected in a recent disagreement about a policy paper to be issued by Directorate-General XIII.[64] The first draft of the paper argued that "because of the strategic importance of Europe's electronics firms," they should have "if not self-sufficiency in all areas, at least the capacity to control this sector's progress at the most advanced level and to put together strategic alliances which guarantee security of supply and mastery of technology" (quoted in *The Economist*, "A Survey of Business in Europe," 8 June 1991, 19). The dirigiste and protectionist tone of this language proved unacceptable to many parties, and after several drafts a final report emerged reflecting an uneasy compromise between the interventionists and the liberalizers.

The report's language recognizes that, in view of the "enabling" nature of the electronics industries and their external effects on the economy as a whole, there are reasons to regard them as "strategic."[65] But the report backs away from broad-based, supply-side measures to promote electronics producers, preferring to emphasize the importance of competition and "a favorable environment" for their revitalization. The report recommends a series of policy initiatives to promote R&D, the diffusion of technology, skill development, and demand growth for the electronics industry.[66] The report also makes recommendations for EC trade policy, with an emphasis on the goal of equitable conditions of competition and market access, especially in semiconductors and consumer electronics. This emphasis is in keeping with Europe's growing commitment to the principle of selective reciprocity—at both the country and the industry levels—in its trade policy.

Among the initiatives proposed in the report are measures to boost demand for electronics products by investing in the development of a "European Nervous System" (ENS) designed to link together different national computer networks, such as those carrying value-added tax, Social Security, and customs data. The ENS idea is a natural stepping stone to Europe's goal of an integrated broadband network. This goal is currently being advanced through the so-called RACE program, a $1.5 billion Community-funded R&D project to explore advanced communications technologies. The RACE program, like the Eureka HDTV program, emphasizes the development of European standards and collaborative R&D as acceptable methods for promoting European capabilities in electronics. Altogether, the Community plans to spend 27 percent of its 1990–94 advanced-technologies R&D budget on information and telecommunications technologies,

---

63. The so-called Cecchini Report (Cecchini 1988, 73–74) concluded that "Failure to meet the demands of competitivity does not mean that the challenges of the Single European Act will not be mastered. They will. But not by Europeans."

64. The recent study by Howell et al. (1992) also emphasizes the ongoing debate and the resulting ambiguities in recent Community pronouncements about appropriate policies for the electronics sector.

65. The report is titled *The European Electronics and Information Technology Industry: State of Play, Issues at Stake and Proposals for Action*, 3 April 1991.

66. In its discussion of ways to stimulate demand growth, the report explicitly mentions the possibility of projects relating to a pan-European HDTV service.

with the remainder scattered throughout a large number of much smaller programs.[67]

The interventionists and the liberalizers tend to agree that the first-best outcome of a successful European strategy in the electronics industry would be the strengthening of indigenous European production and technological capabilities. In a news conference held in conjunction with the release of the Directorate-General XIII report, Commissioner Filippo Pandolfi stated that the aim of Community policies was "to provide opportunities to European companies in the real sense of the word." He added that "we would like European companies to remain European." Citing this goal as justification, he defended the Community's approach of ruling on the participation of non–EC firms in collaborative Community R&D programs on a case-by-case basis. In making decisions about such cases, the Community has emphasized two criteria: the kind and extent of investment by foreign firms in European facilities, and reciprocity. According to these criteria, IBM and other American companies with significant production and research facilities in Europe have been permitted to participate in ESPRIT projects. On the other hand, because European firms have not been included in Sematech, the US–sponsored semiconductor research consortium, the Europeans have invoked the principle of reciprocity to exclude American firms from inclusion in JESSI, a Eureka-sponsored $5 billion collaborative R&D effort in semiconductors.[68]

Where the interventionists and the liberalizers part company is over the correct policy response should a revitalized European electronics industry prove elusive even with a substantial commitment of public R&D support. At one extreme are the committed interventionists, who favor protectionist policies encompassing both trade and foreign direct investment. People of this persuasion have also argued for Community-wide quotas on "foreign" automobiles, whether imported or produced in Europe. At the other extreme are the committed liberalizers, who oppose protectionist policies regardless of the consequences for the European electronics producers. Advocates of liberalization have also argued against Community quotas on automobile imports, even as a temporary transition measure to ease adjustment.

In between these extremes it is possible to discern a more pragmatic policy perspective: if the first-best outcome of a European industry cannot be realized without excessive protection, the second-best outcome is a European production and research base achieved through significant direct investment by the foreign suppliers of Europe's markets. This pragmatic perspective appears to have won in the recent debate over Community-wide quotas on foreign automobiles. Transitional quotas have been adopted for automotive imports, but they have not

---

67. To put this in perspective, however, the total committed to all of the advanced-technologies R&D programs amounts to only 2 percent of the total EC budget; for comparison, the total spent on agricultural support programs in some years has claimed over 70 percent of the total EC budget (Sharp 1991, 164).

68. For more on the JESSI project see Flamm (1990). The discretionary nature of the case-by-case approach is apparent in the recent expulsion of ICL, a British-based computer company, from a number of collaborative R&D projects financed by the Community, after ICL was purchased by Fujitsu. ICL was also expelled from the European Information Technology Roundtable, a private-sector industry creation of which it was a founding member.

been applied to the European production of foreign transplants.[69] This policy, like European trade policies in the VCR, computer, and semiconductor industries, will have the effect of making Europe a fortress against imports but a magnet for foreign direct investment.

With the formal elimination of national import quotas, the formidable political barriers to agreeing upon Community-wide import quotas, and the liberalization of procurement policies, the major policy instrument for discouraging imports in the future is likely to be Europe's antidumping law.[70] Used in conjunction with evolving rules of origin, this law is likely to get tougher and to be used more frequently.[71]

Even in their current form, Europe's antidumping regulations are a potentially powerful barrier to imports. According to a recent GATT study, the Community has interpreted its regulations in a way that makes both the finding of dumping and the proof of injury easy to establish.[72] Moreover, Community antidumping proceedings lack transparency. The Commission itself verifies complaints, limits access to case files, holds informal hearings in accordance with continental law practice (thereby allowing *ex parte* communications), does not require a written record of its deliberations, and grants no automatic right of review. Perhaps most important, if dumping is established, duties are not restricted to the individual exporters found guilty but can be extended to all exporters from the home country of the guilty parties. Exporters who then agree to cut an attractive deal—as the three major Korean companies did in the VCR case—are exempted from dumping duties while exporters who were never found guilty of dumping may be forced to pay them. Many antidumping cases are resolved by undertakings whereby foreign companies agree to increase their European investment or their sourcing of inputs from European suppliers.

Japan, whose electronics producers have been a primary target of Europe's antidumping law, requested in 1989 that a GATT panel investigate the application of Europe's antiscrewdriver regulations. In March 1990 the panel ruled against the Community, but it did so on narrow technical grounds. Although the Eu-

---

69. According to some officials in Brussels, although the formal Community agreement on foreign automobile quotas excludes transplant production, some individual countries, for example France and Italy, may want to cut their own informal deals with the Japanese to limit their total share of a particular national market, including the share supplied from Japanese transplants in Europe. Because of the fragile nature of the Community-wide compromise on this issue, if individual countries violate the spirit of the compromise in this way, the Commission may be forced to look the other way.

70. The possibility of more overt protection cannot be entirely ruled out. Alain Gomez, the chief executive officer of Thomson, is urging an increase in tariffs on semiconductors and consumer electronics by 30 percent to 50 percent for a period of five years. And in the Uruguay Round discussions, the Community has offered less substantial tariff reductions to its trading partners on certain electronics products and has insisted on the need to remove nontariff barriers to foreign market access now facing European consumer electronics goods.

71. In its recent report (1991, 24), Directorate-General XIII emphasized that the antidumping procedure should be used as a last resort and that all available bilateral and multilateral consultative fora should be employed to avoid those situations where the Community has no other choice than to take antidumping measures.

72. For a more complete analysis of European antidumping regulations see GATT (1991, chapter 4) and Hindley (1988, 445–63).

ropeans have suspended suits based on these regulations since the GATT ruling, they remain committed to developing and applying measures to prevent the circumvention of Community antidumping penalties and to increase the penalties for "repeat offenders." The Europeans are currently lobbying for changes in GATT antidumping regulations along these lines.

Even the strongest liberalizers at the Community level such as Sir Leon Brittan, who heads the Competition Commission, defend the Community's antidumping laws on the grounds that they are a legitimate and internationally agreed-upon trade policy instrument to cope with market distortion and unfair competition. The flaw in this argument is that in Europe, as elsewhere, dumping can be demonstrated and countervailed, as it was in the VCR case, without any proof that the conditions of predation and unfair competition prevail. Indeed, according to internationally accepted practice, there is simply no attempt made to determine whether these conditions apply. As a result, Europe's antidumping laws are inherently discriminatory against foreigners, who are *de facto* precluded from business practices that are available to domestic companies as long as such practices cannot be legally demonstrated to be predatory. The discriminatory effect is especially strong in technology-intensive industries, where the economics of production encourage aggressive forward pricing to gain market share and exploit economies of scale and learning. In such industries, national antidumping laws in their current form can actively discourage or effectively rule out normal competitive pricing behavior by foreign suppliers.

Lessons for US Trade and Industrial Policy

The VCR and HDTV stories told in this chapter contain several lessons for US policy. First, the VCR story confirms the findings of previous studies on the effects of voluntary restraint agreements. VRAs suffer from the drawbacks of other protectionist measures: they tend to increase the prices and restrict the supply of foreign products without improving the long-run competitiveness of domestic producers. Moreover, unlike tariffs, which have the same effects but at least add to government revenues, VRAs tend to increase the profits of foreign producers, thereby strengthening their competitive position vis-à-vis domestic producers. Like tariffs, VRAs tend to encourage local investment by foreign producers to jump protectionist barriers, but in the absence of complementary local content policies, such investment is likely to be of the screwdriver variety.

A second lesson from the HDTV story is the growing ineffectiveness of standards as a way to secure a competitive foothold for domestic producers. Some voices in the US HDTV debate have encouraged the development of a distinctive American standard as a way to revitalize American consumer electronics producers. But for the reasons noted above, both the Japanese and the European producers, who already have substantial production and marketing facilities in the United States and better access to long-term capital than many potential American competitors, are likely to emerge as dominant producers of HDTV sets designed to an American standard.

A third lesson to emerge from the long story of European efforts to promote national or regional champions in the electronics industry is the high risk of failure of industrial policies, especially when they concentrate on sheltered domestic producers. The failure of such policies in the European electronics industry is as dramatic as their success in the Japanese semiconductor industry or in the European aircraft industry. Industrial policy by itself is never a guarantee of an industry's success. Nor is the success of an industrial policy—with success defined at sustaining local producers—any guarantee that the policy was economically rational or welfare-improving.

Between 1989 and mid-1990, there was a flurry of interest and lobbying in favor of an activist industrial policy to promote HDTV in the United States. Most of the arguments in favor of such an approach were flawed, as were the specific actions proposed.[73] What finally emerged out of the political fray, however, was a defensible approach that involved the competitive allocation of a limited amount of public funds for precompetitive research on generic technologies, such as high-resolution display technologies, related to HDTV.[74] These funds have been awarded competitively to several groups, and they have not been tied to a single standard. The Eureka-95 approach is less competitive than the US approach, because it unites all of the major European producers in cooperative product development efforts, and because it is tied to a particular standard. Eureka-95 has tried to pick both the winning standards and the winning players in HDTV competition.[75] So far, US programs to support HDTV research have assiduously avoided picking winners of either kind.

Even if the United States emerges from the HDTV race with the frontier digital design, however, there is no guarantee that American producers or the United States as a production location will reap the benefits. No one seriously questions the ability of American companies to innovate. The serious questions concern their ability to commercialize their innovations in ways that increase American living standards. The fate of active-matrix display technology, an innovation developed in the United States but now produced almost entirely by Japanese companies in Japan, may very well be replayed in digital HDTV technology.[76] As Craig Fields, ex-director of the Defense Advanced Projects Research Agency, noted at a June 1991 meeting sponsored by the National Academy of Sciences, American companies remain competitive on the R&D side, but many of them are becoming progressively weaker in the industrial capacities required for con-

---

73. For more on the proposals for an HDTV strategy in the United States see Hart and Tyson (1989).

74. The Defense Advanced Projects Research Agency spent approximately $30 million to promote research on HDTV–related technologies in 1990. In 1991 the agency spent approximately $60 million; the allocation for 1992 is $75 million (Jeffrey Hart, Indiana University, personal communication, 6 April 1992). The National Institute of Standards and Technology has also allocated some research monies to HDTV projects.

75. The Commission's definition of precompetitive research is "projects which competitors agree to do jointly." The Commission defends this definition on the grounds that competitors will not wish to cooperate on market-oriented R&D. But this definition begs a number of competition policy issues, and it overlooks the fact that often it may be in the interest of companies to collude or cooperate at the expense of consumers or market competition. Ultimately, business interests are usually better off with less rather than more competition. Even more than the Commission's publicly supported R&D projects, Eureka's projects tend to cross the line between generic and market-oriented research.

76. For a compelling account of the fate of active-matrix display technology, see Florida and Browdy (1991).

tinued success in technology-intensive production. Even a well-designed, pro-competitive industrial policy in the form of public R&D support for generic technologies cannot substitute for more-fundamental changes in the cost and availability of capital to US firms and in the organization of US manufacturing. Certainly, a misguided protectionist trade policy—such as the recent imposition of dumping duties on Japanese producers of active-matrix displays—cannot (for more on this point see chapter 7).

The final lesson for US policymakers to emerge from the case studies in this chapter concerns the implications of Europe's electronics strategy for global investment flows. Using both protectionist measures, mainly in the form of *de facto* creeping local content requirements, and promotional measures, mainly in the form of R&D subsidies and regional development subsidies tied to European production locations, Europe is actively competing for "quality" investment by global companies.[77] There is a distinctly zero-sum aspect to this competition, since investment in Europe by such companies as IBM, Intel, Fujitsu, and Sony is investment that might instead have gone to US locations.[78] American multinationals may not be harmed by European policies to substitute local production for imports, but all other things being equal, both American exports and America as a production location are adversely affected.

Therefore, the United States should continue to work with the Europeans on agreements to regulate allowable protectionist and promotional policies that affect international investment flows. At the same time, in a world in which direct investment flows are becoming ever more important relative to trade flows, the United States must design its own policies to make it an attractive location for both domestic and foreign multinationals. Foreign direct investment may be only second-best compared with the development of indigenous production and technological capabilities, but it is likely to be distinctly superior to dependence on imports from foreign suppliers who locate their production, employment, and research facilities elsewhere.

---

77. The new study by Howell et al. (1992) reaches a similar conclusion. They argue that both American and Asian firms believe that their ability to sell their products in Europe increasingly depends on maintaining a high level of European production.

78. The European producers of consumer electronics have themselves complained about the tendency of EC member states to outbid one another in subsidies to attract inward investment, and the Competition Commission is trying to make the rules on such behavior more precise and enforceable. The United States should actively support such efforts.

7

A Cautious Activist Agenda for U.S. Policy for High-Technology Industries

Expanding Market Access

The Pros and Cons of Antidumping Remedies

Strategic Threats in High-Technology Industries

Subsidies, Foreign Targeting, and Countervailing Duties

The Need for Complementary Technology and Industrial Policies

Some Concluding Thoughts

Now that the end of the Cold War has dissolved the glue that bound the United States, Europe, and Japan together in defense against a common adversary, their competing economic interests threaten to spill over into increasingly bitter trade conflict. Nowhere is this danger greater than in high-technology industries, to which all three economic superpowers attach special significance both for national security and for the strength of their domestic economies.

Europe and Japan, along with the most successful newly industrializing countries, have targeted these industries for special support. Most of the foreign targets—especially in electronics, telecommunications, aerospace, and biotechnology—are industries that loom large in the American economy, and in most of them American companies retain strong competitive positions. As a result of this targeting and a variety of structural and policy barriers to foreign markets, trade in high-technology industries is no longer free in the classical sense; it is manipulated by government intervention. Nor is comparative advantage in these industries inherited as it is in resource-intensive industries—rather it is created with the help of the often heavy and visible hand of government action.

It can no longer be doubted that foreign intervention in high-technology industries exists and that it works to the competitive disadvantage of American producers. The questions now are whether the harm done to American economic interests warrants a response and what form that response should take.

According to one line of thinking, foreign practices offer no cause for alarm and no need to rethink policy options: foreign subsidies are gifts to American consumers, barriers to foreign markets inflict more pain abroad than at home, and high-technology industries are no more important to the nation's economic well-being than are other economic activities. But these soothing views, often based on ideology rather than analysis, are called into question both by the theoretical insights of the new trade theory and by the empirical evidence presented throughout this book.

As the case studies have demonstrated, foreign promotional and protectionist measures have inflicted substantial harm on American producers. Some of America's most innovative companies, such as Motorola, Cray, Intel, and Boeing, have lost market share, revenues, and potential for creating high-paying jobs for American workers as a result of both barriers to foreign markets and foreign subsidies. Even those studies that indicate that foreign targeting has reduced foreign economic welfare—for example, the analyses by Baldwin and Krugman of European subsidies to Airbus (1988b, discussed in chapter 5) and of Japanese protection of semiconductors (1988a, discussed in chapter 4)—suggest that they have reduced American economic welfare as well. And studies such as those by Katz and Summers (1989) and Dickens (1992), which attempt to account for the deleterious effects of such policies on high-wage job opportunities in the United States, estimate even greater losses to American economic welfare. Moreover, all of these studies employ static approaches, which tend to understate long-run benefits to the targeting country and long-run costs to the United States.

With existing empirical techniques and modeling approaches it is simply impossible to quantify the impact of foreign promotional and protectionist policies on national economic welfare, either in terms of forgone consumer and producer welfare or in terms of the local externalities created by high-technology production. Nonetheless, the evidence presented in this book provides a strong *prima facie* case that this impact is substantial, and this case is buttressed by the economic literature on trade and government policy in high-technology industries. The case is even more compelling in light of the evidence presented in chapter 2 and elsewhere in the book that these industries make important contributions to the nation's overall economic health. Exporting a dollar's worth of oranges may have the same effect on the trade balance as exporting a dollar's worth of computers, but the two have radically different effects on other crucial determinants of economic health, including employment, productivity, wages, skill formation, and investment in research and development.

Confronted with such evidence, a cautious activist such as myself concludes that the continuing relative erosion of American strength in high-technology industries is a legitimate policy concern and that American policies to counter the harmful domestic effects of foreign promotional and protectionist measures are justifiable. However, these conclusions are tempered by the realization that the wrong policy response can easily make matters worse. And they are informed by the recognition that, although foreign practices have played a role, the problems of America's high-technology industries are mainly homegrown and require homegrown solutions.

Drawing on the case studies in chapters 3 through 6, this chapter recommends a policy agenda of cautious activism for maintaining American competitiveness in high-technology industries. Underlying that agenda is the view that the United States should use its trade policies to defend against foreign practices and structural barriers that harm the nation's high-technology producers. But in pursuing this objective it should adopt only approaches that encourage competition and trade and should reject those that impede competition and erect protectionist barriers.[1] Moreover, to the extent feasible, American trade policies should be

---

1. According to a recent survey by Richardson (1992, 13), several new econometric studies by exponents of the new trade theory confirm the maxim that trade liberalization encourages competition, which in turn increases productivity growth and reduces corporate

employed in ways that encourage rather than jeopardize the development of new multilateral rules for high-technology trade. In other words, the trade strategy espoused here is a defensive one—a stopgap measure to defend American economic interests in the absence of multilateral rules, not a sleight-of-hand effort to stymie their development.

As a guide to the following discussion, table 7.1 compares the trade policy actions and international agreements examined in this book according to whether they encompassed rules or outcomes, whether they addressed sectoral or aggregate concerns, whether they were trade promoting or trade restricting, and whether they were bilateral or multilateral in scope. American trade policy has traditionally emphasized rules rather than outcomes. In Bhagwati's terminology, the American objective has been better trade management, not managed trade. But as the following discussion indicates, the distinction between negotiating rules and negotiating outcomes is not as straightforward or pure as Bhagwati's neat dichotomy suggests.

At one end of the negotiating continuum are general multilateral rules that are broadly applicable across all industries and trading partners. The rules of the General Agreement on Tariffs and Trade (GATT) on import tariffs and quotas are examples. At the other end are specific quantitative results or managed trade—agreements formulated in terms of quantities of goods that will be imported or exported, or market shares that will be allocated to foreign producers. Europe's voluntary restraint agreement with Japan on videocassette recorders and the US market access agreement with Japan on semiconductors are examples discussed in this book. Moreover, even managed trade agreements come in different forms. Some are designed to reduce trade, while others are designed to increase it; some are bilateral, while others have multilateral applicability. In the complex world of high-technology trade, the time-honored distinctions between rules and outcomes, between free trade and managed trade, and between bilateralism and multilateralism are no longer adequate. A more complicated vocabulary is necessary to capture a more complicated reality.

Expanding Market Access

Aggressive Unilateralism

On questions of market access, the United States should continue along the path it pioneered in the 1980s: sector-specific negotiations with particular trading partners to secure improved trade and investment opportunities for American producers. Moreover, these negotiations should extend to trade barriers and structural impediments not currently regulated by the GATT, they should seek agreements with multilateral applicability, and they should be backed by a credible threat of retaliation.

Section 301 of US trade law and its temporary Super 301 variant, which embody these approaches, have sparked sharp criticism both at home and abroad for

---

market power. These findings indicate that trade liberalization remains in the national interest even under many conditions of imperfect and strategic competition.

Table 7.1 From multilateral rules to bilaterally managed outcomes: an anatomy of the cases

Case	Sectoral or aggregate concern	Bilateral or multilateral	Rules or outcomes	Trade promoting or trade restricting
Multilateral rules				
GATT agreement on trade in civil aircraft (1979)	Sectoral	Multilateral agreement, but reciprocity limited to signatories	Rules	Trade promoting
Bilateral rules				
Structural Impediments Initiative talks (1989)	Aggregate	US–Japan bilateral agreement with multilateral applicability	Rules	Trade promoting
Market-oriented, sector-specific talks (1985–86)	Sectoral	US–Japan bilateral agreement with multilateral applicability	Rules	Trade promoting
US–EC agreement on trade in commercial aircraft (1992)	Sectoral	US–EC bilateral agreement but may be extended by reciprocal agreements with signatories to the 1979 GATT civil aircraft agreement	Rules and numerical limits on allowable subsidies	Trade promoting

Super 301

· Cellular telephones (1989)	Sectoral	US–Japan bilateral agreement	Rules, but very specific as to product and location within Japan and as to spectrum allocation	Trade promoting
Third-party radios (1989)	Sectoral	US–Japan bilateral agreement with multilateral applicability	Temporary outcome later replaced by rule	Trade promoting
Supercomputers (1990)	Sectoral	US–Japan bilateral agreement with multilateral applicability	Rule	Trade promoting
Bilateral managed trade				
Semiconductor trade agreement (1986): pricing provisions	Sectoral	US–Japan bilateral agreement, but applied to third-country pricing by Japanese companies	Outcome: company-by-company floor on pricing	Trade restricting
Semiconductor trade agreement (1986): market access provisions	Sectoral	US–Japan bilateral agreement with multilateral applicability	Outcome: voluntary import expansion establishing 20 percent share of Japanese market for foreign suppliers	Trade promoting
EC–Japan voluntary export restraint agreement on VCRs (1982–84)	Sectoral	EC–Japan bilateral agreement	Outcome: quantitative limits on exports to Europe from Japan	Trade restricting

their aggressive unilateralism (see Bhagwati and Patrick 1990). They are "unilateral" because they allow the United States to define its own list of unfair foreign practices, including many that are not explicitly proscribed by the GATT; to determine on its own when a trading partner is guilty of such practices; and to demand direct negotiations with US representatives, not arbitration in a multilateral forum, to address them. They are "aggressive" because they allow the United States to threaten or actually impose retaliation to realize its objectives.

The charge that Section 301 and Super 301 are forms of aggressive unilateralism is undeniable. But the premise underlying this book is that aggressive unilateralism is defensible as an interim response to foreign trading practices and structural barriers that harm American economic interests and that are not covered by binding multilateral regulations. The alternative is not a world of free trade; it is a world in which trade and structural barriers can inflict substantial damage on national economic interests, especially in imperfectly competitive technology-intensive industries. In such a world, the United States has three options: accept the damage, try to offset it by promotional or protectionist measures at home, or negotiate to remove its source. Aggressive unilateralism sensibly pursues the third option.

The case studies of trade in cellular telephones, supercomputers, and semiconductors (chapters 3 and 4) demonstrate that Section 301 and Super 301 can be successfully applied to reduce foreign market barriers and increase competition.[2] Neither the intent nor the outcome of US action in these instances was protectionist.

Bayard and Elliott reach a similar conclusion in their forthcoming study of Section 301 and Super 301 cases. They find that almost two-thirds of the cases between 1985 and 1991 resulted in at least partial opening of foreign markets for US companies. Moreover, when Super 301 was applied, it provoked none of the trade wars predicted by some of its opponents.

Aggressive unilateralism has also yielded some real victories in the area of intellectual property protection for American companies. In the semiconductor industry, for example, the Commerce Department has used the Semiconductor Chip Protection Act of 1984 to extend reciprocal protection of semiconductor mask works (a critical early step in semiconductor fabrication) to foreign companies in nations that agree to protect US chip designs. Early in the MOSS (market-oriented, sector-specific) negotiations the Japanese agreed to adopt 10-year protection of original chip design, in conformance with American practice. Since 1984 the Commerce Department has succeeded in fashioning similar bilateral agreements with 18 other nations. In the semiconductor industry, as in other high-technology industries, bilateral reciprocal deals are necessary to secure adequate intellectual property protection for American producers because binding international rules have not yet been developed. Often threats of restrictions on access to the US market have resulted in improved intellectual property protection for American producers.

---

2. Section 301 and Super 301 have also been used with considerable success in the high-technology area to realize greater foreign compliance with American standards of intellectual property protection. For example, threats of restrictions on access to the US market have resulted in improved intellectual property protection for US producers in Thailand, Korea, Taiwan, and Japan.

Despite its effectiveness, there are undeniable risks to aggressive unilateralism even in pursuit of justifiable market-opening objectives. Bilateral trade deals can be trade-diverting, or they can create other unanticipated negative spillovers for nonparticipants. The United States has minimized this risk by using bilateral negotiations to formulate nondiscriminatory, multilateral market-opening arrangements. For example, in most of its negotiations with Japan, the United States has sought improved access for all non-Japanese suppliers, not just American ones.[3] To enhance the multilateral applicability of its trade initiatives, the United States should go further and invite interested nations to participate in the negotiations whenever possible. Such an approach would have made sense in the MOSS talks, the Structural Impediments Initiative (SII) talks, and the semiconductor talks with Japan.

Critics of aggressive unilateralism argue that it also poisons the atmosphere for further progress on the multilateral trading regime. But there is no *a priori* reason why this should be so.[4] It is equally conceivable that American unilateralism may help overcome the inertia that still plagues the Uruguay Round in late 1992. Certainly there is nothing to suggest that American unilateralism, expressed in actions taken under Section 301 or Super 301, caused the breakdown of the round in the first place.[5] To the contrary, the analysis by Bayard and Elliott suggests that Section 301 has actually moved the Uruguay Round negotiations in the direction of improving the GATT's dispute settlement mechanism.

The real danger of aggressive unilateralism is the possible provocation of a mutually destructive trade or subsidy war. US negotiators, acutely aware of this risk, have been much more aggressive in words than in actions. They talked tough in the long disputes on the Motorola and Cray cases, for example, but never introduced any formal retaliatory measures. Likewise, although the United States repeatedly threatened retaliation against continued Airbus subsidies, it ultimately declined to act—a sensible decision in light of the evidence presented in chapter 5.

Indeed, it is often easier to criticize US trade policy for insufficient pressure than for excessive aggression. In the Motorola case (chapter 3), for example, the United States did not retaliate against Japan despite that country's five-year delay in granting Motorola access to the Tokyo-Nagoya cellular telephone market. Similarly, in the 1991 semiconductor trade agreement with Japan (chapter 4), the United States dropped existing retaliatory tariffs on Japanese products, even though Japan had failed to comply with the market share target established in the 1986 agreement. In both instances, Japan's allied bureaucratic and business interests saw the stakes in the underlying trade dispute as zero-sum: what American companies stood to gain, they stood to lose. Therefore, they had every

---

3. The 1992 market access deal for American auto parts in Japan is a dangerous exception to this multilateral principle.

4. Indeed, Robert E. Hudec (1990, 198) has argued that Section 301, which he views as a violation of existing international rules, is a form of legal disobedience that may actually prod America's trading partners to negotiate a comprehensive and enforceable GATT deal.

5. However, America's uncompromising position on European agricultural subsidies—ironically, a position supported by many of the moderate free traders who are outspoken critics of aggressive unilateralism—*was* a precipitating factor.

interest in delaying action, and in acceding to American requests only when they had even more to lose by not doing so.

The cases of US–Japan conflict discussed in chapters 3 and 4 illustrate the role of foreign pressure, or *gaiatsu*, in prodding the Japanese to implement market access agreements. The United States has applied such pressure cautiously, choosing the threat of retaliation over actual retaliation whenever possible. What it has sacrificed in terms of timely response must be balanced against what it has gained by avoiding the costs of protectionist retaliatory measures.

Nonetheless, the history of delayed results from US unilateral initiatives reveals the fundamental limitations of trade policy to redress damages inflicted on domestic producers by foreign trade and structural barriers. The slow resolution of trade policy disputes can be disastrous to American firms or industries, as the 15-year dispute over US access to the Japanese semiconductor market demonstrates. Even when the companies involved can withstand the delay, as Motorola could in the cellular telephone industry, they pay a heavy price in terms of lost revenues. Smaller, less prosperous companies may simply despair of the prospects for breaking into a sheltered foreign market or may find themselves driven out of business by foreign competitors based in those markets.

Some of the delays in American trade policy have been internal, reflecting the failure of US policymakers to react to foreign barriers, in part because to do so might threaten broader geopolitical interests, and in part because the damaging effects of such barriers were simply discounted. For example, in the semiconductor case, as long as US officials believed that it did not matter whether the United States had its own DRAM production capabilities, it was difficult to mount a credible response to Japanese practices.

By the end of the 1980s, however, the American position showed signs of change. The "quick-response" retaliation clause of Super 301 was expressly fashioned to reduce the substantial and costly delays characteristic of past 301 actions. It also sent a powerful strategic signal. Whereas the US government had often looked the other way when foreign practices imposed damages on US producers, Super 301 served notice that it would do so no longer.

The evidence in this book indicates that Super 301 should be extended. It has served American economic interests in a trade-enhancing way. In addition, the United States should oppose a Uruguay Round settlement that seriously curtails the application of Super 301 or of Section 301 when used in response to foreign practices not covered by precise GATT regulations. It is one thing to concede dispute-settlement authority to the GATT when clear-cut GATT rules are violated, but quite another when those rules are vague or ultimately unenforceable.

Nevertheless, the dangers of Section 301 and Super 301 should not be overlooked. Used with less restraint and intelligence they could easily touch off costly retaliatory measures. The United States needs aggressive unilateralism; it does not need obsessive unilateralism. Moreover, it is essential to recognize that American threats are likely to become less effective in the future, as the US market becomes relatively less important for foreign and especially Japanese producers. Finally, although bilateral, sector-specific negotiations can eventually improve market access, they should not be oversold. They usually take a long time to conclude, and the results are often disappointing. Even with a quick-response approach, US producers can rarely expect a resolution to a trade policy complaint in less than a year, and as the Motorola cellular telephone case makes clear, implementation of a resulting trade agreement can take considerably longer. These unavoidable delays mean that trade policy cannot be an effective substitute for a domestic policy response in technology-intensive industries, where one year's delay can destroy a technological advantage. If the health of an American industry is jeopardized by foreign market barriers or unfair competitive practices, the US government should have the capacity and the will to introduce interim domestic assistance measures while it continues to negotiate with its trading partners.[6]

Selective Reciprocity

Critics have also attacked Section 301 and Super 301 for their implicit principle of selective or contingent reciprocity. The GATT is based on the principle of broad-based or diffuse reciprocity: overall access to each national market should be comparable across a broad range of goods and trading partners, but comparable access in particular industries and with particular trading partners is not required. In contrast, the principle of selective reciprocity links access by foreign firms to a particular national market to comparable access in their home markets. The principle of selective reciprocity can be applied to a broad policy area, as the Europeans have done by linking their procurement policy to those of their trading partners, or to a particular industry, as the United States proposed to do during the Uruguay Round telecommunications talks.[7] Selective reciprocity can also be applied on a plurilateral basis. Three examples are the 1979 GATT civil aircraft code, the GATT procurement code, and the GATT subsidy code—in each of these cases reciprocity is restricted to the signatories to the agreement.

Comparable market access with particular trading partners in particular industries has become an increasingly important goal of US trade policy. This goal was apparent in the MOSS talks and in the Motorola and semiconductor cases discussed in this book. There is no denying that the selective reciprocity principle is a dangerous departure from traditional US trade policy. A world in which market access arrangements are negotiated on a bilateral, sector-specific basis is a world in which the benefits of broad-based reciprocity, most-favored-nation treatment, and national treatment are endangered. Selective reciprocity en-

---

6. Along these lines, US trade law should perhaps be amended to provide temporary countervailing subsidy relief once a preliminary finding of a threat of serious injury from unfair foreign trading practices has been made. The possibility of such relief might be limited to priority cases identified in annual trade reviews along the lines of those required by Super 301. A final ruling reversing the preliminary finding or an agreement that eliminates the objectionable practices would terminate the relief. One problem with a countervailing subsidy approach is its potential for misuse. To be effective, such an approach requires a more forward-looking and better-informed trade policy than the United States has at present. Another problem is that a countervailing subsidy approach is likely to be opposed by the stronger companies in an industry, which do not wish to see their weaker competitors kept alive. For more on these points, see below.

7. In the months preceding the stall of the Uruguay Round discussions in December 1990, the United States announced that it did not want to apply the most-favored-nation or nondiscrimination principle to telecommunications, because to do so would allow companies from nations with government-sanctioned or government-owned monopolies in telecommunications to enter the American market, while American firms would be unable to obtain reciprocal opportunities in their markets.

courages preferential trading blocs, and if carried too far can result in retaliation and bilateral trade deals, carving up national markets to achieve "reciprocal" outcomes. In a world of significant structural and policy differences, it is easy to imagine that the difficulties of providing "comparable" market access might encourage negotiators to substitute "comparable" market shares or "results." This is indeed what happened in the US negotiations with Japan over semiconductors.

Despite its many pitfalls, however, selective reciprocity is the most sensible starting point for sectoral trade negotiations.[8] Most of the major trade dilemmas facing the United States and the other developed nations revolve around disputes in specific industries with specific trading partners, where current international rules are either inapplicable or unenforceable. For such disputes, selective reciprocity is the only relevant principle on which to base a resolution. Indeed, Bergsten and Cline (1987, 141) go so far as to argue that "Proposals for reciprocal market opportunities at the sectoral level are an extension of [aggregate reciprocity] and should be acceptable for the same reasons."

Whatever its merits, selective reciprocity is likely to become even more important over time, as Europe continues down the 1992 road, and as the United States continues down the path to a North American free trade area. Indeed, there are those who argue that "reciprocity is the only way to prevent the world economy from regressing into extreme protectionism" (Drucker 1989, 132). The challenge is to dodge the dangers of selective reciprocity while achieving greater comparability of access among different countries.

The cases examined in this book suggest that the United States largely met this challenge during the 1980s. Doing so required detailed sectoral negotiations with specific trading partners to scale back trade barriers and harmonize policies and institutions affecting market access. These are the kinds of negotiations the United States initiated with Europe and other interested nations on civil aircraft trade in 1979 and with Japan on trade in a number of industries, including telecommunications equipment, drugs, medical equipment, financial services, and construction in the 1980s. In several of these cases, negotiations occurred under the gun of threatened US retaliation.

Of the cases in this book that involved American trade policy actions, the only one that did not strictly adhere to the principle of selective reciprocity was the 1989 Super 301 action involving access of American supercomputer producers to the Japanese public procurement market. The evidence in chapter 3 confirms the existence of persistent barriers to this market and their damaging effects on American producers, especially Cray. Moreover, most of what the US negotiators requested was defensible: it would have made Japanese public procurement procedures more transparent and accessible to outsiders. But the US position was not one of complete reciprocity. The United States requested nondiscriminatory treatment of American producers in procurement of supercomputers by public institutions in Japan. But because of national security guidelines, the

---

8. In addition, a developing body of theoretical work indicates that reciprocity can increase the stability of a sequence of cooperative trade agreements among governments and reduce the chance that recurrent negotiations will tend toward noncooperative outcomes (see Richardson 1992, 27).

United States does not grant nondiscriminatory treatment of foreign producers in procurement of supercomputers by public institutions at home.

Ultimately, if the US commitment to aggressive unilateralism for market-opening, procompetitive objectives is to be honored, public procurement practices for supercomputers in both Japan and the United States will have to be harmonized. The inevitable result will be an increase in the Japanese share of the American market. The appropriate American response should concentrate on domestic measures, for example increased funding for the Federal High-Performance Computing and Networking Initiative, to strengthen the competitiveness of American companies. The American supercomputer industry, like many other high-technology successes, was an outgrowth of the nation's defense commitment. It was a long-term vision and public support, not market forces alone, that fostered the industry's development, and both will be necessary to help the industry weather the unavoidable strains of stiffer Japanese competition.

Rules Versus Outcomes

A distinctive feature of the American version of aggressive unilateralism and selective reciprocity has been its emphasis on rules rather than outcomes. But, as noted earlier, this distinction can be overdrawn and misleading, especially when applied to the kinds of high-technology trade conflicts examined in this book.

Between the extremes of multilateral fixed rules and bilateral managed trade are intermediate arrangements, such as those negotiated between the United States and Japan in the MOSS talks, the SII talks, and the 1989 talks on cellular telephones, third-party radios, and supercomputers. In each of these cases, the US lobbied not for outcomes but for rules that would give American and other foreign producers improved market access in Japan. Admittedly, the rules were sometimes quite specific regarding the product, the geographical market, and even the firms in question. On a continuum between trade management through better rules at one end and managed trade through quantitative targets at the other, some US–Japan trade agreements were clearly closer to the latter. Nonetheless, their purpose was to increase competition, not to cartelize the market. Paradoxically, in Japan something akin to managed trade is often required to achieve something akin to a market outcome.

Both the market access provisions of the 1986 and 1991 semiconductor trade agreements between the United States and Japan and the quantitative limits on Japanese VCR exports to Europe are forms of managed trade. The former are examples of what Bhagwati (1983, 83) has called a voluntary import expansion (VIE) agreement, which establishes a minimum target for the share of a country's markets to be satisfied by imports or foreign producers. The latter, in contrast, is an example of a voluntary export restraint (VER) agreement, also sometimes called a voluntary restraint agreement (VRA), which establishes a quantitative limit on a country's exports to one or more of its trading partners and thus implicitly establishes a quantitative limit on those partners' imports from that country.

Both VERS and VIES are routinely criticized by economists, but the evidence in chapters 4 and 6 of this book indicates that the arguments against the former are the more compelling. VERS and other forms of quantitative limits on trade are clearly protectionist in design and intent. There is an extensive literature on VERS demonstrating their protectionist, anticompetitive, and ultimately counterproductive effects on the very domestic producers they are designed to benefit.[9]

In addition, VERS suffer from the drawbacks of other protectionist measures: they tend to increase the prices and restrict the supply of foreign products without necessarily improving the long-run competitiveness of domestic producers. Moreover, unlike tariffs, which have the same effects but at least add to government revenues, VERS tend to increase the profits of foreign producers, thereby strengthening their competitive position vis-à-vis domestic producers over time. Like tariffs, VERS tend to encourage local investment by foreign producers, but in the absence of complementary local content policies such investment is likely to be of the assembly or "screwdriver" variety.

All of these conclusions are confirmed in the study of Japan's VER arrangement with the European Community in VCRs between 1983 and 1985. Because of their documented drawbacks, the United States remains well advised to avoid protectionist managed trade arrangements of the VER or quota variety. Moreover, the United States should support proposals in the Uruguay Round draft text to prohibit new VERS and to phase out existing ones within four years.

In contrast to VERS, which restrict trade, the objective of VIES is to increase trade and foreign competition. VIES are defensible, however, only when there is compelling evidence of impediments to foreign markets. This has certainly been the case in the Japanese markets for semiconductors, telecommunications equipment, and supercomputers. A cautious activist must judge VIES against their real-world alternative. A VIE may be appropriate if the alternative is a situation in which a given national market is reserved for national suppliers. As the analysis in chapter 4 demonstrates, the VIE approach is inferior to the first-best approach of unimpeded market competition; but it is sometimes superior to the do-nothing approach, and almost always superior to a protectionist response.

Opposition among economists to VIES rests on three *a priori* arguments: they cartelize markets, they increase prices by limiting competition, and they violate the nondiscrimination principle of the GATT.[10] None of these arguments have been confirmed, however, by the real-world results of the 1986 and 1991 semi-

---

9. Temporary tariffs or auction quotas are preferable to VERS or other forms of import quotas as a tactic to safeguard domestic producers. Auction quotas allow foreign producers to compete with one another for shares of an overall import quota. In theory, the low-cost producers will offer the highest bids. This will limit the anticompetitive effects of the quota and will hold down its price effects. Moreover, both the tariff and the auction approach mean that at least part of the higher revenues resulting from protection will go to the government imposing the protectionist measures. These revenues can be used to support a restructuring program or countervailing subsidy for domestic producers. For a complete analysis of the costs of VERS and the auction quota alternative see Bergsten et al. (1987).

10. See, for example, Bhagwati (1983) and Schultze and Lawrence (1990, chapter 1 and the comment by Avinash Dixit on my paper in that volume).

conductor trade agreements. Indeed, developments in the Japanese semiconductor market since 1986 suggest that the market access provisions of these agreements have had beneficial, procompetitive effects.

On the supply side, several American companies, anticipating at least a minimum share of the lucrative Japanese market, have increased their investments in sales, distribution, technical support facilities, and production capabilities in Japan. Moreover, because the agreements specify a multilateral VIE covering all non-Japanese suppliers, both Korean and European companies have also been able to increase their shares of the Japanese market. Indeed, the credible long-term threat of the Korean suppliers was one of several factors that broke the Japanese pricing cartel in DRAMs in 1990.

On the demand side, Japanese users of semiconductors have increased their purchases from foreign suppliers, whose share of the Japanese market has grown, especially since mid-1989 when the United States threatened further retaliation. Even more important to long-run market dynamics, Japanese users are now more willing to entertain bids and to design-in products from American suppliers. Several American companies have reported instances of winning contracts that they would not even have been able to bid on except for the pressure of the agreement.

According to these companies, the VIE provisions have partially offset the effects of *keiretsu* impediments to the Japanese market. At a minimum, the semiconductor trade agreement opens a bigger share of this market to competition from foreign suppliers. At a maximum, the resulting competition may finally destabilize the institutional and informal arrangements that impede foreign access. In the minimum outcome, the VIE may benefit only those foreign suppliers that can increase their sales in Japan. In the maximum outcome, the VIE will foster a more competitive marketplace for producers and consumers around the world. Either outcome is preferable to the status quo.

As the evidence in chapter 4 indicates, there is reason to be optimistic that the dynamics of competition triggered by the semiconductor trade agreement will ultimately favor the maximum outcome. This evidence also suggests that the choice posed between more open trade with Japan through VIEs and more open markets in Japan through SII–type negotiations is a false one.[11] A managed trade approach may ultimately produce both more trade with Japan and a more open Japanese marketplace.

The VIE's effects on the terms of competition suggest a general conclusion: US trade policy toward Japan is being used as a substitute for global competition policy or for the extraterritorial application of American antitrust policy. Indeed, as the evidence in chapter 4 indicates, the semiconductor trade agreement did not have dramatic effects on trade flows between the two nations, nor was that its primary objective. One need only recall that the market access target was defined to encompass Japanese sales by all foreign firms. Ownership, not location of production, was the relevant characteristic. In other words, sales by Texas Instruments from its Japanese subsidiaries or by Intel from its East Asian facilities counted toward the target. Such sales were expected to influence the

---

11. Robert Z. Lawrence proposed this dichotomy in his comments on an earlier draft of chapter 4 of this book at the World Trade and Global Competition Conference, held at the Harvard Business School, 1–3 December 1991.

terms of competition between Japanese and foreign companies, regardless of their effects on national trade patterns. Indeed, because of the global reach of most high-technology companies and the oligopolistic nature of the industries in which they function, national trade policies are increasingly used in lieu of enforceable multilateral antitrust policies to affect the terms of market competition. For the foreseeable future, there is really no workable alternative to this second-best approach.

Market Access Issues for the Future

The cases of US–Japan trade competition analyzed in chapters 3 and 4 provide compelling historical evidence of the persistence of structural and policy impediments to the Japanese market. Although formal protection has been phased out, primarily in response to American *gaiatsu*, the peculiar features of Japanese capitalism continue to impede access to foreign suppliers and to shape competition to the advantage of their Japanese rivals. Usually a detailed industry focus is required to identify and counter what are industry-specific impediments to outsiders. This conclusion applies to a whole range of industries—including construction services, financial services, agricultural products, semiconductors, computers, and auto parts—that are continuing sources of US–Japan trade conflict. The access issue is also likely to become more important as it relates to foreign direct investment opportunities in Japan. In both cases, overt barriers actionable under current multilateral rules are not the problem.

If market access is likely to remain a central issue in US–Japan negotiations for the foreseeable future, it is likely to become more important in Europe-Japan negotiations as well. As noted in chapter 1, the Europeans have emphasized the principle of reciprocal market opportunities in designing their 1992 directives. And they have begun to concentrate on reciprocal market access in their bilateral trade talks with Japan. Despite their overt criticism of Section 301 and Super 301, many Europeans envy what they have accomplished and would like to design a similar approach either at the Community level or at the level of the Organization for Economic Cooperation and Development (OECD) or the GATT. There is also growing interest in a European SII-type initiative with Japan.

Market access will also continue to be a source of high-technology trade friction between the United States and Europe. In the European context, however, the issue is likely to remain more straightforward, involving such tangible trade barriers as testing and certification procedures and standards. In addition, many American companies have successfully jumped such barriers by establishing European operations—an option that has proved more difficult to exercise in Japan.

Finally, market access issues are likely to remain significant sources of friction between the United States, Europe, and Japan in such highly regulated industries as telecommunications services, financial services, pharmaceuticals, and medical equipment. These issues will also continue to attract attention where institutional differences between nations are most pronounced—for example, in the organization of science and research, in competition policy, and in environmental regulation. In all of these areas, a combination of harmonization and mutual recognition will be required to defuse trade friction and secure open markets. For the foreseeable future, the realization of these objectives will continue to depend on bilateral or limited multilateral negotiations between interested nations about regulatory standards and practices in particular industries. The resulting agreements, in turn, will be based on the notion of selective reciprocity—reciprocity in particular industries for particular practices between particular nations.[12]

Ultimately, however, open national markets in global high-technology industries will require new multilateral rules and enforcement mechanisms. In the meantime, the makeshift bilateral and plurilateral arrangements hammered out by particular trading partners in particular industries will serve as an imperfect substitute. The GATT or the OECD should survey and analyze such arrangements on a regular basis and summarize their findings for the multilateral community. Information about the results of the bilateral SII talks between Japan and the United States, for example, could provide a model for comparable multilateral agreements.

The Pros and Cons of Antidumping Remedies

Defining and Assessing Dumping in High-Technology Industries

The imperfectly competitive conditions of most high-technology industries provide ample scope for predatory and other restrictive business practices. When domestic suppliers are the culprits, domestic antitrust laws are the appropriate channel for redress. When foreign suppliers are involved, however, these laws are often not applicable, and when they are applicable they are nearly impossible to enforce.[13] As a result, most countries have developed specific trade laws to restrict the anticompetitive practices of foreign firms. Antidumping laws are the most common examples and are allowable under the GATT.[14] Even Sir Leon

---

12. Despite its shortcomings, the 1979 GATT Agreement on Trade in Civil Aircraft is a useful model for similar plurilateral, sectoral agreements in other high-technology fields, for example semiconductors and computers. As chapter 4 argues, such an agreement would be particularly useful in the semiconductor industry, which is characterized by heavy government involvement in all of the major producing nations.

13. The difficulties of using domestic antitrust laws to counter anticompetitive practices in foreign markets are apparent in the US Supreme Court's decision in Zenith's antitrust case against Matsushita. The court ruled that American firms cannot recover antitrust damages solely on the basis of behavior in foreign markets, because American antitrust laws do not seek to regulate the competitive conditions of other nations' economies. American antitrust laws *can* extend to conduct outside US borders, but only when that conduct can be shown to have a direct effect on American commerce. In practice, this condition is extremely hard to demonstrate, especially in light of the difficulties involved in obtaining admissible evidence about the behavior of firms in foreign markets.

14. Under GATT regulations, dumping occurs when a good is sold abroad for a lower price than the seller charges for the same good in the seller's home market. The home market price is usually taken to be the fair market value. In two circumstances, however, GATT regulations allow the construction of an estimate of the fair market value: when there are insufficient sales in the seller's domestic market to allow a determination, or "whenever there is reasonable ground for believing or suspecting that the price at which a product is actually sold in the home market is less than the cost of production." It is the latter condition that is used to justify the cost-based approach to establishing dumping in national dumping laws. The dangers inherent in the vagueness of this definition are manifest.

Brittan, the outspoken free market champion of European competition policy, defends national antidumping laws as a legitimate channel for countering unfair competition by foreign companies. Viewed from this perspective, national antidumping laws are a poor but necessary substitute for enforceable multilateral competition policies.

During the 1980s, both American and European companies frequently resorted to national antidumping laws, particularly in their dealings with Japanese and other East Asian competitors (for evidence see Messerlin 1990). In many of these cases, dumping was defined not in the traditional manner—as selling below an actual home market price or discriminating on price in different markets—but as selling below a constructed measure of average production costs.[15] Both US–Japan friction over semiconductors and Europe-Japan friction over VCRs centered on this definition of dumping. Unfortunately, it suffers from serious shortcomings, particularly where high-technology industries are involved.

The first shortcoming arises from a well-known conclusion of basic microeconomics. Even in perfectly competitive markets, profit-maximizing firms with no significant market power may sometimes find it rational to price below average cost. And the new trade theory contains many examples of how such a pricing strategy can lead to efficient outcomes under imperfectly competitive conditions (for a summary see Deardorff 1989). In short, there is often nothing in such pricing behavior to suggest market power, unfair practices, or predatory malice. This insight—along with the necessarily arbitrary nature of constructing average cost measures for industries where multiproduct firms and huge upfront capital and R&D costs are the order of the day—has led many economists to conclude that the definition of dumping should be restricted, as it was originally, to selling goods abroad for less than they are sold at home.

This conclusion, however, is both politically unrealistic and economically imprudent. It would be naive to imagine that American and European companies would allow a powerful source of trade relief to be so dramatically weakened. And it would be imprudent to overlook the real possibility of pricing below marginal cost as a predatory business tactic, and one that is especially attractive in high-technology industries. According to a growing body of economic literature, pricing below marginal cost or average variable cost may be a sign of predatory behavior, designed to encourage other firms to exit the market, or a sign of preemptive behavior, designed to deter other firms from entering the market (see, e.g., Milgrom 1987, Milgrom and Roberts 1982, and Tirole 1988). Indeed, under certain conditions, such pricing behavior is a sufficient condition for concluding that a firm is pricing strategically to influence the behavior of its rivals. From this perspective, as Flamm (1991) argues, "the economic problem with cost-based definitions of dumping is not necessarily their existence, but their use of the wrong cost concept as the prima facie trigger for consideration of possible intervention." Especially in high-technology industries, where the temptation to discourage entry is great and the costs of curtailed entry are even

---

15. According to the US Department of Commerce, approximately two-thirds of the antidumping investigations processed in 1987 involved allegations that foreign firms were selling below actual or constructed measures of production costs. The cost approach has been used extensively in technology-intensive products for the reasons noted in the text. According to Horlick (1989, 139), since 1980, in approximately 60 percent of all dumping cases in the United States the determination was based on the cost approach.

greater, the possibility of predatory pricing should not be discounted (Milgrom 1987).

A second problem with a cost-based definition of dumping, even one that is appropriately restricted to marginal or average variable cost rather than average total cost, is the likelihood of forward pricing in high-technology industries. In the presence of significant scale and learning economies, prices fall sharply as output increases. This provides a strong incentive to producers—especially new entrants—to set their current price on the basis of some future or forward cost they hope to achieve as they increase production. Forward (or life-cycle) pricing thus means setting prices below contemporaneous costs, whether average or marginal. Unfortunately, the same production conditions that make a forward pricing strategy attractive are also likely to make a predatory pricing strategy attractive. Under these conditions, a simple comparison of contemporaneous price and marginal or average variable cost will fail to distinguish between the two. Additional evidence is required.

Herein lies a third shortcoming of national antidumping rules as they relate to high-technology industries. In the United States, as elsewhere, such rules do not currently require a determination of predatory intent or even a weaker determination of market power or predatory capability. Instead, since 1921 US trade law has defined dumping as sales below "fair value" that injure or threaten to injure American producers, regardless of the seller's intent. Demonstration of the economically defensible rationale behind national antidumping laws—to deter "unfair" or predatory behavior by foreign firms—is simply not required. As a consequence, national antidumping laws can and are used to preclude foreign suppliers from using competitive tactics, like forward pricing, that are permissible to domestic suppliers.

At least under current US procedures,[16] the extensive administrative review required by the US International Trade Commission to establish injury provides a forum for analyzing the predatory intent or predatory capability of foreign suppliers. For example, during the Commission's deliberations on dumping charges against Japanese DRAM producers, representatives of the US Federal Trade Commission testified that the DRAM market was characterized by competitive rather than predatory pricing. In addition, antidumping decisions by the US Department of Commerce and the International Trade Commission can be appealed to the US Court of International Trade. No such restraints apply under current European procedures.[17]

The deficiencies of national antidumping laws as they apply to high-technology industries, coupled with their increasing use, indicate that both national and international antidumping regulations require fundamental revision. As a general rule, dumping should be assessed on the basis of a divergence between

---

16. The discussion here focuses only on what the author believes to be the most egregious shortcomings of US antidumping laws as they apply to high-technology industries. For a complete discussion of American antidumping laws, their applications, and their shortcomings, see Boltuck and Litan (1991).

17. For a more complete analysis of the European antidumping regulations, see chapter 6 of this book and GATT 1991. Antidumping decisions by the Community can be appealed to the European Court of Justice. A study by Hindley (1988) confirms, however, that the court has limited its review to procedural grounds—that is, to making sure that the decisions are consistent with European antidumping statutes.

actual prices in different markets, not on the basis of constructed cost measures. The conditions under which such measures may be used in lieu of actual prices must be more explicitly delineated and restricted. Currently, according to US law, sales in the home market or a third-country market at prices that are below the cost of production may be disregarded in determining dumping if the sales are made "over an *extended* period of time and in *substantial* quantities," and if the prices do not *"permit recovery of all costs within a reasonable period of time in the normal course of trade"* (italics added). The loopholes created by such vague language are obvious. But they are allowable under current GATT regulations, which are equally vague, specifying that cost measures rather than actual prices may be used to assess dumping in cases where home market sales *"in the ordinary course of trade are insufficient or do not permit a proper comparison."*

Such broad and ill-defined concepts as "reasonable period of time" and "normal or ordinary course of trade" invite self-serving interpretations. Moreover, they fail to appreciate the fact that what is reasonable or normal in one national environment may not be reasonable or normal in another. Because Japanese firms tend to have deeper pockets, for example, they are able to weather losses for much longer than their American counterparts. Is such behavior by Japanese firms unfair or predatory? As the analyses in chapters 3 and 4 indicate, often it is, but it is simply impossible to answer this question without further information. The way current antidumping laws work, however, this question is not even asked. If "normal" business behavior by Japanese producers injures or threatens to injure American producers, they can seek and often obtain an antidumping remedy. But injury alone should not be a sufficient condition for obtaining relief. After all, market competition usually injures some firms to the benefit of others. It is only when the injuries involved are the result of unfair or predatory practice or have adverse long-term consequences for market structure and economic welfare that some kind of remedy is required.[18]

As currently written and applied, both national and multilateral (GATT) antidumping laws err in the direction of deterring competitive behavior that is not unfair or predatory. The challenge is to reformulate these laws without going so far in the other direction that they fail to deter behavior that is. One way to address this challenge is to use measures of marginal or average variable cost rather than average total cost as the putative standard for assessing dumping. At a minimum, the methods for calculating average total cost should be modified to eliminate their most egregious biases, including the use of arbitrary profit and overhead markups and the allocation of R&D and startup costs to the year in which they are incurred rather than over the expected life of a product.

A second improvement would be to introduce some mechanism for distinguishing, however imperfectly, between forward pricing and predatory pricing.[19] For example, costs would be estimated for several different levels of

---

18. John H. Jackson (1989, 220–21) is correct to argue that national antidumping laws, for example countervailing duty laws, act more as a buffer between different economic systems than as a response to unfair practices.

19. Several suggestions toward this end were made during the Uruguay Round discussions on antidumping reform. The draft offered by GATT Director General Arthur Dunkel, for example, contains provisions that would require US authorities to ignore high pro-

production or for several different stages of the business cycle or the product life cycle, and an average of such estimates could be used. National antidumping laws should also be modified to incorporate some compulsory procedure for evaluating the market conditions, business practices, industry structure, trade barriers, and structural impediments affecting competition in an industry subject to an antidumping investigation.

A requirement that a dumping complaint demonstrate predatory intent would be too stringent, since intent is notoriously difficult to prove, even in domestic antitrust cases where the evidentiary burden is considerably lighter. But the same is not true of predatory capability. An analysis of market structure would speak to the issue of capability and would allow an assessment of whether dumping is likely to increase or decrease competition in the domestic and the global industry over time.[20] In principle, only injury or the threat of injury to a competitive domestic industry should be subject to redress—a domestic industry with market power should be granted relief only after the offsetting interests of users have been weighed against the interests of producers.

An assessment of predatory capability should also consider whether the foreign suppliers in question have a record of demonstrated offenses in previous dumping cases or in other legal actions involving unfair business practices. A pattern of repeat offenses by foreign producers should be one important piece of evidence in evaluating predatory capability. Foreign-government practices that might encourage or allow dumping or other predatory practices by foreign suppliers should be another.

Finally, the time required to process antidumping complaints in the United States is a justifiable business concern. Even with the fastest procedures permissible under current law, nearly a full year usually passes from the time an antidumping petition is filed to the time an antidumping order is issued. Such delays are especially burdensome for many high-technology industries whose products have short life cycles: foreign producers may have ceased dumping one product and moved on to selling its next-generation successor by the time an antidumping investigation on the first product has run its course.

Undoubtedly, the modifications of US antidumping laws suggested here would make antidumping procedures even more time-consuming. As an antidote, the laws should be amended to allow, or require, the Department of Commerce to monitor imports under certain conditions—for example, when a repeat offender is involved or when there is a presumption of predatory capability or foreign targeting of the industry in question. Under such circumstances, fast-track dumping procedures such as those specified in the 1991 semiconductor trade agreement with Japan are warranted.

---

duction cost estimates during the period of a dumping investigation if lower costs were later achieved.

20. One promising approach is the "two-tier" approach suggested by the OECD. National antitrust authorities would cooperate with the authorities responsible for enforcing national dumping laws. The former would examine the market in question and make a preliminary ruling on whether it is susceptible to successful predation. For those cases that survive, a multifaceted inquiry would then focus on the relationship between prices and costs and examine what factors are behind the observed pricing behavior. Those cases that do not survive the ruling would not be eligible for antidumping relief, although other forms of trade relief would not be ruled out.

The importance of timing to the deterrent effect of the antidumping law can be seen from the experience of the 1986 semiconductor trade agreement. As the discussion in chapter 4 indicates, an antidumping remedy was applied early enough to deter dumping and encourage competition in EPROMS. In contrast, a similar remedy had distinctly anticompetitive effects in DRAMS, because it was applied after most American suppliers had already exited production.

Effective and Sensible Remedies

US trade laws mandate the imposition of dumping duties on the products of foreign suppliers found guilty of dumping. Unless the dumping case is suspended or terminated as part of a broader trade agreement, this remedy is automatic even though it seldom serves the national interest.[21] And negotiated agreements that encourage foreign firms to increase their prices in return for suspension of an antidumping case have been even less effective.

The drawbacks to such agreements are apparent in both the semiconductor and the VCR cases discussed in this book. In both cases, antidumping actions resulted in agreements by the Japanese to raise their prices on products in which they held dominant market shares. These agreements or "price undertakings" brought about higher prices for consumers and higher profits for their producers, most of whom were the very Japanese firms charged with dumping in the first place. No penalties for the injury caused by such behavior were assessed, nor was compensation provided to the injured domestic competitors.

The consequences of the antidumping provisions of the semiconductor trade agreement in the DRAM market vividly demonstrate the potential dangers of price agreements as a remedy against foreign dumping, especially when foreign suppliers already dominate market supply. The Japanese producers agreed to pricing guidelines that required them to increase their prices, in principle not only in the United States but in all other markets including their own. In return, the US firms dropped their dumping charges, and dumping margins were not imposed. This arrangement was meant to avoid making the United States a "high-price island" through the imposition of duties on imported semiconductors. Such duties would have hurt the American computer companies and encouraged them to move production offshore in search of cheaper components.

To limit price increases, the architects of the agreement specified its pricing provisions on a company-by-company basis. Those Japanese companies with lower costs could charge lower prices than their higher-cost Japanese competitors. The intent was to allow competition among Japanese suppliers while discouraging dumping by all of them. Unfortunately, this clever solution overlooked the possibility that the Japanese suppliers, using their overwhelming dominance in the global DRAM market, might choose to cooperate, establishing a de facto price floor that benefited all of them. Under active coordination by

---

21. Under current US law, once an antidumping finding has been made and the International Trade Commission has ruled on the question of injury, the imposition of antidumping duties in the amount of the assessed dumping margins is automatic. It is the automatic feature in the US law that led a spokesperson for the Department of Commerce to comment recently that American laws limit the department's flexibility in clear cases of dumping (*New York Times*, 26 September 1991, C2).

the Ministry of International Trade and Industry (MITI), this is exactly what happened! In the EPROM market, in contrast, where the Japanese suppliers held less than 50 percent of the global market, no such cooperative arrangement was feasible. As a result, EPROM prices were relatively stable, while DRAM prices skyrocketed during the first two and one-half years of the agreement. The interaction between the agreement and the market power of the Japanese firms allowed them to increase their DRAM prices far in excess of those permissible under the agreement and to earn substantial "bubble" profits. These profits in turn were plowed back into investment and R&D in DRAMS, in other parts of the semiconductor industry, and in upstream and downstream electronics products.

In hindsight, it appears that the threatened imposition of company-specific dumping margins might have been preferable to the pricing provisions of the semiconductor agreement, at least as far as DRAM prices were concerned. As often happens in dumping cases, it is likely that the Japanese producers found guilty of dumping would have increased their prices just enough to avoid their dumping margins. But the lower-cost Japanese suppliers would have been able to increase their prices by less than the higher-cost ones, thereby continuing to compete for a share of the American market and moderating the overall price increases that finally occurred. In addition, to the extent that any dumping margins were collected by the American government, they could have been used to help finance a program to rebuild the DRAM production capabilities of American companies.[22]

On the other hand, the evidence in chapter 4 indicates that the Japanese companies, under MITI's leadership, were beginning to exercise their newly won market power in DRAMS before the agreement went into effect. Thus, even the more traditional antidumping remedy might not have prevented the huge price and profit increases enjoyed by the Japanese industry until 1990, when foreign competition, especially from the Koreans, destabilized its cooperative outcome.

In addition, dumping margins, as the American industry feared, would indeed have made the United States a high-price island for semiconductors and encouraged the migration of American users to third-country locations. The only way to avoid such a migratory response to dumping duties on important inputs such as semiconductors and displays would be to extend duties to imports of the finished products embodying them. Thus, for example, it would have been necessary to apply antidumping duties to both imports of Japanese DRAMS and imports of electronics products containing them. Similarly, to be effective, the recent antidumping duties imposed on imports of Japanese liquid crystal displays would also have to be applied to the high-end computers in which they are used. Such extensions of dumping duties to user products would usually prove politically impossible, even when economically justifiable.

Even when appropriately structured, antidumping duties share several major shortcomings with their less attractive price undertaking substitutes. Neither duties nor price agreements provide any compensation to domestic producers for past injuries sustained as a result of dumping. Antidumping duties are applied prospectively from the date that the Department of Commerce makes

---

22. This would have required a change in usual government practices, according to which the proceeds of antidumping cases are not earmarked for the industry's purposes.

a preliminary determination that dumping margins exist. Foreign firms found guilty of dumping are subject to no penalties beyond the duties imposed. Often, these firms increase their prices just enough to avoid paying duties altogether. Any duties collected are paid by American importers, not by foreign producers, and are turned over to the US Treasury, not to the injured domestic producers. Heretofore it has been the principled position of the US government not to earmark such duties for return to the domestic industry. Finally, even though US antidumping laws provide a private right of action under which treble damages can be collected from foreign producers who act with predatory intent, the difficulties of proving such intent have prevented American companies from exercising this right. For all of these reasons, dumping remedies may deter dumping in the future, but they cannot undo the effects of dumping in the past.

Current practices should be modified to address this shortcoming. In particular, the antidumping laws should be amended to include conditions under which at least some percentage of all duties, fines, and other revenues generated by a successful antidumping suit would be disbursed to the injured domestic industry according to a predetermined allocation formula (for example, by market share or according to the percentage decline in firms' revenues or sales). In addition, the laws should allow for penalties and damages for past dumping in certain kinds of cases, including those in which predatory intent, repeat offenders, and explicit foreign targeting policies are involved.

The modifications in the antidumping laws proposed here are only one part of the policy agenda described in this chapter. Taken by themselves, they would curtail a form of relief that has been actively used by many American high-technology producers. For the reasons discussed here, the antidumping relief allowable under US trade law is decidedly second-best, but in the absence of first-best remedies it is often the only option available to American producers. Ultimately, the way to stem the abuses of the antidumping laws is to offer more-effective policies in their place. The health of the nation's high-technology producers would be further imperiled by limiting these laws while failing to do anything else. A cautious activist would be concerned about such an outcome.

Strategic Threats in High-Technology Industries

As just demonstrated, even if dumping is established, the appropriate remedy may be something quite different from antidumping duties or negotiated price agreements. In both the DRAM and the liquid crystal display cases, a more appropriate remedy would have been some form of countervailing subsidy or government support program to offset the damage caused by Japanese dumping and to reduce the strategic threats to American commercial and security interests posed by Japanese market dominance.[23]

---

23. The evidence presented in the semiconductor case indicates dumping with predatory capability and intent. In the absence of a complete analysis of the evidence in the display case, it is impossible to determine whether there was predatory intent or whether the low prices simply represented normal competitive practice. Certainly, given the structure of the industry, predatory capability on the part of the Japanese suppliers was a real pos-

In global high-technology industries, appropriate public policy requires an understanding of the dangers of oligopolistic control. Traditional definitions of market power have concentrated on predatory pricing or the power of a small number of firms to restrict price competition. But as Ernst and O'Connor (1992, 32) argue, in high-technology industries this definition must be broadened to include control over strategic assets and capabilities such as technological knowledge and distribution networks required for effective competition; control over timely access to critical frontier-technology inputs; and the capacity to create or raise entry barriers and to influence the regulatory framework for competition. According to the evidence in their study and in chapter 4 of this study, oligopolistic control by Japanese suppliers is intensifying in several core electronics components, including memory chips, semiconductor equipment and materials, and displays.[24]

But is there any evidence that such control poses strategic threats to the users of such components, either now or in the foreseeable future? Many would say no, pointing to continued competition between Japanese rivals for market share as a source of competitive rather than cooperative or collusive behavior. Others, cautious activists among them, would say that there are several indicators that, taken together, are cause for concern. First, a number of recent studies by the General Accounting Office (GAO), the Defense Science Board, and the National Advisory Committee on Semiconductors (NACS) report that American companies relying on Japanese competitors for such crucial components as DRAMS and displays are sometimes at a competitive disadvantage because they cannot obtain the latest Japanese technology on a timely basis (Defense Science Board Task Force 1990; NACS 1990a and b; US General Accounting Office, National Security and International Affairs Division 1991). In the GAO study, for example, 42 percent of the 59 companies surveyed reported problems in securing state-of-the-art products from their Japanese suppliers, often encountering delays of more than six months.[25]

Second, there is some evidence that the availability of investment capital in certain product areas, such as displays, is limited in the United States by lender perceptions that, once the Japanese have targeted a market, the prospects for American competitors are not auspicious, even when they have a technological

sibility. Whatever the ultimate judgment, it is clear that the remedy chosen to offset the adverse effects of dumping in displays was counterproductive (see chapter 4 for more on this point). For a more complete assessment of the antidumping case in displays see Hart (1992).

24. For a recent study that makes this case in an especially compelling manner, see Borrus and Zysman (1992).

25. Some critics of the GAO study question its credibility on the grounds that the American companies were unwilling to make public their own identity, that of their Japanese suppliers, or the details of the supply difficulties they encountered. Such behavior, however, is understandable if the American firms are indeed dependent on their Japanese suppliers for continued production and if they fear retaliation. Indeed, the unwillingness of the American companies to go public with their accusations can be interpreted as an indicator of their validity. Nor can the evidence presented by these companies to the GAO be dismissed as simply self-serving. In fact, the American companies did not advocate any punitive or protectionist measures against their Japanese suppliers. Instead, they emphasized the need for a stronger American technology base and reduced dependence on the Japanese through the creation of alternative domestic sources of supply.

edge. Private financial institutions such as brokerage houses and investment banks may indeed efficiently gather market information, as economists argue, but this information itself can be affected by the targeting practices of foreign governments. For example, in the words of a recent NACS (1990a) report, "there is a widespread belief among large funding sources that it is suicidal to confront the major Japanese electronics companies directly in developing high-volume display technologies." Without adequate funding, American producers are unable to gain the scale necessary to compete with the Japanese. As a consequence, the global display market remains dangerously concentrated among a few Japanese suppliers operating mainly from Japanese production locations. In a frustrated and ultimately counterproductive effort to obtain capital through higher display prices, the American producers sought and obtained the dumping relief described in chapter 4.

As this and other anecdotes in the NACS report suggest, the pricing and supply control strategies of the Japanese in some electronics components appear to be having a powerful preemptive effect on the strategies of some American companies. A similar conclusion is suggested by the analysis of the semiconductor industry in chapter 4. Ultimately, a credible challenge to Japanese dominance in memory chips has been mounted not by the American companies, who view themselves as competing against the "Japanese system," but by the Korean producers, backed by a credible government commitment to the development of their industry.

Third, chapters 3 and 4 suggest several reasons why a cooperative strategy is more likely to emerge when an industry is dominated by a small number of Japanese suppliers than when it is dominated by a small number of suppliers with diverse home bases. First, there is no credible threat of antitrust prosecution in Japan. Second, information acquired by Japanese firms is regularly exchanged through a number of sanctioned channels, including industry associations, MITI panels, and government-organized and government-sponsored R&D projects. Third, because most large Japanese firms are members of large business groups, they compete with one another in a variety of product markets. It is a well-known presumption in game theory that increased multiproduct competition between firms will increase the costs of deviating from a cooperative strategy in a particular product line. Fourth, because of their financial structure, Japanese firms can credibly threaten to lose money for a substantial period of time to drive out their existing competitors and to deter the entry of new ones.

If the dangers of strategic control by Japanese suppliers in dual-use input industries are as apparent as this analysis suggests, why haven't American suppliers and users joined together in an effort to counter the threat? To some extent they have. Sematech is one such response, as are R&D consortia for display development and a number of cooperative R&D projects spawned by the Semiconductor Research Corporation (SRC) and the Microelectronics and Computer Technologies Corporation (MCC). More prevalent than such cooperative efforts, however, have been private strategies by big American companies to form alliances and joint ventures with their Japanese suppliers and competitors to secure access to the technological knowledge and products they need. It is too early to judge the wisdom of such strategies. Although each of the American companies may gain in the short run by strengthening its individual ties with its Japanese suppliers, all of them might be better off in the long run with a collective response to build alternative sources of supply.

Private solutions by existing firms may impede the entry or expansion of new firms, which may be unable to obtain the supplies of inputs they need to exploit a technological innovation. The NACS report contains anecdotal information about such cases. Ultimately, the only choice facing new market entrants may be the sale of their technology to Japanese suppliers who have both the inputs and the manufacturing prowess required for its profitable commercialization. Overall, the increasing concentration of a number of global markets for electronics inputs implies rising barriers to entry. In light of the beneficial role that new entrants have played in the history of the American electronics industry, this implication is not a promising one.

For all of these reasons, the potential strategic threats posed by foreign oligopolistic control in some high-technology industries should be cause for policy concern, especially when the industries involved provide inputs to a wide variety of downstream users, including the Department of Defense, and especially when this control is exercised by the Japanese.[26] What, then, should be the policy response? At a minimum, an effective monitoring system would seem prudent. One possibility is the use of some threshold rule-of-thumb measure for determining when concentrated foreign control of an industry entails potential competitive and national security risks. Moran (1990), for example, has proposed that a credible national security risk might be presumed to exist whenever four countries or four firms supply more than 50 percent of the world market for a good deemed essential for national defense. This so-called 4-4-50 rule could be used as a threshold for the presumption of a credible commercial risk as well. Applied to the DRAM market, the liquid crystal display market, and the markets for certain kinds of semiconductor equipment and materials, such a measure would indicate potential competitive and national security risks in these dual-use technologies. As the analysis in chapter 5 indicates, industries producing certain aircraft components, such as advanced avionics systems, should also be analyzed for possible excessive dependence on concentrated suppliers.

Initially, regular government monitoring of market structure and competition conditions could be limited to dual-use industries, to industries identified as critical by some nationally sanctioned and politically credible process (such as one organized by the National Academy of Engineers or the Office of Science and Technology Policy in the White House), or to industries explicitly targeted for promotion by foreign governments. The existence of such a monitoring procedure would provide government agencies with the industry-specific information required for wise decisions on a variety of trade policy questions. For example, such information would help the Department of Commerce and the International Trade Commission decide on questions of antidumping, counter-

---

26. Of course, oligopolistic control even when exercised by domestic firms should be a cause for policy alarm. For example, the fact that Intel microprocessors are currently used in 85 percent to 90 percent of the desktop computers in the world gives Intel substantial potential market power. But Intel's exercise of this power has been curtailed by the active and threatened use of American antitrust law by its American competitor Advanced Micro Devices. For more on the use of competition policy in combating the dangers of strategic oligopolistic control, see below.

vailing duties, and safeguard relief under Section 201 of the nation's trade law. It would also help the Committee on Foreign Investment in the United States evaluate the national security implications of foreign direct investment and link its evaluations to antitrust considerations along the lines proposed by Graham and Krugman (1991). Finally, it would help policymakers implement the kinds of industrial and technology policies described in more detail below.

As the semiconductor case indicates, standard antidumping remedies can actually magnify the commercial or national security risks posed by foreign market power by encouraging collusive behavior between foreign suppliers. Under such circumstances, government assistance may be warranted as a form of "anticartel insurance"[27] to encourage a more competitive domestic supply base.[28] A threshold measure of the sort proposed above could be used to evaluate whether such insurance might be required in a particular industry. An anticartel approach might also have the beneficial effect of signaling a US commitment to support domestic producers against predatory attacks by foreign competitors, thereby deterring such attacks in the future.

Ultimately, the dangers created by the concentration of global high-technology industries (whether by foreign producers or by domestic producers) must be contained by enforceable multilateral competition policies.[29] As of this writing the United States is pursuing this goal through bilateral initiatives with both Europe and Japan for greater harmonization of antitrust practices. In the fall of 1991, the United States and the European Community signed an agreement to coordinate enforcement of their antitrust policies. Harmonization of antitrust procedures has also been a major objective of the SII talks with Japan. And the OECD has decided that competition policies should be a priority area for convergence of national differences among its member states.

It is too early to tell whether these initiatives will have an effect. But it seems likely that national differences in competition policy will prove among the most difficult to harmonize or regulate by multilateral rules. Even where national laws appear to be similar in substance—as do, for example, merger laws in the United States and Europe—there are wide variations in interpretation and application. A general prohibition against mergers that "substantially lessen competition" leaves ample scope for discretion on the part of the relevant national authorities. Moreover, behind different interpretations of remarkably similar laws lie different weights on such goals as efficiency and equity and different judgments about the optimality of the market. Both the Europeans and the Japanese, for example, believe that competition can be excessive and that cooperation may

---

27. This term was coined by Kenneth Flamm (1990). As argued below, a similar anti-monopoly rationale was one of several justifications offered by the European governments for their subsidy support of Airbus. The history in chapter 5 indicates that this rationale was not without merit.

28. For more on the notion of a competitive supply base, see Borrus and Zysman (1992).

29. The Havana Charter of the proposed International Trade Organization contained a long chapter on restrictive business practices, including such issues as market access and fair competition. The charter, as well as voluntary codes on restrictive business practices developed by the OECD and the United Nations, are good places to begin the construction of new multilateral competition policies.

sometimes be required to realize the benefits of the market. In the United States, static consumer welfare remains the highest priority of antitrust policy. In Europe, in contrast, pride of place is still given to the objective of European integration—a goal that sometimes better serves the interests of European multinationals than of European consumers. And in Japan, producer interests are still accorded preference over consumer interests by most policy institutions, including the Fair Trade Commission.

Also, as the EC experience elucidates, judicial review and enforcement mechanisms are critical to an effective multilateral competition policy. Since antitrust actions often involve a complaint by one business actor against another, there must be a judicial system whereby cross-national disputes between corporations of different national origins can be adjudicated. Currently such disputes can be played out in one of only two ways: through different national competition policies that have limited extraterritorial applicability, and through trade disputes among national governments sometimes forced to represent the interests of their national firms, even when these interests do not conform to the interests of the nation.

Finally, even if achieved, the harmonization of national differences in competition policy would not mean similar access to all national markets because of remaining national differences in related features of capitalist organization, such as patterns of stock ownership. For example, even if merger and acquisition laws were harmonized between the United States and Japan, it would be much harder for American firms to acquire Japanese firms than for them to acquire American firms. As a result of extensive cross-shareholding among Japanese companies, more than half of their shares are not available for purchase on the open market. In contrast, the shares of most American companies are. This is an important factor behind the bilateral asymmetry in foreign direct investment flows between the United States and Japan. Extensive ownership of corporate shares by German banks fosters a similar asymmetry in mergers and acquisition flows between the United States and Germany.

It is probable that enforceable multilateral competition policies will be a long time in the making. In the meantime, a variety of national trade policies, with an occasional extraterritorial application of national antitrust regulations, will of necessity provide an imperfect substitute. In this regard, the recent announcement by the US Department of Justice that it intends to investigate foreign market practices impeding American exporters for possible infringement of American antitrust laws (*San Francisco Chronicle*, 4 April 1992, B1) is to be applauded. This announcement has important symbolic value because it signals to Japan and other nations that the United States has become more serious about prosecuting restrictive business practices, such as price fixing and group boycotts, that harm American companies in foreign markets. In addition, the announcement may prove to have practical significance as well because harm to American exporters is easier to demonstrate than harm to American consumers, which has been the Justice Department's standard for initiating US antitrust investigations of foreign business practices since 1988.

In announcing its shift in policy, the Justice Department also noted that it was prepared to work with other nations if they take action against restrictive business practices on the basis of their own laws. Cooperative investigations and prosecution of such practices on a bilateral basis could be useful first steps in harmonizing competition policies.[30]

Subsidies, Foreign Targeting, and Countervailing Duties

Subsidies and promotional targeting by governments are the rule rather than the exception in high-technology industries in most countries. Certainly this is the case in most of the industries examined in this book. Whether in the form of defense programs with unintended commercial effects, or in the form of avowedly commercial programs such as export and R&D subsidies, national promotional policies influence the dynamics of trade and competition. Moreover, even though overall subsidies have been cut in the advanced industrial countries, the decline has been concentrated in agriculture and in sunset industries such as steel and shipbuilding. There has been no such tendency in the high-technology realm (OECD 1990b, chapter 1).

Whatever their motive or form, subsidies in high-technology industries, with their characteristic scale and learning economies and imperfectly competitive conditions, can and do influence market outcomes. In such circumstances, commitments by foreign governments to subsidize their producers can change the underlying competitive game played by both foreign and domestic firms to the strategic advantage of the former. This conclusion is apparent in the semiconductor, supercomputer, and aircraft cases examined in this book.

In static trade models, foreign subsidies are gifts that unambiguously increase domestic welfare.[31] Such a sanguine view, however, overlooks the adjustment problems, potential terms-of-trade effects, and dangers to the international trading system posed by such programs. It also overlooks the special benefits of high-technology production that can be denied one nation by the subsidy program of another.

Current GATT regulations recognize that one country's subsidy policies, regardless of intent, can have deleterious effects on the production, employment, profits, and exports of its trading partners. GATT Article VI identifies injurious subsidization as an unfair trading practice, in response to which nations are allowed to adopt countervailing duties (CVDs). The United States has been by far the most active GATT signatory in the use of CVD relief, accounting for some 90 percent of CVD cases launched worldwide between 1980 and 1986 (Hufbauer 1990, 94). During this period, as the US trade deficit mounted and the dollar soared, CVD actions brought by US companies against alleged unfair competition increased sharply (Destler 1991).

GATT regulations unequivocally ban certain kinds of national subsidy policies, primarily those that intentionally and directly encourage exports or discourage

---

30. Along these lines, C. Fred Bergsten (1992) recently proposed a cooperative effort by the Department of Justice and Japan's Fair Trade Commission to carry out joint investigations of alleged anticompetitive business practices in Japan.

31. For example, Dixit (1985, 1990) has demonstrated that, if an industry is perfectly competitive, then in the long run, after unprofitable domestic firms have exited and laid-off workers have found new jobs, even a trade-distorting export subsidy increases economic welfare in the importing country.

imports. For example, export subsidies are explicitly proscribed.[32] This provision motivated the formal GATT complaint by the United States against Germany's exchange rate guarantee for Airbus. As was noted in chapter 5, the other European subsidy programs for Airbus were not explicitly prohibited by GATT Article VI or by the 1979 GATT civil aircraft agreement.

When subsidies are not formally banned by the GATT, CVD relief is permitted but often proves ineffective, for a number of reasons. First, as Spencer (1988) has demonstrated, the appropriate amount for a CVD is difficult to determine and depends on the kind of foreign subsidy involved. A subsidy tied to the purchase of new capital equipment can have very different implications from a subsidy to pay off past debts. The former influences the incentives of the subsidized firm for expansion whereas the latter does not. Therefore, a higher CVD is required in the former case to offset harmful effects on rival domestic firms (Spencer 1988, 315–16).

Second, under current GATT rules and US law, a material injury test is required before a CVD can be imposed. This requirement has two unfortunate ramifications. First, many kinds of subsidies, especially those that encourage investment in physical or R&D capital, are not likely to have effects on competitive outcomes or to show up in material injury for several years. By the time the effects are felt, the subsidies themselves may have been phased out, and it may be impossible to link material injury to them. This lag between subsidies and their effects raises what Bergsten and Cline (1987) have called a "statute of limitations" question for multilateral regulations. For example, the Europeans have often argued that the current strength of American aircraft companies is based on past defense subsidy programs. Although, as chapter 5 indicates, there is some merit to the European position, the question is whether GATT rules should permit remedies today to offset policies that may have been taken much earlier.

A second shortcoming of the material injury test is that it effectively rules out CVDs as a successful deterrent to foreign subsidy practices. In other words, CVDs cannot be used to prevent foreign subsidies that threaten to damage domestic producers in the future. They can only be used to moderate the damage once it has occurred. To operate as an effective deterrent, CVDs would have to be immediate and certain in their application. Countries contemplating a subsidy program would have to expect swift and sure retaliation, particularly when the gain from the subsidy was uncertain (Spencer 1988, 319).

In the real world these conditions are not satisfied. The need to demonstrate material injury makes the CVD process slow and uncertain. Moreover, CVDs are often not imposed even when it is determined that a subsidy falls under GATT rules and is causing material injury. Consequently, the CVD process does not actively discourage foreign governments from using subsidies.

A third shortcoming of the CVD remedy is that it makes the country employing it a high-price island, driving consumers to third-country markets. When the good in question is an input and the consumers in question are themselves producers, this can mean driving production to third-country markets as well. In addition, regardless of the type of good involved, a CVD remedy is powerless

---

32. The draft Dunkel text for the Uruguay Round agreement would extend the red-light category to subsidies that are conditioned on import substitution.

to offset the benefits gained by foreign firms from subsidized operations in other markets in which no CVD relief is applied.

Finally, the CVD approach poses the danger of retaliation. Foreign governments might respond to a CVD action by the United States with a duty of their own, touching off a protectionist trade war. In high-technology industries, where the lag between subsidy and competitive effect can be quite long, and where promotional government intervention on both sides is common, it is quite likely that the imposition of CVD relief by one country will be viewed as unfair, arbitrary, or punitive by the other, encouraging retaliation. Thus, European retaliation to CVD relief by the United States against Airbus subsidies has been a serious possibility, especially in light of European beliefs about the influence of defense programs on the commercial strength of the American producers.

A retaliatory trade war in the aircraft industry would be particularly costly to American companies, which are much more dependent on sales to European markets than Airbus is on sales to the American market. In addition, a trade war would destroy the carefully constructed 1979 GATT civil aircraft code, which abolished the use of protectionist barriers among its signatories. The many cross-national production relationships that exist as a result would also be imperiled. Therefore, it is not surprising that American producers and American trade negotiators have shied away from a CVD or 301 remedy in the Airbus dispute. Moreover, the theoretical literature confirms the wisdom of their position: protectionist measures are usually a costly and welfare-reducing response to foreign subsidies, particularly when they invite strong and harmful retaliation.

Instead of CVD or 301 relief, the United States has used both bilateral and GATT pressure to urge the Europeans to reduce their subsidies for the commercial aircraft industry. As chapter 5 indicates, this approach produced some initial achievements, including the 1979 civil aircraft code itself, an OECD agreement on export credits, and an informal bilateral ban on inducements. But on the big issue of launch and development subsidies, the 1979 code was vague in stipulation and weak in enforcement, reflecting the lack of consensus among its signatories. And the bilateral talks were stalemated over the issue of launch aid during more than five years of sporadic negotiations beginning in 1986. During this period the Europeans defended their subsidies on infant-industry, dual-use, and market structure grounds, all of which had some merit, for the reasons noted in chapter 5. Despite often intense negotiating pressure, the United States was unable to deter the Europeans from their stated objective of building a European producer that would be the technological and commercial equal of its American competitors.

By the end of the 1980s, the Europeans had achieved their goal: Airbus had overtaken McDonnell Douglas to claim the second-largest share of the global market for commercial aircraft, and its aircraft were technologically competitive—perhaps even superior in some respects—to Boeing's. Frustrated by Europe's continued subsidies and alarmed by Airbus's growing competitive challenge, the United States finally lodged formal complaints with the GATT against European subsidy practices in 1991. Following a GATT ruling supporting the US position in early 1992, bilateral negotiations between the United States and Europe intensified, culminating in a bilateral agreement on subsidies announced in July 1992.

As chapter 5 argues, this agreement is a good one for both sides. It restricts the terms, conditions, and amounts of subsidies in the industry and establishes reporting, monitoring, and dispute settlement mechanisms. Moreover, it recognizes a fundamental reality: because of the aircraft industry's underlying economics, subsidies cannot and should not be ruled out altogether. The challenge was to write the subsidy rules as parsimoniously and precisely as possible to encourage beneficial innovation and competition, while at the same time minimizing the risk of rent-shifting subsidies by one side or the other, with deleterious, rent-dissipating consequences for both sides. The July 1992 agreement was a major step toward meeting this challenge.

The aircraft dispute illustrates both the limited effectiveness of national trade policy options and the need for precise, enforceable, multilateral rules to counter foreign targeting programs in high-technology industries. Equally important in this dispute, however, are the formidable barriers to the development of such rules. Even the much-praised Canada–US Free Trade Agreement tabled the subsidy issue because of irreconcilable philosophical differences between the two governments. Such differences are even greater when Europe and Japan are participants at the negotiating table. In technology-intensive industries, where theory suggests that subsidies can be welfare-increasing, philosophical differences are even greater than in agriculture, where the struggle to negotiate multilateral subsidy limits has been long and bitter.

The recent Uruguay Round discussions have identified some of the problems that must be resolved in order to get comprehensive multilateral rules on subsidies in the long run. At a minimum, the rules and conventions regarding the CVD remedy must be made more precise and uniform. Current GATT rules are so imprecise that they permit considerable national latitude in such important areas as how subsidies and CVD margins are calculated.[33] For example, current GATT law has nothing to say about the interest rate that should be used to measure a subsidy arising from a government loan. In bilateral negotiations on Airbus this has been a bone of contention, with the United States arguing that the commercial interest rate should be used and Europe arguing that the relevant interest rate should be the one at which the government can borrow money.[34] Current GATT restrictions are also vague on how to apply the injury test. At present, individual countries can adopt widely different conventions, most of which make the demonstration of injury relatively easy, even when imports are a small fraction of the domestic marketplace and when factors other than subsidized imports are the major determinant of industry difficulties.

Unfortunately, achieving greater specificity in multilateral CVD guidelines is easier said than done. Even if the philosophical and political hurdles could be overcome, daunting technical hurdles will impede the resolution of subsidy

---

33. According to Article 4:2, footnote 2, of the 1979 Tokyo agreement, "an understanding among signatories should be developed setting out the criteria for the calculation of the amount of the subsidy" (see Spencer 1988, 316). The Dunkel draft proposals for the Uruguay Round have embodied some criteria along these lines.

34. The Dunkel draft text for the Uruguay Round proposes that subsidies be measured on the basis of their "cost to the government," indicating that the European position on interest rates may finally prevail.

questions. For example, what guidelines should be established for assessing the commercial subsidy effects of a defense program that has no explicit commercial objective? Or how, if at all, should the subsidy resulting from a precompetitive R&D program be calculated?

One approach to the many puzzles posed by subsidies is to extend the list of those that are explicitly proscribed (the so-called red-light category) and to place a strict quantitative limit on those that are explicitly allowed (the so-called green-light category). The green-light category is in principle limited to subsidies of two kinds: those that are welfare-enhancing, and those that serve acceptable national economic objectives such as regional development and worker adjustment assistance. Green-light subsidies are not countervailable under the GATT. In contrast, the yellow-light category includes actionable subsidies that may be challenged under GATT law or countervailed under national law when they have adverse trade effects as further defined in GATT regulations.

The traffic light approach has encountered difficulties in both the US–Europe bilateral negotiations over Airbus and in the Uruguay Round negotiations. In general, the United States has argued for expanding the red-light category to include certain presently yellow-light or actionable subsidies whenever there is a rebuttable presumption of adverse effects based on specified quantitative tests. The Europeans have opposed the US position.

Whatever finally emerges from the Uruguay Round negotiations is not likely to solve all the problems of controlling industrial targeting and subsidies in high-technology industries. For one thing, these negotiations have not addressed the question of whether subsidies introduced to counter the exercise of market power by foreign suppliers would be permissible under certain conditions. For the reasons enumerated earlier, both the degree of competition and the degree of contestability in high-technology industries are relevant for evaluating the national and global welfare effects of subsidies used to deter the exit of existing producers or to encourage the entry of new ones.

The proposed green light for basic and applied precompetitive R&D programs also raises serious questions because of its potential for abuse. The Uruguay Round definitions for such programs are alarmingly vague: for example, applied research is defined as "investigation or experimental work based on the results of basic industrial research to acquire new knowledge to facilitate the development of specific practical objectives such as the creation of new products, production processes or services." This language, which reflects an uneasy compromise between nations with different philosophical views, reveals that no one really knows what constitutes a precompetitive applied research program. Many scientists and engineers believe that precise distinctions between basic, precompetitive, and applied research cannot be made.

Moreover, even precompetitive research on generic technologies can have significant competitive effects. An R&D program can be precompetitive in its design, but far from neutral in its market consequences; the very large scale integration program in the Japanese semiconductor industry is an obvious example. R&D subsidies, although defensible on general externality grounds, may be the most significant of all subsidies for long-run competition (Spencer 1988). Seen from this perspective, distinctions between allowable R&D subsidies, designed mainly to encourage technological advance, and prohibited R&D subsidies, designed mainly to capture market share from existing technologies, are largely meaningless.

The Uruguay Round's proposed green light for regional development subsidies would create another loophole for national promotional policies in high technology. As noted in chapter 6, individual European governments have used such subsidies to attract quality foreign direct investment in consumer electronics, semiconductors, and computers. Several American states have used similar approaches to lure foreign producers in high-technology industries. As flows of investment become more important relative to flows of trade, competition among the developed nations will increasingly take a locational form: instead of promoting their own national champions in high-technology industries, individual nations (and states) will compete to attract global champions to locate within their borders (see Bergsten 1974). Regional subsidies can be a powerful instrument in such competition.

Multilateral rules that condone certain kinds of subsidies under some circumstances invite abuse. Therefore, any such rules must define the conditions of their use as precisely as possible, must establish strong transparency requirements, and must be backed by timely and credible enforcement mechanisms. If the final Uruguay Round proposals do not satisfy these requirements, as seems likely at this time, the United States should reserve the option of exercising national CVD relief against foreign high-technology targeting programs masquerading as precompetitive R&D or regional subsidies.

Because of the obvious difficulties involved in specifying and enforcing traffic-light subsidy rules, and because of the loopholes that will inevitably remain, some economists have proposed a quantitative cap on infant-industry subsidies by advanced industrial countries.[35] A cap might be set for the total spent on all kinds of subsidies, or individual caps might be set for different categories. The cap approach underlies the 1992 bilateral agreement between the United States and Europe on subsidies for the commercial aircraft industry.

Although it is easy to support such recommendations for new multilateral rules for high-technology trade, it is hard to see their relevance for the near future. The policy challenge for the United States is what to do in the short term. For all of the reasons just given, a CVD response to foreign industrial targeting in high-technology industries is inadequate. The alternative is a countervailing subsidy (CVS) remedy—that is, an action that meets foreign subsidies head on with offsetting subsidies or government assistance at home. A CVS approach has neither the deleterious high-price island effects nor the third-country market effects of the CVD approach. Even more important, it could be a powerful deterrent to foreign subsidies, especially if it were designed to trigger a quick and credible response by the US government before a foreign subsidy program could inflict material injury on American producers. Given the politics

---

35. Bergsten and Cline (1987, 143), for example, argue that "Japan (and the United States and all other advanced industrial countries) should explicitly renounce the right to apply any type of trade distortion for 'infant-industry' purposes. It is simply unacceptable for the two largest and most advanced countries to utilize such devices, which should be reserved for developing countries." Lawrence has also argued (e.g., at a meeting of the Japan Foundation in November 1989) that infant-industry policies should be curtailed or eliminated altogether in the advanced industrial countries.

of US trade policy, however, a CVS solution would only be an option when the threatened American producers are willing to support it.

Despite their obvious advantages over CVDs, CVSs also pose the risk of retaliation. Subsidy wars, like trade wars, can prove mutually destructive. Tit-for-tat subsidies can encourage excessive production and waste resources, depressing prices and profits for all sides and ultimately triggering a protectionist trade war or a market-sharing arrangement.[36] Not all kinds of subsidies, however, share these defects, at least not to the same degree. In this respect, R&D subsidies are preferable to pure production subsidies as a CVS response to foreign targeting.

Obviously, subsidies also differ from duties in their budgetary implications—subsidies are claims on the national budget, whereas duties provide revenues. In this area as in others, a solution to the nation's budgetary crisis is a prerequisite to getting the rest of the policy agenda right.

The Need for Complementary Technology and Industrial Policies

The Inadequacies of Trade Policy

What emerges from the preceding discussion of trade policies is not their strengths but their weaknesses. Even with appropriate modifications, trade policy is incapable of solving the competitive difficulties facing this nation's high-technology producers. Nor should this be surprising, since many of these difficulties have domestic causes that demand domestic solutions. The recent problems of American producers of advanced displays—a critical input in a growing number of consumer, industrial, and military electronics applications—illustrate this point and demonstrate the risks of using trade policy when a domestic policy response is called for.

Advanced display technology was an American invention, but Japanese companies dominate its commercial applications. Although several large American electronics companies—including AT&T, Control Data, Hewlett-Packard, and Texas Instruments—initially produced or considered producing advanced displays, all of them, with the exception of IBM, ultimately opted out of large-scale production. Only a handful of small American firms remain in the business.

The fate of the American display industry reveals some of the domestic factors behind the erosion of the nation's technological edge.[37] The high cost and limited patience of capital top the list. According to Borrus and Hart (1992), capital market conditions were a consideration in the decisions of all of the large American companies to abandon the computer display market. Massive amounts of

---

36. As noted in chapter 5, some Europeans and even some Americans proposed a market-sharing arrangement to end the dispute on subsidies in the aircraft industry. Such an arrangement, however, would reduce trade and competition in the industry, with likely welfare-reducing effects on both sides. In addition, such an arrangement might encourage similar arrangements in other high-technology industries, thereby further undermining the multilateral trading system.

37. For a more detailed analysis of some of these factors, see, for example, Tyson (1988), Cohen and Zysman (1988), Krugman (1990), and Dertouzos et al. (1989).

capital would have been required to establish world-class manufacturing facilities, and would-be investors feared profit-preempting competition by Japanese companies with deeper pockets. Behind these common concerns lay differences in the cost, availability, and patience of capital for Japanese and American companies—differences that have been well documented in several recent studies and were discussed in chapters 3 and 4 (see, e.g, McCauley and Zimmer 1989, Frankel 1991).

Innovative technologies are the major competitive strength of the small American firms still in the display industry; high capital costs are their major competitive weakness. As a recent NACS report notes (1991, 9, citing Henderson 1989), small American startups in advanced electronics technologies must borrow at higher interest rates than their Japanese competitors, are more dependent on equity financing (with its attendant tax disadvantages), and have substantially shorter time horizons because of their dependence on venture capital. Moreover, even their venture investors concede that adequate financing is not available for the most capital-critical stage of development, namely, the transition from prototype development to full manufacturing. It is at this stage that many small American producers are forced to sell their technologies to larger competitors. In electronics, these competitors are frequently Japanese.

The American display producers who brought an antidumping action against their Japanese competitors in 1991 based their case on capital market constraints. They argued that Japanese predation made it impossible for them to obtain the capital necessary to expand production. According to their logic, dumping duties would deter predation and drive display prices up, generating higher earnings and internal funds for investment.

As noted earlier, even if the Japanese display producers were guilty of predatory tactics, the remedies mandated by US antidumping laws could not reverse the damages sustained by the American companies, let alone create the basis for a competitive American display industry. After duties on imports of Japanese displays were imposed in the summer of 1991, the big American manufacturers of laptop computers promptly announced that they would consider moving production offshore. One company has since shifted some of its operations abroad, while others have requested permission to establish duty-exempt "foreign trade zones" for production in the United States. Ultimately, the duties on displays will accomplish little else than to make the United States a high-price location for laptop production. The "relief" won by the American display companies will certainly not provide them with enough additional capital to compete with their much larger Japanese counterparts.

Moreover, using dumping duties for this purpose is indefensible from an economic point of view. US antidumping laws are designed to deter certain kinds of unfair foreign competition, not to raise capital for one industry by shifting revenues from another. Problems in the cost, availability, and patience of capital must be addressed by changes in the nation's monetary and fiscal policies and in its financial institutions, not by ad hoc, protectionist, and ultimately ineffectual trade measures.[38] If the United States wants a domestically

---

38. Most economists attribute the high cost of capital and the low investment rate in the United States to the inadequacy of national saving. For a timely expostion of this view, see the first report of the Competitiveness Policy Council (1992). According to a recent

based display capability, whether for commercial or military reasons or both, it must design policies either to support American producers or to encourage local production by Japanese producers. An off-budget solution in the form of anti-dumping relief will be both ineffective and counterproductive.

The display story also reveals the absence of strategic vision in US policy toward high-technology competition. The reaction of the private venture capital community—that it is foolish to provide financing to an industry targeted or dominated by the Japanese—is understandable. But a similar reaction on the part of the US government is not, especially when the industry in question produces an input with obvious dual-use significance, and when the market power of a relatively small number of Japanese companies poses a potential threat to both commercial and military users. A few agencies of the US government, notably the Defense Advanced Research Projects Agency (DARPA) and the National Institute of Standards and Technology (NIST), have responded to developments in advanced display competition with additional R&D support for American producers. But other voices in the American government have continued to argue loudly against industry-specific programs to support the display industry or any other high-technology industry, including supercomputers, semiconductors, and aircraft, despite their obvious dual-use significance. This remains the dominant view in American policy circles. Certainly, it is impossible to interpret American policy to date as reflecting a credible commitment to maintain American strength in high-technology industries. The contrast between policy in the United States and policy in Europe and Japan is striking.

As the case studies have demonstrated, both Japan and Europe have fashioned a panoply of industrial policies to promote several of their high-technology industries. As a result of its Europe 1992 initiative, the European Community is taking charge of these policies through its financing of large pan-European ventures such as Ariane (aerospace), Eureka (electronics), and JESSI (semiconductors). Airbus, the beneficiary of the most successful European industrial policy to date, is not an EC project but is a pan-European project joining four European nations. MITI and other Japanese government agencies such as the Ministry of Posts and Telecommunications regularly target high-technology industries and support them through an extensive array of tools ranging from direct financing to orchestrating collaborative research to giving administrative guidance. Industrial policy support in Japan is complemented by a number of market access barriers rooted in the nature of business-government relations.

Unlike Europe and Japan, the United States does not have a commercially oriented industrial policy as that term is defined by the US International Trade Commission: "coordinated government actions to direct productive resources to help domestic producers in selected industries become more competitive" (Beltz 1991, chapter 2). On several occasions, however, the United States has had a haphazard and inefficient industrial policy in the form of costly protectionist measures. In this respect the imposition of antidumping duties on ad-

---

set of studies (Porter 1992), however, the structure of American capital markets and the nature of relations between suppliers and customers, investors and managers, and executives and workers may be even more powerful determinants of the availability and price of long-term capital than the national saving rate. These studies indicate that reforms in the system of allocating investment capital within and across companies are needed to provide a competitive capital market environment for American companies.

vanced displays is only the most recent example in a long history of protectionism in such diverse industries as textiles, footwear, color televisions, steel, machine tools, and automobiles. Protection has been the most common form of commercial industrial policy in the United States, in part because it has usually been the only form available and in part because it provides off-budget relief—consumers, not the government, pick up the tab.

Moreover, as the Europeans would be quick to point out, the United States has never been a free market champion when its defense objectives have been at stake. Quite the contrary. The United States has had a coordinated and far-reaching industrial policy to direct resources to particular technologies, industries, and producers for *defense* purposes. And its military industrial policy has provided the basic foundations for the nation's high-technology success stories in computers, semiconductors, advanced telecommunications products, and aircraft. These foundations have included generous R&D subsidies, collaborative research projects, large-scale guaranteed launch markets, and domestic diffusion mechanisms, all of which are features of civilian industrial policies in other nations. Indeed, it is not an exaggeration to say that America's military industrial policy has been the primary driver of technological development and diffusion in the United States since World War II. As the case studies indicate, this policy has had dramatic, albeit unintended, commercial effects.

New Directions

In the aftermath of the Cold War, the challenge is to find ways of reconfiguring the institutions and incentives of the nation's military industrial policy to match the new realities of international competition.[39] Unless this effort is made, there is a very real danger that our government's past commitment to maintaining a high-technology production base will evanesce along with the Cold War.

As a critical first step toward meeting this challenge, the US government must develop an institutional mechanism for assessing competitive and technological trends in global high-technology industries on an ongoing and timely basis. The government should either designate an existing agency or construct a new one to perform several related tasks, including evaluating the likely course of key American industries; comparing these baseline projections with visions of industry paths that would be compatible with a prosperous and competitive economy; and monitoring the activities of foreign governments and firms in these industries to provide an early warning of potential competitive problems in the future.[40]

A government agency of this description is essential to provide the kind of industry-specific information required to make wise decisions on a variety of trade policy questions. Without such information, trade policy institutions are too easily captured by domestic business actors whose private economic interests do not necessarily coincide with those of the nation. As the case studies indicate,

---

39. For more-detailed recommendations for the nation's technology and industrial policies, see Council on Competitiveness (1991), Ross (1992), and National Academy of Sciences (1992).

40. A similar proposal was made by the Competitiveness Policy Council (1992) in its inaugural report.

Motorola, Cray, the Semiconductor Industry Association, and Boeing exerted tremendous influence on the agenda for US trade policy during the 1980s. Because all of these private actors were outward-oriented global players, their trade policy requests concentrated on improving market access abroad rather than reducing it at home. In all of these instances, harried government officials in understaffed and underfunded government agencies found themselves relying heavily on information and industry analyses provided by interested private actors. But interested parties might not always play such a positive role in the future. In contrast, in both Europe and Japan well-financed government agencies provide independent assessments of competitive trends in global high-technology industries to both private and public actors.

In the United States there are a number of institutions that could perform a similar function, among them the National Academy of Sciences, the National Academy of Engineers, the National Science Foundation, the Office of Technology Assessment, an expanded International Trade Commission, and the bipartisan Competitiveness Policy Council formed by the 1988 omnibus trade act. Alternatively, as a recent study by the Carnegie Commission on Science, Technology, and Government (1991) proposed, a new institution could be established for this purpose. In either case, the agency chosen for the task should be responsible for issuing an annual report on the state of the nation's science and technology base and on trends in global high-technology markets.

Another important step in developing a forward-looking policy to support high-technology industries is to shift federal R&D spending from military to dual-use and commercial objectives. Traditionally, the federal government has played an enormous role in what Mowery and Rosenberg (1989b) call the "national innovation system," through the provision of funding for basic research, graduate education in engineering and science, and even university plant and equipment. The bulk of the federal R&D commitment, however, has been concentrated on defense. In 1991 defense still claimed about 60 percent of federal R&D spending, down from a peak of 69 percent in 1987 (National Science Board, *Science and Engineering Indicators*, 1992, 94 and 99). In 1989—the last year for which comparative data are available—defense claimed 66 percent of federal R&D funding in the United States compared with 56 percent in Great Britain, 19 percent in Germany, and 9 percent in Japan (National Science Board, *Science and Engineering Indicators*, 1992, 109). Nondefense R&D as a percentage of GDP has been rising faster in Germany and Japan than in the United States for nearly two decades. As a result, both countries now spend about 50 percent more on nondefense R&D relative to GDP than the United States does.

Undeniably, government support for defense-related R&D has had important spillover benefits for the economy. One need only look at the overwhelming role of the military in supporting R&D in the semiconductor and computer industries during the first decade of their development and its continuing role in the aerospace complex (see chapters 4 and 5). However, in the words of Erich Bloch (1991, 12), "Several factors make it less likely that defense and other mission-oriented R&D will be a primary source of commercial technology development in the years to come." One factor is the collapse of the Soviet threat, which will cause reductions in military R&D budgets. Another is that technological advances in an increasing number of areas—including biotechnology, semiconductor manufacturing, robotics, artificial intelligence, and high-definition displays—are now being driven by civilian, not military applications.

Three trends now shape America's industrial technology base: declining military R&D and procurement budgets; a growing overlap between technologies and materials with both civilian and military applications; and the continued globalization of high-technology markets, which drive the overall direction of innovation. Taken together, these trends suggest that there will be more spin-ons from commercial products to the military sector and fewer spin-offs in the opposite direction.[41] In short, the United States can no longer rely on military R&D spending to provide breakthroughs in commercial technologies, particularly when many other countries have developed civilian R&D programs to do commercially oriented research. In the face of intense foreign competition, the relevant question becomes not whether defense R&D programs might still have commercial spillovers, but whether commercially oriented R&D programs are a more efficient mechanism for generating them.

The United States is just beginning to debate this question in earnest, and there are some promising signs of change. For example, in 1990 the White House Office of Science and Technology Policy accepted the case for a national technology policy, arguing that the public sector ought to "participate with the private sector on precompetitive research on generic, enabling technologies that have the potential to contribute to a broad range of government and commercial applications." D. Allan Bromley, the president's chief science and technology adviser, clarified what the administration means by these terms (Bromley 1990): a generic technology is one that has the potential to be applied to a wide variety of products and processes extending across many industries; precompetitive research is research on a specific technology before its commercial potential has been determined.

Even more dramatically, in March 1991 Bromley released the *Report of the National Critical Technologies Panel,* which identified 22 technologies the panel deemed critical to national economic prosperity and national security. Most of these technologies were also among those judged essential to national defense in a separate list developed by the US Department of Defense (see table 2A.2). Many of the products involved in the trade disputes examined in this book—including semiconductors, supercomputers, liquid crystal and high-resolution displays, and commercial aircraft—appear on both lists. After initial opposition the Bush administration recently endorsed the establishment of a Critical Technologies Institute to be charged with the tasks of identifying crucial emerging technologies and determining which deserve federal support.

Although the nondefense share of the federal R&D budget has grown rapidly, federal funding for most commercial programs remains tiny compared with funding for defense, health, and space, which together claimed 84 percent of the federal R&D budget in 1992 (National Science Board, *Science and Engineering Indicators,* 1991, 99). According to a recent influential study by the National Academy of Sciences, existing federal programs for commercial R&D are not funded at levels that will affect private-sector markets in a significant, measurable way. (National Academy of Sciences, Panel on the Government Role in Civilian

---

41. These trends are identified by Jay Stowsky and Burgess Laird (1992).

Technology, Committee on Science, Engineering, and Public Policy 1992, 94). The National Institute of Standards and Technology, a national laboratory run by the Department of Commerce to promote civilian research programs related to manufacturing, accounts for less than 1 percent of the $22 billion budget for the national laboratories. Out of a total federal R&D budget of about $68 billion in 1992, approximately $1.2 billion will support research programs on manufacturing technologies; half of this amount will be spent by defense-related agencies.[42] Even the Federal High-Performance Computing and Networking Initiative—which many view as a model for joint public-private programs on generic technologies—will have an annual budget of only about $638 million in 1992. That sum pales in comparison with the tens of billions of dollars still being spent on military R&D programs by the Department of Defense.

Any suggestion that the government should provide greater funding for generic technologies with commercial applications sounds alarm bells for many US policymakers and economists, who warn against the dangers of trying to pick winners and losers. And these dangers should not be dismissed. The very act of identifying particular technologies as "critical," as every developed country has done, is an act of picking potential winners. Given technological and market uncertainties and the footloose nature of many technological innovations, especially generic ones, there can be no guarantee that the act of betting taxpayers' money on them—and implicitly betting against others—will pay off.

In addition, there are formidable impediments to the design and efficient execution of public programs to support civilian technologies in the United States. An informed bureaucracy with the capacity to choose between competing claims on the basis of technological merit rather than political clout is a prerequisite. Can the United States meet this requirement? Many observers are skeptical because they believe that the American system is uniquely vulnerable to special interest pressures and pork barrel politics (Spar and Vernon 1989, 1991; Krueger 1990). A recent book edited by Cohen and Noll (1991) demonstrates how political rather than technological concerns have wasted public funds on technology programs with dubious commercial merit in the past.

Some of the political and economic risks associated with federal programs to support civilian technologies can be contained by creating the appropriate institutions and incentives. In particular, there is a growing consensus that such programs should incorporate the following features: the government and the business community should share their costs to ensure serious industry participation and to guide projects into commercially promising areas; projects should be initiated and designed by private firms and should be funded only after they have been competitively reviewed by an independent panel of experts; and the institutions responsible for administering such programs should be insulated as much as possible from continuing budgetary and political pressures.

In fact, the US government already has a few small programs that meet many of these criteria, including the NIST's Advanced Technology Program and the program of cooperative research and development agreements (CRADAS) between

---

42. Estimate offered by Robert M. White, Under Secretary for Technology, US Department of Commerce, at a September 1992 meeting of the Manufacturing Subcouncil of the Competitiveness Policy Council.

the national laboratories and the private sector.[43] Both programs are market-led: project proposals are submitted by private companies and chosen by scientific experts on their technological and commercial merits. The private sector picks the potential winners, and the government provides partial support to reduce the risk and speed the process of technological development and diffusion.

But the government also needs an institutional capability to fund research on precompetitive generic technologies that are likely to be underfunded by individual private companies but are likely to have significant spillover benefits for the nation as a whole. These include new technologies for information processing, advanced materials, microelectronics, transportation, and the environment, most of which appear on the list of critical technologies mentioned above (Borrus 1992). At present the government has no formal mechanism for evaluating and supporting such technologies in a timely and systematic fashion. Existing programs for channelling federal monies to generic nonmilitary technologies are uncoordinated, underfunded, and subject to intense political pressures. Not surprisingly, a recent panel of the National Academy of Sciences concluded that the government needs a new approach that is at once better coordinated and more insulated from political influence to finance research on civilian technologies important to the nation's long-term competitiveness.[44]

Even the best designed programs, however, cannot escape the reality that research is a risky process with uncertain payoffs. Try as they might, neither public nor private investors will always pick winners. But public investors can be cheered by the fact that the social benefits to funding research appear to be so great as to provide a substantial margin for error. In the words of Grossman (1990), a respected economist not known for his support of government intervention in the economy:

> When the introduction and improvement of a new product involve substantial research outlays and costly learning by doing, private firms are often unable to capture more than a fraction of the benefits they create for consumers and for other firms in the industry. . . . It will of course be difficult for the policy analyst to identify the deserving innovations and to delimit the period of government support to the time when substantial externalities are being generated. But the magnitude of the foregone gains that have been estimated for several industries suggest the existence of a margin for error.

Even many who are convinced of the merits of a new technology policy for the United States remain skeptical or hostile toward the notion of industrial policy. Yet the distinction between the two is not nearly as precise as some have suggested. Bromley, for example, favors a government role in developing the basic generic technologies that undergird all of our industrial actvity, but is opposed to using taxpayer dollars for assisting specific industries (*New York Times*, 19 July 1992, 5). Yet greater public funding in support of generic electronics technologies, such as high-performance computing systems, or in support of certain basic or generic biomedical technologies is willy-nilly a form of industrial policy—implicitly favoring certain industries over others.

---

43. For an insightful discussion of the CRADA program see Stowsky and Laird (1992).

44. The panel's report (National Academy of Sciences 1992, chapter 3) describes and contrasts several alternative institutional arrangements for meeting this objective.

In any event, as the case studies in this book demonstrate, civilian industrial policies to address the problems or exploit the opportunities of a particular high-technology industry have proven effective both in Europe and in Japan. Perhaps more amazingly, they have even proven effective in the United States.

Despite what some critics have argued, often on ideological rather than factual grounds, Sematech has been a success relative to its goals. Largely as a consequence of the Sematech program, after a decade of steep decline the share of American producers in the global market for semiconductor equipment rose by three percentage points in 1991 alone. In addition, Sematech, in conjunction with a related industrial policy—the buyout by an American firm of Perkin-Elmer's lithography business, orchestrated with the help of the Defense Department—has fostered the development of a new lithography technology. Micrascan, as this technology is called, challenges the global monopoly of Japanese suppliers in the lithography market. In addition, IBM's access to Micrascan is one reason why Toshiba and Siemens were attracted to participate in a joint venture with IBM for research on 16M DRAMS. Because this venture will operate in the United States, it will provide research monies and jobs for American scientists and engineers.

The nation's limited industrial policy initiatives in high-definition television (HDTV) may also have a positive payoff. As of this writing, it looks as if American companies may leapfrog both their Japanese and their European competitors to develop a digital HDTV technology. Some observers conclude that this outcome confirms the wisdom of keeping the government out of high-technology competition. But this conclusion conveniently overlooks the facts of the case. Whatever the outcome, strategic government intervention both at home and abroad will have played a role. Without the European action in 1986 to delay its introduction, Japan's HDTV standard would have been adopted in Europe and perhaps in the United States, where it was favored by the movie industry. Without the action by the Federal Communications Commission (FCC) to block adoption of the Japanese standard in 1988 on the grounds that it was incompatible with existing American broadcasting standards, there would have been no market incentive for developing an alternative standard. In addition, both DARPA and NIST have provided public funds to support the HDTV-related research programs of some of the firms now participating in the FCC's competition for a new standard. Finally, even though American firms may win the HDTV technology competition, Japanese firms may yet win the HDTV production competition, in part because their strength in related electronics technologies may allow them to act preemptively against their would-be American rivals. The HDTV case clearly confirms the view that strategic interactions between firms and governments manipulate competitive outcomes in high-technology products.

Of course, as noted many times throughout this book, to argue that civilian industrial policies can be effective is not to assert that they are always welfare-improving. Technological and market uncertainties and the limits of contemporary modeling and measurement make it impossible to guarantee that policies targeted at a particular industry will improve national economic welfare in the long run, let alone succeed in the more narrowly defined mission of maintaining or improving an industry's competitiveness. Indeed, the evidence from the case studies in this book suggests that the risk of failure is high. Europe's industrial policy in commercial aircraft may be a success, but its industrial policy in electronics is widely regared to be a failure, at least so far.[45] Even Japan, with its impressive industrial policy track record, has not always succeeded, as demonstrated by the disappointing results of its fifth-generation computing project.

Overall, the evidence presented here argues for a relatively cautious approach to industrial policy, one that limits sector-specific measures to a few technologies or industries that can be characterized as strategic in the military and/or the economic senses defined in chapter 2.[46] The case for such measures is particularly strong when the product in question is a widely used input, such as semiconductors; when market power can be exercised by a small group of foreign suppliers, as in the semiconductor or display industries; or when national security is closely tied to an industry's health, as in the aircraft, semiconductor, and supercomputer industries. The cautious activist also prefers industrial policies that take the form of funding for cooperative, precompetitive R&D consortia whenever possible, because public money spent in this way may at least produce spillover benefits, even if it does not succeed in maintaining the global competitiveness of American companies.

Finally, the cautious activist believes that the challenges of military conversion occasioned by the end of the Cold War require an industrial policy perspective and response. This conclusion emerges most clearly from the analysis in chapter 5 of the difficulties now confronting the commercial aircraft industry. A commercially oriented industrial policy is warranted to reduce the adjustment costs of conversion from military to civilian production, and to ensure that the American industry has the financial and technological wherewithal to meet the inevitable challenge of Airbus in the superjumbo jet market by the end of the 1990s. As the Pentagon slashes its budget and ceases production of weapons prototypes, virtually all of the nation's big military contractors are already looking to the commercial aerospace industry for their salvation. As a result, the United States needs a prosperous commercial industry more than ever before. The country can no longer afford the expensive, defense-oriented industrial policy of the past. And given the certainty of continued policy intervention abroad, it can no longer afford the soothing but largely irrelevant position that market forces alone should determine industry outcomes in the future.

Some Concluding Thoughts

Most of the American trade policy initiatives examined in this book and summarized in table 7.1 have been designed to improve foreign market access for American companies or to counter the effects of foreign targeting programs. Such initiatives are defensible in a world in which trade is manipulated by government intervention, and structural differences impede competition between producers from different nations. The policy task in such a world is to

---

45. According to an insightful analysis by Derian (1990), the failure of Europe's industrial policy in electronics is attributable in large measure to the fact that Europe's electronics producers were sheltered from both domestic and foreign competition. In contrast, the success of the Airbus industrial policy is attributable in large measure to its orientation to the global marketplace.

46. In his recent influential work, Paul R. Krugman (1990, 131) reveals himself to be a cautious activist on the issue of industrial policy.

use the nation's trade policies to serve the national interest, but to do so in ways that foster the development of new multilateral rules, reflecting the growing integration of global high-technology industries.

The GATT may not be dead as some have argued. But even a successful conclusion to the Uruguay Round will leave much more work to be done to formulate precise and binding multilateral rules in such areas as intellectual property protection; antidumping regulations; procedures for testing, certification, and setting standards; industrial targeting; foreign direct investment; and competition policies.

The blueprint for Europe 1992 provides a model of what will ultimately be required at the international level. The Community is designing rules to govern business and member government behavior in all of these areas. The evolution of policy convergence within the Community also indicates the critical role of a supranational judicial system to enforce multilateral regulations, to adjudicate disputes between governments and businesses, and to establish legal precedents.

This vision of deep integration should inform US trade policy at the multilateral level. The American goal should remain the same—more and freer trade, safeguarded by multilateral rules. In pursuing this goal, however, American policymakers must recognize that developing the necessary rules will be a slow process. In the meantime, the United States will continue to face the challenge of preventing further erosion in its relative economic position. The recommendations in this chapter indicate how appropriately designed trade policies can play a constructive role in meeting this challenge.

But even at their best, trade policies will rarely be sufficient. A successful Super 301 action may have been all that was needed to terminate (but not reverse) the damage sustained by Motorola as a result of barriers to Japan's cellular telephone market. But even realization of the market access provisions of the 1991 semiconductor trade agreement with Japan would not restore the share of the global memory market lost by American producers to their Japanese competitors. Nor will enforcement of the recently announced US–Europe agreement on commercial aircraft subsidies undo the market gains won by Airbus as a result of previous European subsidies, or preclude the possibility of future subsidies leading to additional gains. And inappropriate and poorly designed trade remedies, such as the use of antidumping duties in the advanced display industry, will not only fail to realize their narrow objective but may actually harm other parts of the nation's high-technology production base.

Ultimately, the fate of the nation's high-technology industries depends not on the trade battles we fight abroad but on the choices we make at home: in macroeconomic policy, education policy, technology policy, and industrial policy. The policies and institutions that served the nation well when we were the world's unquestioned technological leader require overhaul now that Japan and Europe have emerged as our economic equals. We are fortunate that the collapse of the Soviet military threat provides an opportunity to reconsider national priorities and to shift resources away from the military challenges of the past toward the economic challenges of the future.

References

Abbot, T. A. 1991. "Measuring High-Technology Trade: Contrasting International Trade Administration and Bureau of Census Methodologies and Results." *Journal of Economic and Social Measurement* 17: 17–44.

Aho, C. Michael, and Jonathan David Aronson. 1985. *Trade Talks: America Better Listen!* New York: Council on Foreign Relations.

Alic, John, et al. 1992. *Beyond Spinoff: Military and Commercial Technologies in a Changing World.* Cambridge, MA: Harvard Business School (forthcoming).

Anchordoguy, Marie. 1988. "Mastering the Market: Japanese Government Targeting of the Computer Industry." *International Organization* 42, no. 3 (Summer): 509–43.

Anchordoguy, Marie. 1989. *Computers Inc. Japan's Challenge to* IBM. Cambridge, MA: Harvard University Press.

Anchordoguy, Marie. 1990. "Japanese Industrial Targeting: A Challenge to Free Trade?" Seattle: University of Washington, Jackson School of International Affairs (May).

Anchordoguy, Marie. 1991. "Report on Japanese Policies for the Supercomputer Industry." Contract report for the Office of Technology Assessment (February).

Andersen, E. S. 1991. "Techno-Economic Paradigms as Typical Interfaces between Producers and Users." *Journal of Evolutionary Economics* 1, no. 2 (January): 119–44.

Andrews, John. 1985. "Eternal Triangles—A Survey of the Civil Aerospace Industry." *The Economist* 295 (1 June).

Arrow, Kenneth. 1962. "The Economic Implications of Learning by Doing." *Review of Economic Studies* 29, no. 80 (June): 155–73.

Arthur, W, Brian. 1987. "Self-Reinforcing Mechanisms in Economics." *Working Papers* 111. Stanford, CA: Center for Economic Policy Research.

Arthur, W. Brian. 1990. "Positive Feedbacks in Economics." *Scientific American* 262, no. 2 (February): 92.

Averon, Timothy J. 1982. "Politics and High Technology: The NTT Case." In I. M. Destler and Sato Hideo, eds., *Coping with US-Japanese Economic Conflicts,* 185–242. Lexington, MA: D. C. Heath.

Baily, Martin Neil, and Alok K. Chakrabarti. 1988. *Innovation and the Productivity Crisis.* Washington: Brookings Institution.

Balassa, Bela, and Marcus Noland. 1988. *Japan in the World Economy.* Washington: Institute for International Economics.

Baldwin, Robert, and Paul Krugman. 1988a. "Market Access and International Competition: A Simulation Study of 16K Random Access Memories." In Robert C. Feenstra, ed., *Empirical Methods for International Trade*, 171–97. Cambridge, MA: MIT Press.

Baldwin, Robert, and Paul Krugman. 1988b. "Industrial Policy and International Competition in Wide-bodied Jet Aircraft." In Robert E. Baldwin, ed., *Trade Policy Issues and Empirical Analysis*, 45–71. Chicago: University of Chicago Press for National Bureau of Economic Research.

Bayard, Thomas O., and Kimberly Ann Elliott. 1992. *Reciprocity and Retaliation: An Evaluation of Aggressive Trade Policies*. Washington: Institute for International Economics (forthcoming).

Beltz, Cynthia A. 1991. *High-Tech Maneuvers: Industrial Policy Lessons of* HDTV. Washington: AEI Press.

Bergsten, C. Fred. 1974. "Coming Investment Wars?" *Foreign Affairs* 53 (October): 135–52.

Bergsten, C. Fred, ed. 1991. *International Adjustment and Financing: The Lessons of 1985–1991*. Washington: Institute for International Economics.

Bergsten, C. Fred. 1992. "The Primacy of Economics." *Foreign Policy* 87 (Summer): 3–24.

Bergsten, C. Fred, and William R. Cline. 1987. *The United States–Japan Economic Problem*. POLICY ANALYSES IN INTERNATIONAL ECONOMICS 13, rev. ed. Washington: Institute for International Economics.

Bergsten, C. Fred, and Paula Stern. 1992. "America and Japan: The Key Differences and What to Do About Them."

Bergsten, C. Fred, Kimberly Ann Elliott, Jeffrey J. Schott, and Wendy E. Takacs. 1987. *Auction Quotas and United States Trade Policy* POLICY ANALYSES IN INTERNATIONAL ECONOMICS 19. Washington: Institute for International Economics.

Bhagwati, Jagdish. 1983. *Lectures on International Trade*. Cambridge, MA: MIT Press.

Bhagwati, Jagdish. 1988. *Protectionism*. Cambridge, MA: MIT Press.

Bhagwati, Jagdish. 1991. *The World Trading System at Risk*. Princeton, NJ: Princeton University Press.

Bhagwati, Jagdish, and Hugh Patrick, eds. 1990. *Aggressive Unilateralism*. Ann Arbor: University of Michigan Press.

Bloch, Erich. 1991. "Toward a US Technology Strategy: Enhancing Manufacturing Competitiveness." *Manufacturing Forum Discussion Papers* 1. Washington: National Academy Press (February).

Boeing Commercial Airplane Company. 1982. *International Competition in the Production and Marketing of Commercial Aircraft*. Seattle: Boeing Commercial Airplane Company.

Boltuck, Richard, and Robert Litan, eds. 1991. *Down in the Dumps: Administration of the Unfair Trade Laws*. Washington: Brookings Institution.

Borrus, Michael. 1988. *Competing for Control: America's Stake in Microelectronics*. Cambridge, MA: Ballinger.

Borrus, Michael. 1992. "Investing on the Frontier: How the U.S. Can Reclaim High-Tech Leadership." *The American Prospect* (Fall): 79–87.

Borrus, Michael, and Jeffrey Hart. 1992. "Display's the Thing: The Real Stakes in the Conflict Over High-Resolution Display." *BRIE Working Papers* 52. Berkeley, CA: Berkeley Roundtable on the International Economy (forthcoming).

Borrus, Michael, and John Zysman. 1992. "Industrial Competitiveness and American National Security." In Wayne Sandholtz, Michael Borrus, John Zysman, Ken Conca, Jay Stowsky, Steve Vogel, and Steve Weber, eds., *The Highest Stakes: The Economic Foundations of the Next Security System*, 7–52. London and New York: Oxford Unversity Press.

Borrus, Michael, James Millstein, and John Zysman. 1983. "US-Japanese Competition in the Semiconductor Industry." *Policy Papers in International Affairs* 17. Berkeley: Institute for International Studies, University of California, Berkeley.

Brander, James, and Barbara Spencer. 1985. "Export Subsidies and International Market Share Rivalry." *Journal of International Economics* 18, no. 1–2 (February): 85–100.

Bromley, D. A. 1990. "US Technology Policy: The Path to Competitiveness." Address to the Technology 2000 Meeting, Washington (27 November).

Carnegie Commission on Science, Technology, and Government. 1991. *Technology and Economic Performance: Organizing the Executive Branch for a Stronger National Technology Base.* New York: Carnegie Commission on Science, Technology, and Government (September).

Carrol, S. L. 1972. "Profits in the Airframe Industry." *Quarterly Journal of Economics* 86, no. 4 (November): 547.

Carrol, S. L. 1975. "The Market for Commercial Aircraft." In R. E. Caves and M. J. Roberts, eds., *Regulating the Market*, 145–69. Cambridge, MA: Ballinger.

Castells, Manuel. 1989. *The Informational City: Information Technology, Economic Restructuring and the Urban-Regional Process.* Oxford, England: Basil Blackwell.

Cawson, A., and P. Holmes. 1991. "The New Consumer Electronics." In Christopher Freeman, Margaret Sharp, and William Walker, eds., *Technology and the Future of Europe: Competition and the Global Environment in the 1990s.* London: Pinter.

Cawson, Alan, Kevin Morgan, Douglas Webber, Peter Holmes, and Anne Stevens. 1990. *Hostile Brothers.* Oxford: Clarendon Press.

Choate, Pat. 1990. *Agents of Influence: How Japan's Lobbyists in the United States Manipulate America's Political and Economic System.* New York: Knopf.

Cohen, Linda R., and Roger G. Noll. 1991. *The Technology Pork Barrel.* Washington: Brookings Institution.

Cohen, Stephen, and John Zysman. 1987. *Manufacturing Matters.* New York: Basic Books.

Cohen, Stephen, David Teece, Laura Tyson, and John Zysman. 1984. "Global Competition: The New Reality." *Working Papers of the President's Commission on Industrial Competitiveness*, vol. III. (Reprinted as BRIE *Working Papers* 8. Berkeley: University of California, Berkeley.)

Commission of the European Communities. 1991. *The European Electronics and Information Technology Industry: State of Play, Issues at Stake, and Proposals for Action* (Sec. [91] 565 Final). Brussels: Commission of the European Commnities (3 April).

Competitiveness Policy Council. 1992. *Building a Competitive America: Annual Report to the President and Congress.* Washington: Competitiveness Policy Council (March).

Congressional Budget Office. 1991. "New Directions for the Nation's Public Works." Washington: Congressional Budget Office.

Congressional Budget Office. 1992. "The Budget of the US Government for FY 1993: Special Analysis." Washington: Congressional Budget Office.

Constant, E.W. 1980. *The Origins of the Turbojet Revolution.* Baltimore: Johns Hopkins University Press.

Corker, Robert. 1990. "The Changing Structure of Japanese Trade Flows." *Working Papers* 90/107. Washington: International Monetary Fund (November).

Council on Competitiveness. 1991. *Gaining New Ground: Technology Priorities for America's Future.* Washington: Council on Competitiveness.

Cowhey, Peter F. 1990. "Telecommunications." In Gary Clyde Hufbauer, ed., *Europe 1992: An American Perspective*, 159–224. Washington: Brookings Institution.

Cray Research, Inc. 1991. "The Japanese Public Sector: Problems and Prospects for US Supercomputer Vendors." Minneapolis: Cray Research, Inc. (May).

Davis, Warren, Brent Bartlett, and Thomas Howell. 1992. *Creating Advantage: Semiconductors and Government Industrial Policy in the 1990s.* Washington: Semiconductor Industry Association and Dewey Ballantine (mimeographed).

Deardorff, Alan. 1989. "Economic Perspectives on Antidumping Law." In John H. Jackson and Edwin A. Vermulst, eds., *Antidumping Law and Practice: A Comparative Study*, 23–42. Ann Arbor: University of Michigan Press.

Defense Science Board Task Force. 1990. *Foreign Ownership and Control of US Industry.* Washington: Defense Science Board (June).

Derian, Jean-Claude. 1990. *America's Struggle for Leadership in Technology.* Cambridge, MA: MIT Press.

Dertouzos, Michael L., Richard K. Lester, and Robert M. Solow. 1989. *Made in America.* Cambridge, MA: MIT Press.

Destler, I. M. 1991. "US Trade Policy Making in the Eighties." In Alberto Alesina and Geoffrey Carliner, eds. *The Politics and Economics of the Eighties,* 251–81. Cambridge, MA: National Bureau of Economic Research.

Dickens, William T. 1992. "Good Jobs: Increasing Worker Productivity with Trade and Industrial Policy." Berkeley: Department of Economics, University of California, Berkeley (mimeographed, 11 March).

Dickens, William T., and Kevin Lang. 1988. "Why It Matters What We Trade: A Case for Active Trade Policy." In William T. Dickens, Laura D'Andrea Tyson, and John Zysman, eds., *The Dynamics of Trade and Employment,* 87–112. Cambridge, MA: Ballinger Press.

Dixit, Avinash. 1983. "International Trade Policy for Oligopolistic Industries." *Economic Journal* 94 (supplement): 1–16.

Dixit, Avinash. 1985. "How Should the U.S. Trade Policies in a Changing World Economy?" Presented at the University of Michigan, Ann Arbor, 28–29 March.

Dixit, Avinash. 1988. "Optimal Trade and Industrial Policy for the US Automobile Industry." In Robert Feenstra, ed., *Empirical Methods for International Trade,* 141–65. Cambridge, MA: MIT Press.

Dore, Ronald Phillip. 1986. *Flexible Rigidities: Industrial Policy and Structural Adjustment in the Japanese Economy 1970–80.* Stanford, CA: Stanford University Press.

Dosi, Giovanni. 1981. "Technical Change and Survival: Europe's Semiconductor Industry." *Sussex European Papers* 9. Sussex, England: Sussex European Research Center.

Dosi, Giovanni. 1988. "Sources, Procedures, and Microeconomic Effects of Innovation." *Journal of Economic Literature* 26, no. 3 (September): 1120–71

Dosi, Giovanni, Christopher Freeman, Richard Nelson, Gerald Silverberg, and Luc Soete, eds. 1990. *Technical Change and Economic Theory.* New York: Columbia University Press.

Drucker, Peter. 1989. *The New Realities.* New York: Harper and Row.

Dunning, John. 1989. "Governments, Economic Organization and International Competitiveness." *University of Reading Discussion Papers in International Investment and Business Studies* 130. Reading: University of Reading (March).

Dunning, John. 1990a. *The Globalization of Firms and the Competitiveness of Countries: Some Implications for the Theory of International Production.* Lund, Sweden: Institute of Economic Research, Lund University.

Dunning, John H. 1990b. "Multinational Enterprises and the Globalization of Innovatory Activities." In *International Investment and Business Studies* B, III, 143. Reading, United Kingdom: Department of Economics, University of Reading.

Dunning, John. 1991. "Dunning on Porter: Reshaping the Diamond of Competitive Advantage." *University of Reading Discussion Papers in International Investment and Business Studies* 152. Reading: University of Reading.

Dunning, John, and E. V. Morgan. 1971. *An Economic Study of the City of London.* London: Allen and Unwin.

Encarnation, Dennis. 1990. "Investment and Trade." Cambridge, MA: Harvard Business School (mimeographed).

Ernst, Dieter, and David O'Connor. 1992. *Competing in the Electronics Industry—The Experience of Newly Industrializing Economies.* London: Pinter.

Executive Office of the President, Office of Science and Technology Policy. 1990. *US Technology Policy.* Washington: Government Printing Office (26 September).

Fallows, James. 1989. "Containing Japan." *The Atlantic* 263, no. 5 (May): 40–54

Fazzari, Steven, R. Glen Hubbard, and Bruce Petersen. 1988. "Investment and Finance Reconsidered." *Brookings Papers on Economic Activity* 1:141–96.

Ferguson, Charles. 1988. "From the People Who Brought You Voodoo Economics." *Harvard Business Review* 3 (May-June): 55–62.

Ferguson, Charles. 1989. "DRAMs, Component Suppliers, and the World Electronics Industry: An International Strategic Analysis." VLSI *Memo* 89-554. Cambridge: Massachusetts Institute of Technology (August).

Finan, William, and Chris Anderson. 1991. "The Effects of Exchange Rates on Semiconductor Market Share." Washington: Semiconductor Industry Association (January).

Flamm, Kenneth. 1988. *Creating the Computer: Government Industry and High Technology.* Washington: Brookings Institution.

Flamm, Kenneth. 1989. "Policy and Politics in the International Semiconductor Industry." Paper presented at the SEMI Twelfth Annual Information Services Seminar, Newport Beach, CA (16–18 January).

Flamm, Kenneth. 1990. "Semiconductors." In Gary Clyde Hufbauer, ed., *Europe 1992: An American Perspective*, 225–92. Washington: Brookings Institution.

Flamm, Kenneth. 1991. "Forward Pricing vs. Fair Value: An Analytical Assessment of 'Dumping' in DRAMS." Washington: Brookings Institution (September, mimeographed).

Flamm, Kenneth. 1992. "Measurement of DRAM Prices: Technology and Market Structure." In M. F. Foss, M. Mancer, and A. Young, eds., *Price Measurements and Their Uses.* Chicago: National Bureau of Economic Research and University of Chicago (forthcoming).

Florida, Richard, and David Browdy. 1991. "The Invention That Got Away." *Technology Review* 94, no. 6 (August-September): 43–44.

Foote, Susan Bartlett, and Will Mitchell. 1989. "Selling American Medical Equipment in Japan." *California Management Review* 31, no. 4 (Summer): 146–61.

Frankel, Jeffrey A. 1990. "The SII Outcome: In Whose Best Interest?" *The International Economy* 4, no. 5 (October-November): 70–72.

Frankel, Jeffrey. 1991. "Japanese Finance in the 1980s: A Survey." In Paul Krugman, ed., *Trade with Japan: Has the Door Opened Wider?* 225–68. Chicago: University of Chicago Press.

Fung, K. C. 1991. "Characteristics of Japanese Industrial Groups and Their Potential Impact on U.S.–Japan Trade." Stanford, CA: Stanford University Economics Department.

Garten, Jeffrey. 1992. *A Cold Peace: America, Japan, Germany and the Struggle for Supremacy.* New York: Times Books.

General Agreement on Tariffs and Trade. 1990. *Trade Policy Review Mechanism: Japan 1990.* Geneva: GATT (November).

General Agreement on Tariffs and Trade. 1991. *Trade Policy Review Mechanism: European Communities.* Geneva: GATT (18 March).

Gore, Charles. 1984. *Regions in Question: Space, Development Theory, and Regional Policy.* London and New York: Methuen.

Graham, Edward M., and Paul R. Krugman. 1991. *Foreign Direct Investment in the United States*, 2nd ed. Washington: Institute for International Economics.

Griliches, Zvi. 1990. "The Search for R&D Spillovers." Cambridge, MA: Harvard University (mimeographed).

Grossman, Gene M. 1990. "Promoting New Industrial Activities: A Survey of Recent Arguments and Evidence." OECD *Economic Studies* 14 (Spring): 87–125.

Grossman, Gene, and Elhanan Helpman. 1991. *Innovations and Growth in the Global Economy.* Cambridge, MA: MIT Press.

Guerrieri, Paolo. 1991. "Technology and International Trade Performance of the Most Advanced Countries." BRIE *Working Papers* 49. Berkeley: University of California, Berkeley.

Guerrieri, Paolo, and Carlo Milana. 1991. "Technological and Trade Competition in High-Tech Products." BRIE *Working Papers* 54. Berkeley: University of California, Berkeley.

Hall, Bronwyn. 1990. "The Impact of Corporate Restructuring on Industrial Research and Development." *Brookings Papers on Economic Activity: Microeconomics*, 85-124. Washington: Brookings Institution.

Hall, Bronwyn. 1991. "Corporate Restructuring and Investment Horizons." NBER *Working Papers* 3794 (July). Cambridge, MA: National Bureau of Economic Research.

Hart, Jeffrey. 1992. "The Antidumping Petition of the Advanced Display Manufacturers of America: Origins and Consequences." Bloomington: Indiana Center for Global Business, Indiana University (mimeographed).

Hart, Jeffrey, and Laura D'Andrea Tyson. 1989. "Responding to the Challenge of HDTV." *California Management Review* 31, no. 4 (Summer): 132–45.

Hazard, Heather A., and Herman P. Daems. 1992. "Technical Standards and Competitive Advantage in World Trade: The Case of Television." In David Yoffie, ed., *World Trade and Global Competition*. Cambridge, MA: Harvard Business School Press.

Helpman, Elhanan, and Paul R. Krugman. 1985. *Market Structure and Foreign Trade: Increasing Returns, Imperfect Competition, and the International Economy*. Cambridge, MA: MIT Press.

Henderson, Yolanda K. 1989. "Capital Gains Taxation and the Cost of Capital for Mature and Emerging Corporations." Paper prepared for the American Council for Capital Formation Conference on Saving, (11/13 October).

Heyward, Keith. 1989. *The British Aircraft Industry*. New York: St. Martin's Press.

Hindley, Brian. 1988. "Dumping and the Far East Trade of the European Community." *The World Economy* 2, no. 4 (December): 445–63.

Hirschman, Albert O. 1958. *The Strategy of Economic Development*. New Haven: Yale University Press.

Horlick, Gary. 1989. "The United States Anti-Dumping System." In John H. Jackson and Edwin A. Vermulst, eds., *Antidumping Law and Practice: A Comparative Study*. Ann Arbor: University of Michigan Press.

Hoshi, Takeo, Anil Kashyap, and David Sharfstein. 1988. "Corporate Structure, Liquidity, and Investment: Evidence from Japanese Panel Data." *Quarterly Journal of Economics* 106, no. 1 (February): 33–60.

Howell, Thomas R., William A. Noellert, Janet H. MacLaughlin, and Alan W. Wolff. 1988. *The Microelectronics Race: The Impact of Government Policy on International Competition*. Boulder, CO: Westview Press.

Howell, Thomas R., Brent L. Bartlett, and Warren Davis. 1992. *Creating Advantage: Semiconductors and Government Industrial Policy in the 1990s*. Santa Clara: Semiconductor Industry Association.

Hudec, Robert E. 1990. "Dispute Settlement." In Jeffrey J. Schott, ed., *Completing the Uruguay Round: A Results-Oriented Approach to the GATT Trade Negotiations*, 180–204. Washington: Institute for International Economics.

Hufbauer, Gary Clyde. 1990. "Subsidies." In Jeffrey J. Schott, ed., *Completing the Uruguay Round: A Results-Oriented Approach to the GATT Trade Negotiations*, 93–107. Washington: Institute for International Economics.

Hufbauer, Gary Clyde. 1992. *U.S. Taxation of International Income: Blueprint for Reform*. Washington: Institute for International Economics.

Hufbauer, Gary Clyde, and Howard F. Rosen. 1986. *Trade Policy for Troubled Industries*. POLICY ANALYSES IN INTERNATIONAL ECONOMICS 15. Washington: Institute for International Economics.

Hufbauer, Gary Clyde, and Jeffrey J. Schott. 1992. *North American Free Trade: Issues and Recommendations*

Hufbauer, Gary Clyde, Diane T. Berliner, and Kimberly Ann Elliott. 1986. *Trade Protection in the United States: 31 Case Studies*. Washington: Institute for International Economics.

Industrial Bank of Japan. 1989. "EC 1992 and Japanese Corporations." *Industrial Research* 8 Tokyo: Industrial Bank of Japan (July).

Institute of Electrical and Electronics Engineers. 1988. *US Supercomputer Vulnerability, Report of the Scientific Supercomputer Subcommittee of the Committee on Communication and Information Policy.* Washington: Institute of Electrical and Electronics Engineers (8 August).

Jackson, John H. 1989. *The World Trading System.* Cambridge, MA: MIT Press.

Japan Electronics Almanac. 1989. Tokyo: DEMPA Publications.

Japan Electronics Almanac. 1990. Tokyo: DEMPA Publications.

Johnson, Chalmers. 1982. *MITI and the Japanese Economic Miracle: The Growth of Industrial Policy, 1925–1975.* Stanford, CA: Stanford University Press.

Johnson, Chalmers. 1990. "MITI, MPT, and the Telecom Wars: How Japan Makes Policy for High Technology." In Chalmers Johnson, Laura D'Andrea Tyson, and John Zysman, eds., *Politics and Productivity: How Japan's Development Strategy Works,* 177–240. New York: Harper Business.

Johnson, Chalmers, Laura D'Andrea Tyson, and John Zysman, eds. 1990. *Politics and Productivity: How Japan's Development Strategy Works.* New York: Harper Business.

Jorgensen, Dale. 1971. "Econometric Studies of Investment Behavior: A Review." *Journal of Economic Literature* 9, no. 4 (December): 1111–47.

Julius, D., and S. Thomsen. 1988. "Foreign-Owned Firms, Trade, and Economic Integration." *Tokyo Club Papers* 2. London: Royal Institute for International Affairs.

Kaldor, Nicholas. 1970. "The Case for Regional Policies." *Scottish Journal of Political Economy* 27, no. 3 (November): 337–48.

Kaldor, Nicholas. 1975. "Economic Growth and Verdoorn's Law." *Economic Journal* 85, no. 340 (December): 891–96.

Katz, Lawrence F., and Lawrence H. Summers. 1989. "Industry Rents: Evidence and Implications." *Brookings Papers on Economic Activity: Microeconomics,* 209–75.

Klepper, G. 1990. "Entry into the Market for Large Transport Aircraft." *European Economic Review* 34, no. 4: 775–803.

Kohn, Martin J. 1989. "Structural Impediments Initiative, The Joint DOC/MITI Price Survey: Methodology and Results." Washington: Department of Commerce, International Trade Administration (December).

Krishna, Kala. 1989. "Trade Restrictions as Facilitating Practices." *Journal of International Economics* 26, no. 3-4 (May): 251–70.

Krueger, Anne O. 1990. "Theory and Practice of Commercial Policy: 1945–1990." NBER *Working Papers* 3569. Cambridge, MA: National Bureau of Economic Research (December).

Krugman, Paul R., ed. 1986. *Strategic Trade Policy and the New International Economics.* Cambridge, MA: MIT Press.

Krugman, Paul R. 1987a. "Is Free Trade Passé?" *Journal of Economic Perspectives* 1, no. 2 (Fall): 131–44.

Krugman, Paul R. 1987b. "Strategic Sectors and International Competition." In Robert M. Stern, ed., *US Trade Policies in a Changing World Economy,* 207–32. Cambridge, MA: MIT Press.

Krugman, Paul R. 1988. "Multistage International Competition." In A. Michael Spence and Heather A. Hazard, *International Competitiveness,* 289–300. Cambridge, MA: Ballinger.

Krugman, Paul R. 1990. *The Age of Diminished Expectations: U.S. Economic Policy in the 1990s.* Cambridge, MA: MIT Press.

Krugman, Paul R. 1991a. *Has the Adjustment Process Worked?* POLICY ANALYSES IN INTERNATIONAL ECONOMICS 34. Washington: Institute for International Economics (October).

Krugman, Paul R. 1991b. "Technology and International Competition: Overview." Paper prepared for a National Academy of Engineering symposium on "Linking Trade and

Technology Policies: An International Comparison," National Academy of Sciences, Washington (10–11 June).

Krugman, Paul. 1991c. *Geography and Trade*. Cambridge, MA: MIT Press.

Kuttner, Robert. 1992. "The Slow Growth Trap and the Public Investment Cure." Washington: Economic Policy Institute (September, mimeographed).

Lawrence, Robert Z. 1987. "Imports in Japan: Closed Markets or Minds?" *Brookings Papers on Economic Activity* 2: 517–48.

Lawrence, Robert Z. 1991. "Efficient or Exclusionist? The Import Behavior of Japanese Corporate Groups." *Brookings Papers on Economic Activity* 1:311–30.

Lawrence, Robert Z., and Charles L. Schultze. 1990. "Evaluating the Options." In Robert Z. Lawrence and Charles L. Schultze, eds., *An American Trade Strategy: Options for the 1990s*, 1–41. Washington: Brookings Institution.

Lincoln, Edward J. 1990. *Japan's Unequal Trade*. Washington: Brookings Institution.

Litan, Robert, Robert Z. Lawrence, and Charles L. Schultze. 1990. *American Living Standards*. Washington: Brookings Institution.

Lundvall, B. 1988. "Innovation as an Interactive Process: User-Producer Relations." In Giovanni Dosi et al., *Technical Change and Economic Theory*. London: Frances Pinter.

Malerba, F. 1990. "The Italian System of Innovation." Paper presented at a workshop on the organization of international competitiveness, Brussels (May-June).

Majumdar, Badiul A. 1987. "Upstart or Flying Start? The Rise of Airbus Industrie." *The World Economy* 10, no. 4 (December): 514.

McCauley, Robert, and Steven Zimmer. 1989. "Explaining International Differences in the Cost of Capital." *Quarterly Review of the Federal Reserve Bank of New York* 14, no. 2 (Summer): 7–28.

McDonald, John. 1953. "Jet Airliners: Year of Decision." *Fortune* (April): 125, 248.

Messerlin, Patrick. 1990. "Antidumping." In Jeffrey J. Schott, ed., *Completing the Uruguay Round: A Results-Oriented Approach to the Multilateral Trade Negotiations*, 108–29. Washington: Institute for International Economics.

Micossi, Stefano, and Gianfranco Viesti. 1990. "Japanese Direct Manufacturing Investment in Europe." Paper prepared for the Center for Economic Policy Research Conference on "The Impact of 1992 on European Trade and Industry," London (July).

Milgrom, Paul. 1987. "Predatory Pricing." In J. Eatwell, M. Milgate, and P. Newman, eds., *The New Palgrave: A Dictionary for Economics*, vol. 3, 937–38. London: Macmillan.

Milgrom, Paul, and J. Roberts. 1982. "Limit Pricing Under Incomplete Information." *Econometrica* 50, no. 2 (March): 443–59.

Milner, Henry, and David B. Yoffie. 1989. "Between Free Trade and Protectionism: Strategic Trade Policy and a Theory of Corporate Trade Demands." *International Organization* 43, no. 2 (Spring): 239–72.

MIT Commission on Industrial Productivity. 1989. "The Decline of US Consumer Electronics Manufacturing: History, Hypotheses, and Remedies." In *The Working Papers of the MIT Commission on Industrial Productivity*, vol. 1. Cambridge, MA: MIT Press, 1989.

Moran, Theodore H. 1990. "The Globalization of America's Defense Industries: Managing the Threat of Foreign Dependence." *International Security* 15 (Summer): 57–100.

Moran, Theodore H. 1992. "American Economic Policy and American National Security: Toward Guidelines for National Strategies in the New Era." Paper prepared for the Task Force on Global Security, Council on Foreign Relations (April).

Moran, Theodore H., and David C. Mowery. 1991. "Aerospace and National Security in an Era of Globalization." *CCC Working Papers* 91-2. Berkeley: Center for Research and Management, University of California, Berkeley.

Moritani, Kozuo. 1989. "Impact of the EC Verification on Japan's Automobile and Electronics Industries." *JDB Research Reports* 16. Tokyo: Economic and Industrial Research Department, Japan Development Bank (August).

Mowery, David C. 1987. *Alliance Politics and Economics: Multinational Joint Ventures in Commercial Aircraft.* Cambridge, MA: Ballinger.

Mowery, D. C. 1990. "New Developments in US Technology and Trade Policies: Declining Hegemon, Wounded Giant, or Ambivalent Gulliver?" *Working Papers* 90-1. Berkeley: Consortium on Competitiveness and Cooperation, Center for Research in Management, University of California (April).

Mowery, David C. 1991. "International Collaboration in the Commercial Aircraft Industry: Assessing the Taiwan Aerospace–McDonnel Douglas Agreement." Testimony presented to the Joint Economic Committee, Washington (3 December).

Mowery, David, and Nathan Rosenberg. 1982. "The Commercial Aircraft Industry." In Richard Nelson, ed., *Government and Technical Progress: A Cross-Industry Analysis*, 101–61. New York: Pergamon Press.

Mowery, David C., and Nathan Rosenberg. 1989a. *Technology and the Pursuit of Economic Growth.* Cambridge and New York: Cambridge University Press.

Mowery, David C., and Nathan Rosenberg. 1989b. "New Developments in US Technology Policy: Implications of Competitiveness and International Trade Policy." *California Management Review* 32, no. 1 (Fall): 107–24.

Mowery, David C., and Nathan Rosenberg. 1990. "The U.S. National Innovation System." *CCC Working Papers* 90-3. Berkeley: University of California, Berkeley (September).

Myrdal, Gunnar. 1957. *Economic Theory and Underdeveloped Regions.* London: Gerald Duckworth.

National Advisory Committee on Semiconductors. 1989. *A Strategic Industry at Risk: A Report to the President and the Congress.* Washington: National Advisory Committee on Semiconductors (November).

National Advisory Committee on Semiconductors. 1990a. *Electronics Capital Corporation: A Report of the National Advisory Committee on Semiconductors.* Washington: National Advisory Committee on Semiconductors (July).

National Advisory Committee on Semiconductors. 1990b. *Preserving the Vital Base: America's Semiconductor Materials and Equipment Industry. A Report of the National Advisory Committee on Semiconductors.* Washington: National Advisory Committee on Semiconductors (July).

National Advisory Committee on Semiconductors. 1991. *Toward a National Semiconductor Strategy: Regaining Markets in High-Volume Electronics. Second Annual Report of the National Advisory Committee.* Washington: National Advisory Committee on Semiconductors (February).

National Research Council, Committee on Japan. 1990. "Science, Technology, and the Future of the US-Japan Relationship." *Working Papers.* Washington: National Research Council (March).

Nelson, Richard. 1990. "U.S. Technological Leadership: Where Did It Come From and Where Did it Go?" *Research Policy* 19:117–32.

Newhouse, John. 1982. *The Sporty Game.* New York: Knopf.

Noland, Marcus. 1991. "SII at Nine Months: Notes on the Structural Impediments Initiative." Paper presented at the US–Japan Core Group Meeting of the Institute for International Economics, Tokyo (April).

Nomura Management School. 1986. *Note on the VTR Industry.* Tokyo: Nomura Management School.

Nomura Management School. 1987. *Note on the VTR Industry,* rev. ed. Tokyo: Nomura Management School.

Office of Technology Assessment. 1991a. *Competing Economies: America, Europe, and the Pacific Rim.* Washington: Government Printing Office (October).

Office of Technology Assessment. 1991b. *Government Support of the Large Commercial Aircraft Industries of Japan, Europe, and the United States,* vol. II. Washington: Office of Technology Assessment (22 May).

Office of the US Trade Representative. 1990. *Procedures to Introduce Supercomputers*. Washington: Government Printing Office (15 June).

Okimoto, Daniel I. 1989. *Between MITI and the Market: Japanese Industrial Policy for High Technology*. Stanford, CA: Stanford University Press.

Organization for Economic Cooperation and Development. 1990a. *Technology and Globalization* (OECD-TEP Report). Paris: Organization for Economic Cooperation and Development.

Organization for Economic Cooperation and Development. 1990b. *Industrial Policy in OECD Countries: Annual Review*. Paris: Organization for Economic Cooperation and Development.

Ostry, Sylvia. 1990a. *Governments and Corporations in a Shrinking World*. New York: Council on Foreign Relations.

Ostry, Sylvia. 1990b. "Beyond the Border: The New International Policy Arena." Paper prepared for the OECD Forum for the Future. Paris: Organization for Economic Cooperation and Development (30 October).

Petri, Peter A. 1991. "Market Structure, Comparative Advantage, and Japanese Trade Under the Strong Yen." In Paul R. Krugman, ed., *Trade with Japan: Has the Door Opened Wider?*. Chicago: University of Chicago Press for the National Bureau of Economics Research.

Philips, Almarin. 1971. *Technology and Market Structure: A Study of the Aircraft Industry*. Lexington, MA: Heath Lexington Books.

Piper, W. Stephen. 1980. "Unique Sectoral Agreement Establishes Free Trade Framework." *Journal of World Trade Law* 12, no. 1 (January): 221–53.

Porter, Michael. 1990. *The Competitive Advantage of Nations*. New York: Free Press.

Porter, Michael. 1992. *Capital Choices: Changing the Way America Invests in Industry: A Research Report Presented to the Council on Competitiveness and Co-Sponsored by the Harvard Business School*. Cambridge, MA: Harvard Business School.

Prestowitz, Clyde V., Jr. 1988. *Trading Places: How We Are Giving Our Future to Japan and How to Reclaim It*. New York: Basic Books.

Prestowitz, Clyde V., Jr. 1991. "More Trade IS Better Trade: Life After GATT." *Technology Review* 94 (April): 22–29.

Rae, John B. 1968. *Climb to Greatness: The American Aircraft Industry, 1920–1960*. Cambridge, MA: MIT Press.

Ramseyer, J. Mark. 1984–85. "The Costs of the Consensual Myth: Antitrust Enforcement and Institutional Barriers to Litigation in Japan." *Yale Law Journal* 94:604–45.

Richardson, J. David. 1989. "Empirical Research on Trade Liberalization Under Imperfect Competition: A Survey." *OECD Economic Studies* 12 (Spring): 7–51.

Richardson, J. David. 1990. "The Political Economy of Strategic Trade Policy." *International Organization* 44 (Winter): 107–35.

Richardson, J. David. 1992. "New Trade Theory and Policy a Decade Old: Assessment in a Pacific Context." Paper presented at the First Australian Fulbright Symposium on "Managing International Relations in the 1980s," Canberra (March).

Romer, P. M. 1986. "Increasing Returns and Long-Run Growth." *Journal of Political Economy* 94, no. 5 (October): 1002–37.

Rosenbloom, Richard S., and Michael Cusamano. 1987. "Technological Pioneering and Competitive Advantage: The Birth of the VCR Industry." *California Management Review* 29, no. 4 (Summer) 51–76.

Sabel, Charles. 1989. "Flexible Specialization and the Reemergence of Regional Economies." In P. Hirst and J. Zeitlin, eds., *Reversing Industrial Decline?* 17–70. Oxford, England: Berg.

Salvatore, Dominick. 1990. *The Japanese Trade Challenge and the U.S. Response: Addressing the Structural Causes of the Bilateral Trade Imbalance*. Washington: Economic Policy Institute.

Samuel, Patrick. 1990. "High-Definition Television: A Major Stake for Europe." In John F. Rice, ed., HDTV: The Politics, Policies, and Economics of Tomorrow's Television. New York: Union Square Press.

Sandholtz, Wayne, Michael Borrus, and John Zysman, eds. 1992. The Highest Stakes: The Economic Foundations of the Next Security System. London and New York: Oxford University Press.

Sanekata, Kenji. 1986. "Antitrust in Japan: Recent Trends and Their Socio-political Background." University of British Columbia Law Review 20, no. 2:379–99.

Scott, Allen J. 1988. Metropolis. Berkeley: University of California Press.

Scott, Allen J., and D. P. Angel. 1987. "The US Semiconductor Industry: A Locational Analysis." Environment and Planning 19, no. 7 (July): 875–912.

Scott, Allen J., and Michael Storper. 1987. "High-Technology Industry and Regional Development: A Theoretical Critique and Reconstruction." International Social Science Journal 39, no. 2: (May): 215–32.

Semiconductor Industry Association. 1990a. "Anti-dumping Law Reform and the Semiconductor Industry: A Discussion of the Issues." Washington: Semiconductor Industry Association (February).

Semiconductor Industry Association. 1990b. A Deal is a Deal: Four Years of Experience Under the US-Japan Semiconductor Agreement. Fourth Annual Report to the President. Washington: Semiconductor Industry Association (November).

Semiconductor Industry Association. 1991. Background Information on the US-Japan Semiconductor Trade Agreement. Washington: Semiconductor Industry Association (August).

Sharp, Margaret. 1991. "The Single Market and European Policies for Advanced Technologies." In Christopher Freeman, Margaret Sharp, and William Walker, eds., Technology and the Future of Europe: Competition and the Global Environment in the 1990s. London: Pintner.

Spar, Deborah, and Ray Vernon. 1989. Beyond Globalism: Remaking American Foreign Economic Policy. New York: Free Press.

Spar, Deborah, and Ray Vernon. 1991. Iron Triangles and Revolving Doors: Cases in U.S. Foreign Economic Policy Making. New York: Praeger.

Spencer, Barbara J. 1988. "Countervailing Duty Laws and Subsidies to Imperfectly Competitive Industries." In Robert E. Baldwin, Carl B. Hamilton, and Andre Sapir, eds., Issues in US–EC Trade Relations, 313–35. Chicago: University of Chicago Press.

Spencer, Linda H. 1991. Foreign Investment in the United States: Unencumbered Access. Washington: Economic Strategy Institute.

Spencer, Linda H. 1992. "High Technology Acquisitions: Summary Charts, October 1988–April 1992." Washington: Economic Strategy Institute.

Steinmueller, W. Edward. 1986. "Industry Structure and Government Policies in the US and Japanese Integrated Circuit Industries." Publication no. 105. Stanford, CA: Center for Economic Policy Research, Stanford University (December).

Steinmueller, W. Edward. 1987. "International Joint Ventures in the Integrated Circuit Industry." Publicaation no. 104. Stanford, CA: Center for Economic Policy Research, Stanford University (September).

Storper, Michael, and Richard Walker. 1989. The Capitalist Imperative: Territory, Technology, and Industrial Growth. Oxford, England: Basil Blackwell.

Stowsky, Jay. 1986. "Beating Our Plowshares into Double-Edged Swords: The Impact of Pentagon Policies on the Commercialization of Advanced Technologies." BRIE Working Papers 17. Berkeley: Univesity of California, Berkeley.

Stowsky, Jay. 1987. "The Weakest Link: Semiconductor Production Equipment, Linkages, and the Limits to International Trade." BRIE Working Papers 27. Berkeley: University of California, Berkeley.

Stowsky, Jay. 1989. "Regional Histories and the Cycle of Industrial Innovation: A Review of Some Recent Literature." Berkeley Planning Journal 4: 114–24.

Stowsky, Jay. 1990. "Trapping the Benefits of Technological Innovation: The Development Impacts of Industrial Organization in the Military and the Marketplace." Unpublished doctoral dissertation, Department of City and Regional Planning, University of California, Berkeley (August).

Stowsky, Jay, and Burgess Laird. 1992. "Conversion to Competitiveness: Making the Most of the National Labs." *The American Prospect* (Fall): 91–98.

Technecon Analytic Research. 1991. "The Impact of the 1986 US–Japan Semiconductor Agreement on DRAM Prices." Washington: Semiconductor Industry Association (January).

Thomson, Stephen, and Phedon Nicolaides. 1992. *The Evolution of Japanese Direct Investment in Europe: Death of a Transistor Salesman.* London: Royal Institute of International Affairs.

Thurow, Lester. 1990. "1992: The End of the Line for the Current World Economy." In D. Lessard and C. Antonelli, eds. *Managing the Globalization of Business.* Milan: Scientifica.

Thurow, Lester. 1992. *Head to Head: The Coming Economic Battle Among Japan, Europe, and America.* New York: Morrow.

Tirole, Jean. 1988. *The Theory of Industrial Organization.* Cambridge: MIT Press.

Todd, Daniel, and Jamie Simpson. 1986. *The World Aircraft Industry.* Dover, MA: Auburn House.

Tyson, Laura. 1988. "Competitiveness: An Analysis of the Problem and a Perspective on Future Policy." In Martin K. Starr, ed., *Global Competitiveness, Getting the U.S. Back on Track,* 95–120. New York: Norton.

Tyson, Laura D'Andrea. 1990. "Managed Trade: Making the Best of the Second Best." In Robert Z. Lawrence and Charles L. Schultze, eds., *An American Trade Strategy: Options for the 1990s,* 142–85. Washington: Brookings Institution.

Tyson, Laura D'Andrea. 1991. "They Are Not US: Why American Ownership Still Matters." *The American Prospect* 4 (Winter): 37–48.

Tyson, Laura D'Andrea, and John Zysman, eds. 1983. *American Industry in International Competition.* Ithaca, NY: Cornell University Press.

Tyson, Laura D'Andrea, and John Zysman. 1988. "Trade and Employment: An Overview of the Issues and Evidence." In William T. Dickens, Laura D'Andrea Tyson, and John Zysman, eds., *The Dynamics of Trade and Employment,* 1–40. Cambridge, MA: Ballinger Press.

Tyson, Laura D'Andrea, and John Zysman. 1990. "Developmental Strategy and Production Innovation in Japan." In Chalmers Johnson, Laura D'Andrea Tyson, and John Zysman, eds., *Politics and Productivity: How Japan's Development Strategy Works,* 59–140. New York: Harper Business.

US Congress. Joint Economic Committee. 1992. "McDonnell Douglas–Taiwan Aerospace Deal," hearings, 102nd Cong., 2nd sess. (27 February).

US Department of Commerce, Bureau of Export Administration, Office of Industrial Resource Administration. 1991. *National Security and the State of the US Industrial Base.* Washington: US Department of Commerce (May).

US Department of Commerce, International Trade Administration. 1990. "Joint Report of the U.S.–Japan Working Group on the Structural Impediments Initiative." Washington: US Department of Commerce (18 June).

US General Accounting Office, National Security and International Affairs Division. 1988a. "U.S.–Japan Trade: Trade Data and Industry Views on MOSS Agreements; Fact Sheet for the Honorable Lloyd M. Bentsen, U.S. Senate" (GAO/NSIAD-88-120FS, February). Washington: US General Accounting Office.

US General Accounting Office, National Security and International Affairs Division. 1988b. "U.S.–Japan Trade: Evaluation of the Market-Oriented Sector-Selective Talks; Fact Sheet for the Honorable Lloyd M. Bentsen, U.S. Senate" (GAO/NSIAD-88-205, July). Washington: US General Accounting Office.

US General Accounting Office, National Security and International Affairs Division. 1991. *U.S. Business Access to Certain Foreign State-of-the-Art Technology*. Washington: US General Accounting Office (September).

US International Trade Commission. 1991. *Global Competitiveness of U.S. Advanced Technology Manufacturing Industries: Semiconductors Equipment and Manufactures. Report to the Committee on Finance, United States Senate*. USITC Publication 2434. Washington: US International Trade Commission (September).

van Wolferen, Karel. 1989. *The Enigma of Japanese Power*. London: Macmillan.

Vernon, John M., and Daniel A. Graham. 1971. "Profitability of Monopolization by Vertical Integration." *Journal of Political Economy* 79, no. 4 (July-August): 924–25.

Vietor, Richard, and David Yoffie. 1991. "International Trade and Competition in Global Telecommunications." Cambridge, MA: Harvard Business School (November, mimeographed).

Vogel, David. 1992. "Consumer Protection and Protectionism in Japan." *Journal of Japanese Studies* 18, no. 1 (Winter): 423–44.

von Hippel, Eric. 1988. *The Sources of Innovation*. New York: Oxford University Press.

Winter, Sidney. 1987. "Knowledge and Competence as Strategic Assets." In David Teece, ed., *The Competitive Challenge*, 159–84. Cambridge, MA: Ballinger.

Yager, Loren. 1991. "Price Comparisons Between the Japanese and U.S. Markets." Note #N-3337-CUSJR. Santa Monica, CA: RAND Corporation.

Yamamura, Kozo. 1986. "Caveat Emptor: The Industrial Policy of Japan." In Paul R. Krugman, ed., *Strategic Trade Policy and the New International Economics*, 169–209. Cambridge, MA: MIT Press.

Yamamura, Kozo, and Jan Vandenberg. 1986. "Japan's Rapid Growth Policy on Trial: The Television Case." In Gary Saxonhouse and Kozo Yamamura, eds., *Law and Trade Issues of the Japanese Economy*. Seattle: University of Washington.

Yoffie, David B. 1985. *International Trade and Competition: Cases and Notes in Strategy and Management*. New York: McGraw-Hill.

Yoffie, David B. 1986a. "Protectionism in Video-Tape Recorders: The Second Battle of Poitiers." Cambridge, MA: Harvard Business School (mimeographed).

Yoffie, David B. 1986b. "Protecting World Markets." In Thomas K. McGraw, ed., *America Versus Japan*, 35–75. Cambridge, MA: Harvard Business School Press.

Yoffie, David B. 1988. "Creating Political Advantage." *Harvard Business Review* 3 (May-June): 55–62.

Yoffie, David B., ed. 1990. *International Trade and Competition: Cases and Notes in Strategy and Management*. New York: McGraw-Hill.

Yoffie, David B. 1991a. "Global Semiconductor Industry 1987." *Harvard Business School Cases* 9-388-052, rev. ed. Cambridge, MA: Harvard Business School (October).

Yoffie, David B. 1991b. "Technology Challenges to Trade Policy." Paper presented at the National Academy of Engineering Symposium on "Linking Trade and Technology Policies: An International Comparison," Washington (10–11 June).

Young, Allyn. 1928. "Increasing Returns and Economic Progress." *Economic Journal* 38 (December): 527–42.

Index

ACE consortium 151

Acquisitions, foreign. *See* Foreign direct investment

Active-matrix display technology 143, 250

Adjustment costs 10, 295

Advanced Display Manufacturers of America 141, 143

Advanced displays. *See* Liquid crystal displays

Advanced Micro Devices (AMD) 107, 108, 117, 121, 125, 140, 277

AEG-Telefunken 222, 242

Aérospatiale 155, 160

Aggressive unilateralism 13, 16, 74, 109, 204, 255–61

Agriculture 259

Air carrier industry 156, 163, 165–69, 171, 175, 183, 215. *See also specific airlines*

Air France 175

Air India 203

Airbus Industrie
  Air India deal 203
  A300 model 173, 175, 180–81, 188–89, 193, 197, 202–03, 205
  A310 model 173, 180–81
  A320 model 168, 180–81, 189–90, 202–03, 205, 211
  A330 model 173, 190–91
  A340 model 167, 173, 190–91
  A350 model 156, 210, 211
  commonality of components 164
  consortium members 155
  CVD relief against 282
  Eastern Airlines deal 196–98
  exchange rate guarantees 205–07, 281
  exploitation of market gap 188
  government support for 8–9, 155, 157, 172–76, 192–95, 201–02, 205–10, 215, 254, 278, 282
  launch aid 174
  military sales 160
  production data 158, 159
  proposed joint venture with McDonnell Douglas 191
  technological innovations 189–90
  United Airlines deal 211

Aircraft industry, civil. *See also specific companies*
  alliances and joint ventures 168–69, 189, 191, 192, 195–96
  economics of 161–76
  FDI in 195
  first-mover advantages 168
  GATT agreement on trade in 195–202, 207, 256, 267, 281, 282
  globalization 212
  history 176–92
  impact of defense contracting 157, 169–71, 187, 188
  impact of regulation 188
  industrial organization 168–69
  industrial policy in 157–61, 169–76, 188–89, 192–95, 211–16
  market shares 156

Aircraft industry, civil *(continued)*
  output and trade statistics 158, 159,
    178–81, 196–99
  policy recommendations 160–61,
    214–16
  R&D expenditure 32, 162, 170–71
  relationship with air carrier industry
    166–67, 175–76
  revealed comparative advantage 25
  riskiness 162, 163, 165, 166–68
  role in US trade 26
  scale and scope economies 166
  strategic importance 157–61
  subsidies 172, 193–95
  tendency toward natural monopoly
    156, 161–62, 166, 184
  US–EC 1992 agreement 207–210, 213,
    256, 296
Airlines. *See* Air carrier industry; *specific
    airline*
Alliances and joint ventures. *See also
    specific venture*
  Airbus–McDonnell Douglas 191
  AMD–Fujitsu 125
  European–Japanese 228
  IBM–Siemens 150, 153, 294
  in aircraft industry 168–69, 189, 191,
    192, 195–96
  in cellular telephones 68
  in HDTV 239, 242–43
  in semiconductors 95, 112–13, 125,
    275–76, 294
  in VCRs 222, 228, 231
  Japanese policy toward 93
  JVC–Thomson 222
  Motorola-Toshiba 112, 126
  spillover benefits from 40
  Thomson-Philips 239
  US–Japanese 276
  US policy toward 12
  See also Foreign direct investment
AMD 107, 108, 117, 121, 125, 140, 277
Amdahl 80
American Airlines 182, 183, 185, 186,
    188, 191
American National Standards Institute 7
American Telephone and Telegraph
    Company (AT&T) 67, 70, 90, 98, 105,
    243, 286
Ampex 220
Analog Devices 112
Anchordoguy, Marie 56, 57, 75–77, 79,
    81, 98–100
Anticartel insurance, CVS as 140, 151, 278

Antidumping
  appropriate remedies 272–74
  company-specific margins 273
  compensation of injured parties 274
  countervailing duties 139, 197, 270,
    277, 280–82, 283
  countervailing subsidies 81–82, 139–40,
    285–86
  defining and assessing dumping
    137–38, 267–72
  EC policy 149, 218, 230, 248–49
  fast-track investigations 131, 271
  in GATT 137, 267, 270
  in HDTV 242
  in LCDs 141–42, 287, 288
  in semiconductors 107–10, 131,
    136–43
  in supercomputers 80
  in VCRs 223, 229–33
  policy recommendations 267–74
  procedural delays 271–72
  repeat offenders 271
  SCTA provisions 109–10
Anti-Monopoly Law (Japan) 79, 81, 100
Antiscrewdriver regulations 150, 230,
    248. *See also* Local content policies
Antitrust. *See also* Oligopolistic control
  and joint ventures 151, 152
  enforcement 57, 279
  extension beyond national borders 267
  in Europe 223, 279
  in Japan 57, 81, 84, 100, 120, 122, 276
  in semiconductor industry 81, 90
  in US 90, 279
  preferable to antidumping action 137
  trade policy as substitute for 265, 266
Apple Computer 84, 142, 151
Application-specific integrated circuits
    (ASICs) 110, 113
Ariane 288
Arrow, Kenneth 41
Auction quotas 264
Auto parts 65, 259
Automobile industry 75, 247, 248
Aviation industry. *See* Aircraft industry,
    civil

Bai rule 119
Balassa, Bela 9, 55
Baldwin, Robert 86, 193, 194, 254
Bayard, Thomas O. 258, 259
Beeper-pagers 66–67
Bell Laboratories 88

Bergsten, C. Fred 6, 14, 55, 63, 197, 262, 281, 285
Berkeley Roundtable on the International Economy 1
Bhagwati, Jagdish 5, 28, 30, 53, 73–74, 133, 255, 258, 263–64
Bloch, Erich 28, 290
Blumenthal, W. Michael 197
Boeing
  Air India deal 203
  alliances with foreign firms 189, 192
  defense contracting 160, 169, 170, 182
  early lead in jet technologies 182
  export orientation 26
  impact of McDonnell Douglas–Taiwan Aerospace deal on 213
  influence on policy 290
  position on 1992 US–EC agreement 210
  production data 158, 159
  707 model 178, 179, 182, 183
  720 model 178, 179, 183
  727 model 178, 179, 186
  737 model 178-81, 183, 189
  747 model 163, 167, 172, 180, 181, 185–86
  757 model 172, 175, 180, 181, 189
  767 model 172, 180, 181, 189, 191, 193
  777 model 163, 192
Borman, Frank 197
Borrus, Michael 88, 91, 92, 95, 97, 101, 103, 286
Bosch 239
Brander, James 3
British Aerospace 155, 160
British Airways 189
British Satellite Broadcasting 240
Brittan, Sir Leon 249, 268
Bromley, D. Allan 148, 291, 293
"Bubble" profits 116, 117, 139–41, 273
Bush administration 65, 82, 113, 136
Business groups. See Keiretsu
Buy America Act 184

C-5A transport 170, 185, 187
Camillot, Jean 241
Canada–US Free Trade Agreement 283
Capital, access to 56, 90, 100–01, 142–43, 191, 249, 275–276, 286–88
Caravelle 178, 179
Carnegie Commission on Science, Technology, and Government 290
Carrol, S. L. 170
CASA 155

Cash flow 106
Cautious activism 13–14, 42, 254–55, 274, 275, 295
Cawson, Alan 240
CCIR 238–40
Cecchini Report 246
Cellular telephones
  alliances and joint ventures 68
  in MOSS talks 64
  Motorola case 67–71, 260–61
  US policy toward 259
  use of Section 301 in 256, 258
Central Pharmaceutical Affairs Council (Japan) 61
Choate, Pat 221
Civil Aeronautics Board (CAB) 177
Civil aircraft industry. See Aircraft industry, civil
Clarkson, Larry 213
Classification of high-technology industries 20–21
Cline, William R. 55, 63, 262, 281, 285
CMOS technology 103
Cohen, Linda R. 292
Color television industry 241
Commission of the European Communities 231
Committee on Foreign Investment in the United States 43, 147–49, 212, 278
Committee on Trade in Civil Aircraft 199
"Community producers" 231–33
Compaq Computer 26, 151
Compensation, in high-technology industries 35–39
Competition Commission 249, 251
Competition policy. See Antitrust
Competitiveness, US 1, 2, 254
Competitiveness Policy Council 1, 14, 287, 289, 290
Compliance with trade agreements 65, 66
Computer displays. See Liquid crystal displays
Computer industry, 25, 48, 51–52, 65, 99, 102, 138, 141–42. See also Liquid crystal displays; Software, computer; Supercomputers; specific companies
Concentration, market. See also Oligopolistic control
  FDI and 44, 146
  in aircraft industry 161–62
  in electronics 222, 277
  in Europe 222
  in semiconductor industry 91, 98, 141

Concorde 185
Constant, Edward 177
Consumer electronics 25, 93–95, 99, 217,
    219, 223–24, 237–38, 241–46. *See also*
    Videocassette recorders; *specific
    companies*
Control Data 77, 78, 80, 286
Convair 178, 179, 182, 183
Convenience Radio Phone 68–69
Conversion of military to civilian
    production 295
Cooperative research and development
    agreements (CRADAs) 292
Cost of capital, Japanese advantage in
    100–01
Council on Competitiveness 26, 49–52,
    289
Countervailing duties 139, 197, 270, 277,
    280–82, 283
Countervailing subsidies 139–40, 274,
    285–86
Cray Research 76–82, 132, 254, 259, 262,
    290
"Creeping local content" 8, 43, 235–37,
    251
Critical technologies, lists of 44, 291, 293
Critical Technologies Institute 291
Cross-licensing 90
Cross-shareholding 7, 56, 279
Cross-subsidization 76, 81, 100

Daewoo 231, 232
Daimler-Benz 173, 205, 206
Daini Denden 68–70
David Sarnoff Research Center 243
Davignon, Etienne 245
De Havilland Comet 167, 177, 178, 179,
    182
Defense contracting
    Boeing 160, 169, 170, 182
    impact on aircraft industry 157,
        169–71, 187, 188
    impact on supercomputer industry 82
    impact on semiconductor industry 88
    McDonnell Douglas 160, 170, 211
Defense Advanced Research Projects
    Agency (darpa) 142, 143, 152, 250,
    288, 294
Defense Science Board 146, 149, 275
Delaying tactics, Japanese use of 74
Depreciation, tax treatment of 152
Deregulation, in electronics industry
    245–49

Derian, Jean-Claude 295
Derivatives, in aircraft industry 165
Design-in relationships 113
Destler, I. M. 280
Deutsche Airbus 155, 207
Dickens, William T. 39, 194, 254
Diminished giant syndrome 28, 53
Directorate-General XIII 239, 245, 246, 248
Dispute settlement, in 1992 US–EC
    aircraft agreement 207, 208
Dixit, Avinash 121, 264, 280
Dore, Ronald Phillip 55, 100
Dornbusch, Rudiger 9
Dosi, Giovanni 102
Douglas, Donald 183
Douglas Aircraft Company 182, 183
Dual-use technologies 44, 153, 157, 172,
    276, 277
Dumping. *See* Antidumping
Dunkel, Arthur 270, 281, 283
Dunning, John 4, 43
Dynamic random access memories
    (DRAMs) 99, 101, 103, 136, 138, 139,
    141
    as technology drivers 89
    characteristics 97–98
    dumping of 107, 136–39, 272–74
    exit of US firms from production 101
    Japanese cartelization 117–20, 139–40,
        272–73
    Japanese targeting 97, 101
    market shares 105–06, 125–27
    prices 113–20, 272
    role of Korean firms 123, 126, 127, 265
    targeting by Motorola 112–13, 126

Eastern Airlines 186, 196, 197
Economic geography 41
Economic Strategy Institute 147
Economies of scale and scope 97, 163,
    166, 244
El Al 175
Electronics. *See also specific industries*
    deregulation 245–49
    employment 223
    government procurement 100, 245
    in Europe 26, 217–51, 295
    in NICs 5
    intervention versus liberalization
        245–49
    MOSS talks in 59–60
    R&D in 32, 223
    revealed comparative advantage 19, 25

trade statistics 25, 26, 217, 218
Electronics Industries Association of
    Japan 99, 112, 135
Elliott, Kimberly Ann 258, 259
Employment in high-technology
    industries 18, 31, 35–39, 42–43, 90,
    212, 223
Encarnation, Dennis 55, 93
Enforcement
    of antitrust regulations 57, 81, 120,
        278–79
    of GATT civil aircraft agreement 201,
        282
    of market access rules 74, 267
    of rules governing subsidies 285
Erasable programmable read-only
    memories (EPROMs) 87, 89, 99, 108,
    117, 121–22, 124–25, 136, 138–39
Ernst, Dieter 3, 89, 90, 101, 103, 235, 275
Escape clause, in 1992 US–EC aircraft
    agreement 208, 209
ESPRIT 239, 245, 247
Eureka 239, 240, 243, 245, 250, 288
Europe. See also European Community
    aircraft industry 172–76, 184. See also
        Airbus Industrie
    antitrust in 223
    electronics industry 26, 217–51, 295
    FDI in 7–8, 92, 101–02, 218–20, 236, 251
    fragmentation of markets 102
    impact of unified market 7, 218
    market access in 6–8
    1992 initiative 7, 296
    revealed comparative advantage 19
    semiconductor industry 101–03
    share in global high-technology
        exports 19
    subsidies 8–9
    television industry 221
    VCR industry 219–37
European Association of Consumer
    Electronics Manufacturers 231
European Commission 8, 151
European Community
    agreement with US on aircraft trade
        207–210
    antidumping policy 149, 218, 230,
        248–49
    antitrust policy 223, 279
    HDTV policy 237–44
    industrial policy 219, 288
    procurement policy 7, 101
    promotion of high-technology
        industries 4

semiconductor policy 149–50
    VRA in VCRs 219–24, 229, 255
European Court of Justice 269
European Electronic Components
    Association 151
European Information Technology
    Roundtable 247
European Nervous System 246
Exchange rate guarantees 205–07, 281
Exchange rates 14, 19, 103, 124, 225
Eximbank 175, 198
Exon-Florio amendment 45, 147
Export controls 118
Export financing 175, 198, 199
Export platforms 91
Export subsidies 281
Externalities 3, 12, 32, 39–42, 86, 145,
    293. See also Spillover effects

Fair Trade Commission (Japan) 84, 279
Fairchild 90
Fallows, James 57
Farren, J. Michael 172, 205
Fast-track dumping procedures 131, 271
Federal Aviation Administration 172
Federal Communications Commission
    243, 294
Federal High-Performance Computing
    and Networking Initiative 82, 263,
    292
Ferguson, Charles 106, 114, 119, 120
Fields, Craig 250
Fifth-generation computing project 295
First-mover advantages 3, 69, 74, 86, 89,
    91, 98, 168, 214
Flamm, Kenneth 88, 89, 92, 97, 101–03,
    114, 116, 118–20, 137, 140, 219, 230,
    235, 268, 278
Flash memory 125
Floor prices 224
Fly-by-wire system 168, 189
Foreign direct investment
    advantages and disadvantages 145–46,
        236–37
    and national security 43, 146–49, 278
    as second-best strategy 247
    as substitute for trade 143–49
    effects on market concentration and
        competition 44, 146
    in aircraft industry 195
    in and by Japan 7–8, 87, 92, 112, 145,
        279
    in developing countries 142

Foreign direct investment (*continued*)
  in Europe 7–8, 92, 101–02, 218–20, 236, 251
  in high-technology industries 42–44
  in semiconductor industry 87, 91–93, 101–02, 112, 143–50
  in US 43, 147–49, 212, 278–79
  in VCR industry 228, 233–36
  inducements 285
  performance requirements 147, 148
Foreign market values 110, 114, 117, 131
Foreign trade zones 287
Forest products 59
45 percent rule 230, 231, 241
Forward pricing 89, 101, 137, 249, 269, 270
4-4-50 rule 277
France 8, 155, 172, 173, 175, 188, 222–23, 244
Frankel, Jeffrey 84
Free trade, traditional and moderate positions 9–11, 259
Fujitsu 66, 70, 76, 80, 95, 98, 100, 112, 125, 143, 247, 251
Funai 231, 232
Fung, K. C. 57

Gaiatsu 260, 266
Game theory 276
General Agreement on Tariffs and Trade (GATT)
  agreement on trade in civil aircraft 195–202, 207, 256, 267, 281, 282
  antidumping code 137, 267, 270
  Article VI 280
  Article X 66
  failure to address structural impediments 2, 5, 73, 83
  government procurement code 7, 8, 63, 77, 261
  nondiscrimination principle 134, 135
  ruling on Airbus subsidies 9
  subsidies code 201, 206, 213, 261, 280–81, 284
  Section 301 and 259–60, 266
  selective reciprocity under 261
  study on Japanese trading practices 55
General Electric 167, 185
Germany 8, 19, 155, 173, 188, 205–06, 223, 279, 281, 290
Global Partnership Plan of Action 65
Globalization of markets 291
Goldstar 231, 232

Gomez, Alain 248
Government-business relations, in Japan 57, 73, 98
Government procurement
  in aircraft industry 155, 175–76, 187, 211
  in computer industry 102
  in electronics 100, 245
  in Europe 7–8, 101, 175, 261
  in GATT 7, 8, 63, 77, 261
  in Japan 63, 66–67, 75, 77–82, 95, 99, 134, 262
  in semiconductors 7, 85, 88, 95, 99, 101
  in supercomputers 77–81, 262–63
  in telecommunications 66–67, 75
Graham, Edward M. 11, 42, 45, 278
Great Britain 8, 155, 167, 172, 177, 184, 189, 233, 244, 290
Grossman, Gene 293
Grundig 221–24, 234
Guerrieri, Paolo 5, 19
Guerrieri-Milana classification 19–21
Guidepost system 118, 121
Gulf War 44, 86

Hardened chip technology 152
Harmonization of national policies 5, 59, 60, 63, 80, 218, 219, 262, 263, 266, 278–80, 296
Hart, Jeffrey 286
Havana Charter 278
Helpman, Elhanan 3
Hewlett-Packard 26, 107, 286
High-definition television
  antidumping in 242
  digital systems 242–44, 250
  European policy toward 237–44
  R&D support 237–38
  standards 237–38, 244
  US policy toward 224, 250, 294
High-price island, US as 110, 138, 272, 273, 281–83, 285, 287
High-technology industries
  and national security 44–45
  as source of systemic competition 18
  classification 18, 20, 21
  compensation in 38
  concentration in developed countries 18, 23
  contribution to economic welfare 32–45
  employment and wages 35–39
  erosion of US position 25–28, 46–52
  FDI in 42–44

in Japan 46
oligopoly in 3, 98, 123, 151, 266, 275–77
production and trade statistics 18–19,
    22, 23, 28–29, 34, 54
R&D spending 32–33
relationship to competitiveness 2
returns to capital 39
revealed comparative advantage 24
spillover benefits effects 3, 4, 12–13,
    32, 39–42, 86, 98, 157, 238
strategic importance 3
value added by 34, 35, 37
Hills, Carla A. 81, 206
Hindley, Brian 269
Hitachi 66, 76, 95, 98–99, 108, 111, 117,
    121, 137, 143, 221, 238
Honda 56
Horelick, Gary N. 268
Howell, Thomas 88, 97, 101, 113–14, 117,
    12–21, 126, 231, 251
Hudec, Robert E. 259
Hufbauer, Gary C. 10, 13, 280
Hüls AG 147–49

Imperfect competition 3, 12, 121, 161,
    254, 258, 267–68, 280. *See also*
    Concentration, market; Oligopolistic
    control
ICL 247
Inducements 95, 175, 201, 203, 208, 210,
    282, 285
Industrial policy
    cautious activist approach 295
    costs to consumers 86
    haphazard, in US 288–89, 293
    in aircraft industry 157–61, 169–76,
        188–89, 192–95, 201, 211–16
    in Europe 219, 157, 176, 193, 201, 288,
        294–95
    in HDTV 237–44, 250
    in Japan 6, 93, 223, 288, 294–95
    in semiconductors 85–87, 93–103,
        151–54, 288
    in supercomputers 76, 82, 88
    risk of failure 249–51, 294–5
    trade policy as inadequate substitute
        for 82, 142, 286
Infant-industry protection 69, 76, 86, 93,
    99, 205, 219, 282, 285
Information technology, trade data 218
Institute of Electrical and Electronics
    Engineers 80
Integrated circuits 93–95, 98, 104, 144

Intel 26, 98, 103, 107–08, 117, 121, 130,
    140, 153, 251, 254, 277
Intellectual property protection 59, 97,
    107, 209, 258
Interest rate subsidies 208, 283
International Business Machines (IBM)
    as nonmerchant semiconductor
        producer 90, 98, 105
    cooperative venture with Apple 151
    foreign competition 102
    joint venture with Siemens 133, 150,
        153
    liquid crystal displays 141–42, 286
    participation in European consortia 247
    support of 301 action against Japan 107
International Standard Industrial
    Classification 20, 21
International Trade Commission 290
Intraindustry trade 98
Italy 126

J2T 231, 234
Jackson, John H. 4, 270
Japan
    antitrust policy 57, 81, 84, 100, 120,
        122, 276, 279
    business organization 55–57
    competitive position in
        high-technology industry 18–19,
        22–26, 46, 275–76
    compliance with trade agreements 65
    cost of capital 100–01
    FDI 7–8, 87, 92, 112, 145, 279
    government-business relations 57, 73,
        98
    industrial policy 6, 93, 223, 288,
        294–95
    market closure 6, 54–58, 83–84, 221
    regulation and standards 58
    revealed comparative advantage 19
    semiconductor industry 86–87, 93–101,
        104, 128–131
    structural barriers to trade 55–58
    technological parity with US 54
    trade with US 27, 53
    VCR industry 220–21, 223, 234–36
Japan Automotive Parts Industry
    Association 112
Japan bashing 82
"Japan, Inc." 82
"Japan problem" 53–58
Japanese Aircraft Development
    Corporation 192

JESSI 30, 149, 150, 247, 288
Johnson, Chalmers 55, 57
Joint ventures. *See* Alliances and joint
    ventures
JSMR 71, 72
JVC 220, 234

Katz, Lawrence F. 39, 40, 194, 254
Kawasaki Steel 112
KC-10 170, 187
Keiretsu 56–57, 76–77, 83, 99, 100, 120,
    135–36, 138–39, 221, 265, 276
Kennedy Round 101
Klepper, Gernot 163, 193–94
Kokusai 66
Komoto, Toshio 95
Korea
    encouragement of FDI 91
    role in color TV trade 241
    role in semiconductor trade 111, 123,
        126–27, 133, 265, 276
    role in VCR trade 225, 229, 231
Krishna, Kala 121
Krugman, Paul R. 3, 9, 11, 13–14, 18–19,
    32, 39–42, 44–45, 86, 193–94, 254,
    278, 295
Kuroda, Makuto 77

Laptop computers 141, 142, 287
Large Aircraft Sector Understanding 175
Large-scale integration 95. *See also* Very
    large scale integration
"Laser-beaming" 223
Latin America 92
Launch aid 173–74, 190, 205–07, 282
Lawrence, Robert Z. 9, 55, 56, 135, 264,
    265, 285
Learning curve effects 89, 91, 97, 101,
    163–65
Licensing 60, 67, 72, 93, 228, 234, 241–42
Lincoln, Edward J. 55, 58, 59
Liquid crystal displays 141–43, 220, 273,
    274, 276, 286–88, 296
Litan, Robert 10
Lithography 145, 147, 148, 152
Local content policies 8, 224, 230–36, 241,
    245, 249
Lockheed 157, 170, 171, 173, 180–81, 182,
    185–88, 192, 202
Long-Term Credit Bank of Japan 239
LSI Logic 112, 150
Lufthansa 175

MAC standard for HDTV 239–40, 243, 244
Macroeconomic policy 14, 83, 84
Main banks 56
Malaysia 91
Managed competitive balance 201
Managed trade
    as second-best policy 133–36
    definition 5, 133, 255
    in semiconductors 107, 109, 133, 136,
        151, 263
    in telecommunications 74–75
    in VCRs 219
    versus managed exchange rates 206
Market access and market closure
    in Europe 6–8
    in Europe-Japan negotiations 266
    in telecommunications 64, 73–75
    in Japan 6–7, 54–58, 83–84, 221
    policy recommendations 255–67
    SCTA and 109, 111–13, 131, 133–36
Market-oriented, sector-specific (MOSS)
    talks
    as rules-based approach 263
    assessment 66
    characteristics 256
    goals 59
    in cellular telephones 64
    in electronics 59–60
    in medical equipment and
        pharmaceuticals 60–63
    in telecommunications 63–65, 69, 71, 72
    in third-party radios 71
    on intellectual property 258
    outside participation proposed 259
    reciprocity in 261
Market-sharing arrangements 70, 286
Marshall, Alfred 40
Massachusetts Institute of Technology
    80, 243
Material injury test 281, 283
Materials Research Corporation 146
Matsushita 66–67, 98–99, 112, 220–21,
    233–34, 238, 244, 267
MBB 160, 173, 205
MCA 71–73
McDonald, John 161, 165
McDonnell Douglas
    competition with Lockheed 157,
        185–88, 190, 192
    DC-3 163
    DC-6 163
    DC-8 163, 165, 178–79, 183
    DC-9 178–79
    DC-10 167, 170, 180–81, 187

export orientation 26
defense contracting 160, 170, 211
financial difficulties 156, 211
formation in 167 171, 183
KC-10 170
MD-11 156, 167, 191, 190
MD-12 211–14
MD-80 180–81, 189
production statistics 158–59
proposed joint venture with Airbus
191
Taiwan Aerospace deal 43, 156, 210–14
McGowen, Jackson 187
Medical equipment, MOSS talks in 60–63
Merchant firms, in semiconductor
industry 87, 90, 98
Messerlin, Patrick 268
Mexico 91
Micrascan 153, 294
Microcontrollers 99
Microelectronics and Computer
Technologies Corporation 276
Micron Technology 107, 116, 126
Microprocessors 98, 110, 112, 121, 127,
140
Microsoft 151
Milana, Carlo 19
Milgrom, Paul 268
Military contracting. *See* Defense
contracting
Ministry of Health and Welfare (Japan)
60, 61
Ministry of International Trade and
Industry (MITI)
assessments of technological standings
46
conduct of industrial policy 288
relationship with Japanese businesses
98
role in cellular telephone case 69
role in semiconductor case 96, 99, 110,
118–19, 121, 127, 132, 136, 145, 273
role in VCR case 229, 233
subsidies offered by 221
Ministry of Posts and
Telecommunications (Japan) 64, 65,
67–75, 98, 134, 239, 288
MIPPS 151
MIT Commission on Industrial
Productivity 221
Mitsubishi 98, 99, 112, 143, 221, 233
Mobile Radio Center (MRC) 71, 72, 75
Moderate free trade position 259
Monitoring of foreign oligopoly 277

Monitoring of trade agreements 66, 207
Monsanto 147, 148
Moran, Theodore H. 11, 13, 44, 132, 169,
171, 194, 196, 211, 277
Mosbacher, Robert A. 7
Mostek 117
Motorola
cellular telephone dispute 66–71, 259,
260
diversification 100
export orientation 26
foreign investment 112, 130
influence on policy 290
joint venture with Toshiba 112, 126
targeting of DRAMs 112–13, 126
third-party radio dispute 71–73
use of American suppliers 153
Moving band of protection 79, 98
Mowery, David C. 87, 90, 132, 155, 162,
165, 169, 171, 177, 194, 196, 199, 211,
290
Multilateralism 5, 10, 66, 83, 255
Muse standard for HDTV 239, 243

National Academy of Engineers 277, 290
National Academy of Sciences 54, 290,
291, 293
National Advisory Committee on
Aeronautics 170
National Advisory Committee on
Semiconductors 142, 275–77, 287
National Aeronautics and Space
Administration 170, 172
National Broadcasting Company of
Japan 238
National Health Insurance (Japan) 60, 61
National Institute of Standards and
Technology 250, 288, 292, 294
National Science Foundation 290
National security. *See also* Defense
contracting
as rationale for trade intervention 11
FDI and 43, 147–49, 278
high-technology industries and 44–45
risk of foreign control of an industry
277
supercomputers and 80
trade conflict and 6
National Semiconductor 98, 108, 124, 125
National treatment 6, 64, 66
NEC 66–68, 76, 78, 80, 95, 98, 100, 111,
117, 119, 143
Nelson, Richard 28, 42, 88

New growth theory 12
Newhouse, John 185, 186
Newly industrializing countries 4, 5, 25.
    See also specific country
Nikon 146, 148, 152
Nippon Idou Tsushin Corporation (IDO)
    68–70
Nippon Sanso 146, 147
Nippon Telegraph and Telephone (NTT)
    63, 64, 66–70, 73, 75–77, 95, 98–100,
    134
Nissan 76
NMB Semiconductor 56
NMOS technology 103
Nokia 222
Noland, Marcus 55, 84
Noll, Roger G. 292
Nondiscrimination 6, 64, 134, 261, 264
NTSC broadcast standard 238

O'Connor, David 3, 89, 90, 101, 103, 235,
    275
Office of Science and Technology Policy
    277, 291
Office of Technology Assessment 8, 173,
    290
Office of the US Trade Representative
    66, 93
Oki Electric 66, 112, 117
Okimoto, Daniel I. 58
Oligopoly in high-technology industries
    3, 98, 123, 151, 266, 275–77. *See also*
    Antitrust; Concentration, market;
    Imperfect competition
Omnibus Trade and Competitiveness
    Act of 1988 45, 69
Organization for Economic Cooperation
    and Development (OECD) 3, 19–21,
    151, 175, 199, 203, 213, 266, 278,
    282
Orion 231, 232
Ostry, Sylvia 5, 18, 31

PAL broadcasting standard 238–40, 242,
    244
Pan American World Airways 183, 186,
    202
Pandolfi, Filippo 247
Patents 59, 92, 107
Performance requirements 147, 148
Perkin-Elmer 147–49, 153, 294
Petri, Peter A. 57

Pharmaceuticals, MOSS talks on 60–63
Philips 221–24, 238–39, 241, 243, 244
Pi rule 119
Pierson, Jean 192
Plowden Report 177, 184
Point-of-sales affiliates 92
Poitiers 222
Policy recommendations
    aggressive unilateralism 255–61
    antidumping 142, 267–74
    countervailing duties/subsidies 270,
        274, 277, 280–83, 285–86
    domestic policy 151–54, 286–96
    foreign direct investment 147–49, 251
    in aircraft industry 160–61, 214–16
    market access 255–67
    plurilateral agreement in
        semiconductors 151
    proposed critical technologies agency
        289, 290
    R&D funding 142, 290–91
    rules versus outcomes 263–66
    sectoral negotiations 84
    selective reciprocity 261–63
    subsidies 280–86
Polysilicon 148
Porter, Michael 18, 31, 41, 91, 287
Pratt & Whitney 16
Precompetitive R&D 250, 284, 291, 293
Predatory pricing 137, 268–69, 270–71,
    274, 275
Prestowitz, Clyde V., Jr. 6, 55, 57–59, 63,
    64, 88, 92, 95, 107, 204, 214
Price discounting 77–79, 81, 89
Price undertakings. *See* Undertakings
Procedural delays in trade disputes 260
Procurement. *See* Government
    procurement
Product differentiation 166, 171, 185
Product families 162–65, 193
Propfans 189, 190
Protectionism
    infant-industry 69, 76, 86, 93, 99, 205,
        219, 282, 285
    use of intervention to head off 11
    versus cautious activism 13
Public broadcasting 238, 240
Public procurement. *See* Government
    procurement

Quick-response approach 260
Quotas, import 92, 93, 221, 224, 229, 241,
    245, 247, 264

Regulation. *See also* Antidumping;
   Antitrust; Rules versus outcomes;
   Standards.
   antiscrewdriver 150, 230, 248
   export controls 118
   impact on airline industry 188
   in electronics industry 245–49
   international harmonization 5, 59, 60,
      63, 80, 218, 219, 262, 263, 266,
      278–80, 296
   local content 8, 224, 230–36, 241, 245,
      249
   national differences in, as trade barrier
      4, 6
   rules of origin 8, 101, 149, 218, 242, 248
   testing and certification 58, 60–64, 67,
      266
   transparency 60, 61, 64, 72, 78, 79, 207,
      208, 248, 262, 285
Research and development (R&D)
   consortia 276
   foreign participation in 59
   in aircraft industry 32, 162, 170–71
   in electronics 32, 223
   in Europe 219
   in HDTV 237–38
   in semiconductor industry 89, 95–97,
      117, 150–54
   in supercomputers 82
   military versus civilian 290
   MITI sponsorship 96
   national differences in organization
      and funding 59–60
   precompetitive 250, 284, 291, 293
   spending in US 33, 89
   spillover benefits 32
   subsidies to 284–86
   tax credit 14, 152
RACE program 246
RCA 220
Reagan administration 1, 58, 203
Reciprocity
   EC policy on 247, 266
   in semiconductors 109
   in supercomputers 80, 262–63
   selective 7, 13, 261–63, 267
Relational handshake 100
Retaliation 255, 259–60, 262, 282, 286. *See
   also* Sanctions, trade
Revealed comparative advantage 19–25
Richardson, J. David 3, 14, 254, 262
Risk, in aircraft industry 162, 163, 165,
   166–68
Rolls-Royce 184, 187, 189

Rosen, Howard F. 13
Rosenberg, Nathan 87, 90, 155, 162, 165,
   177, 199, 290
Rules of origin 8, 101, 149, 218, 242, 248
Rules versus outcomes 5, 59, 66, 73, 74,
   255, 263–66

Salvatore, Dominick 55
Samsung 123, 127, 231, 232
Sanctions, trade 114, 131, 132, 136. *See
   also* Retaliation
Sandholtz, Wayne 6, 44
Sanyo 221
Scale and scope economies 97, 163, 166,
   244
Schott, Jeffrey J. 10
Schultze, Charles L. 264
"Screwdriver" operations 228
SECAM broadcast standard 238
Section 301
   and multilateral trading regime
      259–60, 266
   as aggressive unilateralism 255–59
   as legal disobedience 259
   dangers 260–61
   in aircraft industry 203
   in cellular telephones 258
   in semiconductor industry 107–09
   SIA petition under 107–09
   supported by President Reagan 203
Sector-specific negotiations 83–84, 255,
   260. *See also* Market-oriented,
   sector-specific (MOSS) talks
Selective reciprocity 13, 261–63, 267
Sematech 95, 143, 148, 150, 152–54, 157,
   247, 276, 294
Semi-Gas Systems 146–48
Semiconductor Chip Protection Act 107,
   258
Semiconductor equipment industry 114,
   145–48, 153–54
Semiconductor industry. *See also specific
   companies, specific products*
   consumer electronics and 224
   dumping and antidumping in 107–10,
      131, 136–43, 268, 272–73, 274, 278
   foreign market shares in Japan 93, 113
   economic structure and significance
      86, 88–91
   employment 90
   FDI 87, 91–93, 101–02, 112, 143–50
   government intervention in 85–87
   history 88–92

Semiconductor industry *(continued)*
in Europe 101–03, 149–50
in Japan 86–87, 93–101, 104, 128–131
in Korea 123, 126–27, 133, 265, 276
industrial policy in 154
investment patterns 89, 106
national market shares 103–06
need for plurilateral trade agreement
151, 267
R&D 89, 95–97, 117, 150–54
reciprocity in 109
role of innovation 90
technological spillovers 86
trade patterns 92–93
US policy toward 88–92, 94, 128–29,
151–54, 260
Semiconductor Industry Association 107,
110, 114, 136, 151, 203, 290
Semiconductor materials industry 145,
146
Semiconductor Research Corporation 276
Semiconductor trade agreement
alliances and joint ventures 95, 112–13,
125, 275–76, 294
antidumping provisions 131, 136–43,
149, 272
as managed trade 133–36, 255, 263
assessment 87, 109, 132–33, 259
background 106–08
confidential side letter 109
effects on competition 132–33, 264–66
effects on FDI 143, 149
effects on market access 111–13, 131,
133–36, 149, 257, 265
effects on prices 113–24, 257
effects on trade patterns 124–30
encouragement of Japanese
cartelization 119–24, 135, 138
firm-specific price setting 110, 138–39
1991 extension 130–32
provisions on third-country markets
110
terms 109–10
SGS-Thomson 125
Shared mobile radio systems. *See*
Third-party radio systems
Sharp 221, 233
Sharp, Margaret 245
Shikoku Tsuhan 72
Shrontz, Frank A. 210
Shultz, George P. 66, 204
Siemens 102, 123, 127, 133, 150, 153, 223,
294
Sigma project 59

Silicon Valley 41
Silicon Valley Group 148
Singapore 91
Singapore Airlines 167
Single European Act 241, 246
Sky TV 240
Smith, C. R. 182
Software, computer 59, 76, 151, 219
Sony 92, 112, 143, 146, 220, 221, 234, 238,
244, 251
Southeast Asia 91, 92. *See also* Newly
industrializing countries; *specific
country*
Spain 155
Spencer, Barbara J. 3, 281
Spillover effects 3, 4, 12–13, 32, 39–42,
86, 98, 157, 238. *See also* Externalities
Standard Industrial Classification 20, 21
Standards. *See also* Regulation
in Europe 218, 221
in HDTV 219, 237–39, 241–42, 244
in telecommunications 63–64, 67
in television industry 221
ineffectiveness as promotional tool 249
Static random access memories (SRAMs)
89, 121
"Statute of limitations" for CVDs 281
Steinmueller, W. Edward 90-92, 98
Stowsky, Jay 291, 293
Strategic trade theory 3–4, 39, 161, 171,
268
Structural differences, as source of trade
conflict 30–31
Structural Impediments Initiative (SII)
83–84, 256, 259, 263, 267, 278
Subsidies
countervailing 139–40, 274, 285–86
export 281
for infant industries 285
for R&D programs 284–86
for regional development 285
in aircraft industry 8–9, 161, 172,
193–95, 207, 215, 259
in computer industry 102
in electronics industry 9
in Europe 8–9, 233, 251, 259
in GATT 201, 206, 213, 261, 280–81, 284
in Japan 8, 221, 233
in Korea 126, 233
in supercomputers 81–82
in VCRs 233
interest rate 208, 283
policy recommendations 280–86
traffic-light approach 284

US–EC agreement on 9, 282–83, 285
Summers, Lawrence H. 39, 40, 194, 254
Super 301 16, 69, 79, 113, 136, 255–59, 260–62, 266, 296
Supercomputer industry. *See also specific companies*
  dumping of 80
  government procurement 77–81, 262–63
  in MOSS talks 77
  industrial policy in 82
  market shares 78, 80
  national security and 80
  R&D in 82
  reciprocity in 80, 262–63
  subsidies 81–82, 139–40, 285–86
  US–Japan agreements on 77–82
  use of Section 301 in 257–58
Supersonic transport program 172, 185
SVG 153

Taiwan 43, 91, 111, 126, 140, 156, 210–14
Taiwan Aerospace Corporation 43, 156, 210–14
Tariffs 55, 91–93, 101, 114, 151, 184, 224, 229, 259
Taxation 14, 91, 112, 152, 246
Technecon Analytic Research 116
Technology drivers 89, 124
Technology policy 291–93. *See also* Industrial policy; Research and development
Telecommunications, 261. *See also specific product*
  government procurement in 7, 66–67, 75
  in Uruguay Round 261
  MOSS talks in 63–65
  reciprocity in 261
  standards 63–64, 67
  testing and certification 63, 64, 67
  trade data 218
  US–Japan trade 65
Telecommunications Deliberation Council (Japan) 64, 67
Telefunken 222, 242
Television industry. *See* Color television industry; High-definition television; *specific companies*
Terms-of-trade effects 10, 11
Testing and certification 58, 60–64, 67, 266

Texas Instruments
  diversification 100
  foreign investment 112, 126, 233
  forward pricing by 89, 101, 137
  impact of SCTA on 116
  intrafirm technology transfer 40
  Japanese patent applications 107
  joint venture with Sony 92
  role in US antidumping action 139
Third-party radios 67, 71, 73, 75, 134, 257, 263
Thomson 102, 220, 222, 234, 238, 239, 241, 243, 244
Thorn-EMI 222, 239, 242
Thornton, Dean D. 192, 203
Tohoku University 78
Tokyo Round 66, 101, 198
Toshiba 66, 98, 99, 112, 120, 126, 143, 150, 153, 221, 238, 294
Totsu 66
Trade Act of 1974 77
Trade warfare 259, 282
Traditional free trade position 9–10
Traffic light approach to subsidies 284
Trans World Airlines 186
Transparency 60, 61, 64, 72, 78, 79, 207, 208, 248, 262, 285
Trident 178, 179
Turbofans and turbojets 176, 178–81, 184
Tyson, Laura D. 11, 55, 74, 79, 98

U.S. Memories Consortium 123, 126, 140
Undertakings 138, 149, 230, 232, 233, 248, 272 273
Unilateralism, aggressive 13, 16, 74, 109, 204, 255–61
Unisys 26
United Airlines 168, 192, 211
United Kingdom. *See* Great Britain
United Nations 278
United States
  antitrust policy 90, 279
  as high-price island 138, 272, 273, 281–83, 285, 287
  competitiveness 1, 2, 254
  eroding position in high-technology industry 25–28, 46–52
  FDI in 43, 147–49, 212, 278–79
  haphazard industrial policy 288–89, 293
  HDTV policy 224, 250, 294
  international competitive standing 1, 3, 25, 46, 47–52

United States *(continued)*
  policy recommendations for. *See*
    Policy recommendations
  policy toward joint ventures 12
  policy toward cellular telephones 259
  policy toward semiconductor industry
    88–92, 94, 128–29, 151–54, 260
  R&D spending 33, 89
  revealed comparative advantage 19, 25
  trade statistics 14, 19, 22, 24–29, 53–55,
    62, 94, 105–08, 116, 129, 196–99, 218,
    236
Uruguay Round 2, 5, 248, 259–61, 264,
  270, 281, 283, 285, 296
US Court of International Trade 269
US Department of Commerce 20, 21, 80,
  108, 110, 114, 146, 258, 268, 269, 273,
  277
US Department of Defense 44, 114, 142,
  152, 291
US Department of Justice 146, 147, 279
US Department of Transportation 172
US Export-Import Bank 175, 198
US Federal Trade Commission 137, 269
US Food and Drug Administration 61
US General Accounting Office 275
US International Trade Commission 7,
  137, 269, 272, 277, 288
US National Research Council 26
US Supreme Court 267
US Trade Representative 69

Value added by high-technology
  industries 34, 35, 37
Van Wolferen, Karel 57
Vertical integration 55–56, 76, 142, 168–69
Very large scale integration program 97,
  284
Videocassette recorders (VCR). *See also*
  specific companies
  costs of protection 226
  dumping and antidumping in 223,
    229–33, 268, 272
  early industry history 220–22
  Europe-Japan VRA 219–24, 229, 255, 257
  European policy in 219–37
  FDI in 228, 234–36
  in Japan 220–21, 223, 234–36
  market shares 229, 234, 235
  price effects of VRA 225–28
  role of Korean producers 225, 229, 231
  subsidies 233
  trade data 227, 236
Vogel, David 58, 60
Voluntary export restraints (VERs) 134,
  263–66
Voluntary import expansions (VIEs) 134,
  263–66
Voluntary restraint agreement
  definition 263
  disadvantages 249
  Europe-Japan, in VCRs 219–24, 229,
    255
  Europe-Korea, in VCRs 233
  proposed for semiconductors 109

Wages in high-technology industries
  35–39
White, Robert M. 292
Williams, Linn 131
Wolf, John 212

Yamamura, Kozo 55, 56
Yoffie, David B. 107, 222
Young, Allyn 40

Zenith 241, 243, 267
Zysman, John 11, 55, 79, 98

Other Publications from the
Institute for International Economics

POLICY ANALYSES IN INTERNATIONAL ECONOMICS Series

1 **The Lending Policies of the International Monetary Fund**
John Williamson/*August 1982*
ISBN paper 0-88132-000-5   72 pp.

2 **"Reciprocity": A New Approach to World Trade Policy?**
William R. Cline/*September 1982*
ISBN paper 0-88132-001-3   41 pp.

3 **Trade Policy in the 1980s**
C. Fred Bergsten and William R. Cline/*November 1982*
(out of print)   ISBN paper 0-88132-002-1   84 pp.
Partially reproduced in the book *Trade Policy in the 1980s*.

4 **International Debt and the Stability of the World Economy**
William R. Cline/*September 1983*
ISBN paper 0-88132-010-2   134 pp.

5 **The Exchange Rate System**
John Williamson/*September 1983, rev. June 1985*
(out of print)   ISBN paper 0-88132-034-X   61 pp.

6 **Economic Sanctions in Support of Foreign Policy Goals**
Gary Clyde Hufbauer and Jeffrey J. Schott/*October 1983*
ISBN paper 0-88132-014-5   109 pp.

7 **A New SDR Allocation?**
John Williamson/*March 1984*
ISBN paper 0-88132-028-5   61 pp.

8 **An International Standard for Monetary Stabilization**
Ronald I. McKinnon/*March 1984*
(out of print)   ISBN paper 0-88132-018-8   108 pp.

9 **The Yen/Dollar Agreement: Liberalizing Japanese Capital Markets**
Jeffrey A. Frankel/*December 1984*
ISBN paper 0-88132-035-8   86 pp.

10 **Bank Lending to Developing Countries: The Policy Alternatives**
C. Fred Bergsten, William R. Cline, and John Williamson/*April 1985*
ISBN paper 0-88132-032-3   221 pp.

11 **Trading for Growth: The Next Round of Trade Negotiations**
Gary Clyde Hufbauer and Jeffrey J. Schott/*September 1985*
ISBN paper 0-88132-033-1   109 pp.

12 **Financial Intermediation Beyond the Debt Crisis**
Donald R. Lessard and John Williamson/*September 1985*
ISBN paper 0-88132-021-8   130 pp.

13 **The United States–Japan Economic Problem**
C. Fred Bergsten and William R. Cline/*October 1985, rev. January 1987*
ISBN paper 0-88132-060-9   180 pp.

14 **Deficits and the Dollar: The World Economy at Risk**
Stephen Marris/*December 1985, rev. November 1987*
ISBN paper 0-88132-067-6   415 pp.

15 Trade Policy for Troubled Industries
Gary Clyde Hufbauer and Howard F. Rosen/*March 1986*
ISBN paper 0-88132-020-X   111 pp.

16 The United States and Canada: The Quest for Free Trade
Paul Wonnacott with an Appendix by John Williamson/*March 1987*
ISBN paper 0-88132-056-0   188 pp.

17 Adjusting to Success: Balance of Payments Policy in the
East Asian NICs
Bela Balassa and John Williamson/*June 1987, rev. April 1990*
ISBN paper 0-88132-101-X   160 pp.

18 Mobilizing Bank Lending to Debtor Countries
William R. Cline/*June 1987*
ISBN paper 0-88132-062-5   100 pp.

19 Auction Quotas and United States Trade Policy
C. Fred Bergsten, Kimberly Ann Elliott, Jeffrey J. Schott, and
Wendy E. Takacs/*September 1987*
ISBN paper 0-88132-050-1   254 pp.

20 Agriculture and the GATT: Rewriting the Rules
Dale E. Hathaway/*September 1987*
ISBN paper 0-88132-052-8   169 pp.

21 Anti-Protection: Changing Forces in United States Trade Politics
I. M. Destler and John S. Odell/*September 1987*
ISBN paper 0-88132-043-9   220 pp.

22 Targets and Indicators: A Blueprint for the International Coordination
of Economic Policy
John Williamson and Marcus H. Miller/*September 1987*
ISBN paper 0-88132-051-X   118 pp.

23 Capital Flight: The Problem and Policy Responses
Donald R. Lessard and John Williamson/*December 1987*
ISBN paper 0-88132-059-5   80 pp.

24 United States–Canada Free Trade: An Evaluation of the Agreement
Jeffrey J. Schott/*April 1988*
ISBN paper 0-88132-072-2   48 pp.

25 Voluntary Approaches to Debt Relief
John Williamson/*September 1988, rev. May 1989*
ISBN paper 0-88132-098-6   80 pp.

26 American Trade Adjustment: The Global Impact
William R. Cline/*March 1989*
ISBN paper 0-88132-095-1   98 pp.

27 More Free Trade Areas?
Jeffrey J. Schott/*May 1989*
ISBN paper 0-88132-085-4   88 pp.

28 The Progress of Policy Reform in Latin America
John Williamson/*January 1990*
ISBN paper 0-88132-100-1   106 pp.

29 The Global Trade Negotiations: What Can Be Achieved?
Jeffrey J. Schott/*September 1990*
ISBN paper 0-88132-137-0   72 pp.

30 Economic Policy Coordination: Requiem or Prologue?
Wendy Dobson/*April 1991*
ISBN paper 0-88132-102-8   162 pp.

31 The Economic Opening of Eastern Europe
John Williamson/*May 1991*
ISBN paper 0-88132-186-9   92 pp.

32 Eastern Europe and the Soviet Union in the World Economy
Susan M. Collins and Dani Rodrik/*May 1991*
ISBN paper 0-88132-157-5   152 pp.

33 African Economic Reform: The External Dimension
Carol Lancaster/*June 1991*
ISBN paper 0-88132-096-X   82 pp.

34 Has the Adjustment Process Worked?
Paul R. Krugman/*October 1991*
ISBN paper 0-88132-116-8   80 pp.

35 From Soviet disUnion to Eastern Economic Community?
Oleh Havrylyshyn and John Williamson/*October 1991*
ISBN paper 0-88132-192-3   84 pp.

36 Global Warming: The Economic Stakes
William R. Cline/*May 1992*
ISBN paper 0-88132-172-9   128 pp.

37 Trade and Payments After Soviet Disintegration
John Williamson/*June 1992*
ISBN paper 0-88132-173-7   96 pp.

BOOKS

IMF Conditionality
John Williamson, editor/*1983*
ISBN cloth 0-88132-006-4   695 pp.

Trade Policy in the 1980s
William R. Cline, editor/*1983*
ISBN cloth 0-88132-008-1   810 pp.
ISBN paper 0-88132-031-5   810 pp.

Subsidies in International Trade
Gary Clyde Hufbauer and Joanna Shelton Erb/*1984*
ISBN cloth 0-88132-004-8   299 pp.

International Debt: Systemic Risk and Policy Response
William R. Cline/*1984*
ISBN cloth 0-88132-015-3   336 pp.

Trade Protection in the United States: 31 Case Studies
Gary Clyde Hufbauer, Diane E. Berliner, and Kimberly Ann Elliott/*1986*
ISBN paper 0-88132-040-4   371 pp.

Toward Renewed Economic Growth in Latin America
Bela Balassa, Gerardo M. Bueno, Pedro-Pablo Kuczynski, and Mario
  Henrique Simonsen/*1986*
(out of print)   ISBN paper 0-88132-045-5   205 pp.

Capital Flight and Third World Debt
Donald R. Lessard and John Williamson, editors/*1987*
(out of print)   ISBN paper 0-88132-053-6   270 pp.

The Canada–United States Free Trade Agreement:
The Global Impact
Jeffrey J. Schott and Murray G. Smith, editors/*1988*
                  ISBN paper 0-88132-073-0   211 pp.

World Agricultural Trade: Building a Consensus
William M. Miner and Dale E. Hathaway, editors/*1988*
                  ISBN paper 0-88132-071-3   226 pp.

Japan in the World Economy
Bela Balassa and Marcus Noland/*1988*
                  ISBN paper 0-88132-041-2   306 pp.

America in the World Economy: A Strategy for the 1990s
C. Fred Bergsten/*1988*
                  ISBN cloth 0-88132-089-7   235 pp.
                  ISBN paper 0-88132-082-X   235 pp.

Managing the Dollar: From the Plaza to the Louvre
Yoichi Funabashi/*1988, rev. 1989*
                  ISBN paper 0-88132-097-8   307 pp.

United States External Adjustment and the World Economy
William R. Cline/*May 1989*
                  ISBN paper 0-88132-048-X   392 pp.

Free Trade Areas and U.S. Trade Policy
Jeffrey J. Schott, editor/*May 1989*
                  ISBN paper 0-88132-094-3   400 pp.

Dollar Politics: Exchange Rate Policymaking in the United States
I. M. Destler and C. Randall Henning/*September 1989*
                  ISBN paper 0-88132-079-X   192 pp.

Latin American Adjustment: How Much Has Happened?
John Williamson, editor/*April 1990*
                  ISBN paper 0-88132-125-7   480 pp.

The Future of World Trade in Textiles and Apparel
William R. Cline/*1987, rev. June 1990*
                  ISBN paper 0-88132-110-9   344 pp.

Completing the Uruguay Round: A Results-Oriented Approach to the
GATT Trade Negotiations
Jeffrey J. Schott, editor/*September 1990*
                  ISBN paper 0-88132-130-3   256 pp.

Economic Sanctions Reconsidered (in two volumes)
  Economic Sanctions Reconsidered: History and Current Policy
    (also sold separately, see below)
  Economic Sanctions Reconsidered: Supplemental Case Histories
Gary Clyde Hufbauer, Jeffrey J. Schott, and Kimberly Ann Elliott/*1985,*
  rev. December 1990
                  ISBN cloth 0-88132-115-X   928 pp.
                  ISBN paper 0-88132-105-2   928 pp.

Economic Sanctions Reconsidered: History and Current Policy
Gary Clyde Hufbauer, Jeffrey J. Schott, and Kimberly Ann Elliott/
  December 1990
                  ISBN cloth 0-88132-136-2   288 pp.
                  ISBN paper 0-88132-140-0   288 pp.

Pacific Basin Developing Countries: Prospects for the Future
Marcus Noland/*January 1991*

    ISBN cloth 0-88132-141-9   250 pp.

Pacific Basin Developing Countries: Prospects for the Future		
Marcus Noland/*January 1991*		
	ISBN cloth 0-88132-141-9	250 pp.
	ISBN paper 0-88132-081-1	250 pp.
Currency Convertibility in Eastern Europe		
John Williamson, editor/*September 1991*		
	ISBN cloth 0-88132-144-3	396 pp.
	ISBN paper 0-88132-128-1	396 pp.
Foreign Direct Investment in the United States		
Edward M. Graham and Paul R. Krugman/*1989, rev. October 1991*		
	ISBN paper 0-88132-139-7	200 pp.
International Adjustment and Financing: The Lessons of 1985–1991		
C. Fred Bergsten, editor/*January 1992*		
	ISBN cloth 0-88132-142-7	336 pp.
	ISBN paper 0-88132-112-5	336 pp.
North American Free Trade: Issues and Recommendations		
Gary Clyde Hufbauer and Jeffrey J. Schott/*April 1992*		
	ISBN cloth 0-88132-145-1	392 pp.
	ISBN paper 0-88132-120-6	392 pp.
American Trade Politics		
I. M. Destler/*1986, rev. June 1992*		
	ISBN cloth 0-88132-164-8	400 pp.
	ISBN paper 0-88132-188-5	400 pp.
Narrowing the U.S. Current Account Deficit: A Sectoral Assessment		
Allen J. Lenz/*June 1992*		
	ISBN cloth 0-88132-148-6	640 pp.
	ISBN paper 0-88132-103-6	640 pp.
The Economics of Global Warming		
William R. Cline/*June 1992*		
	ISBN cloth 0-88132-150-8	420 pp.
	ISBN paper 0-88132-132-X	420 pp.
U.S. Taxation of International Income: Blueprint for Reform		
Gary Clyde Hufbauer, assisted by Joanna M. van Rooij/*October 1992*		
	ISBN cloth 0-88132-178-8	304 pp.
	ISBN paper 0-88132-134-6	304 pp.
Who's Bashing Whom? Trade Conflict in High-Technology Industries		
Laura D'Andrea Tyson/*November 1992*		
	ISBN cloth 0-88132-151-6	352 pp.
	ISBN paper 0-88132-106-0	352 pp.

SPECIAL REPORTS

1	**Promoting World Recovery: A Statement on Global Economic Strategy**	
	by Twenty-six Economists from Fourteen Countries/*December 1982*	
	(out of print) ISBN paper 0-88132-013-7	45 pp.
2	**Prospects for Adjustment in Argentina, Brazil, and Mexico:**	
	Responding to the Debt Crisis	
	John Williamson, editor/*June 1983*	
	(out of print) ISBN paper 0-88132-016-1	71 pp.

3   Inflation and Indexation: Argentina, Brazil, and Israel
    John Williamson, editor/*March 1985*
                        ISBN paper 0-88132-037-4   191 pp.

4   Global Economic Imbalances
    C. Fred Bergsten, editor/*March 1986*
                        ISBN cloth 0-88132-038-2   126 pp.
                        ISBN paper 0-88132-042-0   126 pp.

5   African Debt and Financing
    Carol Lancaster and John Williamson, editors/*May 1986*
    (out of print)   ISBN paper 0-88132-044-7   229 pp.

6   Resolving the Global Economic Crisis: After Wall Street
    Thirty-three Economists from Thirteen Countries/*December 1987*
                        ISBN paper 0-88132-070-6   30 pp.

7   World Economic Problems
    Kimberly Ann Elliott and John Williamson, editors/*April 1988*
                        ISBN paper 0-88132-055-2   298 pp.

    Reforming World Agricultural Trade
    Twenty-nine Professionals from Seventeen Countries/*1988*
                        ISBN paper 0-88132-088-9   42 pp.

8   Economic Relations Between the United States and Korea:
    Conflict or Cooperation?
    Thomas O. Bayard and Soo-Gil Young, editors/*January 1989*
                        ISBN paper 0-88132-068-4   192 pp.

FORTHCOMING

A World Savings Shortage?
Paul R. Krugman

Sizing Up U.S. Export Disincentives
J. David Richardson

The Globalization of Industry and National Economic Policies
C. Fred Bergsten and Edward M. Graham

Trading for the Environment
John Whalley

The Effects of Foreign-Exchange Intervention
Kathryn Dominguez and Jeffrey A. Frankel

The Future of the World Trading System
John Whalley

Adjusting to Volatile Energy Prices
Philip K. Verleger, Jr.

National Security and the World Economy
Ellen L. Frost

The United States as a Debtor Country
C. Fred Bergsten and Shafiqul Islam

International Monetary Policymaking in the United States, Germany, and Japan
C. Randall Henning

The Economic Consequences of Soviet Disintegration
John Williamson

Reciprocity and Retaliation: An Evaluation of Tough Trade Policies
Thomas O. Bayard and Kimberly Ann Elliott

Global Competition Policy
Edward M. Graham and J. David Richardson

The Dynamics of Korean Economic Development
Soon Cho

Equilibrium Exchange Rates: An Update
John Williamson

The United States and Japan in the 1990s
C. Fred Bergsten, I. M. Destler, and Marcus Noland

Toward Freer Trade in the Western Hemisphere
Gary Clyde Hufbauer and Jeffrey J. Schott

The New Tripolar World Economy: Toward Collective Leadership
C. Fred Bergsten and C. Randall Henning

Korea in the World Economy
Il SaKong

The Costs of U.S. Trade Barriers
Gary Clyde Hufbauer and Kimberly Ann Elliott

Comparing the Costs of Protection: Europe, Japan, and the United States
Gary Clyde Hufbauer and Kimberly Ann Elliott, editors

The Politics of Economic Reform
John Williamson

Third World Debt: A Reappraisal
William R. Cline

The New Europe in the World Economy
Gary Clyde Hufbauer

Prospects for World Growth
Rudiger Dornbusch